Ned Wynkoop
and the Lonely Road from
Sand Creek

Ned Wynkoop
and the Lonely Road from
Sand Creek

By Louis Kraft

University of Oklahoma Press : Norman

Also by Louis Kraft

The Final Showdown (New York, 1992)
Custer and the Cheyenne: George Armstrong Custer's Winter Campaign on the Southern Plains (El Segundo, Calif., 1995)
Gatewood & Geronimo (Albuquerque, 2000)
Lt. Charles Gatewood & His Apache Wars Memoir (editor and author of additional text) (Lincoln, Nebr., 2005)

Library of Congress Cataloging-in-Publication Data

Kraft, Louis, 1947–
  Ned Wynkoop and the lonely road from Sand Creek / by Louis Kraft.
     p. cm.
  Includes bibliographical references and index.
  ISBN 978-0-8061-4226-5 (hardcover : alk. paper) 1. Wynkoop, Edward Wanshaer, b. 1836. 2. Pioneers—Colorado—Biography. 3. Indian agents—Colorado—Biography. 4. Colorado—History—To 1876. 5. Colorado—History—Civil War, 1861–1865. 6. Sand Creek Massacre, Colo., 1864. I. Title.
  F780.W96K73 2011
  978.8'02092—dc22
  [B]   2011016101

For my little girl
who has become a beautiful woman—
Marissa Lauren Kraft

Contents

List of Illustrations ix

Preface and Acknowledgments xi

Prologue: Formative Years 3

1. Gone A-westering 8

2. To Civilization and Back 20

3. The Streets of Denver 34

4. A Bad Man from Kansas 45

5. Civil War 64

6. The Winds of Change 79

7. Prelude to Infamy 92

8. Wynkoop's Gamble 105

9. Perfidy 116

10. A People Divided 139

11. Walking between the Races 157

12. Hancock's War 178

13. Hope and Discontent 203

14. A Matter of Conscience 227

Epilogue 254

Notes 271

Bibliography 313

Index 323

Illustrations

FIGURES

Ned Wynkoop, 1852   7

Pawnee Land Office/Kansas Territorial Legislature building
   in Lecompton   9

William Byers   39

Park McLure and O. J. Goldrick, Denver Post Office   46

Rose Wakely   50

Louise Wakely Wynkoop   59

Ned Wynkoop, 1861   67

Samuel F. Tappan   77

Ivory calendar presented to Wynkoop   83

First Colorado Volunteer Cavalry officers, 1863   86

Southern Cheyenne and Arapaho leaders arriving in Denver,
   September 28, 1864   120

Wynkoop and Indian chiefs after Camp Weld council   124

Bull Bear and Black Kettle   125

Scott Anthony   127

John Chivington   132

Ledger drawing of George Bent   135

Silas Soule, 1865   149

Southern Cheyenne Pawnee Fork village, Kansas   190

Ned Wynkoop and Dick Curtis, April 1867   193

Wynkoop observes April 1867 Hancock-Kiowa meeting   195

Wynkoop's Upper Arkansas Agency at Fort Larned   200

Louise Wynkoop with her first son, late 1860s   202

Arapaho chief Little Raven   207

Edmund Guerrier   231
Cooper Union, where Wynkoop spoke, 1868   248
Washita women and children prisoners, 1870   252
Ned Wynkoop, 1875   258
Ned Wynkoop and Capt. Jack Crawford   263

MAPS

Kansas Territory/State and vicinity   xvii
Colorado Territory and vicinity   xviii

Preface and Acknowledgments

Many years ago, while searching for an Indian agent to use in a novel, I discovered Edward W. Wynkoop. Unfortunately, the research did not pan out, since I was looking for a villain. Instead, I found a man who broke the rules because of his humanity and took a stand against what he considered the murder of innocent people. In so doing, he became a true westerner. By that I mean a man of his times. Although I never completed the novel, my research on Ned Wynkoop has never ended, and one of the results is this book.

This biography of Wynkoop focuses on his western experiences, in particular his years dealing with Indians. A literate man, he left many reports, letters, and even an unfinished first draft of an autobiography, written in 1876. Since Wynkoop wrote it more than a decade after the events he described, his memory failed him on occasion, as was the case with others who wrote about their experiences on the frontier, such as Lieutenant Charles Gatewood (Sixth U.S. Cavalry) and mixed-blood Cheyenne George Bent.[1] Wynkoop checked facts when available, but when they were not available, he did the best he could. This does not mean that he lied or attempted to rewrite history to his advantage. He had a point of view, which, as often happens, changed with the passage of time. Also, memories take on a life of their own as the years pass. Unfortunately, Wynkoop's "Unfinished Colorado History" abruptly stops in 1866. Actually, it is possible that Wynkoop never expected his manuscript to be printed. The first sentence states: "If this narrative should ever be read by any beside my personal friends and relatives I have an apology to make for what I fear must be inevitable in simply detailing the experiences of the humble writer viz[.] the frequent use of the personal pronoun."[2]

· · ·

Many people and institutions have played a major part in this project. For more than twenty years dating back to the 1980s, when it was the New Mexico History Library, the Fray Angélico Chávez History

Library, New Mexico History Museum (Santa Fe), has played the leading role in my understanding of Wynkoop. Former librarian Orlando
Romero allowed me special access to the *Wynkoop Scrapbook,* which
is in the Edward W. Wynkoop Collection. After Orlando's retirement,
curator Tomas Jaehn has continued to open the door and make me welcome. Aiding me in far too many ways to list, he has constantly looked
for ways to bring me back to Santa Fe, including setting up speaking
engagements and creating the Louis Kraft Collection. Over the years
Tomas has become a good friend, and his encouragement, support, and
help cannot be overstated. The Stephen H. Hart Library at the Colorado
Historical Society/History Colorado (Denver) houses the Edward W.
Wynkoop Papers, and like the people at the Chávez, the staff, including
library director Rebecca Lintz, photo librarian Jenny Vega (who also
handled the permissions), Caitlin Deane, and Barbara Dey, among others,
have been terrific. Their holdings are extensive and include a wealth of
information on many of the key players of the 1860s Indian wars. The
Western History Department of the Denver Public Library is another
goldmine for researchers of this turbulent time, and its staff, including
Wendell Cox, Coi Drummond-Gehrig, Bruce Hanson, Sheila O'Hare,
Janice Prater, and Joan Harms, has assisted me for years, offering suggestions and tracking leads. Coi, who handles digital image sales and research, was particularly helpful with some of the key images in this book
(as was Jenny Vega at History Colorado). Images add immeasurably to a
book. Thank you, ladies.

Two people from totally different institutions round out the founda-
tion of my research—Kim Walters and George Elmore. Kim, who is
director of the Braun Research Library, Autry National Center of the
American West (Los Angeles, California), and Marilyn Kim, rights and
reproductions coordinator, have provided expert advice on the library's
holdings, including the extensive photo collection and magnificent
George Bird Grinnell Collection, which is invaluable to anyone interested in the Southern Cheyennes. Across town, their coworker, Marva R.
Felchlin, director of the Autry Research Library, Autry National Center
of the American West (Los Angeles), made it possible for me to view ob-
scure books. I can't say how much I appreciate Kim Walters's friendship
and ongoing support of my projects. George Elmore is chief historian
at the Fort Larned National Historic Site (Kansas). He is an expert on
the 1867 Hancock Expedition as well as the military presence at the
fort. He and the entire fort staff have aided my Wynkoop research, and

I have spent many happy days walking the grounds and accessing their archival material. He teamed up with Leo Oliva (about whom more later) to give me a private tour tracking the April 1867 military march to the Pawnee Fork village site, concluding with our walking the grounds. George has always been ready to answer my spur-of-the moment phone questions. Like Kim's, his enthusiasm, encouragement, and friendship are always present.

The National Archives in Washington, D.C., has provided advice on microfilm collections. Melissa T. Salazar, senior archivist of the New Mexico State Records Center and Archives (Santa Fe), has been instrumental in my understanding of Wynkoop's later life. Site Administrator Tim Rues, Kansas State Historical Society, gave me a private tour of Constitution Hall, a national landmark in Lecompton. This building housed the Kansas Territorial Legislature and the Pawnee Land Office, where Wynkoop worked upon his arrival in the territory. Carol Salomon, archives librarian, Cooper Union (New York City), aided my search for a Wynkoop–Peter Cooper connection, as did Joan Boyle, an independent researcher. Museum Curator Sharon A. Small at the Little Bighorn Battlefield National Monument (Crow Agency, Montana) kindly allowed me to use an image of the Washita prisoners, and Photo Archivist Daniel Kosharek at the Palace of the Governors, New Mexico History Museum Photo Archives (Santa Fe) permitted me to use a key Wynkoop portrait. Other institutions include the Kansas State Historical Society; the Oklahoma Historical Society (Oklahoma City); Harold B. Lee Library, Brigham Young University (Provo, Utah); Beinecke Library, Yale University (New Haven, Connecticut); Tutt Library, Colorado College (Colorado Springs); the Charles E. Young Research Library at UCLA (Los Angeles); and the Central Los Angeles Public Library, which houses a terrific history department on the lower level of the Tom Bradley Wing.

I am grateful to owner Michael Perrin, Valley Photo Service, North Hollywood, California, Noe Torres, and especially Sevan Ghazaryan, who always took that extra step to help me.

Minoma Littlehawk, a National Park ranger who recently completed studying the Cheyenne language at the Cheyenne-Arapaho College in Weatherford, Oklahoma, has been a tremendous help to me in learning the spelling and pronunciation of Cheyenne words. She presented my questions not only to Southern Cheyenne chief Lawrence Hart but also to Carol Joyce Bullcoming, her language professor at the college, and Cheyenne language expert Christine Starr of Hammon, Oklahoma.

Byron Strom, custodian of the Anne E. Hemphill Collection (Des Moines, Iowa), allowed me access to the Silas and Hersa Coberly Soule letters and family photos. Historian Scott Zesch (Art, Texas) kindly shared his research on the capture and release of Melinda Ann Caudle. Before Denver became a favorite destination of mine, in the 1980s Joan Reese performed initial Wynkoop research for me. More recently I shared notes and compared research with Kit Carson Historian Lee Burke (Dallas, Texas) to clarify the Wynkoop-Carson connection.

Four people played a major role in the development of the Wynkoop project. W. Charles Bennett, Jr., a writer/historian and former assistant director of the Palace of the Governors (Santa Fe) has shown me the wondrous treasures that the Palace preserves. On another visit to Santa Fe he led a fence-hopping visit to the National Cemetery to do something I avoid—seeing a grave. Over the years he has provided tips, advice, great stories, his Southwest knowledge, and his Wynkoop research. Historian/writer Leo Oliva has been the leading player in saving the Cheyenne/Sioux village site on the Pawnee Fork in Kansas that General Winfield Hancock destroyed in 1867. His hard work was rewarded on June 17, 2010, when it was added to the National Register of Historic Places, a major coup for the understanding of the Plains Indian wars and the preservation of their sites. This recognition has been a long time coming, and Leo's effort has been Herculean. I don't know where to begin when documenting his endeavors on my behalf. He has invited me to Kansas to talk, initiated the first Wynkoop one-man show, and constantly aided my research. He and his wife, Bonita, who kindly allowed me to use a detail from one of her drawings of Fort Larned, have opened their home to me many times. Christopher H. Wynkoop (d. December 25, 2009), an expert on Ned Wynkoop and creator of a magnificent web site (the Wynkoop Family Research Library), was perhaps the most detail-oriented person I've ever known. He was always available, always willing to help, and I miss him. The fourth person is George Elmore at Fort Larned (already mentioned). In 2007 all four contributed detailed reviews of the first complete Wynkoop draft. It goes without saying that their comments improved the manuscript.

Many writers and historians have offered encouragement and support, including Johnny D. Boggs, Gary McCarthy, Paul Andrew Hutton, Robert Utley, Durwood Ball, Deb Goodrich, Eric Niderost, George Carmichael, Mike Koury, Michael Blake, and Greg Lalire (editor of *Wild*

West), among others, including John Monnett, whose suggestions have been invaluable.

Aaron Cohen, owner of Guidon Books (Scottsdale, Arizona) passed away in December 2010. After we met in the 1970s, he became one of the most influential people in my professional life. I can't tell you how supportive Aaron was of my writing, or how many enjoyable hours I spent in his shop chatting with him. He was a wonderful person, and I'll never forget him.

I would be remiss if I didn't mention my good friend Tom Eubanks, who has directed all the Wynkoop one-man dramas that have played in four states and have evolved into *Cheyenne Blood*. Tom's contribution has been extraordinary, for he has constantly questioned and challenged me, and by so doing, allowed me to view Ned Wynkoop in ways I might have missed if I had confined my research to traditional methods.

In 1990 my cherished daughter Marissa Kraft and I tracked the people and events that led to the 1867 Medicine Lodge Peace council in Kansas for *The Final Showdown* (1992), a book in which Wynkoop and Black Kettle play key roles. Since then Marissa has spent many days following endless trails (most recently, tracking Custer in Montana). She has worked the microfilm machine in the New Mexico State Records Center and Archives and has meticulously transcribed the *Wynkoop Scrapbook* at the Chávez History Library. Good times.

At the cost of precious days together, my lady, best friend, and love, Diane Moon, has supported the Wynkoop project 100 percent. Our missed time is gone, lost forever, but as Errol Flynn's Custer says to Olivia de Havilland's Libbie in *They Died with Their Boots On,* "The more sadness in parting—the more joy in the reunion." As in the film, so alas in reality: life doesn't always turn out as we hope. Diane was my life, and without her my time walking this earth is a little emptier.

Working with the University of Oklahoma Press has been a very enjoyable experience. The staff and their freelancers have done everything possible to bring *Ned Wynkoop and the Lonely Road from Sand Creek* to publication. Emmy Ezzell, assistant director and production manager, ensured, as she did years back with *Gatewood & Geronimo*, that the typesetting and printing process moved forward smoothly and on schedule, answering questions and offering advice. Bill Nelson, a freelance cartographer, immediately understood my needs and took my rough drafts and created absolutely terrific maps. In my humble opinion, a writer's best friend is his copyeditor, and Elizabeth Hadas—Beth—easily became my best friend as we worked together in a give-and-take environment to eliminate errors and improve the text—my favorite part of the entire process for it is here that a manuscript comes to life. Managing editor Steven Baker kept me informed and involved during the entire production process. Realizing that I like an open-door, hands-on approach, he ensured that this was possible and at all times was receptive to my suggestions. All . . . thank you.

This volume has been a project with the University of Oklahoma Press long before editor-in-chief Charles Rankin and I agreed upon the contract. Chuck has been a driving force behind the Wynkoop project for years, and during our time together he has done everything possible to aid my research and improve the text. He has patiently listened to me and, regardless of our differences of opinion, has always stood behind the project 100 percent. I can never fully express my appreciation for all he has done to bring the Wynkoop manuscript to publication . . . other than to say, "Thank you, Chuck, thank you."

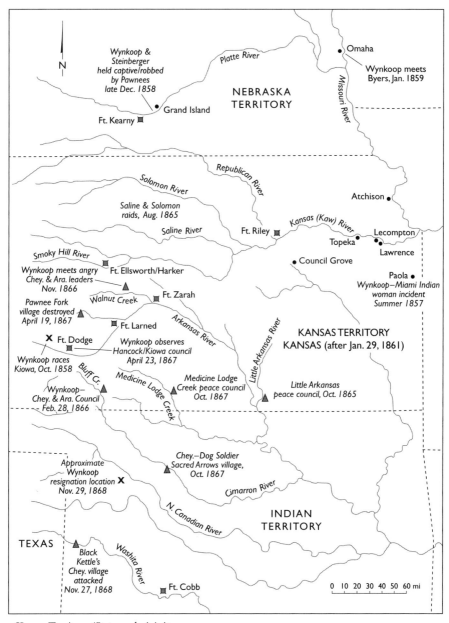

N

*Wynkoop &
Steinberger
held captive/robbed
by Pawnees
late Dec. 1858*

NEBRASKA
TERRITORY

Platte River

Omaha

Missouri River

*Wynkoop meets
Byers, Jan. 1859*

Ft. Kearny   Grand Island

Republican River

Solomon River

Atchison

*Saline & Solomon
raids, Aug. 1865*

Saline River

Ft. Riley

Kansas (Kaw) River

Lecompton

Topeka

Lawrence

Smoky Hill River

*Wynkoop meets angry
Chey. & Ara. leaders
Nov. 1866*

Ft. Ellsworth/Harker

Council Grove

Walnut Creek   Ft. Zarah

*Pawnee Fork
village destroyed
April 19, 1867*

Ft. Larned

Arkansas River

Paola
*Wynkoop–Miami Indian
woman incident
Summer 1857*

X Ft. Dodge

*Wynkoop observes
Hancock/Kiowa council
April 23, 1867*

Little Arkansas River

KANSAS TERRITORY
KANSAS (after Jan. 29, 1861)

*Wynkoop races
Kiowa, Oct. 1858*

Bluff Cr.

Medicine Lodge Creek

*Medicine Lodge
Creek peace council
Oct. 1867*

*Little Arkansas
peace council, Oct. 1865*

*Wynkoop–
Chey. & Ara. Council
Feb. 28, 1866*

*Approximate
Wynkoop
resignation location
Nov. 29, 1868* X

*Chey.–Dog Soldier
Sacred Arrows village,
Oct. 1867*

Cimarron River

N. Canadian River

INDIAN
TERRITORY

TEXAS

*Black
Kettle's
Chey. village
attacked
Nov. 27, 1868*

Washita River

Ft. Cobb

0 10 20 30 40 50 60 mi

Kansas Territory/State and vicinity

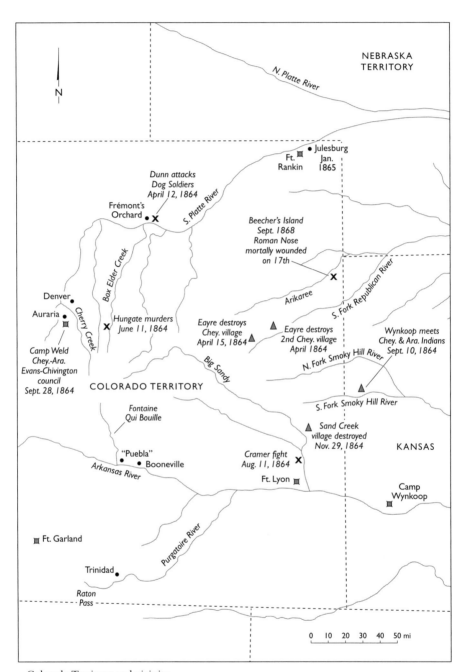

Colorado Territory and vicinity

Ned Wynkoop
and the Lonely Road from
Sand Creek

Formative Years

The late 1850s presented a hopeful prospect for Americans struggling with recession, though one marred by the ever-growing threat of civil war. Promises of a new beginning, land, and riches and the lingering slogan Manifest Destiny powered westward migration. Many believed it was their right to better themselves on the ever-expanding frontier, and few dared speak out against the mode of conquest. Those who did often found themselves the objects of public ridicule or worse.

Edward Wanshaer Wynkoop (1836–91) came of age during this time of westward expansion and began his life on the frontier holding a host of prejudices. His courage to change, however, made him stand apart from most of his contemporaries. His early years were marked by a close relationship with his mother and older siblings that was intensified by the struggle to survive, and this set the tone for Wynkoop's future, as did a family life filled with love, religion, a thirst for knowledge, an appreciation of the arts, the quest to succeed, and loyalty to country. As the youngest of seven children, Wynkoop was especially influenced by this environment.

Wynkoop's father, John Wanshaer Wynkoop, was born September 9, 1794, in Newton, Bucks County, Pennsylvania, and was already a skilled cabinetmaker by his eighteenth birthday. He became known "as a man of great cultivation and refinement."[1] During the War of 1812, when the British Army amassed along the Canadian border in the fall of 1813 in preparation for invading the United States, he enlisted in the

Pennsylvania Militia in early 1814. Wynkoop served first with Fenton's Fifth Regiment and then with Bache's Second Regiment of Light Infantry, where he rose to the rank of quartermaster sergeant.[2]

After the war ended, John Wynkoop moved to Philadelphia, where he became a merchant. Later he engaged in coal mining and owned lime kilns in Montgomery County, Pennsylvania. While still in his twenties, he met and wooed Angeline Catherine Estill (born c. 1803) of Philadelphia. Both John and Angeline were Episcopalians of Dutch heritage. They married on March 4, 1819, and began their family the following year when Francis Murray was born. During the next ten years their brood continued to increase with the birth of Anna Maria (b. January 26, 1821), Emily (b. 1824), John Estill (b. May 9, 1825), Charles Shippen (b. 1828, and named after one of his father's business partners), and George (b. 1830).[3]

During the 1830s Wynkoop prospered. He expanded his business opportunities and owned, wholly or in part, numerous properties in Spring Garden, a district of Philadelphia.[4] A man of property, he set aside time to dabble in something that gave him pleasure, composing poetry. In 1832 he wrote a number of verses that he dedicated "To sister Mary." The *Home Journal* (New York) eventually published the poems under the title "The Voyage of Life" (February 23, 1856).[5]

During his children's formative years, John Wynkoop not only provided them with material comforts but also instilled in them a strong sense of country and duty, an entrepreneurial attitude toward life, and an appreciation of the arts.

Angeline gave birth to her last child, Edward Wanshaer Wynkoop, on June 19, 1836.[6] The newborn would never know the life his older siblings shared, for their lives, and his, were about to change forever. The family's fortunes took a downturn shortly after Edward's birth. Needing money, John Wynkoop sold a store in Spring Garden to Robert Ray, a carpenter, in October 1836. Financial difficulties continued, and on May 30, 1837, Wynkoop sold his half of the remaining properties in the Spring Garden area to pay off additional creditors.[7] A month later, on July 1, 1837, John Wynkoop died at his half-brother George Campbell Wynkoop's house in Pottsville, Pennsylvania.[8] Angeline, a widow at thirty-four, now had to fend for her family alone. But the death of John brought everyone together, and the family survived. Two of the children, Francis, seventeen, and Anna, sixteen, were almost adults, while

Emily, thirteen, and John, twelve, were close behind. All the children took young Edward, now just a year old, under their care. While they may have spoiled him, they were endowed with their father's views and values, and they introduced him to the arts and literature and instilled in him loyalty to country and racial tolerance.

During these formative years Edward's brothers and sisters affectionately called him Neddy. Anna wrote poetry, and one of her poems, "Let Neddy plant the Willow, &c," was a warm tribute to her youngest brother's eagerness to participate. Like most youngsters, Edward eventually outgrew his nickname. By the time he neared maturity he preferred to be called Ned or Ed, names that remained with him for the rest of his life.[9]

By spring 1847, when Edward was almost ten years old, the household had dwindled as some of his older siblings had left home to make their own way in life. Francis enlisted in the First Pennsylvania Volunteers on December 1, 1846, at Pottsville, Pennsylvania, and on December 18 was elected colonel. On the evening of April 12, 1847, he sat in his tent in camp at Mountain Pass, Mexico, just forty miles from Antonio López de Santa Ana and his massive army of 15,000 men in Veracruz. (After Santa Ana conquered the Alamo in 1836, he was defeated by Sam Houston's Texans at the Battle of San Jacinto. Two years later he defeated the French at Veracruz. President and dictator of Mexico from 1841 until overthrown in 1845, Santa Ana had returned to power with the outbreak of war with the United States in 1846.) On that April night Francis anticipated his coming death. As he pondered his future and recorded his thoughts in his Bible, Anna's poem, "Let Neddy plant the Willow, &c," comforted him.[10]

Ten-year-old Neddy Wynkoop had learned of his father's military experiences and he had heard of Santa Ana and Mexico, but he was too young to appreciate the American conquest of California and the war with Mexico. Still, he knew that Frank, as he called Francis, was fighting in Mexico as a member of General Winfield Scott's staff.[11] Realizing that he might never see his older brother again, he prayed for his safe return.

The Americans defeated the Mexicans and on August 8, 1848, Frank Wynkoop mustered out of his regiment in Philadelphia. During the conflict he had observed how badly both officers and soldiers treated their Irish comrades, and it bothered him. Two years later, in 1850, when Frank managed Wynkoop's Shanty in Hempfield Township, Westmoreland County, Pennsylvania, he made a point of only hiring men of Irish descent, somewhere between sixty and eighty employees.[12] Even the teenaged Ned Wynkoop realized the chance his brother was taking by hiring people looked down upon by most whites.

By 1852, Ned Wynkoop had become a striking sixteen-year-old. Confident and dapper almost to the point of being a dandy, he posed for a daguerreotype portrait.[13] The young Wynkoop excelled at school, and his command of the English language would serve him well throughout his life.[14]

Ned Wynkoop's third oldest brother, Charles , also had an artistic bent, but instead of crafting the written word, he craved the theatrical spotlight. Likely he performed as an amateur in Philadelphia before turning professional, performances his youngest brother heard of or saw. By 1855 Charlie, as he preferred to be called, managed his own theatrical company known as McKensie's Vaudeville Troupe. Using the stage name Charles McKensie, he began touring southern states. It was at this time that he met Scottish actress Catharine Sinclair Carmichael, who had her own troupe, the Katie Estelle Company. Four years his junior, Katie had immigrated to the United States with her parents when she was fourteen. Their relationship blossomed, and she and Charlie were married at the Christ Church in Raleigh, North Carolina, on August 30, 1855. After their union, they toured together and Charlie assumed management of her company.[15]

But it was not just Ned's brothers who ventured far afield. Sister Emily married Dr. Thomas Kempton in 1851, only to have him die nine months later. She married again in 1854.[16] Her second husband, William Brindle, rose to the rank of lieutenant colonel in the Second Regiment of Pennsylvania Volunteers during the Mexican War.[17]

Two years after their marriage, Brindle took a position with the United States Pawnee Land Office, in Lecompton, Kansas Territory, a pro-slavery stronghold, and Emily traveled west with her husband in September 1856.

The first survey by the Pawnee Land Office, completed in 1856, included 1,864,141 acres approved for sale along the eastern borders of Nebraska and Kansas Territories. Surveyor General John C. Calhoun estimated that the number of acres available for sale would expand to 2,860,000 by June 1857.[18]

Although Brindle has sometimes been called surveyor general, he actually became the receiver in the office. Soon after his arrival, Brindle

Ned Wynkoop at the age of sixteen in 1852. Daguerreotype in author's collection.

began writing editorial pieces for the Lecompton *Democrat*, and often his three-to-four-column articles supported abolitionists and damned slavery, making him a marked man.[19]

Of all Ned Wynkoop's siblings' life choices, Emily's would have the biggest impact on him, for it was her move to Kansas that became the deciding factor in his going "a-westering."

CHAPTER ONE

Gone A-westering

Edward W. Wynkoop stood out in any crowd. According to his son, Frank, he was "six feet three inches tall, broad-shouldered and athletically built," which made him tower above most of his contemporaries.[1] By summer 1856, when just twenty, he had decided to leave home and make his fortune. Emily, knowing her younger brother was anxious to begin his adult life, insisted he follow her to Lecompton, in the rolling hills of northeastern Kansas Territory. Built in 1854 on a bluff above the south bank of the Kaw (or Kansas) River, the town (originally named Bald Eagle) had just become the first capital of Kansas Territory.

On his way to Lecompton by the fall of 1856, Wynkoop took a "train to Pittsburgh, a boat down the Ohio to the Mississippi, and a steamer up the Mississippi to the Missouri."[2] Here he boarded the steamer *F. X. Aubry* for Fort Leavenworth, Kansas Territory. But floating ice hindered progress, and the captain put Wynkoop and the other passengers ashore to walk. Twenty-two miles later they found food and shelter.[3] Upon his arrival at Lecompton, Emily welcomed him into her home, a log cabin, and Brindle hired him as a general clerk in the Receiver's Department of the Pawnee Land Office, which occupied the first floor of a two-story wooden building that also had a basement.[4] To avoid being flooded when the Kaw River overflowed, it was built above a perpendicular cut into a small hill. A wide wooden staircase led up to the front entry of the building. The second floor housed the territorial legislature.[5]

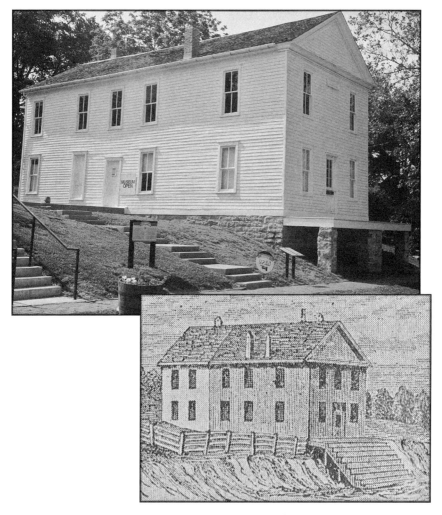

The Lecompton building that housed the Pawnee Land Office on the first floor and the Kansas Territorial Legislature on the second floor in the late 1850s. It was here that Wynkoop worked for his brother-in-law William Brindle upon his arrival in Kansas Territory, and it was here he met the fifth territorial governor of Kansas, James W. Denver. The photograph shows what the building, a national landmark, looks like today. Woodcut in author's collection; photograph © 2008 by Louis Kraft.

At first, Wynkoop found his new life in Lecompton invigorating. This would not last, since his duties as clerk did not inspire him. But one day when he arrived at the office, he was surprised to see Brindle standing by his desk "with a Bowie Knife peeping from under one side of his coat tail and a Six shooter from the other."[6] Wynkoop knew that Brindle condemned slavery, not a popular or safe view in Lecompton, and he was aware that free-staters and border ruffians, those opposed to slavery and those for it, made Lecompton a powder keg ready to explode. Up to now, though, Wynkoop had been on the outside looking in.

The threat was real, as Wynkoop—who shared the upstairs of the Brindles' cabin with three other Pennsylvanians, the Petrikin brothers (Hardman and Henry) and George Crawford—would soon learn. Hardman served as head clerk in the Receiver's Department; Henry was evidence clerk. Shortly after Wynkoop's arrival, Emily, who was known to her inner circle as "Joan of Arc," and Brindle invited him to join co-conspirators Crawford and the Petrikins in plotting against border ruffians.[7] Taking him into their confidence, they showed him the arsenal that Brindle maintained in the cabin—muskets in the cellar and on the upstairs floor. Brindle had every intention of protecting his home against invasion.

The image his brother-in-law presented in the office, combined with the arsenal, made it clear to Wynkoop that survival skills were critical. Violence had become common as free-state advocates and slavers struggled to control the territory. So in his spare time Wynkoop worked at mastering the art of self-defense. Gaining confidence as his skill improved, and in stark contrast to "the frantic struggles of the speculators in their endeavor to snatch up the most valuable lands," he quietly completed the transformation.[8] "In those dark days and darker nights," George Crawford later explained, "when assassination lurked in alleys, and prowled upon the streets, and listened through the keyholes, we whispered or quietly muttered many an hour away together."[9] Joining his friends and coworkers, all of whom "were armed like Brigands," Wynkoop wore buckskin and packed a Bowie knife and revolver.[10]

One evening Wynkoop ate dinner at the Brindle residence before returning to the land office. A young Quaker, a new hire of Brindle's who had just arrived from Pennsylvania, sat at the table for the first time. Finished eating, Wynkoop excused himself, stood, and buckled on his weapons. The Quaker watched him in horror. "I should consider myself no better than a murderer," he said, "were I to go armed in that fashion; why do you do it?"[11] Acclimated to Lecompton, Wynkoop looked at the newcomer. "Never mind, my boy," he drawled, "if you stay here long you will find out." And the newcomer did, ultimately arming himself "with a bigger pistol and a longer Bowie Knife."

By the time the territorial legislature met in January 1857, the population of Lecompton exceeded one thousand. The fast-growing town was a proslavery hotbed that housed four churches, a school, a livery stable, three hotels, six dry goods stores, a number of law offices, the land office, surveyor general's office, the capitol building, a U.S. courthouse, and a great many saloons. Choice town lots sold for $500 to $1,000 each. That year hundreds of settlers came to the Pawnee Land Office to record their claims, many of which were contested at the courthouse. One or two stores, the land office, lawyers, and saloons all did a booming business. During this time Wynkoop was continually aware of the discontent that seethed on the streets, but his clerical duties kept him too busy to conspire with his housemates.[12]

In February the legislature passed a bill to create a constitution for entry into the Union as a slave state. John W. Geary, third territorial governor of Kansas (July 31, 1856–March 20, 1857), vetoed the bill, but the legislature immediately overruled him, which aggravated the antislavery group. Fed up with the incendiary atmosphere, Geary submitted his resignation. Incoming President James Buchanan ignored the resignation and fired Geary, effective March 20.[13] Robert J. Walker became the fourth territorial governor on May 27, 1857.[14]

Prior to the establishment of Nebraska and Kansas territories, many eastern Indians had been removed to the lands west of the Missouri River. As whites migrated westward they discovered that much of the reservation land granted to the displaced Indians was attractive for settlement. The Peoria, Kaskaskia, Piankeshaw, Wea, and Miami Indians signed over most of their reservation lands to the United States in May and June 1854. Held in trust, this territory included 400,000 acres of Kaskaskia and Peoria, 150,000 acres of Piankeshaw and Wea, and 400,000 acres of Miami reservation lands.

By early June 1857 the Pawnee Land Office relocated temporarily to Paola, a small town near the Missouri border, about forty-five miles southeast of Lecompton. The move to Paola did not provide a respite from the tensions in Lecompton for Wynkoop or his companions.

Determined to obtain as much land as possible, proslavers from Missouri crossed the border. This set up yet another opportunity for bloodshed as free-staters also intended to control the land in the area.[15]

That June tensions between the feuding sides drove the situation to a crisis. Before violence could erupt, Governor Walker addressed a mob from a wagon parked in front of the Paola Land Office. Wynkoop stood to the side and watched as Walker spoke to the belligerent gathering, "composed of hundreds armed to the teeth, about equally divided between free-state and pro-slavery men."[16] When no one responded to his words, an unnerved governor hastily climbed into the land office through a window behind the wagon. Charles Foster, an attorney and free-stater, leaped onto the wagon and denounced Walker and the U.S. government. His words agitated the crowd, which began to grumble. Realizing his peril, Foster jumped off the wagon and disappeared. Seeing an opportunity, New Yorker Edwin O. Perrin, who traveled with the governor, climbed out of the window that Walker had used for his exit. He attempted without success to calm the restless crowd. Supporters of Foster's views drew their guns and began yelling. A rider charged the wagon. Brandishing a pistol, he demanded to know if Perrin's goal was to insult Foster. Unnerved, Perrin blurted a negative response and dove through the window.

With their weapons drawn, the antagonists backed away from each other, lining opposite sides of the street. Quietly watching the spectacle, Wynkoop kept his distance and maintained a firm grip on his revolver and knife. He later described the scene, tongue firmly in cheek. "Not being interested [in] either side, [I] looked on feeling somewhat like the old woman who saw her husband and the Bear fighting." Although his politics were already well formed, he was not yet ready to take a public stand.

Suddenly Commissioner of Land Sales Robert Stevens leaped onto the wagon to address the crowd. He warned them that if they started shooting, he would shut down the land office. Both sides knew the ownership of land would play an important part in the territory's entry into the union, whether as a free or a slave state. Although the selling of human chattel remained a growing concern in American politics, on that day land sales ruled in Kansas Territory. As Wynkoop later remembered, "land sales progressed without any further excitement." He nonchalantly added, "Occasionally a man was killed but that thing had become monotonous."

One day in Paola, Wynkoop with some companions from the land office, including his well-armed Quaker friend, decided to have a drink. While walking down the street they came upon an old man hanging by his ankles from a tree. A group of ruffians poked their prisoner, prodding him to confess to a robbery he claimed he had not committed. Wynkoop's party pushed their way to the front and cut the tethered man down. When the accusers complained, the Quaker cracked one of them over the head with his revolver, ending the confrontation.[17]

As the days passed there would be additional incidents, some more serious than others. Once as Wynkoop and some friends were strolling down a road bordered on both sides by a wooden fence, they were startled to see a Miami Indian woman galloping toward them. As Wynkoop and the others scrambled, she changed directions and tried to ride them down. Missing one of the white men, she aimed at another. Realizing she was drunk, Wynkoop leaped onto the fence, and cockily made mocking and offensive gestures at her. She immediately charged him, pulled a pepper-box pistol from her blanket, and pointed it at him. Wynkoop flipped over backward onto the grass. Looking up from flat on his back, he watched as she drew a bead on him. He began rolling, then regained his feet and ran. She did not shoot, but Wynkoop never lived it down. No matter how hard he tried to silence his companions he failed to hush up the incident, for they had too much fun telling and then retelling the story. He later proclaimed, "I have never run away from a Squaw since."[18]

Wynkoop's sense of humor grew right along with his manliness. Over the coming years he would take potshots at his own bravery, underplaying the danger of some of the situations in which he found himself.

Soon after the incident on the streets of Paola, Brindle closed the land office. He had over $800,000 in gold coin, and now faced the daunting prospect of safely transporting it to the U.S. subtreasury in St. Louis. As Brindle's brother-in-law, Wynkoop was privy to the threats that the shipment of gold would never reach its destination.

The most direct route was the road to Kansas City and then the Missouri River to St. Louis. Brindle and Wynkoop decided that the best course of action was not to deny anything, which gave the impression that they would take the quickest route north. On the day of their departure, they set out on the Kansas City road at 3:00 P.M. Their party consisted of four wagons manned by mixed-bloods hauling the money, the land office's attachés, and an armed guard. In all, the Brindle-Wynkoop party consisted of "nineteen well armed men."[19]

The wagon train slowly made its way north, continuing long after dark. Finally, two hours after sunset, when Brindle and Wynkoop felt certain no one was following them, they changed direction and headed west onto the grassland. After they finally called a halt, one of the guards reported that he heard voices. As it turned out, a well-armed band of ruffians was hunting them. At midnight, the moon offered enough light to travel and the convoy continued the journey. They reached Leavenworth City, not Kansas City as previously advertised, and their ultimate destination, St. Louis, without further incident. After making the delivery Wynkoop and Brindle returned to Lecompton. The trip gave Wynkoop a foretaste of battle. No bullets had been fired, no blood drawn, but he had become a veteran of a conflict that did not take prisoners. This was a lesson he would not forget.

During the summer of 1857 United States stocks began falling at alarming rates. On August 24 the stock market crashed, initiating a panic that swept the country. In New York City alone, more than 40,000 people lost their jobs. The panic produced high prices, a large excess of goods, and an "orgy of railroad construction" that spiraled out of control. The panic soon deepened into a depression. The frontier borderlands suffered more than the Northeast and the mid-Atlantic states. With the massive influx of immigrants to western territories, the land market should have continued to boom, but low prices combined with the abundance of prime land marked the end of a promising future.[20]

Violence stemming from the slavery issue continued and then escalated. Simply walking the streets of Lecompton put one at risk. Free-state views did not sit well in a predominantly proslavery land. Even though he had developed survival skills, Wynkoop questioned his prospects. He was earning a living, but that was all. Bleeding Kansas had little to offer beyond an early grave. With well-defined views on slavery, he avoided confrontations by declining to discuss the subject. Young and ambitious, Wynkoop looked for a more positive future.

The governor's office constantly changed occupants, and on May 12, 1858, James W. Denver became Kansas Territory's fifth governor. As the territorial congress convened on the second floor of the land office,

Wynkoop found himself in close proximity to the governor and the congress. At an opportune time he stepped up to Denver and introduced himself, mentioning that his older brother Frank, who had died in December 1857, had been Denver's comrade during the Mexican War. Frank's recent death opened the door. Wynkoop's boldness led to a friendship, and Denver, who liked Wynkoop, took him into his confidence. On one of Wynkoop's visits to the governor's office, Denver showed him a large map of a newly discovered gold region then known only as Pike's Peak, at the eastern base of the Rocky Mountains. Denver spoke of his plans for turning the area into a territory known as Shoshonee, which, according to Wynkoop's memory, took in portions of New Mexico, Kansas, and Nebraska territories.[21] The name would change, but the plan and its scope would survive.

In the spring of 1858, rumors of gold discoveries east of the Rocky Mountains began sweeping through Kansas Territory. Like many in Lecompton, Ned Wynkoop found himself caught up in the excitement. At the beginning of September 1858 he attended a meeting in Lecompton to set up a land development project in the gold region. Eager to make his fortune and anxious to put bleeding Kansas behind him, he joined the outfit. Denver heard of the plans, and on September 21 he bestowed official positions upon some of the members of the group. By this time he had recognized Wynkoop's potential and named him sheriff of Arapahoe County, a massive area in the western portion of the territory. Wynkoop would later express the opinion that his position as sheriff was as worthless as the paper it was printed on, but in 1858 he had every intention of using his appointment for all it was worth. He was now known as Sheriff Wynkoop. Other appointed officials included Hickory Rogers, chairman of supervisors, who carried blank commissions to use as he deemed appropriate; Lucillias J. Winchester and Joseph McCubbin, supervisors; Hampton L. Boan, clerk of supervisors; H. P. A. Smith, a friend of Denver's from his California days, probate judge; and John H. St. Mathews, county attorney. While Denver envisioned his newly commissioned officers organizing Arapahoe County, setting up a town-site, and selling lots, several members of the expedition were intent primarily on mining.[22]

Wynkoop and sixteen heavily armed companions set out for Topeka. Some of them, including Wynkoop, rode good horses; the rest drove wagons. At Topeka they provisioned themselves for one year. They knew their objective: the confluence of Cherry Creek and the South Platte River, some ninety miles north of Pike's Peak. The guidebooks touted the central route, which followed first the Kaw River and then the Smoky Hill River or the Republican River, as the most direct. This route had the advantage of beginning in Topeka, but Wynkoop and his companions decided against it. They realized that the central route was poorly documented. Fall had arrived, and, with weather conditions now a concern, the Santa Fe Trail to the Arkansas River was clearly the only viable route. Before traveling south to the Santa Fe Trail, they backtracked to Lawrence, where they set out for the famed road on September 23. As Wynkoop put it, "excitement and exhilaration" super-seded "any sense of disaster."[23] Following the trail, they reached Council Grove, Kansas Territory, then the outskirts of civilization, on September 27. Here one of the miners traded a horse to a Kaw (Kansa) Indian for a mule. Finally, on October 1, 1858, Smith and Wynkoop led the wagon train onto the plains.

As the newly commissioned officials rode westward on the Santa Fe Trail they saw buffalo and Indians, but the journey progressed without incident until some three hundred miles west of Council Grove, when a large group of Kiowa and Comanche warriors approached the cara-van. During the meeting a Kiowa spotted the recently traded-for mule. Using sign language, he indicated that Kaws had stolen it from him and that he wanted it back. After speaking among themselves, the whites refused to hand over the animal.

This angered the Indians. They waved their weapons and shouted. The threat was clear, but nothing happened. The whites cautiously de-parted, and the Comanches and Kiowas did not follow them. By night-fall there was no sign of the Indians, and Wynkoop's group relaxed—a bit prematurely, for the next morning the warriors reappeared and kept pace with the caravan. Not knowing the Indians' intentions and fearing attack, Wynkoop and his companions kept their weapons close. Tense hours passed. Then, before noon, a number of warriors approached the wagon train and the Kiowa asked for the mule. The whites again refused the request.

The Indians pulled away, then returned to the caravan, but not close enough to talk. Instead, they followed the train, maintaining a safe gap between the two groups. While tension among the whites grew, Wynkoop, in his ignorance, rode some distance from the wagon train.

One of the Kiowas approached him and, using sign language, challenged him to a horse race. Wynkoop understood the man's intention, and off they charged, running neck and neck. Wynkoop was slightly ahead when his rifle bounced off the pommel of his saddle and discharged, the ball narrowly missing the Indian's mount. Thinking he had been attacked, the Kiowa shouted and pulled away. Wynkoop yanked his mount to a halt and cautiously approached the man. He frantically attempted to sign that he did not mean to shoot. He had never used sign language before. The Indian did not seem to understand his apology, which was probably muddled.

Upon hearing the shot, the other warriors yelled and charged. Before Wynkoop could react, he found himself surrounded. Unnerved, he quickly realized he did not face the "noble savages" of the James Fenimore Cooper novels. Nor were they "Poor Lo," the idealized Indians of the eastern press. He faced living, breathing warriors, well-armed adversaries capable of killing him. He looked toward his companions. Instead of rushing to his rescue, they quickly circled the wagons. Alone and surrounded, Wynkoop thought he would be killed. Then the Kiowa he raced spoke. Wynkoop did not understand the man's words, but to his great relief the warriors rode off and he realized that he had been spared.

That day the Comanches and Kiowas camped near the whites. When evening arrived Wynkoop and his cohorts spent a long restless night holding their weapons and peering into the blackness. Nothing happened, and the next morning they discovered that the Indians had left. Unsure how they had avoided hostilities, Wynkoop and the others dismissed the lack of a skirmish as pure luck. Years later, when he came to understand Indians, Wynkoop knew better, deciding that "they are not the first to precipitate a war, and whenever Indian hostilities have taken place war has been forced upon them by the action of the whites."[24]

The Indian threat gone, the Rogers-Smith-Wynkoop outfit plodded onward, day in and day out, until they finally reached a stream known as Fontaine Qui Bouille, or Fountain Creek, which drained into the Arkansas River twenty-five miles south of Pike's Peak. Several Mexican hunters and two whites from New Mexico had set up camp in a long-abandoned adobe building known as Puebla. (Built as a trading post in 1841 or 1842, the post shut down in 1843 when the Mexican government banned commerce with white trappers. Mexican farmers occupied the adobe structure until an attack on Christmas Day 1854 by

Jicarilla Apache and Ute warriors.) The hunters advised Wynkoop and Smith that early snowstorms made it risky for them to attempt crossing the 8,000-foot Palmer Divide until spring. Disappointed, they discussed the situation with their companions and as a group decided to set up camp north of the ruins and wait out the winter.[25]

Unknown to Smith and Wynkoop, another land development outfit, which had set out from Leavenworth on October 3, was camped six miles east of the ruins. One evening while two of the Smith-Wynkoop men were gathering hay, a member of the other party saw them, and soon after William Larimer, Jr., who had decided to investigate, entered their camp. A teetotaler who was opposed to slavery, the forty-nine-year-old Larimer had been a politician, banker, and railroad builder in Pennsylvania, where he also served in the militia. After moving to Nebraska Territory in 1855, he founded Larimer City. When rumors of gold at the base of the Rockies surfaced, he changed his career direction once again.

Larimer's company was not as large as the Lecompton train, but it was better outfitted. The party included his eighteen-year-old son, William H. H. Larimer, Charles A. Lawrence, Richard E. Whitsett, Folsom Dorsett, and M. M. Jewett. Relying only on a four-yoke ox wagon, they hauled everything they would need to set up a land claim, including tools, nails, pine planks, glass for windows, and provisions for a year.

As the men talked, Wynkoop realized that neither outfit was skilled at real estate exploitation. When Smith and Wynkoop mentioned the snowstorms and reported that Lieutenant Marcy had lost men and livestock the previous May while attempting to pass through Palmer Divide, Larimer dismissed their fears, urging them to attempt the crossing immediately. At first Rogers, Smith, and Wynkoop hesitated, but Larimer's persistence won out and they agreed to push on to Cherry Creek. Next, Larimer persuaded the two groups to join forces. Using a blank commission, Rogers named Larimer treasurer and made him one of Governor Denver's officers of the now-merged organization.[26]

The two groups agreed to meet at a common junction that was reachable in one day. Unfortunately, they celebrated their union long into the night and relaxed their guard. The next morning, they discovered that all their saddle animals had been stolen. They blamed the Mexican hunting party, who were now gone. Luckily the travelers still had their mules and oxen, and decided to press on. But now Wynkoop and the others who had ridden horses traveled on foot. When they reached Palmer Divide they had better luck than Marcy's party. They saw scattered bones and could tell how deep the snow must have been judging by where trees had been cut. They camped at the Point of Rocks. That night twelve inches of snow fell, but next morning Larimer, Wynkoop, and company continued their march, plodding slowly forward, and walked out of the snow. According to Hickory Rogers, they reached the headwaters of Cherry Creek on the evening of October 30, 1858. With no further reason for haste, they rested and hunted, feasting on deer, antelope, and wild turkey. Setting out once again, they passed Montana City, the most advanced of the towns sprouting up in the area, and seven miles later reached the junction of Cherry Creek and the South Platte River on November 2.[27]

CHAPTER TWO

To Civilization and Back

As Ned Wynkoop, William Larimer, and their party looked at the land they had traveled so far to reach that November 1858, they realized they had a problem: they were too late to claim the prime acreage. Georgians, New Mexicans, and Nebraskans had laid out the town of Auraria on the west side of Cherry Creek, and the St. Charles Town Company, a land-development organization from Lawrence, Kansas Territory, had surveyed the land east of the creek.[1]

As it happened, however, most of the St. Charles group had set out for Lecompton to file the paperwork for their proposed city. Feeling secure, they had left only three men behind to protect their interests. One of the men, Charles Nichols, had also come from Lawrence. The other two were mountain men living in the area, William McGaa, sometimes known as Jack Jones, and John Simpson Smith. Good friends and always together, McGaa had a Sioux wife and Smith had a Cheyenne wife.[2]

As soon as Larimer, who had begun to assume control, realized that the St. Charles people had departed, he, H. P. A. Smith, and Wynkoop moved quickly. Hickory Rogers spread the word that Governor Denver sanctioned the Lecompton-Leavenworth group, that they had commissions, and that they would now take charge of the area. Rogers's pronouncement did not sit well with those already on the South Platte, especially the men from Georgia. They told the newcomers they would not hesitate to hang any of Denver's so-called officers if they attempted "to exercise any official functions."[3] Wynkoop and his companions took the threat seriously. Still, they had commissions and could show them to doubters. Larimer, Smith, and Wynkoop had no intention of walking away from this rich land.

Larimer, probate judge Smith, and Sheriff Wynkoop went to visit McGaa on the night of November 17 and invited the Lecompton-Leavenworth group, the Lawrence party, and anyone else who might be interested in forming a new town company, to join them. Larimer wanted those with him added to the St. Charles Town Company register. Such an action, McGaa explained, required a two-thirds vote of the company, which was impossible since the majority of the members were not present. Angry at the answer, Larimer said he had the power to declare the Right and Title of the St. Charles Town Company null and void, that he would evict them, and that if McGaa, Smith, or Nichols returned they'd be killed. In the face of this threat, they accepted the new order.[4]

The pleasantries finished, "ardent spirits" were served, and Larimer took charge. The gathering discussed setting up a town company, this one with Governor Denver's sanction, but they settled nothing that night. During a second meeting, again at McGaa's, they named the proposed city east of Cherry Creek "Golden City." By this time Larimer, Smith, Wynkoop, and company had physical control of the land, but Larimer realized that they still had work to do. He called for yet another meeting at McGaa's on the evening of November 22. At this meeting E. P. Stout became president of the organization. Larimer became donating agent, which gave him the power to run the proposed town. None of the former St. Charles representatives objected, and they became members of the company. At this meeting forty-one members drew up papers that created the Denver City Town Company and adopted a constitution.

Realizing the value of official confirmation, that night Larimer told the assembly that they needed volunteers to represent the company and return to Lecompton. Winter was approaching and the weather had begun to change, with temperatures dropping below freezing after dark. They could not wait until spring, Larimer told the gathering; they must act now. Someone had to incorporate the Denver City Town Company, print stock certificates, and ensure that they did not lose their new property. Wynkoop had done everything possible during the trip west to increase his value to the land development outfit. He now saw an opportunity to play a key role in the township's success. The group had already gambled and safely passed through the Palmer Divide; surely a winter passage back to civilization could not be more trying. Wynkoop stepped forward, as did Albert B. Steinberger, another Pennsylvanian.

Later that night of November 22 when Golden City was questioned as a suitable name, Wynkoop spoke up, saying that they should call the town Denver, in honor of the territorial governor. Larimer liked the idea, most everyone agreed, and the motion passed.[5]

But all did not go smoothly for Governor Denver's appointed officials. Their presence bothered many of the men who had preceded them to the area, including G. N. Hill of Auraria. "We thought we were out of the pale of civilization, and would be allowed to regulate our domestic affairs to our own liking," Hill said.[6] Another meeting was called, this time by the citizens of the South Platte, who invited Wynkoop, H. P. A. Smith, and Larimer. The disgruntled men told Denver's appointees they did not want them "to administer justice," that *they* would choose who ruled the area. Not finished, they demanded that the newcomers resign their commissions, but Wynkoop and his companions refused to quit, saying they needed to think it over. "If they do not resign," Hill wryly commented, "look out for squally times in the valley of the South Platte."

The infant town of Denver City boasted a dozen houses by November 28. With plenty of water in the creeks, everyone had high hopes of finding gold. "The weather is not favorable for digging and nearly everyone is fixing for winter; still some are digging and doing well," William Larimer wrote his wife, Rachel McMasters.[7] "We found gold in small quantities along the banks of the Platte River as well as on Cherry Creek," Wynkoop remembered, "but no mining to any extent was carried on at that season [for] it was too late to prospect in the mountains where it was supposed to exist in quantities."[8]

On December 1, 1858, the men of the South Platte held yet another meeting with Larimer, Wynkoop, and Governor Denver's appointees. Wynkoop resigned as sheriff and the large gathering appointed McGaa to take his place effective the next day.[9] Ned Wynkoop knew the value of the office of sheriff of Arapahoe County. Although he had resigned, he had no intention turning his back on his appointment.

Snow fell, temperatures continued to fall, dropping below zero, and creeks froze, with rivers not far behind. Ned Wynkoop and Albert Steinberger must have questioned their chances of surviving the trip they had volunteered to undertake. Not knowing what awaited them, they packed supplies on a wagon pulled by two mules. They also accepted letters to transport east. Larimer had orders for Wynkoop to give his son John a map of Denver City after he created lithographs of it in the territorial capital. Bundled up in layers of clothing, Wynkoop and Steinberger climbed aboard the wagon and set out for Lecompton on December 3. Wynkoop had heard that the South Platte River route was the shortest distance between the gold fields and their destination, and they chose it so as to reach Lecompton as quickly as possible.[10]

That first day Wynkoop and Steinberger huddled against the cold as the wagon bounced and slid over the icy ground. Whatever they had expected, this was worse. Wynkoop's feet froze. He was in a bad way, and, as neither he nor Steinberger knew what to do, Wynkoop feared he might lose his feet. Luckily they happened upon white hunters who took care of him, saving his feet. On the second day, Wynkoop and Steinberger camped in an Arapaho village; this tribe often occupied land near the South Platte and Cherry Creek. While in the village they traded for an Indian pony. The next day two Arapaho warriors guided them until they were headed in the right direction, and that afternoon they found a decent camp. Bad weather continued to slow their progress, and the scarcity of game on the barren plain increased the amount of time they had to dedicate to finding food. At times they went days without seeing a tree as they slowly made their way over the rolling swells of land.[11]

Finally, after traveling four hundred miles, Wynkoop and Steinberger reached Fort Kearney, Nebraska Territory, on the southern bank of the Platte River. They rested that night and the following morning. Wanting to reach the north shore of the shallow river, Wynkoop asked if they could safely cross over the ice and was told they could.

Setting out from Fort Kearney that same afternoon, Wynkoop and Steinberger traveled to where they had been directed to cross. Looking at the expanse of ice, which he thought might be a mile wide, Wynkoop eased the wagon onto the ice and then maintained a slow pace. As they approached the middle of the river, the ice suddenly broke. The mules, Indian pony, and wagon plunged into the river. With the mules frantically flailing about and the Indian pony struggling to climb back onto firm ice, Wynkoop and Steinberger jumped into the water and unhooked the team. One of the mules worked its way back onto the ice, but the other gave up. Pulling themselves onto the ice, Wynkoop and Steinberger lassoed the mule still in the water, and, using the other mule, hauled it out of the water. But their efforts were in vain, for the mule died within minutes.[12]

By this time night had fallen, the wagon was still underwater, and they were sopping wet. Abandoning the wagon, they hustled to reach the north shore. Using the pony and the surviving mule, they dragged the dead mule behind them. Their clothing frozen stiff, the two men did not dare sleep. Instead, they moved about until exhausted, then sat on the dead mule before getting up and moving about again. Wolves, lured by the carcass, circled the white men in the blackness, yipping and howling. The predators ventured so close that Wynkoop heard the patter of their paws on the ice.

In the morning Wynkoop and Steinberger had a bit of luck. A herder who worked for Russell, Majors and Waddell, a freighting company, happened upon them. Wynkoop, who knew the local agent, jotted a note and asked the herder to deliver it. The herder agreed, and later that day men working for Russell, Majors and Waddell arrived. They hauled the wagon out of the water and pulled it to shore. Hitching the remaining mule and the pony to the wagon, Wynkoop and Steinberger continued their journey. The lack of sleep caught up to them, and they struggled to stay awake as the wagon bounced over the prairie. After a while they saw the settlement of Grand Island in the distance above the banks of the Platte. Although anxious to reach the town, Wynkoop did not push the animals.

Without warning, a party of warriors charged and forced the wagon to a halt. Dirty and poorly dressed, the Indians looked to Wynkoop like beggars. He attempted to start the wagon, but the warriors refused to let him pass. A mixed-blood pushed his mount forward and said in English that the white men would remain where they were until his companions decided they could leave. The warriors were Pawnees, he said, and lived on a nearby reservation—in other words, these were "civilized" Indians.[13]

As he had during his initial trek westward, Wynkoop and Steinberger had safely passed through land occupied by what Wynkoop called "wild" and "uncivilized" Indians—Cheyennes, Arapahos, and Sioux—without being molested. Before they reached Fort Kearney, Arapahos had sheltered them and provided them with food—something Wynkoop never forgot. Writing years later, he used the words "wild" and "uncivilized" to distinguish Indians who lived free on the prairie from Indians who had already been forced onto reservations, whom he called "civilized." Wynkoop did not have a good opinion of reservation Indians, believing that "they had succeeded in acquiring all the vices of the white man without being troubled with any of his virtues."[14]

Using the mixed-blood to interpret, the Pawnees began to interrogate the whites. They wanted to know the whereabouts of their tribal enemies—Cheyennes, Arapahos, and Sioux. Although Wynkoop and Steinberger had had some contact, they did not provide an answer. Next, the mixed-blood asked if they had seen any buffalo, and Wynkoop again answered negatively. The interrogation continued until the Pawnees ran out of questions and Wynkoop attempted to move the wagon. The warriors screamed, and some leaped off their mounts and grabbed the bridle traces of the white men's livestock. One Pawnee jerked the mule's bit so violently that the animal bled from the mouth. Other warriors grabbed the wagon's wheels to keep it from moving. Warriors leaped onto the wagon and rummaged through what remained of the supplies. After an hour the Pawnees had all they wanted but still refused to free the white men. Uneasy over what might happen next, Wynkoop reached for his rifle. Immediately the warriors pointed their weapons at him and Steinberger. He released his grip and nervously waited.

Another Pawnee rode up, and the mixed-blood announced that he was a chief. Using the interpreter, Wynkoop asked if they could go, and the chief signaled for the warriors to release the whites. Wynkoop used a blacksnake, a heavy whip, to start the animals toward Grand Island. When it became obvious that the Pawnees were not pursuing them, Wynkoop allowed the tired livestock to slow to a walk.

But the encounter had not ended. When they were half a mile from the town, they heard someone yelling. Turning, Wynkoop saw a Pawnee riding toward them. When the warrior drew close, he signed that he wanted them to stop. Wynkoop recognized him as the man who had made the mule bleed. As he approached the wagon, the Pawnee held up moccasins and shouted "swap, swap." Wynkoop could not believe what he heard. It was almost as if the warrior felt he had done no wrong. Still frightened, but now also angry, Wynkoop pulled the wagon to a halt and looked about. The other Pawnees had disappeared; the warrior was alone. "I motioned to him to come on," Wynkoop remembered, "saying Yes we'll Swap." The warrior dismounted and walked to the wagon. When he was close, Wynkoop swung the blacksnake with all his might, striking the warrior across the face, slicing the skin almost as if he had cut him with a knife. The Pawnee screamed and ran. At the same time, Wynkoop lashed the animals into a mad dash toward the settlement and safety.

Wynkoop and Steinberger reached Omaha, Nebraska Territory, on January 5, 1859. To Wynkoop's surprise, he and Steinberger "created an immense sensation" as they were the first travelers from the Rockies to reach the city with news of gold finds.[15] Up to then all the people of Omaha had heard were conflicting rumors. Wynkoop and Steinberger, although unknown in the city, found themselves in demand, for, as Wynkoop reported, "we were supposed to be somewhat reliable."

They announced who they were and from where they had recently departed. But that was it. Wynkoop and Steinberger were dirty, hungry, and worn out. They checked into the recently opened Herndon House, the first major hotel in Omaha.[16]

Alone in his room, Ned Wynkoop stepped to the mirror and looked at himself. "I must confess it was as horrible a looking specimen of humanity as ever I gazed upon," he later wrote.[17] "Dressed in buckskin from head to foot, an otter skin cap and Indian moccasins; long matted hair falling below the shoulders; unshaven and dirty face; belt around the waist with Pistols and Bowie Knife attached I seemed to be a cross between a Malay pirate and a Digger Indian." The hard journey had added darker edges to his appearance, and in the coming years much of what he described would continue to characterize his appearance. He liked wearing buckskin and fur caps, often armed himself with revolvers and Bowie knives, at times wore his hair on the long side, and from this time forward always let his whiskers grow.

Crowds of people followed Wynkoop and Steinberger whenever they appeared on the street. Answering the population's questions, the two reported "the most flattering and cheering accounts of the mines, confirming all that has heretofore been published."[18] Steinberger produced a small piece of gold that was "part of eight dollars washed in one day by him."

Wynkoop and Steinberger's stopover in Omaha would prove fortuitous, especially for Ned. During their short stay in the town a publisher named William Newton Byers sought them out. Byers had already set his sights on the Rocky Mountain gold region, but before making the move to the area he had another project in development: a book on the gold fields. He wanted the travelers to submit their comments to him for publication. Wynkoop and Steinberger liked the idea and before continuing on to Lecompton they gave Byers and John Kellom a report of their findings, a wondrous tale of gold discovery at Cherry Creek, the south bank of the South Platte River, and the surrounding region. Their comments about the various gold finds along the creeks, including the Georgia Company which in fact had found gold in decent quantities, gave the account a ring of truth.[19]

At every stop en route to Lecompton, which they reached in early January 1859, Wynkoop and Steinberger continued to be mobbed by crowds eager for news of the gold region. The trip had taken thirty-two days, not counting layovers.[20] "We willingly furnished all the information we were possessed of, but that was but limited," Wynkoop later admitted, and, although he did not realize it yet, the information was also inaccurate.[21]

Wynkoop's brother George, who had been in Lecompton for almost a year and had become partners with one of the Petrikin brothers, welcomed him back. George had gone into business as a land agent and had become a dealer in land warrants. The office he shared with Petrikin was across the street from the Pawnee Land Office and one door south of the executive office.[22]

Ned Wynkoop's newfound celebrity in Lecompton did not distract him from getting on with business. His main mission was to file papers to incorporate the Denver City Town Company. He printed the certificates but was too late to file the necessary paperwork, for representatives from the Lawrence party had already filed the documents for the St. Charles Town Company.[23] After the arduous journey he and Steinberger had just completed, Wynkoop did not intend to walk away without a fight.

But times had changed. James Denver's term as governor of Kansas Territory had ended on October 10, 1858. Samuel Medary became the next governor of the territory, replacing Acting Governor Hugh Sleight Walsh in December.[24] Knowing he needed help, Wynkoop turned to his brother George, offering him a full share of stock in the as-yet-unincorporated town site if he would influence members of the legislature to vote against the St. Charles petition. But George's efforts failed. The Lawrence group provided evidence that they had been the first on the land, had surveyed it, and intended to build a town. They pointed out that after they had left Cherry Creek for Lecompton, Wynkoop and cohorts arrived in the area and jumped their claim. Refusing to accept defeat, Wynkoop met with the St. Charles representatives and offered to stop his efforts to block the passage of their bill if they allowed William Larimer, Charles Lawrence, and himself become members of their corporation. Wynkoop's proposal could not have been better timed, for the St. Charles men were anxious to have their bill presented before the current session of the Territorial Legislature. They accepted his proposition, and the act to incorporate the St. Charles Town Company passed on January 11, 1859. The newly enacted bill proclaimed that Frank M. Cobb, Theodore C. Dixon (Dickson), Adnah French, William Hartley, Jr., William McGall (McGaa), Charles Nichols, Loyd Nichols, along with Larimer, Lawrence, and Wynkoop and their associates and successors, had the power to issue stock and enact laws as necessary to govern and manage the newly formed 960-acre town of St. Charles.[25]

Ned and George Wynkoop, walking away from the proceedings with a major victory, naïvely thought their fortunes made. More important, Wynkoop had discovered that he had no fear of stepping forward and speaking up. To pull off his coup, he had knowingly withheld information during his negotiation to get himself, Larimer, and Lawrence added to the bill. When he and Steinberger left Cherry Creek, he knew that the Denver men were erecting buildings as quickly as possible. By remaining silent, Wynkoop misled the St. Charles group into believing that there would be no construction on the land until after they returned to the area.[26]

Ned Wynkoop had failed and yet he had succeeded. He and the other key players in the Denver City Town Company still played leading roles in the gold region's future. With this victory securely in place, Wynkoop and Steinberger returned to Omaha. Byers had opened the door during their first visit, and Wynkoop knew the value of giving the editor what he wanted. He and Steinberger supplied Byers with a description of the trail they had used to return to Lecompton and spoke of the wealth waiting to be reaped by anyone who dared to travel to Cherry Creek.[27] Wynkoop was only a few years younger than the ambitious editor/publisher, and this meeting set in motion a long relationship.

Wynkoop found himself front and center in a frenzy of publicity. The paper reported that he and Steinberger would soon team up with Antoine Janis to lead a party westward and penetrate the mountains until they reached the Grand River, a tributary of the Colorado River.[28] At best this information, pure publicity with no basis in fact, was wishful thinking. The trip never came close to happening.

Wynkoop and Steinberger returned to Lecompton, reaching it this time on January 23, 1859.[29] Adnah French had been elected president of the St. Charles Town Company. With the land problem removed, Wynkoop began to look to his future. Knowing that French and his colleagues did not plan to return to Cherry Creek until June at the earliest, he decided to leave for the area as quickly as possible.[30] As his supposed knowledge of the new golden land kept his celebrity alive, he realized he could lead a party of gold seekers to the new El Dorado. A four-story stone hotel known as the Rowena House had recently opened just a few doors from the Pawnee Land Office. When Wynkoop met the proprietor of the hotel, S. O. Hemenway, they hit it off. Soon after, Hemenway began promoting a party to the Rocky Mountain gold region that would be led by Wynkoop. Steinberger dropped out of the proposed venture at an undisclosed date. From the end of January through May, Hemenway ran advertisements in the *Kansas National Democrat* pitching Wynkoop's experience traveling to and from the gold fields and setting prices and deadlines for adventurers to join his protégé's return to Cherry Creek. The ad solicited volunteers to apply by March 15, 1859 and invited all interested parties to attend a meeting in April.[31]

Capitalizing on the paid advertisement, Wynkoop provided another newspaper, the *Herald of Freedom,* with a story that made him out as one of the foremost pathfinders to and from the Rockies. Using his title of "sheriff," the newspaper claimed that he knew "the different routes, and is acquainted with the most favorable points for watering, wooding, grazing and camping."[32] Applicants had to furnish a down payment of fifty dollars by March 15. The total cost would be one hundred dollars per person, and this included one hundred pounds of baggage, with an additional charge for extra weight.

At this time Ned Wynkoop heard unfavorable comments about Governor Denver's officers in the gold region, including threats to hang Denver's appointees. Loyal to his sponsor and determined to protect his position, he confronted the accusers in the press. "Permit me . . . sir," he stated, "to pronounce these statements base and malicious falsifications."[33] This seems to have been his first effort to use the press to promote his opinions. And although he would not fine-tune this technique until the 1860s, he grasped the power of the printed word and from this time forward never shied away from expressing his views in print.

On February 11, 1859, Governor Samuel Medary approved the act that incorporated the St. Charles Town Company. Wynkoop, Larimer, Lawrence, and "their associates and successors" were now officially members of the corporation.[34]

News of gold discoveries continued to generate interest. On April 9 prospective gold seekers met at Rowena Hall (not to be confused with Rowena House). Ned and George Wynkoop joined the group. Word of mouth combined with the ads and news articles had turned Ned into a celebrity, and he found himself the centerpiece of the meeting. As the first item of business, the gathering nominated George to chair the meeting, and he accepted. Taking charge of the meeting, George set up committees to decide upon a route to the gold region, plan provisions, and set a departure date. Ned Wynkoop and Hemenway played key roles in these committees, which decided to depart on April 28 and use the southern or Arkansas River route, which Ned Wynkoop championed.[35]

The group needed someone to lead the caravan, and now Wynkoop's celebrity came into play. He quietly watched while he was nominated and then appointed unanimously. As the leader of the expedition, he would command and conduct the train. His appointment in place, he stepped before the gathering and thanked them for their confidence. Describing his two trips between Lecompton and Cherry Creek, he made it clear why he preferred the southern route. Wynkoop's impromptu talk eliminated any debate for the Platte River route.

Before the evening ended, the group settled upon one final committee to draft the rules and regulations that the members of the party would obey during the trip. Ned Wynkoop shared this responsibility with John Wimsatt and J. Statts. They would report at the follow-up meeting at Rowena Hall on the evening of April 16.

Ned and George Wynkoop departed the hotel completely satisfied with the evening's results, Ned envisioning his return to the land of his future and George hoping to see this same land for the first time. But the trip did not take place. What happened is unknown, but most likely the company did not secure enough financing to set the venture in motion.[36]

Still, Ned Wynkoop knew that a caravan to the Rockies was his ticket back to Cherry Creek. Lecompton, as territorial capital, remained the perfect place to join a wagon train headed west, and his experience traveling to and from the gold fields kept him in demand. Wynkoop had learned a lot about the world and about himself during his return to Lecompton, and now he put it to good use, keeping his name in the minds of men considering the journey.

While Ned bided his time in Kansas, a movement began at the base of the Rocky Mountains in spring 1859 to break away from Kansas Territory. Representatives from Auraria, Denver City, Arapahoe, Eldorado, El Paso, and Fountain City met in Auraria to create a proposal for statehood and a new territory. Statehood was wishful thinking, but the territory was not. Jefferson Territory, although never sanctioned by the United States, separated a good deal of land east of the Rockies from Kansas Territory. The upstart government established a legislature with two houses and a supreme court, but without the ability to collect taxes they had little power.[37] As a result, the territory was soon governed only by vigilantism, duels, miner's courts, survival of the fittest, and general lawlessness.

As the muggy summer of 1859 arrived in Lecompton, Wynkoop was frustrated by inactivity. He knew he needed to act if he had any chance of returning to the gold fields, but nothing happened. Finally, at the end of July, he met with a group of potential emigrants to the gold region. Negotiations continued into August before Wynkoop agreed to lead them to Cherry Creek. By this time mining was no longer the main reason for migrating. R. M. Nance, one of Wynkoop's conscriptions, had no intention of working a mine. He planned to haul wines, liquor, two billiard tables, and all the other necessities for opening a saloon. John S. Wimsatt, who had joined Wynkoop's aborted attempt to return to the gold region in the spring, D. Doyle, J. S. McGee, Mm. [sic] McDowell, H. Bariny, and L. Hunt rounded out the group. After provisioning, Wynkoop, who was now known as "Marshal" E. W. Wynkoop, led the party out of Lecompton on Monday, September 5, 1859.[38]

On this passage across the prairie, Wynkoop's popularity quickly disintegrated into acrimony and accusations. As Wynkoop and his recruits plodded across the plains, they encountered what Wynkoop would term a "stampede" of disillusioned men scrambling back to civilization. Many of the first rush of miners had not met with much success and were stymied by the lack of supplies at affordable prices. The result was a steady stream of the defeated returning to their former lives. Wynkoop likened them to "a routed army," many of whom starved to death. As he remembered, "we met them every day; traveling in all kinds of modes; on foot, horseback, with wheelbarrows; while some were harnessed up like horses dragging every sort of vehicle; [some] were begging for food, while many curses loud and deep were leveled at the heads of those who were accused of bringing in false reports to the States."[39] Having promoted the gold fields to newspapers and to editor William Byers, Wynkoop cringed inwardly at the accusations of the defeated and did what he could to keep those he led moving forward. He knew he was dangerously close to calamity. When men stumbling back to the territories and the states recognized him, he found himself in harm's way; once he came close to being lynched. According to Wynkoop, it was his belief in the mineral wealth of the area, combined with "cooler heads of the infuriated mob," that saved him when he faced the rope. Looking back, Wynkoop wrote, "I might have committed an error of judgment but had not intentionally deceived the public."

Shortly before Wynkoop's return to Denver, Apollo Hall, on the west side of Larimer Street between E and F streets, and a block from Jump's Hall, opened on September 14, 1859. Unafraid of the competition, Ed Jump, who soon renamed his establishment the Criterion Saloon, bragged about the food and liquor he offered in his dining room and bar. Not to be outdone, the two-story clapboard Apollo Hall offered a restaurant, gambling, and saloon on the first floor, and a hall with a stage at one end on the second floor.[40]

On September 27, 1859, while Ned Wynkoop's caravan plodded across the prairie, a twenty-three-year-old actress named Louise Matilda Brown Wakely (b. September 17, 1836) and her two younger sisters, Rose (b. November 18, 1842) and Flora (b. about 1845) arrived in Denver. Originally from London, England, of English heritage with Welsh, Scottish, Irish, and Polish kinship, Louise came to America in 1854 with her siblings, mother, Matilda Louise Brown (b. 1814 in London), and stepfather, George D. Wakely (b. 1823 in England), who earned his living as a "daguerreoanist."[41] The three sisters were members of Colonel Charles R. Thorne's Star Company. William Larimer knew Thorne, who then performed in Kansas, and invited him to bring his theatrical troupe to Denver.[42] Six days after their arrival Louise "Haydee" and Rose (who used the professional name M'lle Haydee) made their acting debut in Denver with Thorne's Star Company at the Apollo Theatre in the drama *Cross of Gold,* or *The Maid of Croisay.* Rose played Therese, the Maid of Croisay, while Louise played Manette. Thorne played the lead, a French soldier named Serg't Austerlitz. The sold-out crowd paid $2.50 per ticket. Although enthusiastic and boisterous, they did not hinder the performance, and all went well until dinner concluded on the first floor. As the patrons turned to drink and gambling in the saloon, their voices competed with the actors, making it difficult for them to be heard above the din. That night the troupe also performed the farce *Two Gregories.* Rose, still billed as M'lle Haydee, played Fanchette, and Louise, now billed as Miss Louise, played Mrs. Gregory. Flora, billed as Miss Flora Wakely, sang the ballad "Maggie's By My Side" between the two per-formances.[43] The evening had been a huge success, but the atmosphere disgusted Thorne and he soon left Denver.

Shortly after Louise and her sisters' debut before the footlights, Ned Wynkoop completed his less-than-triumphant return to the shanty town that had grown into Denver City. Instead of returning to a scat-tering of shacks on a wide expanse east of Cherry Creek, he found a boomtown. No returning hero, Wynkoop now faced the same issues that the defeated had faced. His position as sheriff paid, but only upon arrest and conviction. This did not bring in a lot of money as he had no authority within the city limits. He was going to have to find a better way to survive on the frontier.

CHAPTER THREE

The Streets of Denver

Shortly after Ned Wynkoop's return to Denver in the fall of 1859, his appointment as sheriff of Arapahoe County came under fire, a continuation of the rumblings that had begun in late 1858. Some critics held that the creation of Jefferson Territory severed all ties to Kansas Territory, thus eliminating Wynkoop's appointment as sheriff. Even though his sponsor, James Denver, was gone, Wynkoop had no intention of walking away from the position. Times were lean and he needed the money. The county, his jurisdiction, still existed; he refused to resign.[1]

An actor's life might have been exciting and glamorous, but the pay was no better than Wynkoop's unreliable sheriff's salary. However, occasional benefit performances paid star actors the entire box office take, after expenses. The Apollo Theatre listed the December 7, 1859, performance of *Skatara, the Mountain Chieftain* as a benefit for Louise Wakely. Albert Steinberger, who, having returned to Denver, was now a budding playwright, wrote the script, which promoted Denver, the mountains, and Jefferson Territory. George Wynkoop played Whitcomb, a fictional governor of the territory.[2]

Ned Wynkoop made his debut on the Denver stage that evening, playing Hardicamp, a mountaineer, a part for which he was well suited. Taking a role in the play allowed him not only to remember his formative years in Pennsylvania but to act out his recent adventures. The rehearsals and time spent with the cast, especially with Steinberger and George, proved an exciting respite from daily life. He found that he liked the theatrical world, and this made the possibility of hearing catcalls from a rowdy audience bearable. More important, Wynkoop's initiation to the theatrical world placed him in close proximity to Louise Wakely.

By early 1860, George Wynkoop, like Ned, was getting involved in the city's growth. On February 11, at an Arapahoe County Claim Club meeting he attended with Ned in Auraria, George nominated himself secretary and recorder, and won the position unopposed. The Claim Club, after declaring that it "sometimes becomes necessary for persons to associate themselves together for certain purposes, such as the protection of life and property," revised their constitution.[3]

Although the threat of violence had become a constant in Denver City, Sheriff Ned Wynkoop's apprehension-and-conviction-based pay remained inadequate. As one of the pioneering members of the Denver City Town Company, he had a claim on Clear Creek that brought in money when he worked it, but it did not provide a steady income. There were bills to pay, and by the end of February 1860 he needed cash. The threat of homelessness, combined with loneliness, made the theater all the more alluring, and the attraction that Wynkoop and Louise first experienced in late 1859 refused to fade. Sometime after the New Year he began courting her. At twenty-three, unmarried, and with the "Haydee" Star Company's future uncertain, Louise was open to the tall, buckskin-clad Wynkoop's advances. For Wynkoop, the timing was also right, for when Louise entered his life, she changed it. If he had been involved with women previously, the relationships had not amounted to much and were long forgotten. This one was real and would eventually deepen into intimacy.

Ned Wynkoop owned a number of Denver city lots, and when he decided to sell one of them, it did not take him long to find a buyer. Thomas W. Thorne, Charles Thorne's second son and the company's leading juvenile comedian, had refused to leave Denver with his father and older brother, William. Wynkoop had made his acquaintance through Louise, and on March 1, 1860, he sold Thorne Denver City lot number 17 in block 35 for two hundred dollars.[4]

With money no longer a concern and Louise in his life, his appointment as sheriff felt less tenuous. He had learned the value of befriending highly placed officials, and greenbacks made it easier for him to associate with leading citizens of the city. Acting Territorial Governor L. W. Bliss became a friend. If not on sociable terms with Dr. Joseph S. Stone, who currently served as a member of the Legislative Assembly, Wynkoop knew him.

Although slightly more civilized than the roughnecks who pounded the bars and brutally struck out at any provocation, the so-called cultured leaders of the new land harbored the same potential for violence as their underlings. On March 5, 1860, Bliss and Stone attended a dinner party at the Broadwell House in Denver. Built during the winter of 1859–60 by James M. Broadwell, the two-story building on the corner of G and Larimer streets soon became *the* hotel in town. Wynkoop also attended the affair, which began at one o'clock in the afternoon.

That day would become the turning point in Stone's life and introduce Wynkoop to the so-called field of honor. Dueling was illegal, but this did not stop those who felt that the best way to eliminate adversaries was to kill them.

Stone and Bliss did not get along. During a toast Bliss made a point of insulting Stone without naming him. Dr. Stone stood and asked if Bliss meant him. "I do," Bliss replied, "Do you wish to see me?"[5] Stone declined and stormed out of the room.

Clearly Bliss had instigated the confrontation and wanted to face Stone. As soon as the doctor left the room, Bliss, knowing that Stone could not ignore what had happened, approached Wynkoop and asked him "to act as his friend—accepting, and making any terms, or obligations for him." Even though Wynkoop, as sheriff, represented the law, he agreed to act as Bliss's second.

That afternoon, shortly after five, Captain William Bates and Colonel Thomas Warren called upon Wynkoop and presented him with Stone's challenge to Bliss. Wynkoop took the handwritten note, read it, and promised to deliver Bliss's response the next day.

The following morning Wynkoop wrote a note to Warren, stating that the governor would accept the challenge: shotguns at thirty paces, "one or more shots, as circumstances may require." This would be a duel to the death. Wynkoop set the time at 3:00 P.M. the next day, March 7, "on the banks of Cherry Creek." Warren and Bates quickly accepted for Stone.

By March 7 the location had changed slightly to the north side of the South Platte River across from Denver. Stone and his seconds arrived on the grounds first, with Bliss, Wynkoop, and company arriving by carriage a few minutes later. By the appointed time a crowd of somewhere between six and eight hundred had gathered along the Platte to watch. Wynkoop read the Articles of Agreement, which defined exactly what would happen when the two men faced each other. Stone won the coin toss and chose his position. According to Wynkoop, clouds obscured the sun behind Bliss's left shoulder and gusts of wind blew in Bliss's face.

Minutes ticked. Someone asked if anyone could propose a compromise, but neither Wynkoop nor Stone's seconds offered an alternative. The combatants walked the required steps, then turned to face each other. Wynkoop and his assistant, J. B. Caven, remained with Bliss while Stone's seconds stayed with him. Warren took the lead and gave the combatants several practice signals. Both duelists said they understood the procedure, and received their weapons. Wynkoop and the other seconds retired to a safe distance. Warren gave the signal and Stone fired, with Bliss shooting an instant later. Stone's shots fell short while Bliss's hit the mark. The gunshot entered Stone's left thigh and penetrated his bladder. He groaned as he fell to the ground.

Ned Wynkoop's life had changed. He had stepped outside the law without suffering the consequences. But he was spending less time hobnobbing with Denver society as his romance with Louise Wakely blossomed. While he and Louise enjoyed their courtship, the Wakely sisters' theatrical careers had not been going well since Colonel Thorne, who had brought them to Denver in his troupe, had left the city. Madam Wakely, the sisters' mother, now ran the company by default. Rose was absolutely stunning. Her forte was her physical beauty and sensual dancing.[6] She was the star even though she did not play the most demanding roles. Unfortunately the troupe was forced to use amateurs to fill most of the male roles. This did not lead to riveting performances or productions that rose above mediocrity. With the first theatrical season in Denver over, Madam Wakely contacted Major Hadley, of Mountain City, which would soon become part of Central City, and arranged for M'lle Haydee and her sisters to do a season in his two-story log cabin. The women would perform on the second floor. Drunks and rowdies were now less likely to interrupt performances, for the bottom floor housed a barber shop, meat market, and bakery.[7]

With one of his mining claims along Clear Creek, Wynkoop had an opportunity to be in the vicinity of the Louise's new employment near

Gregory Gulch. Since his duties as sheriff were sporadic and he only worked his mining claims when he felt like it, he had free time and could follow Louise to Mountain City.[8] Upon Louise and her sisters' arrival in the town with their mother, Hal Sayre attended the Mountain City performances. "Miss Millie," as Sayre claimed the locals called M'lle Haydee since they had problems pronouncing her French name, "did her work very well." Continuing, he said, "I am sorry that I can not say so much for her support . . . her sisters were not brilliant." And here Sayre totally upset the general opinion that Louise's teenaged sister, Rose, who excelled as a dancer, was the lone M'lle Haydee, for he named Miss Millie's choice of male companions. "Miss Wakely did not continue long to adorn the stage," Sayre wrote. "She had many suitors but of all these[,] the young lady soon displayed a preference for Ned Wyncoop [sic]." Sayre made no mistake in his identification of the tall mustached wooer and his lady. Louise's time in the mountains did not survive the theatrical season.

Louise and Wynkoop needed privacy, which made living with her mother, stepfather, and sisters trying. When he asked her to move to Denver and live with him, she accepted. Louise's decision not to complete the Haydee Star Company's first season in Mountain City must have upset her mother, and perhaps her sisters, for her departure reduced the Haydee Star Company's star power by one-third. Louise had made her decision, though, and she left with her man.[9]

On April 6, 1860, the Larimer Street Bridge over Cherry Creek was completed, linking Denver City with Auraria. The two cities had officially merged three days before, on April 3, becoming Denver.[10]

That spring George Wynkoop, who had published a newspaper called the *Minersville Bulletin* in Pennsylvania, worked as a printer at William Byers's *Rocky Mountain News*.[11] Byers—the same Byers Ned Wynkoop met in Omaha—had appeared in Denver on April 17, 1859, and within six days began printing a weekly newspaper with a printing press he brought with him. His guide mapping out the routes to the gold fields, the publication for which Wynkoop had provided information, was more propaganda than actual fact. But this did not matter to the entrepreneurial Byers, who saw his future in the new land he promoted. He had decided upon the title of his newspaper before his arrival in Denver City. Byers, like William Larimer, worked hard to become one of the driving forces in the booming town.[12]

Rocky Mountain News publisher and editor William Byers, photographed by Rinehart. Most likely the image was made shortly after Byers's arrival in Denver, Colorado Territory, in April 1859. Wynkoop, who met Byers in Nebraska Territory in late 1858, had a long and ever-changing relationship with him. Courtesy History Colorado (scan #10028274).

Up to now Ned Wynkoop's brother Charlie had done well. He had become an actor and moved to the South, where he toured with and managed wife Katie Estelle's touring company. Their daughter, Mai Twiggs Wynkoop, was born on May 19, 1859. Early in 1860 Charlie appeared in Denver and Byers hired him as a printer. By this time Ned and Byers had become friends, and Ned most likely influenced Byers to hire his brothers. Byers, who had no fear of printing what he believed, nevertheless took the precaution of keeping guns within arm's reach in the newspaper office.[13]

In mid-April 1860, George Wynkoop took the Denver City Town Company to court. He claimed that his brother Ned, as agent for the company, had offered him a full share of company stock in early 1859 to use his influence and prevent the St. Charles Town Company's charter from becoming law. George had worked diligently to this end at a "great expense of time and money."[14] When he failed, the Denver City Town Company, claiming that Ned Wynkoop had overstepped his authority as agent, refused to honor the contract. George Wynkoop sued for $11,600 in damages. The trial lasted three days, and the jury found in his favor, but awarded him only $1,175.

. . .

In mid-July 1860, William Byers secured backing to purchase the additional printing equipment he needed to turn the *Rocky Mountain News* into a daily newspaper. To make this happen he took on additional partners and dissolved his original company, replacing it with the News Printing Company.[15] Byers began printing his daily in August, and attempted to put his competition out of business by setting his advertising rates so low that for them to win a bid they had to do the work virtually for free.[16] As he began to print daily, he stepped up his attacks on what he considered the less-than-desirable elements of Denver. On July 29, when he refused to retract a story about gamblers George Steele and Carl Wood, they dragged him from the *News* office at gunpoint. Before the situation spiraled out of control another gambler, Charles Harrison, hustled him away from his captors. Soon after, when Steele and Wood with two other hard cases, John Rucker and James Ennis, attacked the *News* office, the editor and his staff returned fire. A mob gathered, shot and killed Steele, and captured Rucker and Wood; Ennis escaped.[17]

While Byers waged his private war against anyone who opposed his vision of Denver's future, Ned Wynkoop continued his struggle with the proverbial wolf that pounded on his and Louise's door. By the middle of August he sold yet another piece of property (lot 28, block 293) for the grand price of $10.00 to O. F. Wadsworth.[18] The remote location probably contributed to the reduced price.

But there was more to Wynkoop's life than the mere struggle to survive, which remained constant. He still craved the elusive gold strike, but now Louise provided him with the impetus to move in new directions.

As Jefferson Territory toiled for legitimacy and as the United States spiraled toward conflict, Wynkoop began to speak his mind. He was not a supporter of Jefferson Territory, and as the upcoming presidential election neared, he no longer suppressed his view on slavery.

During the last year and a half the growth of Denver had exploded, but the expansion had now slowed. Men who had come to make their fortune continued to flee the area in droves, broke. Their exodus discouraged speculators and hampered the development of the city. Still, Denver now boasted everything more established cities had, though in more primitive form. There were hotels, liveries, warehouses, medical offices, general stores, bakeries, theaters, as well as the ever-present saloons.[19] And with the growth came increasing violence. The risks of shootings, stabbings, and beatings made walking the streets of Denver dangerous after nightfall.

In August 1860 Arapahoe County, Kansas Territory, participated in its first United States Federal census. As with all such tasks it was impossible to catch everyone as the collectors worked their way from door to door. In Denver, they found Ned Wynkoop at home, while missing Charles Harrison and Park McLure, two southerners who would soon play pivotal roles in his life. Wynkoop listed his occupation as "Speculator," not sheriff or miner. The omissions say a lot about the validity of his appointed occupation, his success at working his claims, and the amount of money his so-called professions brought in.

At this time Louise lived with him. The census reported her name as "Louisa." Although she was born the same year as Ned, she sliced three years off her age, listing it as twenty. They did not live alone. A third person shared Wynkoop's lodging: Charles Montande, a twenty-year-old.[20]

According to the census the rest of the Wakelys still resided in Mountain City; Matilda, George, Rose, and Flora. As expected, Rose (eighteen years) and Flora (fifteen years) listed their occupations as actress. Matilda called herself a housekeeper, which downplayed her management of the theatrical troupe in Mountain City. She claimed that she was forty years old, cutting six years off her age. Wakely listed his profession as "daguerreoanist."[21]

Regardless of how Ned Wynkoop decided to describe himself in the census, his life had begun to change. Although one of his goals in setting out for Pike's Peak had been to make his fortune, so far he had remained just one step ahead of his creditors, but now he had Louise's well-being to consider. In later years, Wynkoop enjoyed telling a tale that accentuated his impecunious state at this time of his life. He and his companions, the story goes, stole a stub-tailed cow from an unnamed military post so they could have milk. Before abducting the animal one of his companions purchased from a slaughterhouse a full tail the same color as the cow in question and attached it to the stub-tailed cow. When the commanding officer of the fort appeared looking for his missing animal, Wynkoop and cohorts professed their innocence. Pointing to the stolen animal, they asked "But she hasn't a stub-tail, has she?"[22] The officer looked at the cow with the full tail and agreed. "Well, she isn't your cow, then," Wynkoop said.

Since being sheriff paid only on arrest and conviction, and since his mines do not seem to have done well (contrary to his claims), Wynkoop began to supplement his income by moonlighting as a bartender at Charles Harrison's Criterion Saloon on Larimer Street between F and G Streets. Harrison, whom his friends called Charlie, remained one of Byers's print targets. A southerner, he claimed to have killed eleven men and three women, and as recently as July 12, 1860, had killed a black man named Stark—unintentionally, he claimed, as he had aimed at another man. After purchasing the Criterion from Ed Jump, Harrison refitted it, later claiming he stocked the "choicest liquors" found in Denver. Now an ornate two-story white frame building, the Criterion flourished. With a first-class hotel on the second floor, it offered dancing, dining, drinking, and gambling on the first.[23] Julia Lambert, who lived through Colorado's turbulent early years, described Harrison as "a fine-looking man and always dressed in perfect style, with plenty of diamonds."[24]

Wynkoop's decision to work at the Criterion marked a pronounced change in his life. As his association with businessmen and city officials diminished, his involvement with men who did not hesitate to use weapons increased. Harrison, along with Denver's first postmaster, Park McLure, soon became his constant companions, and soon Wynkoop became known as "a wildcat sort of fellow, and generally in debt."[25] He also heard himself called "a 'bad man from Kansas,' who wore buckskin breeches and carried a [B]owie-knife and revolver in his belt."[26] In spite of this change in his image, he remained friends with William Byers.

In the summer of 1860, the dissension that would soon divide America and thrust the country into war reached Colorado. As the national election approached, tensions grew as men took sides. In late September, Governor Robert Steele announced that the first election of the provisional government of Jefferson Territory would take place in October. The editor of *The Western Mountaineer* (Golden City) did not hide his opinion of the prospects and reported the story with a total lack of enthusiasm.[27]

Nevertheless, Golden was the site of a meeting on October 9 of delegates to the Territory of Jefferson including Park McLure and William Byers, two of Denver's representatives. For four days and nights they discussed the future of the territory and how they would present themselves at the Thirtieth Congress in Washington. A turbulent atmosphere marked the convention. According to *The Western Mountaineer,* the "sessions abounded in scurrilous and disreputable personalities" and "nearly all the trouble originated with about half a dozen of the Denver delegation."[28]

On October 22, Governor Steele's territorial ticket handily won the unrecognized Territory of Jefferson's first election for territorial, county, and town officials. The victory split the gold region in two. The new city government that William Byers and others strong-armed into existence did not help matters. Many discontents harbored extreme prejudice against the upstart government. Some, like Ned Wynkoop, who remained loyal to former Kansas Territorial Governor James Denver's original plans, vocally opposed what they considered illegal. Of course, Wynkoop had another reason for his loyalty. According to *The Western Mountaineer* the new Denver government wanted to clear the streets of gamblers, something Wynkoop did not want to see as Harrison's Criterion thrived on the gamblers' presence.[29]

Regardless of his loyalty to Denver and Harrison and his unhappiness with the new territory, Wynkoop saw the election as an opportunity and he took it. He ran for sheriff on the county ticket in Denver and won the October 22 election. This immediately removed the stigma of being Governor Denver's appointee. More important, it placed him on payroll. The following day, the *Rocky Mountain News* published a constitution for the people of Denver, in which the duties for sheriff were listed under section 13.[30]

William Byers was among those who saw the secession in a positive light, for it transferred the power of the gold region from the far-off administration of Kansas Territory to the city of Denver and the surrounding towns. While Byers, who used the *Rocky Mountain News* as a weapon to espouse his views, could ignore a friend's shenanigans, he refused to turn his back on his own political views. Ned Wynkoop had been elected to office, but his stance against the new territory bothered Byers. Although the publisher did not attack his friend in print, he would not forget the political chasm that now separated them.[31]

CHAPTER FOUR

A Bad Man from Kansas

On Friday, November 2, 1860, Ned Wynkoop, Charlie Harrison, and perhaps eighteen other men drank and talked late into the night at the Criterion. Earlier that day, Postmaster Park McClure had been jailed by a people's court.[1] Considered by William Larimer "rough in his manners and of a quarrelsome disposition," McClure had seen a less-than-flattering story about himself in the *St. Louis Democrat* by "Observer," a pseudonym O. J. Goldrick used. At gunpoint McLure demanded and obtained a signed retraction of the "false and slanderous" words. This was not a wise move, for Goldrick, who had opened Denver's first school in 1859 and also reported for the *Rocky Mountain News,* complained.[2] McLure quickly found himself under arrest and standing before Judge Jacob Downing. Totally defiant, McLure said he did not recognize Denver's municipal government, would not be tried, and walked out the door. Arrested again that night, he was tried, found guilty, and ordered to pay a $2,000 bond to guarantee he would not disrupt the peace for one year. When McLure refused to pay the bond, Downing ordered him confined inside the C. A. Cook & Company building.

Shortly before 1 A.M. on Saturday, Harrison, Wynkoop, and company converged on the Cook & Company building, stormed it, and overwhelmed the guards. With McLure freed, they returned to the saloon to celebrate.[3] News of the escape spread quickly, and later that morning McLure and a few friends barricaded themselves inside the post office.

That afternoon of November 3 City Marshal James Shaffer led two hundred men toward the post office. On Larimer Street the posse, which

The image in the foreground depicts Postmaster Park McLure demanding that O. J. Goldrick, a schoolmaster and editor, retract a story he wrote about him. The image in the background is the Denver Post Office. Built in 1860, the building also housed the offices of the Central Overland, California & Pike's Peak Express Company. Wynkoop would have stood in the line in the foreground while waiting to obtain his mail in December 1860. Both images are from A. D. Richardson, *Beyond the Mississippi* (1867). Author's collection.

resembled a lynch mob, paused briefly at the Apollo Theatre, perhaps to bolster their courage with liquor before continuing to the post office. While Shaffer's enlistees positioned themselves to cut off any chance of escape, someone inside the building yelled "Fire!" The posse scattered without firing a shot.[4]

Before Shaffer could reassemble his men, Wynkoop approached the marshal and offered his services as mediator. Shaffer and Wynkoop knew each other, for their paths had crossed not only on the streets of Denver but also at Apollo Hall. The marshal had acted with Wynkoop in *Skatara, the Mountain Chieftain* and was a member of the Amateur Dramatic Association. Wynkoop hoped to secure a peaceful solution to a potentially violent situation. Although the two men were on good terms, nothing came of Wynkoop's offer.[5]

On November 4 Shaffer distributed handbills calling for the citizens of Denver to assemble in front of Apollo Hall at 9:00 A.M. on the fifth to decide how to handle the McLure problem. When Shaffer called for a vote, an overwhelming majority denied McLure the benefit of a second trial. He would pay the bond or face the consequences. Shaffer again had two hundred men at his back when he returned to the post office, but McLure had vanished. Without hesitating, Shaffer hustled to McLure's rented quarters on Ferry Street. Again, the marshal failed to find his man.

While Shaffer's men searched the neighborhood, Wynkoop reappeared and mingled with the mob as he looked for Shaffer. When he found him, Wynkoop said he would deliver McLure to the Star Saloon and Restaurant; then told Shaffer to meet him there. As soon as Wynkoop left, the marshal marched his posse to the Star Saloon. Ki Harrison, owner of the Star (no relation to Charlie), greeted him, but that was it. Wynkoop did not appear, and there was no sign of McLure.

While Shaffer fumed, Wynkoop, as he had twice before, worked his way through the marshal's posse. He entered the saloon alone and strode up to the lawman. By now it was obvious that Wynkoop had no intention of placing his friend's life at risk. He told Shaffer that McLure would arrive at Judge Downing's office within five minutes and pay the bond. He then turned and left. True to Wynkoop's word, McLure appeared and made good on the bond.

Byers could not resist editorializing that he hoped it would "be a long time" before the press would again "chronicle events similar to those which have transpired within the last three days."[6] Byers never backed away from stating his mind. At the same time, he generally remained loyal to his friends. Ned Wynkoop's actions irritated him more than once during the standoff, but Byers again refused to chastise his friend in print.

Even though lawlessness continued to plague Denver, national politics grabbed more and more headlines. By early evening on November 12, when presidential election results began to drift westward from the States, the threat of victory by antislavery Republican candidate Abraham Lincoln devastated the proponents of slavery and set in motion events that would split the country in two and impact the Rocky Mountain gold region. Though outnumbered by Union supporters, slavery advocates were boisterous in Denver, as Wynkoop knew, since many were his friends. As he was a Democrat, they expected him to support their cause, but Wynkoop did not. With Lincoln's victory almost certain, he knew that his stance on the preservation of the Union would affect his life.[7]

"For the first time since the issue between slavery and freedom has been before the people of the union," the *Western Mountaineer* proclaimed, "the advocates of the [Republican party] have triumphed."[8] In the same article, the *Mountaineer* pointed out that had the Republicans resisted the 1856 election, they would have been guilty of treason; so the southern states would be now if they fell in line with South Carolina's insistence on secession.

On election night, as initial results reached the city by wire, those who supported the Union swarmed over the streets of Denver. The stars and stripes flew, bonfires illuminated the thoroughfares, and the victors drank and fired their weapons into the air. Jubilant speakers damned the secessionists and praised the victory from a podium set up before a coal yard on Fifth Street. On this night, the Southern sympathizers sensibly kept a low profile.[9]

On November 15 the *Mountaineer* took potshots at both Wynkoop and McLure. In an untitled statement related to Jefferson Territory politics, the editors singled out Wynkoop's choice of companions and actions: "Vice stings even in our pleasures, but virtue consoles even in our pains. If Bliss [who wounded Dr. Stone] would shun the former, and cleave unto the latter, he would realize how happy *we* are. Try it on, Ned."[10] Their attack on McLure was stronger: "McLure still survives! If the Provisional government under which he acts can corr[a]l the old man, let us know it."[11] Surprisingly the newspaper's condemnation of

McLure's total disregard for the law did not hinder his participation in territorial legislative proceedings. On November 21 he succeeded in getting himself appointed to two committees: "State Organization" and "Revision of the Code."[12]

Soon after McLure's confrontation with the law died down, Wynkoop became entangled in something completely different. Living with Louise, and having acted on stage with her, he met and knew her sisters, Rose and Flora. Rose began seeing a gambler named Thomas Evans, a dandy with a reputation similar to Harrison's for being a dangerous man. Knowing this, Rose kept the relationship secret from her mother and sisters. That November, when her mother and stepfather left Denver to travel "in the mountains," she disappeared. When Evans also turned up missing, word spread that he had kidnapped her. Since the abduction was in his jurisdiction, outside the city limits, Sheriff Wynkoop set out to save Louise's sister.

During the winter of 1858–59 Ned Wynkoop had proved that the best and shortest route to the states was along the Platte, and now he followed the South Platte northeast. Near Julesburg he overtook the fleeing couple on their way back to civilization. Here circumstances took a strange turn. Rose told Wynkoop that Evans did not abduct her, she had eloped with him. Whether her story was true or not, Sheriff Wynkoop could not return empty-handed; he had come too far. Besides, Louise was waiting, wondering what had happened to her sister.

A snowstorm began the morning of November 19 and lasted all day, covering the ground with six inches of snow. On that cold and miserable day, with a shackled Evans and an angry Rose in tow, Wynkoop rode into Denver, observed by what must have seemed like the entire town.[13] Four days later, "Judge" Park McLure scheduled the trial of Evans. William Byers appeared at the designated location at 10:00 A.M., thinking he had a scoop for the afternoon edition of his paper. After waiting for an hour he realized he had wasted his time and left. The afternoon paper made his view clear: he wanted a full explanation of what happened.[14]

For all of the parties involved, excepting Rose and Evans, the entire matter quickly spiraled into unreality. Miners expressed disgust over the deflowering of perhaps the prettiest actress in early Denver, while those close to the young performer struggled to accept the facts. In a bizarre ending to the melodrama, Ki Harrison quietly married Rose and Evans

Rose Wakely, Louise Wynkoop's sister. Known as M'lle Haydee, she was renowned for her exotic dances, but also performed credibly on the stage. In fall 1860 she eloped with gambler Thomas Evans, providing Ned Wynkoop the opportunity to make a heroic rescue. Denver Public Library, Western History Collection, Daguerreotype by George D. Wakely, Call Number F-11482.

at his establishment on November 24. Almost two weeks passed before the *Western Mountaineer* reported the event. "So poor Rose has gone in the *hey-dee* of youth; we trust her joy will not be *evan-escent*."[15]

By this time Wynkoop often found himself in Charlie Harrison's presence, even when not working at the Criterion. On the afternoon of Sunday, December 2, 1860, Wynkoop was at the Criterion, when he and Harrison learned that another of Charlie's employees, Andy Goff, had been struck in the head with a revolver by James Cochrane and lay close to death. They immediately set out to find Cochrane. As soon as they did, they began cursing him. Their anger built until they yanked out their pistols, but they managed not to lose control or fire a shot. The incident ended without bloodshed.[16]

That night, while Wynkoop tended bar at the Criterion, James Hill entered the saloon, worked his way through the crowded room, and strode up to Wynkoop. Before Wynkoop sensed Hill's presence, Hill grabbed him and spun him around. As Wynkoop faced the taller man he realized that Hill had been drinking. Wanting nothing to do with Hill, Wynkoop broke free of the man's grasp and walked away. His attempt to avoid a fight failed, however, for Hill pushed after him and grabbed him a second time, becoming loud and threatening. Surprisingly, Hill's anger had nothing to do with the altercation with Cochrane earlier that day. Instead, he lashed out at Wynkoop's recent victory as sheriff in the Jefferson Territory election in October. Hill also alluded to a woman. His patience gone, and angered at Hill's relentless attack, Wynkoop became the aggressor. He told Hill that he had heard he intended to "whip" him. Then, losing his temper, Wynkoop called Hill "a G[o]d d[am]n liar."[17]

Hill yanked out his pistol. Wynkoop studied him, then asked if he intended to frighten him. If so, Wynkoop continued, "[You have] found the wrong man."[18] Refusing to back down, Hill snapped: "I don't draw my pistol unless I design to use it."[19] Those nearby stopped their conversations and watched, as did Charlie Harrison, who was farther away. Wynkoop casually drew his revolver and asked Hill to holster his weapon. When Hill refused, Wynkoop clubbed his gun in preparation for hitting him.

Harrison had seen enough and rushed to the two men, saying that he did not want any of his friends shooting each other. If Hill wanted to shoot someone, Harrison told him to shoot him. Another bartender, O. B. Thomas, joined the confrontation and talked Wynkoop into holstering his revolver and moving to the end of the bar near the water cooler.

With Wynkoop no longer a threat, Hill resheathed his pistol. Harrison placed his arm about Hill's shoulder in a friendly way and led him to the bar to have a drink. Having calmed Wynkoop down, Thomas returned to his position behind the bar. Satisfied that the situation was under control, Harrison walked away. As Hill leaned on the bar Thomas asked him if he would step outside to talk. Hill snapped he would not go outside with a son of a bitch. Harrison heard the comment and stormed back to Hill. "[I will] allow no man to call [my] bartender a son of a b[itc]h," he said.[20]

Hill reached for his revolver, but Harrison grabbed his hand. In the fight for the gun, Harrison jammed his finger between the trigger and guard. At the same time he drew his revolver with the other hand and fired four times at point-blank range, hitting Hill twice. At the first explosion everyone in the saloon scrambled to get out of the line of fire. They need not have bothered, for the shooting had ended. Shot in the chest and abdomen, Hill fell to the floor face first, landing on top of his pistol.[21]

Notified of the shooting, Dr. Peck hustled to the Criterion. He found Hill still alive and had him moved first to Murdock's store on the next block, and then to the hospital. To kill the pain Peck gave Hill brandy, and Hill talked freely as he drank. According to C. A. Cromwell, who stood at the wounded man's side, Hill said "he wanted to see Wynkoop—then said that he did not; contradicting himself several times."[22] After half an hour, Hill collapsed. He died at three the next morning.

Frontier justice was quick and unbending. Charlie Harrison's trial began on December 4 and concluded the next day. Judge William M. Slaughter released the jury to make their determination at 6:00 P.M. After fourteen hours they were locked at "ten for acquittal and two for conviction."[23] Even though some of the testimony was conflicting, Judge Slaughter, unhappy over what had been printed in the press and unwilling to spend more money on the case, decided against a retrial. Byers took exception to this outcome. He wanted Denver to take the next step toward becoming a civilized city, and this included eliminating the bad element, represented by Harrison and company. He also wanted the carrying of firearms prohibited, which was wishful thinking in 1860.

Wynkoop had again played a leading role in events that Byers found distasteful. But again the newspaperman refused to attack his friend in print.[24]

As 1860 drew to a close, money pressures in the East combined with Abraham Lincoln's presidential victory kept the threat of secession alive. Still, as the *Western Mountaineer* reported on December 13, many thought that secession was "hardly probable . . . notwithstanding all the bluster of South Carolina."[25] Nevertheless, this story would dominate the news in the states and territories well into the New Year.

Wynkoop must have wondered if 1860 would ever end. As December dragged on, Patrick Waters replaced Harrison as the leading name in Denver headlines. On December 10, M. C. Fisher's freight train arrived in Denver. In addition to his cargo Fisher brought in a wagon covered with blood that he had found in a river bottom. Someone recognized the wagon as belonging to Thomas R. Freeman, a farmer who lived by himself just south of Denver. Freeman could not make a living farming, and during the winter months he purchased hay from neighbors to sell in Denver. The blood and gore on the wagon suggested that he had been murdered.[26]

Ned Wynkoop appointed W. T. Shortridge deputy sheriff and sent him to investigate the murder. Patrick Waters had departed the area but did not bother to cover his trail, apparently thinking that no one knew about Freeman's demise or that Freeman had hired him. Shortridge, who stopped at each homestead he passed, easily tracked the unknown killer. Reaching Cottonwood Springs, Nebraska Territory, he found his man in bed. Waters had Freeman's rifle and horse in his possession. Shortridge brought Waters to Denver by stagecoach, arriving on the morning of December 15.[27]

At an early evening meeting of the A. F. & A. Masons on Sunday, December 16, the lodge appointed members Wynkoop, Byers, L. Pollard, Thomas, and John Wanless to find out how Thomas Freeman died, locate his body, and return it to Denver for proper burial. The gathering voted not to hinder Waters's defense. Wynkoop told the gathering that he would take Waters on the search for the dead man.[28]

Wynkoop acted quickly, leaving that evening with a posse to which he had added eight or nine more men, including Charlie Harrison. During the ride Waters maintained his innocence and refused to help. Late that night, with his posse worn out and no clue where the corpse had been stashed, Wynkoop called off the search. The next morning when he resumed the hunt, Waters remained uncooperative. Wynkoop decided to force the situation. He threatened to hang Waters if he did not talk. Giving the prisoner time to mull over his situation, Wynkoop took the posse aside and explained his ruse, making it clear that if he made a move to carry out the threat, Waters was not to be lifted off the ground. Everyone in on the deception, Wynkoop returned to Waters, who remained adamant that he had not killed Freeman. Tired of wasting time, Wynkoop ordered the posse to hang Waters. A rope was tossed over a tree limb and a noose placed around Waters's neck. The threat of lynching did the trick, and Waters confessed. He admitted having shot Freeman with the dead man's shotgun at point-blank range from behind while riding in his wagon on November 30. After telling Wynkoop that it was an accident, he led the sheriff to where he had hidden the body. The frozen corpse was covered with hay, approximately 125 steps from the road, two miles below Fort Lupton, and thirty miles from Denver. Wynkoop, his posse, and the doomed man returned Denver that evening.[29]

The next day, December 18, Wynkoop accompanied Judge Waggoner to the post office, where, as usual, they waited in line to obtain their mail. Waggoner was first, and after collecting several newspapers from the East, he stepped aside and began reading one of them. Next in line, Wynkoop asked for his mail. Typically, he was in arrears. When Postmaster Park McLure heard of Wynkoop's presence, he stormed to the front counter and waved Wynkoop's mail in the air as he yelled at him to pay what he owed—five dollars. McLure then turned to leave. "No one's going anywhere," Wynkoop drawled. He snatched his letters from McLure's hand and strode out of the building with McLure screaming threats at his back.[30]

The approach of war undoubtedly had as much to do with this encounter as the delinquent bill, for neither Wynkoop nor McLure made any attempt to hide their opposing views.[31] Lincoln's election had polarized their positions and trumped Wynkoop's recent actions on McLure's behalf.

Later that day the A. F. & A. Masons met at Harrison's Criterion and thanked Wynkoop for his prompt actions. After voting to hold Waters for trial at the Criterion, the group briefly adjourned before reconvening to bury Freeman.[32]

A People's Court assembled near, but not inside, the Criterion on the morning of December 19. A motion by the assembly named Colonel William Person judge. The court named Wynkoop marshal, and he left to gather twenty-four men for jury selection. When he returned with the potential jurors, the prosecution and defense took turns interviewing them until they eliminated six each. The court adjourned until 2:00 P.M., when the Patrick Waters trial began.[33]

The next day the weather turned cold, and the court moved inside the Criterion. Deputy Shortridge, John Wanless, Mr. Burns, Mr. Ewing, Ned Wynkoop, Charles Harrison, Dr. Farner, John Martin, and Mr. Marr testified for the prosecution, while Mr. Sharp and Mr. Murdock were the only defense witnesses.[34] The result was a foregone conclusion; Waters received a death sentence.

On the west, or Highland, side of the South Platte River, near the F Street bridge, laborers erected a gallows with a drop on a scaffold. A little before 3:00 P.M. on December 21, Sheriff Wynkoop, Deputy Sheriff Shortridge, and a number of men sworn in as deputies for the occasion assembled in front of the Criterion. Waters stepped from the saloon, and Wynkoop escorted his prisoner to the gallows. Waters prayed, confessed his guilt, and at nine minutes past the hour died when the fall broke his neck.[35]

On the next mail day, Monday, December 31, Wynkoop once again waited in line until it was his turn to stroll into the post office. He found his box empty. Before he left, McLure appeared and cursed him, adding that he would receive no additional mail until he paid his bill. Wynkoop calmly "stepped to the side desk, and instead of counting his ducats, penned a challenge."[36] The heated exchange continued, prompting Wynkoop to invite McLure to step forward so he could mop the floor with him. Refusing, McLure penned his own challenge. Wynkoop immediately accepted it, and they set a date.

Dueling, although outlawed, continued to occur frequently. At times Wynkoop ignored his position as sheriff and walked the deadly ground between law-abiding and lawless behavior. In the past his appearances on dueling fields alternated between being an observer and a second. Now he would play a leading role. As Wynkoop knew how to handle guns, both rifle and revolver, he was not a good man to cross.[37]

William Byers hesitated, not wanting to write anything about the affair. He merely reported, "It is whispered around our streets that a hostile encounter will occur at some convenient place, between two of our well-known citizens, on Wednesday next."[38] Byers did not want this duel to come off, and refused to publicize it by providing any details.

As the date of the duel neared, according to Amos Steck, McLure sent a friend to visit Wynkoop and tell him that McLure "could hit larks on the wing."[39] These tough words did not intimidate Wynkoop, who drawled "Larks don't have guns." Just prior to the appointed day, a buckskin-clad Wynkoop gave an impromptu performance of his expertise with rifles in the streets of Denver, consistently hitting targets the size of silver dollars at thirty to sixty paces.[40]

One of McLure's friends, a milliner named M. E. Cody, saw Wynkoop's performance and hustled to the post office to report what she saw. "Mackey," she told McLure, "you are a dead duck if you face that Kansas jayhawker."[41] McLure remained grimly silent. Wynkoop's shooting exhibition created a gambling frenzy as men began placing bets on the outcome, with all the smart money on Wynkoop. At the specified time on January 2, 1861, the duelists met near the Catholic Church under construction on F Street and Stout. As the crowd grew to almost fifteen hundred, including an undertaker, the seconds reviewed their instructions. At the last moment, McLure made a public apology. He went so far as to hand over Wynkoop's mail, offering him one year's free postal service.[42] An undated clipping in the *Wynkoop Scrapbook* praised Wynkoop and McLure's "high-toned sense of honor and their acknowledged bravery," reporting that the highly anticipated duel ended without bloodshed.[43] These kind words did not represent Byers's view of the featured players in Denver City's ongoing melodrama.

Wynkoop and McLure had survived potential disaster and arrived at a peaceful settlement, but when they walked away from the duel both knew their friendship had ended.

Looking back on these days, Wynkoop would later say "almost always there exists a certain state of society in newly settled countries which sometimes renders an appeal to arms absolutely necessary[.] In Colorado in 58–59 & 60 the 'Code' was universally recognized; and it would have required more nerve for a gentleman to refuse a challenge than to accept one."[44]

His latest crisis ended, Wynkoop resumed his duties as sheriff. When the January 8, 1861, edition of the *Western Mountaineer* announced that a body had been discovered three miles outside of Denver, Wynkoop rode out to bury it that morning. Before interring the dead man, Wynkoop removed some of his clothing and clipped a lock of his hair in the hope that the items might help identify the corpse. While attending to his macabre task, he discovered an empty laudanum bottle, which suggested that the deceased had committed suicide. Wynkoop completed the burial, and delivered the clothing and hair to the *Mountaineer*'s office in Golden City.[45]

Ever since Wynkoop had perturbed Byers by his refusal to support the upstart Territory of Jefferson, the editor had refrained from going after him in print. This truce was over, never to return. With the Wynkoop-McLure confrontation still fresh, Byers took dead aim at dueling. He printed a guest correspondent's view, which compared the act of facing each other on a field of honor with murder. His resolution: hang the victor "to the nearest tree."[46]

While fighting the war against the continued violence in the city, Byers also fought for supremacy over his closest rival, the *Daily Denver Mountaineer,* which should not be confused with the *Western Mountaineer.* In January, when the Denver Post Office awarded the *Denver Mountaineer* the "letter list," Byers was livid. The *Rocky Mountain News* had a distribution twice that of his competition, and by law, he should have won the award, which was based upon circulation. Since Byers had taken the postmaster to task in print at every opportunity, McLure must have smiled when he told Byers that he had considered the *News* for the award. McLure's decision would cost Byers money.[47]

The year 1861 had begun ominously for Ned Wynkoop. With potential violence surrounding him and the threat of civil war growing daily, to relieve the tension he resumed his amateur theatrical career in January. That month he began rehearsals for *Pizarro* with Louise and Flora. His romance with Louise had flourished. They continued to live together, and she undoubtedly helped him prepare his role of Rolla in *Pizarro.* That January she conceived their first child.

On January 29 Kansas became a state. That night in Denver Ned Wynkoop and Ki Harrison participated in the organization of a military company named the Jefferson Rangers. Harrison became captain and Wynkoop first lieutenant. In direct contrast to the militia that Captain Park McLure commanded, the Denver Guards, which supported the southern cause, the Rangers staunchly backed the Union. Wynkoop and Harrison began drilling their recruits the next day.[48]

Pizarro premiered at the Apollo on February 1, and, according to the *Rocky Mountain News,* Ned Wynkoop "acquitted himself with much credit." With "a capital voice," he performed "gracefully and easily, and with training and experience would make a first rate actor."[49] Continuing, the *News* reported that the "Misses Wakely as Elvira and Cora, attracted much attention. Miss Louisa particularly, was perfect in her part, and acted throughout with dignity and grace."

The following night the Denver Amateur Dramatic Society assembled at the office of a member named Winchester. Wynkoop, James Shaffer, and Albert Steinberger all attended, as did a number of women. At the beginning of the assembly the group called upon Wynkoop to chair the meeting. He accepted, and later that evening the gathering elected him president. The association voted on a number of resolutions. Their agenda went beyond amateur theatricals. The mining boom had not panned out for many, and legions of homeless men roamed Denver looking for handouts. Wynkoop's way with words put him in a position to take the lead on something that mattered—the poor and destitute. To date Wynkoop had been a man about town, strutting and speaking as he liked, almost as if he did not have a care in the world. Now he had a mission. The next day Wynkoop visited Byers at his office and handed him the previous night's minutes to publish.[50]

By this time Wynkoop had created quite a name for himself while also making himself a target for potshots. A little over a month after he and McLure resolved their problem, the *Rocky Mountain News* received a letter from Golden City. Dr. Joseph Stone, who had clung to life for months after L. W. Bliss shot him, refused to fade away after dying on October 11, 1860, and again linked Wynkoop with Bliss. After publicizing a dance class on Thursday evenings, the letter stated: "The question is often asked, 'Why don't Bliss come up oftener?' Now, Ned, *do* come up, and try what a little *innocent* amusement will do to soothe your troubled spirit."[51] A junior editor at the *News* could not resist having some fun and added his own endnote: "We repel indignantly the imputation implied by that last word in Italics."

That February the chasm that divided the United States not only dominated national politics but also affected the people of Denver, including Wynkoop. When an Act of Congress created Colorado Territory on February 28, replacing the unrecognized Jefferson Territory (October 24, 1859–February 28, 1861), outgoing President James Buchanan

Portrait of Louise Wakely. If this image was made in 1861, Louise's father-in-law, George Wakely, took it before Louise's first pregnancy began to show or after her first son was born that October, when she was Mrs. Wynkoop. Denver Public Library, Western History Collection, Daguerreotype by George D. Wakely, Call Number F6190.

signed the document. The creation of the territory meant that the Union remained in control of the mineral-rich area. Soon after Lincoln took the oath of office on March 4, 1861, he named William Gilpin Colorado's first territorial governor. Gilpin had served with Charles Frémont on his second expedition and participated in the Mexican War, after which he toured the Rocky Mountains in the late 1840s. During the 1850s he had touted the new territory's bountiful mineral prospects.[52]

On March 5, 1861, the day after Lincoln's inauguration, Wynkoop reached the pinnacle of his acting career when he played the lead role in *The Drunkard* at the Apollo Theatre. He played the part of Middleton, an alcoholic whose tremors were so severe that he could no longer lift a glass of spirits to his mouth. He sobbed in frustration, his head sinking to his arms on the bar. He began trembling to the point of explosion. Slowly he forced himself erect, and drawing a handkerchief from his pocket, and taking "hold of one corner with his left hand, [he] spasmodically worked the cloth around back of his neck, over his right shoulder, fumblingly grasped the diagonally opposite corner and the glass with his right hand, and still fitfully shaking slowly drew the stimulant to his mouth and gulped it down. Revived, he exclaimed: 'My last!'"[53] The audience exploded with cheers and applause.

Wynkoop's performance garnered him a sensational review in the *Rocky Mountain News*. "Mr. Wynkoop deserves more than a passing notice," the reviewer proclaimed.[54] "His rendition of the *Drunkard* was given with most thrilling effect, and in the scenes of delirium,—in the intensity and strength of his *mania,*—he exhibited more than ordinary histrionic ability. . . . [Wynkoop's delirium tremens] will never fade from our memory, [as] it was more vividly before us last night than we have seen it for years." As a modern historian wryly surmised, "the crowd's enthusiasm derived partially from the common knowledge that Wynkoop was no more averse to taking a drink off the stage than on it."[55] Regardless of how he pronounced his surname, he now found himself addressed as "Winecoop," as his drinking buddies forever had fun at his expense for his crowning moment on the stage.

Also during that first week of March 1861 the schism that would soon cast the country into war reached Colorado Territory, leading to the disbanding of the Denver Guards and Jefferson Rangers. The Rangers had recently defended the streets of West Denver (former Auraria) when a group of ruffians known as the Bummers terrorized the town.

Tempers flared and tensions grew as Union sympathizers and secession-ists expressed their views more and more vehemently. Wynkoop severed all ties with anyone favoring secession.[56]

In the course of the previous year Wynkoop and City Marshall James Shaffer had had numerous run-ins. With city elections approaching, and Shaffer running for reelection, Wynkoop decided to challenge the in-cumbent. Although Wynkoop was well known and well liked, his recent past came into play in a way he did not expect. As the race for the of-fice of marshal began to heat up, Byers decided to speak out. He and Wynkoop had enjoyed each other's company; indeed, Byers's paper had refused to print negative items about the sheriff even though some of his actions approached lawlessness. This changed on March 20 when Byers ran an editorial on the front page of the *Rocky Mountain News*. Without mentioning Wynkoop's name, Byers opined that "No man should be elected City Marshal who is not conscientiously and by example a strict law and order man. . . . We want no man for City Marshal whose sympa-thies will influence him to protect and screen those who are disturbers of the peace and violators of law."[57]

Byers's public condemnation of Wynkoop angered rival publisher James T. Coleman, who never missed a chance to confront his com-petitor in print. In the March 31 issue of his paper, the *Daily Denver Mountaineer,* the Sunday before the election, Coleman accused Shaffer of "non-return of fines" in an effort to influence voters. According to Byers, as soon as Wynkoop heard the story, he "condemn[ed] the whole proceeding."[58] Although Byers supported Shaffer, he wrote of Wynkoop: "He is too much of a gentleman to lend himself to any such shameful work."

Before the counting of the ballots for the East Division of the City was complete, the election judges broke for dinner. Although they locked up the ballot box before departing, Byers claimed that sixty to eighty extra ballots made it into the box before the judges returned from dinner. The extra ballots, the *News* stated, made Wynkoop the victor. Winner or not, Wynkoop wanted nothing to do with deceit and submitted "A Card" to the *News* which damned the fraud.[59] Wynkoop's condemnation pleased Byers, who wanted him to drop out of the election.

Wynkoop decided to withdraw from the race since without the "extra" votes he obviously had not won. Then friends made him aware of "A Card" they intended to print in the *News* on April 4, the day before the second election. They urged him to stay the course because he only needed a few extra votes to secure victory. Wynkoop changed his mind accordingly, angering Byers, who demonstrated not only his ruthlessness but also the power he wielded. Friends they were, and perhaps friends they would remain, but on this day Byers would have his way. To date Byers had not named Wynkoop in print when he disagreed with him, but now everything had changed. "And so, in reference to the 'stuffing' frauds, Mr. W. also disclaims all complicity with, and publicly denounces, this dishonorable method of increasing the vote," Byers proclaimed.[60] "We believe him to be animated with all the impulses, and possessed of all the instincts of a gentleman," he continued. Then he attacked. Anyone reading the rest of the article must have cringed; certainly Ned Wynkoop cringed. Byers made it clear to everyone that he would go after anyone who confronted him. "At the time of our legal organization last fall, Mr. Wynkoop was opposed to the City Government. He publicly denied its authority, refused to acknowledge its legality, and, on a well remembered occasion, entered one of our courts, took possession of one of the city's prisoners, and in the face of public opinion sought to screen the prisoner from a judicial investigation." It got worse, much worse.

Ned Wynkoop had lost the election. He should have known better, should have dropped out of the race, but he did not. Perhaps Coleman's support influenced his decision. Angered by Byers's recent attack on Wynkoop, Coleman praised the sheriff, applauding his involvement with the McLure breakout the previous November. Since Shaffer had not defended his honesty, Coleman again questioned the marshal's integrity and moral character, stating "Those accusations still remain unanswered, and we therefore are at liberty to take them as true."[61] He urged everyone to vote for Wynkoop.

The second Election Day arrived and Wynkoop's supporters, the Laborer Party, walked the streets displaying banners and playing musical instruments as they touted their man. Fights broke out, but by late evening it appeared that Wynkoop had won decisively. His supporters claimed victory, but their claim was premature. The next day the *News* reported the results: Shaffer, 671; Wynkoop, 508. Not surprised but nevertheless pleased, Byers immediately attempted to patch up his relationship with Wynkoop. "We have no desire to exult over the defeat of Mr. Wynkoop," he printed in the April 6 daily of the *News*.[62] "He has acted, so far as we can learn, with all fairness and honor through both elections, and has publicly rebuked and condemned every fraudulent attempt to increase his vote."

Wynkoop had lost the election, but he continued to earn a salary as sheriff. Nevertheless, the election results marked the beginning of the end of this portion of his life.

CHAPTER FIVE

Civil War

At 4:30 A.M. on April 12, 1861, Brigadier General Pierre Beauregard (CSA), tired of waiting for Major Robert Anderson (First U.S. Artillery) to yield, began bombarding Fort Sumter, an unfinished fortress at the mouth of Charleston harbor. Thirty-three and a half hours later, Anderson surrendered.[1] The United States declared war on the Confederate States of America on April 15, 1861.

The war affected life in Denver from the start. The Criterion became the unofficial headquarters for Denver's secessionists, and, knowing Charlie Harrison's temper and inclination for violence firsthand, Ned Wynkoop wisely kept his distance from the establishment.[2] He focused on helping the ever-increasing number of people in Denver who had no employment and no way of surviving. On May 9, presiding over a meeting of the Denver City Amateur Dramatic Association, he announced that Jack Langrishe, an actor and impresario who had recently arrived in Denver, "had generously offered to give an entertainment for the benefit of the poor" on May 14.[3] Wynkoop wanted to postpone the Dramatic Association's next play, *Honeymoon,* also a benefit for the poor, until a week after Langrishe's benefit to ensure it pulled in as much money as possible. The motion passed. *Honeymoon* was scheduled to play on May 22, but when the date arrived, it was pushed out to May 27. The timing could not have been better. Governor Gilpin arrived in Denver that day and attended the performance.[4]

In spite of this coup, Wynkoop's theatrical career had ended, although he probably did not know it yet. Denver now resembled Lecompton, with armed men cautiously walking the streets. As summer approached, posters nailed about Denver offered to buy percussion caps and ammunition to use against the federal government. A rumored Confederate invasion of the Southwest made Colorado Territory vulnerable. According to Methodist Episcopal Reverend John M. Chivington, the secessionists still in the city, although outnumbered, intended to steal as much gold dust as possible and then join the Confederacy. The forty-two-year-old from Ohio had been a missionary in Nebraska Territory prior to migrating to Denver in May 1860 where he became presiding elder. Chivington praised Governor Gilpin's decision "to checkmate that state of affairs" and prepare to block a Confederate invasion, even though he had no money and no official authority from the War Department.[5] Wynkoop credited Gilpin with the guts to act "upon his own responsibility."[6] He felt that if the governor had hesitated and waited for a response from Washington, the "delay might have proved fatal" to the territory.

In June 1861 the governor created two companies of the First Regiment of Colorado Volunteers. Company A recruited in Denver while Company B recruited in Central City. The two companies had only a handful of officers and none held a rank higher than captain.[7] Although Wynkoop was still treading the fine line between law and lawlessness, he no longer meandered aimlessly. He now knew what he would do. He enlisted and on July 31 received a commission as second lieutenant.[8] "I went into the service to help my country in her time of trouble," he said, "not to play soldier."[9]

On August 10, 1861, the women of Eureka, near Central City, hosted a festival for Company B. Captain Samuel Tappan, who commanded Company B, marched his men to the event. Even though Company A was not invited, Wynkoop, who was visiting Central City, also attended the fête. Upon the troops' arrival in Eureka, Tappan spoke to the assembly. After two women presented Company B with a Bible, the men ate a light meal. The event concluded with a series of talks, only one of which captured Tappan's attention—Lieutenant Wynkoop's. After speaking about Company A, Wynkoop, whom Tappan called an "inimitable Wolf," focused his attention on the duties of officers and men before tackling the heated topic of politics. His words were biting and at times "facetious," garnering him "roars of laughter."[10]

Amid the unrest that gripped the territory, Wynkoop and Louise's relationship flourished. His enlistment, along with her pregnancy, led to their betrothal. They married on August 21, 1861, at her stepfather's house on Larimer Street, with the Reverend John H. Kehler, Denver's first Episcopal minister, presiding. Kehler, who had arrived in Denver in late 1859 or early 1860, had met Wynkoop while serving as rector of St. John's Church in the Wilderness. When the war broke out, Kehler became the chaplain for the First Colorado Volunteer Regiment.[11]

Wynkoop did not remain a second lieutenant long. Tappan, who had been promoted to lieutenant colonel and still remembered Wynkoop's impressive performance in Eureka, supported his promotion to captain of Company A.[12] Surprisingly, William Byers harbored no animosity toward Wynkoop in spite of his transgressions in Denver. "Our military looking friend, Ned Wynkoop, stepped at once from a Second Lieutenancy to the Captaincy of his company," Byers reported in his paper, "and we may here remark, none are better fitted for their positions, than is Ned for the one he now occupies."[13] James Shaffer served under Wynkoop in Company A, as first lieutenant.[14]

At this time the bearded Reverend Chivington joined the First Colorado. At six feet, seven inches and 250 pounds, Chivington was a powerful-looking man who made Wynkoop look frail. Governor Gilpin asked him to become regimental chaplain, but he wanted a fighting commission. Although he had no military experience, Chivington had two factors in his favor: he feared no man and was charismatic in front of an audience. Gilpin granted his request.[15]

Captain Wynkoop spent the remainder of 1861 in garrison duty at Camp Weld, which was under construction. Getting the troops ready to operate as a cohesive unit became his main concern. Wynkoop and First Lieutenant Shaffer saw to it that the noncommissioned officers drilled Company A on a daily basis. The recruits, anxious to see action, pushed themselves. By the middle of September 1861, Companies A and B had noticeably improved, and Lieutenant Colonel Tappan invited council members from Denver to observe the men maneuvering through their drills on the evening of September 13. At 5:30 Wynkoop and Shaffer assisted Tappan as portions of Companies A and B performed for the visitors, marching to fife and drum. The presentation proved successful and impressed the dignitaries.[16]

Major E. W. Wynkoop, Capt
Co. A. and later Major
1st Colo Cav. 1861

Carte de visite of Edward Wynkoop by George Wakely at his Denver studio. The image was taken shortly after Wynkoop became a captain in the First Colorado Volunteer Regiment in 1861. This is the quintessential portrait of Wynkoop, capturing his poise and cockiness. Courtesy History Colorado (Scan #10038738).

By October Wynkoop and Chivington were becoming friends, thanks to Wynkoop's religious beliefs, along with his propensity to voice his opinions. This month also saw the birth of the Wynkoops' first child, Edward Estill, born on October 6, one and a half months after their marriage. (In later years their marriage would be pushed forward to January 1861 and their son's birth to October 6, 1862.) Apart from the initial scandalized gossip at the baby's birth so soon after their marriage, his arrival made them a family and filled Ned and Louise with pride and happiness.[17]

Wynkoop had experienced massive changes—enlistment, marriage, the birth of his son—in just a few months. Although he was still a man unto himself, he no longer straddled the boundaries between law and lawless. Now he was guided by duty and conscience.

Days turned into weeks and not much changed for Wynkoop and the other volunteers. The men drilled while Wynkoop and the other officers learned how to perform their duties. Enlisting additional recruits became one of Wynkoop's ongoing functions, and he often advertised in newspapers.[18]

. . .

In July 1861, Brigadier General Henry H. Sibley (CSA) was directed to organize an invasion force and drive the Federal troops from the Southwest. Sibley, a West Point graduate who had served previously in the Southwest, first against Santa Ana's Mexican army and then against the Navajo Indians, had little respect for the fighting ability of the people born to the area. His army, known as Sibley's Brigade, comprised the Fourth Texas Mounted Volunteers (810 officers and men), Fifth Texas Mounted Volunteers (835 officers and men), half of the Seventh Texas Mounted Volunteers (414 officers and men), and an artillery battery.

The Confederates did not keep the invasion secret when they set out from San Antonio, Texas, in mid-October 1861. Everyone from Chivington and Wynkoop to the rawest recruit in the First Colorado knew of the advance. This did not concern Sibley or his command, for they considered the First Colorado no more worthy a foe than the inhabitants of the Southwest, labeling the regiment the "Pet Lambs." But Sibley had miscalculated. The recruits of the First Colorado were not native to the Southwest. Boisterous in their loyalty to the Union, by January 1862 they had been pounded into a battle-ready military unit.[19]

The time for pomp and bold proclamations had ended. Knowing Sibley's Brigade presented a threat to the gold fields of Colorado and recognizing that the men of the First Colorado wanted action, Chivington and Wynkoop authored a petition on February 5, 1862, that every officer stationed at Camp Weld signed. They wanted Colonel John Slough, who commanded the First Colorado, to allow their regiment to support General Canby's defense of the Southwest.[20]

The next day officers of the First Colorado elected representatives to oversee matters beyond the realm of the military. Colonel Slough became president, Captain Scott Anthony (Company E) vice president, and Wynkoop secretary.[21]

Wynkoop was also instrumental in creating a theatrical center on the post. On February 7 when the Camp Weld Dramatic Hall officially opened, he addressed the crowd. According to the *Rocky Mountain News,* his address was "a literary morceaux [*sic*] of much spirit, patriotic sentiment, and smooth, sonorous, stately style; characterized by an animation, appropriateness and elegance, creditable to the Captain, and not unworthy [of] the accomplished genius of many of those professional lit-[t]erateurs who occupy names and niches in the poetic pages of the precise and polished periodicals of the day."[22]

The time for drilling and waiting came to an end. On February 22, 1862, the First Colorado Volunteer Regiment, with Captain Edward Wynkoop commanding Company A, departed Camp Weld and marched toward New Mexico Territory. Hindered by deep snow and frigid temperatures, the command did not reach the mouth of Plum Creek, four miles north of Colorado City, until the night of February 27.[23]

On the morning of February 28 orders rang out for the men to form ranks for the day's march. That morning Wynkoop's Company A camped near Company I, which consisted mostly of German immigrants. As Wynkoop's company prepared to move out, Lieutenant Charles Kerber, who commanded Company I, refused to obey orders. When Colonel Slough rode up to Kerber, the lieutenant complained that all the companies had three transport wagons except for Company I. Kerber, who felt the slight was because his men were German, demanded a third wagon, threatening that they would not fall into line if they did not get it. Slough responded to the insubordination by ordering Wynkoop's men "to load [their Springfield-rifled muskets] with ball cartridge and disarm Company I."[24] Kerber defiantly stated "that no one company could

disarm" his men, in response to which Slough directed Captain Anthony's Company E to load their muskets. Drawing his revolver, Slough
pointed it at Kerber, who in turned ordered his men to aim their muskets at the colonel.

Chivington charged forward, yelling "You shoot, Kerber, and we'll put
sixty holes though you." Slough yanked his mount about, told Chivington not to make camp that day until the men marched four to six miles
south of Colorado City, and rode off. Chivington told Kerber that the
next wagon the regiment commandeered would belong to Company I,
ending the confrontation.

Continuing southward, the First Colorado followed the Fontaine Qui
Bouille (Fountain Creek), fording it just before it emptied into the Arkansas River, which they also crossed before stopping for the night. At
this camp the men suffered through a heavy snowstorm that turned into
a relentless downpour. Wynkoop and his men, along with most of the
regiment, were cold, soaked to the skin, and miserable as they had few
tents. The inclement weather forced a temporary halt to the command's
progress. On the second night at the camp (March 1, 1862) a messenger
rode into the muddy bivouac to speak with Slough. The news was not
good. Sibley's Confederate forces had defeated Canby's Union command
at Valverde, a short distance north of Fort Craig on the Río Grande in
New Mexico Territory on February 21. Slough shared the information
with Chivington, Wynkoop, and the other officers.[25]

The news added urgency to the First Colorado's need to confront the
invading southerners. Making forced marches, the Pike's Peakers reached
the Purgatoire River, where they were joined by members of the First
Colorado recently garrisoned at Fort Wise, in southeastern Colorado
Territory. Wynkoop and his companions greeted the newcomers with
cheers and hugs. By the next day the command camped at the base of the
mountains three-quarters of a mile from Trinidad, and that night many
Coloradans invaded the town to drink and let off steam. As Wynkoop
liked companionship and lifting a glass, he probably joined the revelers.
Chivington, commenting later on the First Colorado's night in Trinidad, wrote, "It seemed to me that his Satanic Majesty must have had a
going-up-and-down place somewhere on the banks of the Purgatoire,
and from about the time we went into camp until we broke camp and
left there the next morning he held high carnival."[26]

The command reached Bent's Old Fort on March 4. The next day they left the Arkansas River and began a seventy-five-mile march southward over barren prairie with little water and few trees. By this time, a foot-weary Wynkoop must have wondered if he would engage the enemy before his boots and legs gave out. On March 7, after another forty miles, Wynkoop and his companions reached the Raton Pass. A day later they were halfway up the steep pass, reaching the summit at noon on March 9. Wynkoop and the men had just begun the descent when a courier from Fort Union, New Mexico Territory, appeared and spoke with Slough. Sibley's army was close, he reported. According to Colonel Gabriel René Paul, who commanded the post, only the arrival of the Pike's Peakers could prevent the loss of Fort Union. Slough updated Tappan, Chivington, and Wynkoop, but not the soldiers.[27]

Continuing down the pass, the First Colorado reached the Red River by three o'clock. During the halt a mail coach headed for Fort Union and Santa Fe stopped at the bivouac, and Slough, claiming he needed detailed information, boarded it. Left in command, Chivington jettisoned all the supplies except the arms and two blankets per man. He then announced that only eighty miles separated the First Colorado from the rebels. Amidst cheers, he began a forced march that continued through the night. After just a short break before dawn Chivington continued moving all through the next day. Finally, with a harsh wind adding to their misery, the leading remnants of the First Colorado—those on horseback or wagon—plodded into Fort Union at dark on March 11. Wynkoop, Anthony, and the rest of the infantry still afoot dragged themselves into the stone fort at 9:00 P.M.[28]

On March 14 the Quartermaster Department issued arms and additional clothing to the Colorado Volunteers. Rumors abounded but nothing happened until March 22, when Slough, who had rejoined the command, was instructed to remain at Fort Union. He ignored the orders. With Colonel Paul, who as senior officer thought he should be in command, the Colorado Volunteers, two light batteries, and two companies of the Fifth U.S. Infantry (Captain William Lewis), Slough set out at noon on March 23 to retake Santa Fe. A twenty-two-mile march brought them to Las Vegas, New Mexico Territory. The next day the march resumed. Traversing a rocky terrain dotted with juniper and piñon pine, the Coloradans began to file into Bernal Springs about noon. Soon after their arrival they discovered they had no blankets. Captains Wynkoop, Downing, and Anthony (Companies A, D, and E; about 180 men), who did not reach Bernal Springs until March 25, had the blankets in their wagons.

There would be no rest for Wynkoop or the men and officers of Companies A, D, and E. Within an hour of their arrival they were again on the move. Wynkoop, Downing, and Anthony's companies joined eighty-eight mounted Colorado First Volunteers (Company F, Captain Samuel H. Cook) who had arrived the previous day, and more than one hundred troops of the First U.S. Cavalry (Captain Charles J. Walker) and Third U.S. Cavalry (Captain George W. Howland). As on previous days, the march was long and the worn-out men did not halt until they reached Kozlowski's Ranch at the eastern end of Glorieta Pass at ten that night. As Wynkoop and his men began to retire they heard rumors that six hundred Texans had recently departed Santa Fe and were close.[29]

On the morning of March 26 Chivington left camp at Kozlowski's Ranch and set out for Johnson's Ranch in Apache Canyon at the western entrance to Glorieta Pass. His command consisted of the First Colorado, Wynkoop (Company A), 60 men; Company C, 28 men; Downing (Company D), 60 men; Anthony (Company E), 60 men; First Regiment Cavalry Colorado Volunteers, Cook (Company F), 88 men; plus 12 additional Colorado Volunteers; as well as Howland (Company K, Third U.S. Cavalry), 10 men; Captain Walker (Company E, Third U.S. Cavalry), 50 men; Captain Lord (Companies D and G, First U.S. Cavalry), 50 men, for a grand total of 418 men.[30]

Early that afternoon the command entered the eastern entrance of Glorieta Pass at Pigeon's Ranch, a stage stop in Apache Canyon.[31] The pass, 7,641 feet above sea level, consisted of jagged ravines and rugged hills where the abundant piñon, juniper, and ponderosa pines greatly hindered visibility. Glorieta Mesa, 500 feet above the canyon floor, flanked the southern side of the pass. Johnson's Ranch, at the western end of the pass, was still six miles away.[32] Sometime after 2:00 P.M. they came to a sudden halt. Before them stood two hundred fifty to three hundred Confederate soldiers. Two cannons under the command of Major Charles L. Pyron (Second Texas Mounted Rifles) opened fire.[33]

Chivington ordered Wynkoop and Anthony, who were on the left, to advance along the base of Glorieta Mesa and act as skirmishers as they moved through the trees. Anthony's Company E led, with Wynkoop's Company A right behind. On the right, Downing also moved along the base of the mountain with his men firing as they advanced. Chivington dismounted all the cavalry, except those under Cook, who were to charge as soon as the enemy broke and retreated. While Cook held his position, Howland, Walker, and Lord's dismounted men joined the fray.[34] Howland moved along the base of the mountain on the right while Walker supported Wynkoop "in clearing the hills to the left and front of our position."[35] Lord followed Wynkoop and Walker. Downing began to flank the Confederate line while Anthony, Wynkoop, and Walker continued their steady advance on the left hillside. "Some little skirmishing occurred . . . at long range," Walker continued, "but the enemy fell back so rapidly that we scarcely got sight of them." Afraid of being overrun and cut off, Pyron's command and battery hastily retreated. After a mile and a half, they halted and prepared to confront the Union advance again.

But the Federals did not appear. Slough had ordered his army back to Kozlowski's Ranch. The next day, March 27, both armies tended to their wounded. While Slough pondered his next move, spies reported some twelve to fourteen hundred Confederate soldiers bivouacked in Apache Canyon at Johnson's Ranch.[36]

At 8:30 A.M. on March 28, Chivington led two battalions from Kozlowski's Ranch back toward Glorieta Pass. Captain Lewis commanded the first battalion, which consisted of Companies A and G, Fifth Infantry (sixty men); Company B, First Colorado Volunteers (seventy-eight men); and Captain James H. Ford's company of Second Colorado Volunteers (strength not reported). Captain Edward Wynkoop commanded the second battalion, First Colorado Volunteers, which consisted of Company A (Lt. Shaffer, sixty-eight men), Company E (Capt. Anthony, seventy-one men), and Company H (Capt. George L. Sanborn, about eighty men). An hour after setting out, Chivington's two battalions bore to the left and followed the Galisteo Road, which led to the pueblo of the same name.[37]

By 10:00 A.M. Chivington's command had covered perhaps four miles. The trail toward the top of Glorieta Mesa was not an easy climb. Half an hour later Wynkoop, Shaffer, and the volunteers had still not reached the top. Suddenly they heard explosions and gunfire below. Slough, who had set out with thirteen hundred men half an hour after them, had engaged the Texans near Pigeon's Ranch.[38]

With their comrades engaged in the canyon, Wynkoop, Shaffer, and Chivington's command slowly worked their way around and through the heavy vegetation on the mesa top. Sounds of the engagement below drifted upward. Wynkoop walked a mile, then another. Each step separated him and his comrades farther from the fight below. The noon hour came and went. Wynkoop, Shaffer, and the soldiers pushed onward. The men began to show signs of fatigue. The fight in the canyon could no longer be heard. After working their way though the thick vegetation for eight miles, they reached their destination. It was 1:30 P.M. Chivington, Wynkoop, several other officers, and a guide cautiously worked their way to the edge of the mesa and peered down at their objective, Johnson's Ranch.[39]

Chivington and Wynkoop saw the Confederate supply train, perhaps eighty wagons, one field piece, and two hundred soldiers. After Chivington discussed the mode of attack, Wynkoop led thirty of his men down the northern face of the mesa. Spreading out, they found positions that guaranteed a view of the camp below. When Wynkoop signaled that his men were ready, the rest of the command began their descent. As soon as the Texans realized they were under attack, they opened fire. Wynkoop yelled for his men to cover Chivington's men as they advanced down the mountainside. His sharpshooters targeted the Confederate gun crew and any rebels shooting at their comrades. When Chivington's men reached the base of the mesa they yelled and cursed as they swarmed through the encampment, surrounding the buildings and wagons, killing three Confederates, and wounding several others. Captain Lewis and the Fifth U.S. Infantry overran the lone cannon and spiked the gun. Almost as suddenly as the fight began, it ended, with most of the Texans fleeing up the cliffs on the opposite side of the canyon or toward the western entrance to the pass. "The wagons were all heavily loaded with ammunition, clothing, subsistence, and forage," Chivington reported.[40] He ordered his men to destroy everything. During the burning of the wagons, the Federals suffered their only casualty. Private Ritter, of Wynkoop's Company A, suffered severe wounds when one of the ammunition wagons exploded. The Federals captured seventeen soldiers and approximately thirty mules and horses while recovering five of their comrades who had been taken that day at Pigeon's Ranch. Chivington singled out Lewis for gallantry but did not ignore the rest of his men. "Both officers and men performed their duty efficiently," he reported. "I repeat, all, ALL, did well."

With the total destruction of the Confederate supply train complete, Chivington, not knowing the strength or closeness of the enemy, wisely retreated to the top of the mesa. Here he received orders to rejoin Colonel Slough, who had once again retreated to Kozlowski's Ranch. The Confederates under Lieutenant Colonel William Scurry had driven the Federal forces from the canyon. According to Scurry, the Union lost seventy-five dead with many more wounded while the Confederates suffered thirty-three dead and thirty-five wounded. Scurry had won the battle and should have claimed victory.

But by the time Wynkoop, the battle-weary and footsore Pike's Peakers, and members of the Fifth U.S. Infantry limped into Slough's encampment at ten that night, the Confederates, aware that their supply train had been destroyed, retreated toward Santa Fe. Chivington claimed that his force had killed twenty-seven and wounded sixty-three, but more important, his surprise attack on the Texans' rear guard turned defeat into victory.[41]

Slough's performance during the battle did not sit well with his command. John Chivington had led the Pet Lambs to victory at Johnson's Ranch, and it was he the First Coloradans cheered. Not happy with Chivington's sudden popularity, Slough tendered his resignation to Canby, who accepted it on April 9, 1862.[42] Chivington, seeing an opportunity, circulated a petition requesting that he be promoted to fill the vacant position.[43]

As Chivington maneuvered to become colonel of the regiment, Sibley called off the invasion and departed Albuquerque for Texas. Even though the time was perfect to strike a decisive blow against the retreating Confederates, on April 13 Canby, instead of pursuing the enemy, moved to reunite his command near the pueblo of Tijeras at Carnuel Canyon. Knowing the rebels were in retreat, Wynkoop, Chivington, and the rest of the First Colorado celebrated long into the night. It was at Tijeras that Lieutenant Colonel Tappan realized he could not hold out against Chivington's immense popularity. He waived his right, which in turn freed Canby to appoint Chivington the regiment's colonel.[44] About this time the First Regiment of Colorado Infantry underwent a name change and became the First Regiment of Colorado Cavalry.[45]

The changes did not stop with Chivington's promotion and the renaming of the regiment. Many of the officers in the First Colorado also received field promotions. On April 14, Canby promoted Wynkoop to acting major of the regiment, pending approval of the governor of Colorado Territory.[46] The newly appointed major retained his second in command; James Shaffer became captain of Company A.[47]

The victory celebration was short-lived. Union scouts entered Los Lunas, south of Albuquerque, and watched Confederate officers dancing with Hispanic women in a cantina. The enemy was too close to ignore, and Canby's combined force of twenty-four hundred men moved toward the enemy position. They camped within a mile of Peralta, which shared a border with Los Lunas, and where, as it turned out, the Texans bivouacked. Chivington approached Canby and requested permission to make a night raid with just the Coloradans. The general denied the request.[48]

Soon after reveille woke Wynkoop and his comrades on the morning of April 15, Sibley's brass band blared "Dixie." A company of New Mexican Volunteers rushed the pueblo and exchanged shots with the Confederates before returning to the Union camp. The Southerners' artillery began bombarding the Federal supply train, forcing it to move back so as not to lose supplies or mules. Union artillery returned fire but did little damage. During the initial stages of the fight that became known as the Battle of Peralta, Canby moved with a portion of his command to gain the other side of Los Lunas, on the west bank of the Río Grande. After the general's departure, Colonel Paul, who was second in command, met with the officers who had not departed with Canby and proposed attacking. Wynkoop stepped forward and volunteered to lead the assault. Paul accepted his offer and ordered Chivington to follow in support. Although the field was "covered with low, heavy timber, cut up by wide sloughy *acequias,* and crossed and recrossed by adobe walls," which favored an infantry advance, Paul, perhaps foolishly, ordered the cavalry to advance on the right.[49] Paul told Chivington to keep him informed, then left to rejoin the New Mexican regulars. Within minutes Chivington ordered Wynkoop to begin the assault. The major deployed the first battalion of Coloradans as skirmishers, and they began to maneuver through the muddy irrigation ditches on foot. According to Chivington, when Wynkoop reached the halfway point between the Union encampment and the Confederate battery, he "in a most stentorian voice . . . ordered the troops to rally on their chief, and they concentrated on him."[50] Acting upon Wynkoop's order, Chivington, who did not bother to update Paul, brought the second battalion of Coloradans up to support

Carte de visite of Lt. Col. Samuel F. Tappan (First Colorado Volunteer Regiment) in 1861. Although he and Wynkoop were never close, and Tappan went after Wynkoop when John Chivington became colonel of the regiment in April 1862, their views on the Indian situation eventually connected them. Courtesy History Colorado (Scan #10038744).

the assault. Within minutes Wynkoop's charge overran and captured the Confederate battery that had kept the Federals at bay for over five hours. Paul, who heard gunfire, rode forward. When he found Chivington, he complained about not being notified of the attack. When Chivington declared he did not need support, Paul blurted, "You wanted the credit of the whole thing yourself."

When Canby returned to the front, he did not want a full-scale battle, so Wynkoop's victorious charge marked the end of the fight at Peralta.

As ordered, Wynkoop retired to the Federal line.[51] Both sides retained their positions, pounding each other with artillery fire throughout the day until the Union soldiers retired to their previous night's camp where they reunited with Canby's command.[52]

That night, with a sandstorm raging, the Confederates left their sick, wounded, and dead behind and crossed the icy Río Grande to Los Lunas. On April 16 a ferocious storm of wind, sand, and snow raked the land, making it almost impossible to breathe. As Sibley's Brigade limped southward, Canby's army followed them on the east side of the Río Grande. The Union general did not want prisoners, nor did he crave more blood. He had one objective—to drive the Texans out of the Southwest.[53]

On May 15, 1862, Samuel Tappan wrote to his cousin, Lewis, attacking Wynkoop's actions at Peralta. "Wynkoop went out, discharged a few rounds and then retired without orders."[54] "Had I known of his retiring without orders," he continued, "I should have advanced on the enemy, but conceiving it impossible for him to back out without orders, I supposed when he came back that Gen[.] Canby had changed the programme of attack, and rested quiet." Tappan claimed he did not learn of Wynkoop's disobedience until days later. "Had I known it at the time the young man who aspires to be a major would have been charged with cowardice." Chivington, who supported Wynkoop's advance, and who would soon censure anyone who failed to be aggressive, had nothing negative to say about his subordinate's actions that day. Of course, Wynkoop was a Chivington man, and Chivington now basked in all the laurels of Glorieta, making the newly promoted major a safer target for Tappan's frustration and anger.

CHAPTER SIX

The Winds of Change

Even though the Confederate Army was in retreat and had withdrawn from New Mexico Territory, the Union command feared another invasion. This delayed Major Edward Wynkoop's return to Colorado, and by May 1862 he found himself stationed at Fort Craig.[1] Unwilling to be separated from Louise any longer, Wynkoop ignored the risk and sent her word to join him. She conceived their second child soon after her arrival.[2]

While at Fort Craig Wynkoop learned that the body of a Confederate officer, Major Henry Raguet, who was shot from his horse and died at Pigeon's Ranch on March 28, had been transferred to Santa Fe and buried at the Masonic Cemetery. Raguet, a Mason, was also a distant cousin of Wynkoop's. At the first opportunity, Wynkoop took Louise and traveled to Santa Fe to investigate.[3] They checked into La Fonda Hotel, where some friends gave them a chocolate cake. Wynkoop stepped out while Louise remained in the room reading. Apparently drawn by the cake, rats appeared in the room, and Louise scrambled onto a chair and drew her skirts about her. Wynkoop returned, but when he opened the door, the rats disappeared. When his wife told him what had happened, he chuckled at her distress. "Well, just sit quietly for a moment and we'll see what happens," she snapped.[4] Sure enough, the rats reappeared, and both Wynkoops quickly stepped onto their chairs. With rats circling them, Wynkoop drew his revolver and began firing. The rats fled, the proprietor appeared, and they were ushered to a new room.

After visiting Raguet's grave, which he marked so it could later be found, the Wynkoops returned to Fort Craig. On June 2 Wynkoop wrote to Raguet's father at Nacogdoches, Texas, offering his assistance if in the future the family wanted to move Raguet's body.[5]

Wynkoop's time at Fort Craig did not last long. In July he was ordered to Polvadera, a supply depot on the Río Grande eleven miles south of Fort Craig. He spent the remainder of the summer commanding the depot and watching for raiders or signs of another invasion. Wynkoop saw nothing. Feeling that Polvadera was safe and knowing that his officers missed their loved ones, he invited them to bring their wives and children to Polvadera. By midsummer a number of wives and children had arrived, boosting the men's morale and relieving the monotony of guard duty at an isolated post. As summer drew to a close it became apparent that the Texans did not plan another invasion. His services no longer needed in New Mexico, Wynkoop was sent with Companies H and K to Denver City to await further orders.[6] Wynkoop told his men that their families could make the journey to Colorado. When he led his command out of Polvadera, some of the women and children joined the march. They walked with the soldiers, giving the convoy the look of a huge family outing as the caravan worked its way northward.[7] The harsh New Mexico desert was hard on the women and children, including Wynkoop's own wife and child, who was less than a year old. By the time the travelers reached Santa Fe, he knew he needed to do something. As commanding officer, he was able to acquire an ambulance to transport his baggage. The wagon carried his luggage; it also carried Louise, baby Edward, and some of the other women and children. When Brigadier General James H. Carleton, who commanded the Department of New Mexico, heard how Major Wynkoop had used the conveyance, he accused him of using it for personal reasons. Wynkoop had obtained the wagon for Louise and his son, but as a commanding officer returning to Colorado Territory on orders, he did not think he had used it illegally. Wynkoop, who never backed down when he felt himself in the right, informed Carleton "that no such thing has occurred," and charges that the ambulance had been misused were dropped.[8]

Wynkoop and his command reached Fort Garland, Colorado Territory, on September 29. On October 24, 1862, he received orders to continue to Denver City and report to Chivington for duty. On his way north, he commanded at Colorado City for a short time in December 1862.[9]

Colorado's gratitude for the repulsion of the Confederate invasion had not faded during the summer and fall. When Wynkoop reached Denver, cheering crowds lined the streets to welcome the volunteers home as conquering heroes. Ever popular among his officers and men, Wynkoop now found himself the toast of Denver. By this time Chivington controlled the District of Colorado, which was part of the Central District of Missouri.[10] Wynkoop and the colonel remained friends. As Frank, Wynkoop's son, remembered, his parents and Chivington "got along fine. They were friends, early day pioneers."[11]

During the war, Louise often split her time between residing alone and living with her husband at the various army posts to which he was assigned.[12] By January 1863, Wynkoop again found himself stationed at Camp Weld, and a very pregnant Louise joined him. On February 1 she delivered their second child, Emily Reveille.[13]

The next day a Free Mason by the name of C. E. Cooke shot himself after an argument with his wife. Even though Wynkoop did not know the deceased, he attended the funeral, for as a Free Mason he felt honor-bound to pay his respects to a fallen comrade. After the service he rode in the funeral procession as it wound through the streets of Denver to the graveyard. The drawn-out line of mourners slowly proceeded along Larimer Street until it reached Cherry Creek. As Wynkoop began to cross the Larimer Street bridge, "the clattering of hooves upon the bridge" frightened the black horse he rode, which reared.[14] Wynkoop fought to rein in the animal, which continued to fight his commands and rear until "opposite the Post Office." Wynkoop had almost succeeded in controlling the animal when it reared again and fell over backward, landing on him. Some bystanders pulled the flailing animal off Wynkoop, and Dr. Pollock assisted him into the Post Office, where he examined him. Pollock found that Wynkoop "had received a severe contusion of the lower part of the spine, very painful." Although not believed serious, the injury caused Wynkoop increasing pain with the passage of time.[15]

February 1863 inched forward and Wynkoop seemingly recovered from the fall. On February 25 a group of Union supporters convened at the Denver Theatre. That evening Wynkoop, Chivington, and Byers, among others, were elected vice presidents. A letter that Wynkoop had recently drafted was read that night. His main concern was that, as a Democrat, his choice of political party carried "with it a suspicion of disloyalty" to the Union, and he did not want his name "to be so sullied."[16] Sixteen officers of the First Colorado who were also Democrats signed it.

With Chivington, his subordinate officers, and the Denver populace continuing to acknowledge Wynkoop's ability to command, on February 27 the military and civilian population cosponsored a ceremony in his honor. The mayor of Denver, Amos Steck, opened the proceedings by praising Wynkoop's contributions to the preservation of the Union and presented Wynkoop with a strawberry roan named Sam.[17] Wynkoop also received a pocket calendar made of ivory cut into rectangular sheets and hinged at one end and ornamented with a silver shield and latch. The ivory leaves, one for each day of the week, fanned out for entries that could be erased after use. The inscription read: "Maj. E. W. Wynkoop 1st Colorado Cav."[18]

Called to the podium, Wynkoop, who loved the spotlight, thanked everyone for what he considered an "unmerited compliment." He told the gathering that he had made every effort to make friends since his arrival in Colorado Territory. Then, making the most of his easy way with words, he added, "[T]hank God I have still some."[19] With the crowd eager for him to continue, he moved to the topic that drove him. "Since treason has raised its venomous head"—and this was exactly how Wynkoop viewed the rebellion—"may [I] assist in hunting this foul and fiendish rebel lion to its death." Next, he shared his greatest hope, "[that] *our Union is saved!*" In closing, Wynkoop downplayed his part in the Union victory at Glorieta, then bared his soul to the crowd. "[I]f my country requires my poor life as a sacrifice . . . I desire no *nobler* grave than the spot on which I 'render up my spirit to the God who gave it.'" Wynkoop had wooed and won the crowd, and his popularity soared. Thrilled by his reception, an elated Wynkoop had no idea of the winds of change that had begun to blow. The indigenous people of the West would soon replace the Confederates as enemies, posing a threat even more deadly.

. . .

Before the coming of the white man, the words "enemy" and "stranger" were almost synonymous to the Plains Indians.[20] Alone or in small groups, strangers would be attacked. With the coming of mountain men and explorers, skirmishes sometimes occurred, but most of the fighting remained intertribal throughout the first half of the nineteenth century.

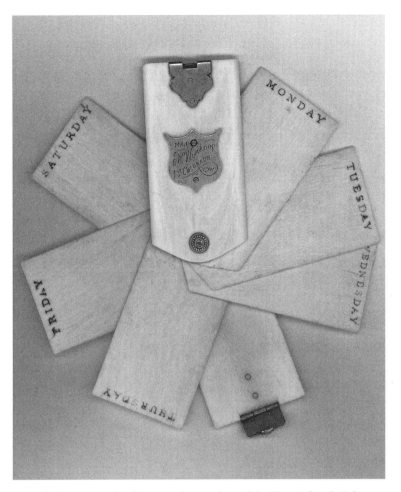

An ivory calendar presented to Wynkoop by members of the First Colorado Volunteer Cavalry shortly after his return to Denver in early 1863. The ivory leaves were erasable, allowing Wynkoop to schedule a week. Author's collection.

By the 1860s numerous tribes roamed the central and southern plains and mountains. Four of them dominated the others: the Kiowas, Comanches, Arapahos, and Southern Cheyennes. Along with the Utes and the Plains (or Kiowa) Apaches, these groups would soon take center stage in Wynkoop's life.

That spring of 1863 Southern Cheyennes, Arapahos, and Kiowas visiting Washington, D.C., were warned by government officials not to take sides in the war between the states. After the Indians had returned to their homelands, Confederate sympathizers approached the Cheyennes, Arapahos, Kiowas, Comanches, and their traditional enemy, the Osages, and asked them to join Texas troops and annihilate Fort Lyon (Colorado Territory) and Fort Larned (Kansas). The recruiting efforts failed. The Indians wanted nothing to do with the white man's war.[21]

By spring 1863, over a year since the victory at Glorieta, the threat of another invasion by the Texans had receded, but rumors of another assault on the Southwest did not cease. After returning to Denver Wynkoop spent his time in garrison at Camp Weld, where he became commanding officer on April 22.[22] This was a monotonous duty, interrupted only by the flare-up in May of his injury from the February riding incident, and "on or about May 20, 1863," the regimental surgeon treated him.[23]

That same May approximately twenty-two Confederate officers volunteered to enlist Indian tribes in Kansas to launch a war against Union sympathizers in New Mexico and Colorado territories. Among the Confederate officers were Wynkoop's old associates Charles Harrison, now a captain in the Fourth Confederate Missouri Cavalry, and Park McLure.[24]

On May 15 Osage warriors came upon the Confederates near the settlement of Humboldt in southeastern Kansas. When questioned, the whites said they belonged to the Union garrison at Humboldt. Well acquainted with Troop G, Ninth U.S. Kansas Cavalry, then stationed there, the Indians demanded the whites accompany them to Humboldt. Instead, Harrison and cohorts opened fire. One Osage died. Later that day a party of two hundred Osage warriors caught up to the Southerners near the Verdigris River and killed all of them in a running fight.[25] Wynkoop probably never learned of his former friends' fate.

By this time, Indians were little more than a memory to Wynkoop, but this was about to change. When whites invaded their homeland on the eastern slopes of the Rockies during the gold rush of 1858–59, the Utes struggled to get over the shock, but by 1862 they began to raid sporadically. That year a movement in Colorado Territory to remove them from their land became a priority for territorial politicians.[26]

But at the end of June 1863, before treaty talks could be arranged, Ute warriors again raided settlements in the northwestern portion of Colorado Territory. As the depredations increased, Special Order No. 121 instructed Wynkoop to lead a punitive expedition to Fort Bridger,

Nebraska Territory. His battalion consisted of companies A and G, First Colorado Volunteer Cavalry.[27] Orders explicitly stated his command could consist of officers, noncommissioned officers, privates, servants of officers, people employed by the quartermaster and commissary departments, a guide, officers from other regiments, and personal friends, but "no camp followers, except the regular sutler."[28] All who accompanied Wynkoop had to subscribe to an oath of allegiance to the United States.

Suddenly, Wynkoop found himself front and center in a potential Indian war. Intent on proving his mettle, he marched eighty miles north from Camp Weld to Camp Collins, Colorado Territory. After collecting three additional companies (M and B; Company I also joined him after being outfitted), he set out for Fort Bridger. He would support Brigadier General Patrick Edward Connor, commander of the Military District of Utah and Nevada, in bringing depredating Utes and Shoshones to bay.[29] On July 10, Wynkoop's orders were expanded: "Great caution should be observed not to get into trouble with any party of Indians who are peacefully disposed."[30] Although Chivington had complete confidence in Wynkoop as an officer and field commander, he intended to join the punitive expedition.

On July 11 Wynkoop's assignment became complicated. Lieutenant Silas Soule, acting assistant adjutant general for the First Colorado, informed Wynkoop that a large number of Southern Cheyenne and Arapaho warriors had congregated near Camp Collins on the southern bank of the Cache la Poudre River, a tributary of the South Platte. The Indians wanted to join Wynkoop's command, wage war against the Utes, and collect as much plunder as possible. Orders forbade Wynkoop to allow this.[31]

The Cache la Poudre was not the only place where Southern Cheyennes and Arapahos appeared in large numbers. They also gathered at Fort Larned in Kansas, along with Kiowas, Comanches, and Plains Apaches. According to Brigadier General Thomas Ewing, Jr., they were "friendly or not as occasion prompts."[32] Although these tribes followed the buffalo herds as they migrated across the prairie, they also expected to receive their annual allotments of supplies from the federal government. Their numbers were estimated by the total of lodges, somewhere between four and five thousand. This large an assembly represented the possibility of violence. When a sixteen-year-old sentry named Isaac

Wynkoop and officers of the First Colorado Volunteer Cavalry in 1863. *Sitting, left to right:* Capt. Samuel M. Robbins, Dr. John F. Hamilton, Maj. Edward W. Wynkoop, Col. James A. Ford. *Standing, left to right:* Lt. Silas S. Soule, Capt. James M. Shaffer, Capt. Samuel H. Cook. As city marshal of Denver, Shaffer occasionally confronted Wynkoop. However, after the formation of the regiment and during the Glorieta campaign, Shaffer served as Wynkoop's second-in-command. Courtesy History Colorado (Scan #10028910).

Marrs shot and killed a warrior named Little Heart late one night at Fort Larned, the Indians, angry over the murder, became "indignant and threatening."

By July 17 Wynkoop found himself en route to a location one hundred miles south of Fort Halleck. Chivington set out to intercept him. Finding him seven days later, the colonel remained with Wynkoop for three days. Before he left, Chivington made sure that Wynkoop understood his orders "to recover, if possible, the stock [the Utes] stole from the Overland Stage Line and others, and to chastise them if they refused to give them up. . . . [Wynkoop was to] penetrate the country to the headwaters of Bear, White, and Snake Rivers."[33] As soon as Chivington departed, Wynkoop, supplied for fifteen days, resumed sole control of his command.

With his destination again Fort Bridger, Wynkoop marched north toward Nebraska Territory. Moving through rolling hills filled with buffalo grass, he climbed the high plains and had almost reached 7,000 feet as he approached the Virginia Dale Stage Station on the Overland Trail, south of the northern border of Colorado Territory. Here a courier overtook him. General Connor had come to terms with the Indians, marking the end of the uprising. With Connor no longer requiring his support, Wynkoop marched back toward Camp Weld.[34]

Just before he reached Denver, a communiqué from Chivington overtook him. The violence had not ended; the Utes continued to raid near Fort Halleck. Unsure what to do, Wynkoop left his command, who stayed where they were while he rushed to Denver to meet with his commander. Chivington ordered him to remain in the field and recover the stolen stock. If Wynkoop could recover the property peacefully, fine. If not, Chivington wanted him to attack the Indians.[35]

With new orders in hand, Wynkoop made it a point to talk with the Denver press. He was determined, he claimed, "to penetrate to the villages and hiding places of the red thieves and murderers, and administer a lesson the survivors will not soon forget."[36] The "Indian fighter," as the press labeled him, rejoined his command. Then he did an about-face and again headed north "for the purpose of hunting down and punishing the aforementioned Indians using my own discretion in regard to the manner of doing so."[37] With his destination again Fort Halleck, Wynkoop pushed his men. At Camp Collins, he ordered the sabers left behind. Revolvers and carbines would serve him better when he caught up to the Indians. He also left Company B in garrison at the post.

The Utes' tracks made it obvious where they were headed, and Wynkoop set out immediately, keeping scouting parties continuously in his advance. He traveled thirty miles westward along the Overland Mail route. The track then turned to the south into country he did not know. Relying upon his compass, Wynkoop pressed forward. Eighty miles later, he reached the northwestern entrance to North Park, near the North Platte River.

Even though the trail was hot, Wynkoop camped to lighten his load. During the halt Chivington appeared to discuss strategy, and they decided that if Wynkoop decreased the size of his command he had a chance to strike the Indians. Wynkoop handpicked 160 men. Next, he packed rations for fifteen days on fifty mules that had never served as pack animals. Saying goodbye to Chivington, a hopeful Wynkoop set out once again.

Leaving the wagons behind seemed a logical choice to increase his speed, but it did not take Wynkoop long to realize the drawbacks of the decision. The pack mules were unmanageable. Wastage quickly reduced fifteen days of rations to ten. Fortunately, North Park was a hunter's paradise. The men feasted on grouse, deer, elk, bear, antelope, or fish every night. A march of two days brought them to the southwestern extreme of the area. By this time the Utes' trail had become faint. Pressing onward, Wynkoop pushed his men and livestock. He crossed a mountain range and entered a valley called Old Park. Here, the Utes, probably considering themselves safe from pursuit, made no attempt to hide their trail. Certain that the Indians did not know he was tracking them, Wynkoop now hoped the war party would lead him to their village. Continuing the march, he had every intention of following the trail no matter where it led.

Following the westward-moving trail, Wynkoop force marched the next eighty miles in two days. The tracks wound through terrain that was almost impassable. Now west of Middle Park, Wynkoop crossed two snow ranges, a number of small mountains, and the Bear and White rivers. Before reaching the Grand River, he came upon a sulfur spring that had formed in the shape of a caldron. The constant overflow of the boiling spray had formed a circular land mass some sixty-eight feet above the river where the earth spewed forth the scalding water. As they crossed the area, the clip-clopping of horses' hooves on the surface echoed eerily—a sound that made Wynkoop think that at any point he and his command could plunge through the surface into boiling water.

At the Grand River, the trail again turned south, and Wynkoop followed it. Soon, the trail turned westward. His scouts continued to report that the Utes had no more than a day's lead, but Wynkoop no longer believed them. The trail looked no fresher than when he began the pursuit, and worse, it now branched off in many directions. Unsure of his location (in all likelihood he was near the Grand and Bunkara rivers), Wynkoop made a quick assessment. With his supply of flour totally gone and his rations getting dangerously low, it did not look promising. Game was now almost nonexistent. The long marches had been hard on both men and livestock; privation showed on everyone's face. As the animals could not last much longer, Wynkoop knew that even if he did catch his prey he would not pose much of a threat. To continue seemed foolhardy. Considering the safety of his command, Wynkoop decided to return to civilization before disaster struck.

He considered pushing on to Fort Garland in southern Colorado with his officers, but then changed his mind. More than 150 miles southwest of South Park, and at risk of having his command disintegrate, he called off the hunt and limped back toward civilization. Three days later, he reached Georgia Gulch, where he secured much-needed flour.[38] In the course of the expedition, Wynkoop and his men had passed through portions of present-day Wyoming, Colorado, Idaho, and Utah.

Although proud of how well his command had functioned, Wynkoop surely had mixed feelings at best. By the time he returned to Denver, his command was dirty and emaciated, a sad sight to see. His quest to preserve his country had changed from a war in support of his country to a war with Indians. When he fought the Confederates he had put his life on the line for his beliefs. Indians were not opponents in a battle. They were an unseen foe who refused to fight. Not once had he seen even one of the raiding warriors. Shockingly, this did not matter in the eyes of the Colorado press, who presented Wynkoop as a hero.

As soon as his new career as Indian fighter began, it was put on hold. In September Wynkoop was ordered to Fort Laramie, Nebraska Territory, for quartermaster duty. This did not last long; he was back in command of Camp Weld by October 1863.[39]

On October 7, John Evans, Colorado's second territorial governor, along with other territorial dignitaries, signed a treaty with the Tabeguache band of Ute Indians. Even though most of the Ute bands on the eastern side of the Continental Divide—notably the Southern Utes (Capote and Muache or Mohuache), whose land in the San Luis Valley had been targeted—did not attend the treaty talks, they would be affected by the outcome. It did not matter what the Utes in attendance understood or, more important, what those *not* in attendance believed, for the paper had been signed. The Utes no longer had the right to roam their land in Middle Park or the Arkansas and San Luis valleys. But the treaty was not just a land grab. Article 3 stated "Any citizen of the United

States may mine, without interference or molestation, in any part of the country hereby reserved to said Indians where gold or other metals or minerals may be found."[40]

Shortly after the signing of the Ute treaty and Wynkoop's return to Colorado Territory, Evans began voicing his concerns over the possibility of an Indian war. He had actively supported Abraham Lincoln's bid to become president in 1860. However, after Lincoln took office in 1861, he declined an offer to become territorial governor of Washington Territory. The following year he agreed to become the second governor of Colorado Territory, replacing William Gilpin in 1862. Appointed by Lincoln on March 31, 1862, he did not arrive in Denver until May.[41] In November 1863 Evans forwarded William Dole, commissioner of Indian affairs, an anonymous statement that forewarned the future: "The C[o]manches, Apaches, Kiowas, the southern band of Arapahoes and *all* of the Cheyennes with the Sioux, have pledged one another to go to war with the whites as soon as they can procure ammunition in the spring."[42] Without identifying his informant, Evans closed his letter by saying "I am fully satisfied with the truthfulness of his statement."

Although the threat of widespread Indian troubles was worrisome, the war raging in the East remained the main concern in Colorado Territory. On December 2, 1863, the entire city of Denver turned out to celebrate Union army movements in Virginia and Tennessee. Jubilant, boisterous men crowded the streets, drinking, talking, cheering. Throngs hovered near the newspaper and telegraph offices, waiting for word of another rebel defeat. Patriotism reached fever pitch, and those who harbored sympathies for the Southern cause kept their opinions to themselves.

Not wanting to miss the celebration, Wynkoop led an impromptu parade of the First Colorado Volunteer Cavalry and a section of the Battery up and down the main streets of Denver late that afternoon. With the band blasting martial airs, Wynkoop's troops, mounted on "prancing steeds [with] fluttering banners, [made] a gay and imposing cavalcade. Salutes were fired at the crossing of the main streets, and cheer upon cheer rung throughout the city for hours."[43] Just before sundown, Wynkoop led the enthusiastic troops back to Camp Weld. Any attempt at order long gone, the exit of the city turned into a full charge, "with a continuous yell that would have struck terror to the hearts of Stuart's famous Black Horse Cavalry."

Not long after that December parade, Wynkoop received word that his mother, who still lived in Philadelphia, was ill. His upbringing had made his family the most important thing in his life. More than seven long years had passed since he had been home. As he had not had any time off since enlisting in the service, he applied to Secretary of War Edwin M. Stanton, for a leave of absence on December 8, 1863.[44]

Within a month of his application for leave Wynkoop had an answer; permission granted for forty days. There was a caveat. "Any officer absent from duty with leave, except for sickness or wounds, shall, during absence, receive half of the pay and allowances prescribed by law, and no more."[45]

Wynkoop did not head east immediately. Instead, he delayed his leave and continued to command Camp Weld through February 1864.[46] The daily routine of running a military post continued to dominate his time. The war in the East seemed distant, his efforts to save the Union a faded memory. With thoughts of the Ute expedition also receding into the past, the heroic Indian Fighter with zero notches on his revolver ceased to exist. Intent upon seeing his mother, Wynkoop set out for the East on March 17, 1864.[47]

CHAPTER SEVEN

Prelude to Infamy

By mid-April 1864 Ned Wynkoop's forty-day leave was over. On the day of his departure, he said goodbye to his mother and set out with his family for the frontier. As he traveled to Colorado, he was unaware that relations between whites and Cheyennes had begun to disintegrate. Of Algonquian lineage, Cheyennes were originally pastoral hunters in the Great Lakes region of Minnesota. With the introduction of the horse in the mid-eighteenth century, their culture changed. No longer sedentary, they followed the movement of game herds onto the Great Plains. By the 1820s the buffalo had become the centerpiece of their lifeway, and a number of bands followed the annual buffalo migration as far south as the Arkansas River and beyond. Finding the country to their liking, they stayed, splitting the tribe into two, the Northern and Southern Cheyennes.[1]

The Southern Cheyennes called themselves the Tsistsistas.[2] Tsistsistas "has been translated to mean 'the People,' 'people alike,' 'our people,' [or possibly] 'related to one another,' or 'similarly bred.' [Sometimes] their name has also been translated as 'gashed' or 'cut people.' The white man came up with the word 'Cheyenne,' from the [Siouan] word, 'Shai ena,' which translates to 'people who speak with a strange tongue.'"[3]

During the winter of 1837–38 a Cheyenne military society known as the Dog Men became outlaws, banished by the Southern Cheyennes when one of their leaders killed a tribal member. By 1856 the Dog Soldiers (a white term) had become the third division within the Cheyenne tribe, ranging between the Republican and Smoky Hill Rivers.[4] The Northern Cheyennes (Ohméséhesos) lived north of the Platte River; the Southern Cheyennes roamed along the Arkansas River.

On April 12 Second Lieutenant Clark Dunn (First Colorado Volunteer Cavalry) with fifteen men of his command (Companies H and C, forty men) came upon a group of Dog Soldiers north of the South Platte River in the hills east of Frémont's Orchard, Colorado Territory. The warriors were en route to join a Northern Cheyenne raid on the Crows. W. D. Ripley, a rancher, claimed the warriors had stolen his horses; the Indians claimed they found loose mules which they wanted to return. Dunn reportedly attempted to negotiate, only to be attacked. In stark contrast, the Dog Men claimed Dunn attacked without provocation. The rest of Dunn's command appeared and, according to the lieutenant, on water-bloated horses that had already ridden seventy-five miles that day, the soldiers chased as many as forty-five Dog Soldiers fifteen or sixteen miles. Four of Dunn's men were injured, and they wounded ten or fifteen and killed eight or ten Indians before calling off the fight. The Dog Men claimed—again, in stark contrast—that when the soldiers attacked they killed an officer, the soldiers fled, they did not give chase, and they returned to the villages on the Smoky Hill. By their own account they suffered three wounded and no deaths.[5]

Dunn's fight was just one of several that Wynkoop would hear about soon after he and his family arrived in Denver on April 26.[6] That day he reported to Chivington, and the colonel placed him in command of Camp Weld.[7]

Three days later Wynkoop visited William Byers to hear the latest news. Seeing the potential of Dunn's encounter and wanting Indians removed from the territory as obstacles to progress, Byers printed inflammatory editorials that enraged and frightened the Denver population. The *Commonwealth* took exception to Byers's fear tactics and declared that there was "not the slightest cause for any general scare."[8] After castigating Byers, it called on "every man [to] shoulder his gun and join in a war of extermination against these miserable wretches." Wynkoop agreed. "[T]he cry of war rang through the Territory," he later wrote.[9] Before leaving the *News* office, Wynkoop told Byers that he was "glad to get back," that "Colorado, State or no State," was where he wanted to be.[10]

By this time Wynkoop had heard of other attacks on Cheyennes. When government freighters Jackman and Irwin reported livestock stolen near

Big Sandy in Bijou Basin seventy-five miles southeast of Denver (Southern Cheyennes later said they found the animals wandering), Lieutenant George S. Eayre (Independent Battery, Colorado Volunteer Artillery) set out from Camp Weld. He used Big Sandy's official name in his report but soon officers would begin calling it Sand Creek. Eayre commanded fifty-four men with two 12-pounder mountain howitzers. Lieutenant Phillips (First Colorado Volunteer Cavalry) with twenty-six men from Company D accompanied him. On April 15 Eayre found Southern Cheyenne Crow Chief's village of seventy lodges near the headwaters of the Republican. According to the lieutenant all the Indians fled upon his appearance except one, who wounded one of his men. The Cheyennes claimed the soldiers attacked without attempting to talk. After destroying the deserted village, Eayre found another village on the Republican. Again the Cheyennes ran, and again Eayre destroyed their homes.[11]

The attacks made the Southern Cheyennes aware that white soldiers could and would attack without provocation. At the same time it gave Chivington the reason he needed for a more aggressive attitude toward potentially hostile Indians. Several days after Wynkoop resumed command of Camp Weld, Chivington realized he was wasting the major's capabilities by keeping him near Denver. Knowing that the garrisons along the upper Arkansas were inadequately manned to repel a rebel invasion or an Indian attack, Chivington issued new orders on May 2, sending Wynkoop to Fort Lyon to replace Major Scott Anthony.[12] Wynkoop and Anthony had fought side by side at Glorieta but had never become friends. Like Wynkoop, Anthony, a New Yorker, had migrated west to make his fortune, reaching Kansas (1857) and then Colorado (1860). He had dabbled in mining before opening a store in Oro City.[13]

Wynkoop reached Fort Lyon on the evening of May 8. Located on the Arkansas River in the southeastern portion of the territory, Fort Lyon, a sandstone garrison, included Bent's New Fort, the trading post on the hill above the fort that trader William Bent had built in 1853 and sold to the military in 1859. First named Fort Fauntleroy and then Fort Wise, it became Fort Lyon in June 1862.[14]

Although he had still not fired a round at an Indian, with the growing unrest Wynkoop must have figured his chance would come. Assuming command the following morning, May 9, he asked about the local Indian situation and inspected the post. The inspection revealed that the quarters were dilapidated and, worse, that no vegetables were available.

Because his orders included preparing the garrison to withstand an assault, he decided to repair the buildings. With the surgeon's support, he requested that the commissary supply vegetables.

That day he heard that Southern Cheyennes were camped near the fort. Supposedly they had not attacked any whites, and he assumed they did not pose a threat. Nevertheless, they were Indians, and he wanted Chivington to clarify his assignment. "I would like to receive from headquarters full and thorough instructions in regard to the course I shall adopt in reference to the Indians."[15]

Wynkoop was not the only one concerned about defending against the danger the tribes presented. As the sporadic incidents increased in violence and destruction, Governor Evans realized that the Indians posed a real threat to the white population. He wrote Major General Samuel Curtis, who commanded the Department of Kansas, requesting reinforcements. Curtis, a West Point graduate, had retired from the military prior to the Civil War only to receive a second commission as colonel in 1861. After a victory over the Confederates at Pea Ridge, Arkansas (March 6–8, 1862), he became a major general of volunteers. Curtis admitted to Evans that the military posts on the upper Arkansas were weak and in danger of being overrun but refused the request for reinforcements on the grounds that the need "to crush rebel armies in Virginia and Tennessee" made Kansas and the rest of the frontier vulnerable to Confederate attacks.[16] Curtis then asked Evans to "dispense with all the Federal troops you can spare."

When Chivington answered Wynkoop, he ignored the Indian question and addressed another rebel invasion. Wynkoop received instructions to send scouts to the Red River to watch for signs of a new Confederate penetration into the Southwest. Wynkoop's orders included establishing a picket, a military detachment ready to meet an enemy advance, on the Arkansas in southeastern Colorado. The threat was not an idle one, as the Federals feared another raid into Kansas by William Quantrill. The Confederate guerilla and his men had attacked and destroyed Lawrence, Kansas, an antislavery stronghold, on August 21, 1863, killing 150–200 people. Chivington declared the new dictum the result of an "an increasing evil in this district."[17] Fearing that officers and men might not return to duty after a vacation, Chivington told Wynkoop that all requests for a leave of absence would be refused. He also forbade officers to employ soldiers as servants.

Almost as an afterthought Chivington addressed the Indian unrest, but not as Wynkoop had hoped. After returning to Camp Weld, Eayre had set out a second time and disappeared. If he appeared at Fort Lyon, Chivington wanted Wynkoop to detain him until he could issue new orders.

As ordered, Wynkoop established pickets along the Arkansas and sent scouts to the Red River to learn whatever they could about Confederate movements in the vicinity. These actions spread his command over a vast area and reduced his immediate command drastically. Wynkoop realized that if Fort Lyon were attacked he might not be able to defend it, nor would he be able to mount punitive or rescue expeditions should the need arise. Accordingly, he soon recalled some of the troops he had stationed in the field.[18]

While Wynkoop prepared for an attack, Southern Cheyenne Chiefs Black Kettle and Lean Bear, nervous they might be attacked, moved from near Fort Larned north to Ash Creek. Here Eayre found them on May 16. When Lean Bear approached the troops to say his village was peaceful, soldiers shot and killed him. Outraged Cheyennes attacked, their numbers growing by the minute. Black Kettle rode among the warriors, yelling "Do not make war!"[19] Facing overwhelming numbers, Eayre retreated with angry warriors—those Black Kettle could not stop—in pursuit. Eayre reached Fort Larned and reported he had driven off the Cheyennes. He first claimed the soldiers had killed three chiefs and twenty-five warriors, while losing four dead and three wounded, but later admitted he fought a seven- or eight-mile running battle, lost three or four men, and killed only one unnamed chief.[20]

That same May 16 Wynkoop received a surprise. The military considered Fort Lyon temporary, and instructed him to do "what is absolutely necessary" with little expense.[21] On the positive side, antiscorbutics, used to prevent scurvy, were en route to Fort Lyon (sent by the sanitary commission of Denver), and Chivington had requested 10,000 pounds of potatoes for the post.

Moreover, headquarters did not ignore Wynkoop's Indian concerns, ordering him to learn if any Southern Cheyennes had participated in raids along the Smoky Hill, Republican, or Platte River. "If they did, they should be punished; if not, and if they commit no offense, of course they will not be molested, but must be watched."

Dutifully, Wynkoop set about fortifying and repairing the post. He took pride in the initial work as he incurred zero cost to the government. Then, with a firm grip on his course of action, Wynkoop issued his own orders: Sell no alcohol to the Southern Cheyennes and arrest William Bent's half-Cheyenne son George if he appeared at the fort.[22] George Bent, captured as a Confederate prisoner of war on August 30, 1862, was released to his father six days later when he signed an oath of allegiance to the United States. Since returning to Colorado he had lived with the Southern Cheyennes and refused to honor his pledge, often berating Union soldiers, calling them "damn Yankees."[23]

Predictably, Eayre's unjustified actions (he killed a total of three Indians) angered the Southern Cheyennes. They began raiding the stage road between Forts Riley and Larned. This caused panic among the whites, who abandoned the ranches and stations along the road. Warriors took what they wanted from the deserted structures and then destroyed them. Kiowa War Chief Satanta (Set-t'ainte, Sa-Tan-Tee, White Bear) raided the horse herd at Fort Larned. Soon after when Arapaho Chief Left Hand (Niwot, Nor-wan-che) approached the post to talk, soldiers fired at him. Eayre's actions had set off a war between the Arkansas and Platte rivers.[24]

Five days after Eayre attacked Black Kettle's village, on May 21, Lieutenant Luther Wilson, who commanded Camp Wynkoop (a picket sixty miles east of Fort Lyon), sent Wynkoop word of a large congregation of Southern Cheyennes in his vicinity. Wynkoop immediately ordered Wilson to find out if any of them had taken part in the recent clashes. If so, Wynkoop intended to attack.[25] At this time he began receiving alarming reports that combined facts with rumor—Comanches and Kiowas joined the Cheyennes; Kiowas raided near Fort Larned, south of the Arkansas; Cheyennes attacked and annihilated a company of soldiers.[26]

But the Southern Cheyennes were not just fighting white soldiers. A war party en route to or from raiding Utes, passed close to Booneville, about eighty miles west of Fort Lyon. As whites had attacked their villages, the Southern Cheyennes now struck at random. "[W]omen have been grossly abused," civilian H. M. Fosdick claimed, "cattle killed, farmers driven from their lands, and fear and danger have run riot."[27]

Uncertain over the extent of the Indian uprising, Chivington admonished Wynkoop to warn his officers camped at outposts to remain constantly alert. In a startling turnabout from his previous stance, on May 31 Chivington addressed the Indian situation. "The Cheyennes will have to be soundly whipped before they will be quiet," he wrote Wynkoop. "If any of them are caught in your vicinity kill them, as that is the only way."[28]

By the end of May 1864, Companies A and E of the First Colorado were en route to Fort Lyon from Camp Weld and companies B, C, and G would set out for the fort no later than June 1. This represented good news for Wynkoop. The Indian threat was real, and the major hoped that one of the troops would deliver the much-needed supplies he had requested.[29]

With firefights exploding north, east, and south of Denver, Governor Evans intensified his campaign for military reinforcements to the territory. He distributed letters describing his fear for the safety of the white population of Colorado. "It will be destruction and death for Colorado if our lines of communication are cut off," he wrote Curtis on June 3.[30] "We are now short of provisions and but few trains are on the way."

As June began Wynkoop had a good understanding of his surroundings and situation, and was in a position to act accordingly. But by the third of the month the anticipated reinforcements had still not arrived. Wynkoop's immediate command consisted of exactly 129 officers and men. The unknown status of the impending Southern invasion also demanded his attention. Even though two howitzers belonging to him had been detained at Fort Larned, a confident Wynkoop informed headquarters, "I will be as vigilant as possible—give them another taste of Pigeon's Ranch and Apache Cañon and see how they like it. I can hold my own against twice my number."[31] Brave words—most likely bolstered by the knowledge that reinforcements would soon arrive.

To date Wynkoop and Lieutenant Silas S. Soule had had little contact except through official communications. Since August 1863 Soule (Company D) had been on detached duty in Denver acting as adjutant and performing recruiting duty. On April 12, 1864, he received a promotion to captain. At the beginning of June, Soule and Company D set out for his new assignment as Wynkoop's second in command, arriving at Fort Lyon on the fifth.[32]

Wynkoop had always been a capable person. By June 1864 his ability to deal with adversity had garnered him respectability and a reputation as a man capable of doing what had to be done. He faced an unenviable situation at Fort Lyon. Spies had reported Southern scouts along the Arkansas River and, to the south, on the Red River, but they provided no details of actual rebel movements. With the added threat of an Indian uprising, Wynkoop found himself juggling responsibilities and vacillating on how he should deal with the various threats. The South needed to secure mineral-rich Colorado, and the Cheyennes threatened the white population in the territory. Deciding that the Confederate threat was greater, Wynkoop sent Lieutenant Horace Baldwin to Fort Garland, Colorado, 130 miles southwest of Fort Lyon. The major asked Lieutenant Colonel Samuel Tappan, who commanded the post, for two howitzers. Tappan balked at Wynkoop's request.[33]

About the time Wynkoop sent his request to Tappan, reinforcements began arriving at Fort Lyon, improving his ability to defend the region. Aware that Chivington considered Camp Wynkoop vulnerable, and per the colonel's orders, Wynkoop reinforced the outpost. He instructed Lieutenant Wilson to be wary of Indian attack and told him he wanted the illegal distribution of whisky to Indians by traders stopped.[34]

With additional troops, Wynkoop hoped to lead an exploratory expedition to determine the South's strength locally as soon as the artillery pieces arrived. But Tappan never sent the howitzers, and Wynkoop continued to feel the twofold threat. However, as rumors of a Kiowa-Cheyenne-Southern alliance persisted and raids initiated by Kiowas and other Indians on the Arkansas became concerns, the fear of another rebel invasion diminished. To Wynkoop's relief, Chivington came through and provided him every man he could spare. By June 8 Fort Lyon had ten companies of cavalry at the post, within sixty miles of it, or en route. As troops arrived, Wynkoop reassigned many to outlying garrisons along the Arkansas, which in turn kept the fort undermanned.[35]

While Wynkoop worked at distributing the soldiers under his command, June saw an escalation of Indian attacks. Feeling that war had been forced upon them, Southern Cheyennes, Dog Men, and Arapahos joined forces with the Brûlé Sioux. Not confining their attacks to southeastern Colorado Territory, warriors raided along the Platte River, running off stock at every opportunity. Cheyennes assaulted Coal Creek, ten miles from Denver. Then, on June 11, in an unconnected raid, Arapahos attacked a cabin on the Isaac Van Wormer ranch near Box Elder Creek.

When the mutilated bodies of Nathan Hungate (who worked for Van Wormer); his wife Ellen, who had also been raped; and their daughters Laura, not yet four, and Florence, who was less than a year old, were brought to Denver and displayed for all to see, outrage was instantaneous. Many cried out for extermination. Bloodlust mingled with fear and panic. Residents of Denver boarded up their windows, and farmers deserted their homes and fled to the city. The panic was not confined to Denver or the Platte. As the raids escalated, the citizens of the Arkansas Valley near Fort Lyon abandoned homes and crops.[36]

The waters of the Arkansas overflowed in mid-June 1864, forcing the laundresses at Fort Lyon to scramble from the riverbank and move to the north side of the post. When the river threatened the stables, Wynkoop evacuated the horses to higher ground. Scurvy had become another of the major's problems, but luckily the promised train of supplies arrived with one barrel of antiscorbutics on June 17. Wynkoop and his officers bought the liquid for $1.25 per gallon and shared it with the troops.

The flooding waters, combined with humidity, created the perfect breeding ground for mosquitoes. Chivington, who visited Fort Lyon to observe the Indian situation, as well as to evaluate rumors of amassing Confederate troops, was attacked by the swarming insects. At this time Wynkoop's forces, which were in constant flux, had dwindled to two companies (E and D) at the fort. On June 18 Chivington arrived at Camp Wynkoop to examine that post.[37] Currently Lieutenant John Oster (First Colorado Volunteer Cavalry) commanded Wynkoop's lone patrol in the field (fifteen men). Oster's extended scouting trip south into New Mexico lasted eleven days (June 7–17), and covered 464 miles. Although rumors hinted that a "large body of Texans" was in the area, the lieutenant saw nothing but the trail of "some horses and mules" that was ten days old.[38]

While Wynkoop worked at fortifying southeast Colorado against an attack, on June 27 Governor Evans issued a proclamation titled "To the Friendly Indians of the Plains."[39] Hoping to separate friendly from warring Indians, he had the letter distributed, asking all who were not at war to report to specified areas—the Cheyennes and Arapahos on the Arkansas to report to Agent Colley at Fort Lyon, the Comanches and Kiowas to report to Fort Larned, the Arapahos and Cheyennes on the Upper Platte to report to Camp Collins on Cache-la-Poudre, and the Sioux to report to Fort Laramie, Nebraska Territory.

As July 1864 began, Chivington returned to Fort Lyon. During this stay at the post, he met the Southern Cheyenne One-Eye (Ochinee, Lone Bear), who told him he wanted to return to his people but was frightened of being stopped by soldiers. Chivington wrote him a safe conduct pass.[40]

Pleased with how Wynkoop was handling his duties, Chivington returned to Denver. His satisfaction would not last. About the middle of June, Curtis had instructed Wynkoop to send troops to Fort Larned in Kansas. Instead of doing as ordered, Wynkoop forwarded the order to Chivington for approval before obeying it (most likely because he felt desperately short of men). Curtis arrived at Fort Larned on the evening of July 29, "just as four companies of the First Colorado arrived."[41] The general chastised Chivington, claiming Wynkoop's delay in sending reinforcements caused the loss of lives and stock in Kansas. Curtis then criticized Chivington's interest in Colorado politics. Signing the communication "Truly, your friend," Curtis told Chivington, "I fear your attention is too much attracted by other matters than your command." Curtis wanted his subordinate to focus on the Indian war.

The threat of violence to whites living in the territory did not abate. At 10:00 P.M. on August 7 Wynkoop heard that Indians had attacked a wagon train seven miles from Fort Lyon. The raiders, supposedly Kiowas and Comanches, crossed the Arkansas to join other warriors on the south side. Wynkoop immediately sent word to Captain Isaac Gray (Company E) at Camp Wynkoop to cross the river and block the retreat of the marauders should they pass his way. Taking eighty men (Capt. Soule, Company D; Lt. Ira Quinby, Company K; and Lt. Horace Baldwin, Company G), and one howitzer, Wynkoop set out. While searching for a trail to follow, he received a dispatch from Bent's Ranch informing him that Kiowa war chieftain Satanta and other chiefs had appeared there that evening. The war party then moved downriver and attacked a family named Rood, killing everyone.

Wynkoop pushed his men toward Bent's Ranch but saw no sign of Indians until he reached a house that had recently been attacked. The building was deserted, and Wynkoop later heard that four men had held off a war party, killing one warrior. Wynkoop proceeded as far as Bent's Ranch, seeing the pony tracks of fourteen "red devils," as he called them. The raiding party changed direction and moved quickly toward the Cimarron.

Although Wynkoop began the pursuit with eighty men, after two nights of constant riding, all of which proved fruitless, his command had dwindled to fifty. The other mounts had become unserviceable, greatly hindering his mobility. Calling off the hunt, Wynkoop limped back to Fort Lyon with his command, arriving on August 9. An exhausted Wynkoop had again failed to engage the enemy.

"I am well convinced Satanta with one thousand or more warriors of the Kiowas and Comanches is located over on the Cimarron or in that vicinity," Wynkoop reported.[42] Like other officers, even though he only saw pony tracks for fourteen warriors, he inflated his estimate. Nevertheless, he was unnerved. Feeling his force insufficient to mount another pursuit, he requested reinforcements. "If it is possible I would command in the field to punish this fiend Satanta and his murdering crew."

With no end to the Indian war in sight, in August 1864 John Evans and Henry M. Teller (who eventually became secretary of the interior) led the campaign for Colorado statehood. When they selected their candidates early that month, they chose Chivington to run for congressional representative, something the colonel should have declined as Curtis had already warned him to steer clear of politics. The Evans-Teller-Chivington triumvirate met with heavy opposition from anti-staters, who wanted neither statehood nor a constitution.[43]

Amid the heated political battle a desperate Evans began a barrage of communications describing the situation in the territory and requesting assistance. On August 10 he warned W. P. Dole, commissioner of Indian Affairs, of "the largest Indian war this country ever had."[44] He wanted Dole to "get me authority to raise a regiment of 100-days' mounted men." The next day Evans wrote Curtis that if the tribal alliance moved westward "we shall be in great danger of being destroyed."[45]

On August 11 Sergeant Kenyon, searching for a stray horse north of Fort Lyon, raced for the post. Fifteen warriors chased him, halting in view of the commissary building. Within ten minutes Wynkoop had thirty men in the saddle. He divided the troops into two commands led by Lieutenants Joseph Cramer and Horace Baldwin.

By the time Cramer came in contact with fourteen raiders, only six men were riding serviceable horses. The rest of the mounts had played out, and the men followed as best they could. As Cramer engaged the Indians in a five-to-six-mile running fight, most of the Starr carbines malfunctioned. Still, Cramer claimed he wounded four warriors and captured one pony. By this time, he had advanced approximately twenty-five miles from Fort Lyon. With all his horses now worn out, he pressed on but did not again engage the enemy. After traveling another twenty miles, he reached Sand Creek, as he called it, northeast of Fort Lyon. Here, Cramer saw signs that perhaps 150 Indians had recently crossed the creek, but a heavy rainfall spoiled his ammunition and he called off the pursuit.[46]

Hearing that Cramer had engaged the enemy near Sand Creek, Wynkoop dispatched Lieutenant Quinby with thirty men to reinforce Cramer that evening. Then, concerned for Cramer's safety and anxious to engage the enemy, Wynkoop decided to find out for himself what was going on at Sand Creek. That night he left Captain Isaac Gray, who had recently returned to Fort Lyon, in command. With Soule and chief of cavalry Captain Samuel Robbins, he led a combination of cavalry and battery out of Fort Lyon and headed toward Sand Creek. Soon after he left, a thunderstorm pounded the mounted riders. Wynkoop struggled to maintain his course. After six weary hours he reached Sand Creek. There was no sign of Cramer or the warring Indians, who he thought were Kiowas or Arapahos. Again failing to engage warring Indians, a concerned Wynkoop returned to Fort Lyon.

He need not have worried; Cramer returned safely on August 12. When Wynkoop heard that only two of the eleven Starr carbines Cramer's men carried functioned properly he was livid, complaining in his August 13 report that they were "absolutely worthless, it being impossible to discharge over two-thirds of them."[47] Ever the warrior, he added, "it is my intention to kill all Indians I may come across until I receive orders to the contrary from headquarters."

Back in Denver Evans had good news. General Curtis authorized the enlistment of a volunteer regiment to serve for 100 days. On August 13 Byers printed Evans's proclamation that the Secretary of War had authorized the enlistment of a regiment of cavalry to fight Indians.[48]

Evans continued his pressure. On August 18 he wired Secretary of War Edward M. Stanton of the escalating Indian depredations. "Our lines of communication are cut, and our crops . . . cannot be gathered by our scattered population. Large bodies of Indians are undoubtedly near to Denver, and we are in danger of destruction both from attacks

of Indians and starvation. . . . It is impossible to exaggerate our danger."[49]
He then wrote to Curtis, "We look to you to keep the Platte line open;
otherwise our condition is hopeless."[50]

As the summer advanced, Wynkoop heard stories of three white
women held captive by Cheyennes.[51] Everyone dreaded falling into the
hands of Indians; for women, it was considered "a fate worse than death."
Certainly, as the years passed, the saying "Save the last bullet for yourself"
held real meaning for many. "I do not desire to enter into the sickening
details of that terrible Summer of '64," Wynkoop later wrote, "suffice it
to say that after the Indians were once aroused [*sic*] they were rapacious
in their cruelty."[52]

CHAPTER EIGHT

Wynkoop's Gamble

On September 4, 1864, Major E. W. Wynkoop was speaking with several officers and post trader Dexter Colley in his office at Fort Lyon. A soldier entered the room, interrupting the conversation to say that a sergeant and two soldiers who had set out for Denver to muster out of the service were outside with captured Indians. Since joining the military, Wynkoop had done much posturing about killing Indians. He felt they were degraded, stood in the way of progress, and "must make way for civilization or be trampled on."[1] As far as Wynkoop was concerned, Indians "had no rights that we were bound to respect, in fact . . . had nothing but the instincts of a wild beast, and should be treated accordingly." Before stepping outside, Wynkoop suggested they rough up the prisoners. Colley agreed.

As soon as they stepped outside, Colley recognized the Cheyennes. Wynkoop, who did not know them, pushed past Colley and demanded they get off their horses. Colley rushed to Wynkoop and told him that he knew the Indians, that they were Southern Cheyennes, and were friendly. Continuing, he told the major that his father, Cheyenne-Arapaho agent Samuel Colley, relied on one of them "a great deal for information."[2]

Since the Indians arrived with the soldiers, Wynkoop assumed that his men had apprehended them. This angered him. "I reprimanded the Sergeant for taking prisoners," Wynkoop remembered, "reminding him of the existing orders" to kill all Indians.[3] According to Wynkoop, the sergeant stood up to him, saying he had come upon the Cheyennes as they neared Fort Lyon. He said he fired at the Indians but when he saw them "hold up a paper and make signs of peace," he decided not to kill them and return to the fort.

The sergeant handed Wynkoop the papers, which turned out to be letters Southern Cheyenne Chief Black Kettle had dictated to Edmund Guerrier and George Bent, mixed-blood Cheyennes. Wynkoop looked at the Cheyennes, One-Eye, who was Agent Colley's informant; his wife; and Min-im-mie (Eagle Head, Minimic, Mah-nim-ic). He led everyone into his office. Once inside, he read the letters. Both were dated August 29, 1864. Bent's letter was addressed to Agent Colley and Guerrier's to the military commander of Fort Lyon.[4]

The letters offered to make peace providing the whites also made peace with the Arapahos, Comanches, Kiowas, Plains Apaches, and Sioux. Bent's said, "We have seven prisoners of you which we are will-ing to give up providing you give up yours."[5] This interested Wynkoop, since he certainly wanted to free the white hostages. However, the next sentence gave him pause. "There are three war parties out yet and two of Arapahoes, they have been out some time and expect now soon."

Wynkoop knew nothing about Indians except they could be frighten-ing and were hard to engage in battle. Not sure what he wanted to do but knowing he wanted to talk with the Cheyennes, he sent for someone he had kept his distance from since the Denver City Town Company seized the land that eventually became Denver in November 1858. John Smith had first come in contact with Southern Cheyennes while work-ing for William Bent during the 1830s. He had married into the tribe and knew the language.[6] Smith currently partnered with Dexter Colley, and their ethics were questionable. Trader William Bent saw boxes that Colley and Smith traded to the Indians marked "U.S. Upper Arkansas Agency," and later stated: "It is hard to identify Indian goods, but I am satisfied that a portion of the goods [they] traded with the Indians were annuity goods."[7] Robert Bent, William's son, swore that he had "heard the Indians charge Major [Samuel] Colley with trading their own goods to them."[8] The scheme was simple: Agent Colley withheld annuities from his wards and later his son and Smith sold the plunder to Indians.

Wynkoop was not aware of Smith's ethics or lack thereof, nor did he care. He needed someone to translate immediately. When Smith arrived at his office he appointed him post interpreter.

Through Smith, Wynkoop began to question One-Eye, asking why he had risked death to deliver the letters. Before answering, One-Eye wrapped himself in his blanket and, according to Wynkoop, said "I thought I would be killed, but I knew that paper would be found upon my dead body, that you would see it, and it might give peace to my people once more."[9] Continuing, Wynkoop asked One-Eye if he thought his people were sincere and would give up white prisoners. One-Eye replied "that at the risk of his life he would guarantee their sincerity."[10]

Twelve years later Wynkoop romanticized the interrogation. "I was bewildered with an exhibition of such patriotism on the part of two savages," he wrote, "and felt myself in the presence of superior beings; and these were the representatives of a race that I had heretofore looked upon without exception as being cruel[,] treacherous, and blood-thirsty."[11] Perhaps by then he had read too many James Fenimore Cooper novels or perhaps he was trying to justify his actions that September of 1864.

Wynkoop continued questioning the Cheyennes, and learned of a massive village approximately 140 miles northeast of Fort Lyon. In late August 1864 the Cheyennes and their allies, led by Dog Soldiers, continued to strike isolated whites along the Platte River. As the war dragged toward fall, a number of tribal bands interested in ending hostilities congregated near the headwaters of the Smoky Hill just inside the Kansas line at a place called Big Timbers. With large cottonwood trees and little underbrush, it had long been a favorite campsite for the Southern Cheyennes and Arapahos.[12]

A state of war existed. Wynkoop did not have enough troops to mount a force that could survive an attack. Regardless of his after-the-fact justification of his actions, he was foolish even to consider meeting warring Indians. At the same time, he felt that the Indians would free their captives to obtain peace. He hesitated. One-Eye saw Wynkoop's vacillation and told him to act quickly before the village broke up and the tribal bands moved in different directions.[13] But Wynkoop refused to be pushed. The letters stated the Indians held seven white captives. Women? If Wynkoop thought about Louise, he must have shuddered. To gain time, he locked the Cheyennes up. Before enlisting in the military Wynkoop had survived by his own hook. Not much had changed since he became an officer, and at times it appeared he had a lack of respect for the chain of command.

He had recently received a detachment of infantry from the Department of New Mexico, and he decided to leave them to defend the post. His decision made, he assembled his officers. When he told them he would meet the Indians, they called him a fool and the mission suicide. Wynkoop refused to listen to them. He had a chance to rescue prisoners and end a war, and he had no intention of missing the opportunity. Speed was imperative. Knowing he had to act quickly and could not wait for a reply, he made no attempt to alert his superiors of his plans. By not informing them, he eliminated any negative response on their part. This decision guaranteed him complete control.

The Indians' admission that war parties still roamed the land made the proposed mission perilous, and Wynkoop asked for volunteers. Regardless of their misgivings, a number of officers and troopers volunteered.

Ned Wynkoop led his command of 127, including Soule and Cramer, along with two howitzers and John Smith, out of the safe confines of Fort Lyon on September 6. He also took the three Cheyenne prisoners, along with another Southern Cheyenne known only as "The Fool." He told the Indians that he would kill them if he met with treachery. Wynkoop headed for what he called "the Bunch of Timber" on a tributary of the Smoky Hill.[14]

When the column neared its destination on the third day, Wynkoop saw signs that Indians were near. He sent Min-im-mie to the village to tell the Indian leaders that he came because he had read their letter. When Min-im-mie returned to the command, Wynkoop moved to the left for a mile and halted for the night.

The next morning, September 10, Wynkoop approached the as-yet-unseen village. After traveling about four miles, the command suddenly came face-to-face with a battle line of seven hundred to eight hundred painted and screaming warriors.[15] George Bent, who rode with the warriors, said, "They lined up facing the troops with bows strung, and for a time, it looked very much like war."[16] Wynkoop rightly surmised that he faced a "hostile demonstration." He probably cursed himself for a fool for ignoring his officers' advice. He yelled for his men to form their own battle line. Wynkoop then slowly advanced on the Indian line that blocked his line of march, further agitating the warriors.[17]

Before getting too close to the Indians, Wynkoop halted. Hoping to avoid a clash he sent One-Eye between the lines to tell the screaming horde that he came because he understood they wanted to end the war and would free white prisoners. After One-Eye reached the Indian line he disappeared. Wynkoop watched as warriors brandished weapons and yelled obscenities. Tense moments passed. Wynkoop must have felt that he had been duped; still, he held One-Eye's wife, Min-im-mie, and The Fool hostage. When One-Eye did not return, Wynkoop felt certain the Indians would attack.

But before they did, a Cheyenne—perhaps Black Kettle—shouted above the din. He asked what the soldiers wanted. After hearing Smith's translation, Wynkoop told Smith to say that he "came there to talk."[18] This the Cheyenne questioned. He wanted to know why the *vi'ho'i* brought soldiers, cannons, and prepared to fight. Wynkoop countered that "he came prepared to defend himself in case of any treachery."

The Cheyenne accepted this explanation, and they continued to shout across the open space until they agreed the Indians would lead the soldiers to the village. As the march began, warriors surrounded Wynkoop's command, placing the soldiers at their mercy. Wynkoop later claimed the village contained 4,000 people. After riding about two miles, the warriors halted. The troops set up camp while Wynkoop, Soule, Cramer, Lieutenant Charles Phillips, and Smith rode with the warriors to a grove of large trees along the south fork of the Smoky Hill not too far inside Kansas. Wynkoop never saw the village; he was perhaps a mile or two shy of it. It was here he would meet Tsistsistas Black Kettle, Big Wolf, and White Antelope; Dog Man Bull Bear; and Arapahos Left Hand, Little Raven, Neva, and Big Mouth.

Word of the arrival of the *vi'ho'i* spread quickly. Indians converged on the grove, the chiefs taking their places around the council circle while the warriors found spots behind them. As Wynkoop waited he saw George Bent arrive and sit with the chiefs.

Before anything happened, a pipe was passed and Wynkoop, his companions, and the chiefs smoked. Finally the council began. With all eyes watching him, some glaring, Wynkoop explained that he had received the letters that Black Kettle had dictated and that he visited their village to see if he could work out an understanding. He said "he had come for peace and not for war."[19] He told the chiefs that if they gave up the prisoners it would show the sincerity of their desire to end the war. Continuing, Wynkoop offered to take the leaders to talk with the "Great Father in Denver, [where] he had no doubt peace would be made, and that he would return them in safety to their tribes; that he was not great enough chief himself to make any treaty with them that would be binding." In conclusion, Wynkoop told the chiefs that they should bring their people to Fort Lyon "in compliance with the governor's proclamation" and not communicate with their brethren still waging war.

In reference to Black Kettle's letter, Wynkoop told the chiefs that he knew nothing of Indian prisoners and could not promise their return. At that point he told the chiefs "that he was acting upon his own responsibility and would pledge them nothing but what he knew he could fulfill."

As soon as Smith finished translating Wynkoop's last words, the question again came up: "[W]hy had he brought his men and guns" if he came to make peace? Remaining calm, Wynkoop told Smith to say that he knew there were bad Indians and he wanted enough men in case "they did not act in good faith." To this point during the six-hour negotiation with the Indians, Smith appeared unruffled, in control. Wynkoop repeated that "he hoped they could understand each other so that they would have no trouble." Then, pushing, Wynkoop again stated he wanted the white prisoners so he could "return them to their homes."

Shortly after the parley began, mounted warriors invaded the bivouac Wynkoop's troops had set up on the Smoky Hill. According to Sergeant B. N. Forbes (Company D), there were "about five Indians to every white man."[20] This estimate translates to over five hundred warriors. All were heavily armed. With their bows strung and arrows nocked they quickly seized control of the camp. Some of the warriors knew English curse words and verbally assaulted the troopers. Forcing the soldiers away from the howitzers, they also raided the provision wagon.

Before the situation spiraled into disaster, a nervous Lieutenant George Hardin hustled to the council ground and spoke to his commander. An outraged Wynkoop interrupted the proceedings and expressed his anger at the warriors' invasion of his camp. Black Kettle left the council, rode to the white camp, and yelled for the warriors to mount and leave. They did, but as a parting gesture they set the prairie on fire. With flames and smoke gusting toward them, the soldiers hastily packed and abandoned the ground. They marched almost twelve miles before daring to halt and set up a new camp along Hackberry Creek.

In the meantime, the council continued. The squat, barrel-chested Bull Bear (O-to-ah-nac-co) spoke. A leading war chief of the Dog Men, he was open to peace if it benefited the People, but he was still angry over the murder of his brother, Lean Bear, at Ash Creek the previous May when he tried to stop an attack upon his and Black Kettle's village.[21]

Suddenly Bull Bear leaped to his feet, stormed Wynkoop, and demanded he stand. Wynkoop stood, holding his ground as the chief sized him up. Turning to the council, Bull Bear pointed at Wynkoop. "This white man thinks we are children," he said, "but I tell him we are neither Papooses or Squaws, that we are men, warriors, Chiefs; we have said to him, we want to trade; we have given many horses and many Buffaloe [sic] robes to other tribes for these white prisoners; we now say we will trade them for peace. And this white soldier Chief, says, 'give me the White Prisoners, and I will give you nothing in return'; does he think we are fools that he comes to laugh at us[?]"[22] His words ignited an explosion of voices.

As the clamor grew, Wynkoop moved back to Smith and sat. He detected a change in the trader's demeanor when he asked him to translate Bull Bear's words. Smith obeyed, but then said, "I have now got to talk for my life."[23] This admission jolted Wynkoop, who saw and heard the uproar. He yelled to Bent to confirm the accuracy of Smith's words, and translate for him when necessary. Bent consented.

The uproar grew. The chiefs and warriors who surrounded Wynkoop reminded him of "snarling wolves."[24] Then he glanced at Black Kettle, who "sat calm[,] dignified, im[m]ovable, with a slight smile upon his lips, and a brightness upon his face."

This was Wynkoop's introduction to Black Kettle or, as he would come to call him, Make-tava-tah. As a youngster, Make-tava-tah (Moka-tovatah, Ma-ta-ve-ta, Ma-ta-ve-to, Moke-ta-va-to) had joined the Bow String warrior society, but switched to the Crooked Lances (or Bone Scrapers) when he became a man. He was born into the Hairy People clan (Hí-vãi-tä-nü). His clan affiliation changed to the Wuh´tapiu when he married Little Sage Woman, whom he lost when Utes captured her in a fight at the head of the Cimarron River in 1848. Black Kettle became a leader in the Wuh´tapiu clan and, in 1855, became a chief. As a warrior he had led raids but now, in his fifty-second year, he dedicated himself to protecting the Tsistsistas who followed his lead.[25]

"He saw my bewilderment, I might say my trep[i]dation," Wynkoop continued, "and as his eye caught mine, he gave me a look of encouragement."[26] Although he did not realize it at that moment, Wynkoop had found a soul mate, someone who would join him on the precarious boundary between the races. He later claimed that Black Kettle's "dignity and lofty bearing, combined with his sagacity and intelligence, had that moral effect which placed him in the position of a potentate. The whole force of his nature was concentrated in the one idea of how best to act for the good of his race; he knew the power of the white man, and was aware that thence might spring most of the evils that could befall his people."[27]

Wynkoop was about to embark on a journey across the line that separated whites and Indians. Soon he would become what late twentieth-century historians called a "cultural broker, acting "as a conduit for goods, services, and information" between races.[28]

Wynkoop had "come through the fire," as he termed it, to meet with the Southern Cheyennes.[29] Black Kettle's look had eased his fear somewhat. Vigilant, teetering on a precipice, Wynkoop knew that his life depended upon his every word. At that moment his only concerns were obtaining the white prisoners, getting the chiefs to Denver, and surviving.

Left Hand voiced his anger next. He had been peaceful and had even offered to help recover stock stolen from Fort Larned in Kansas. His offer had been ignored. During the summer when he approached the fort, soldiers had fired at him.[30] After that his young men rode the war trail with the Dog Men and Kiowas. Little Raven (Nah-ka-he-se, Oh-has-tee) agreed with Bull Bear that "no peace could be brought about."[31]

As the tension grew, Bull Bear again saw his chance to agitate. He yelled "the only thing left [is] to fight."[32] The tone of the voices surrounding Wynkoop put him on edge; he did not need a translation. "[T]he whites [a]re not to be trusted," Bull Bear bellowed.

But before it got worse, One-Eye pushed forward, surprising Wynkoop, who had not seen him since he rode between the lines. One-Eye said he felt "ashamed" and did not want to live if the Tsistsistas harmed the *vi´ho´i*.[33]

It was at this point that Black Kettle took control of the council. He spoke quietly to One-Eye, telling him to sit. He then waved his hand for silence, and after obtaining it he stood, wrapped his blanket around himself, and crossed to Wynkoop. The chief took the major's hand and pulled him upright. He embraced Wynkoop twice before leading him to the center of the council. "This white man is not here to laugh at us," Black Kettle said, "nor does he regard us as children, but on the contrary unlike the balance of his race, he comes with confidence in the pledges given by the Red man. He has been told . . . that he should come and go unharmed." Black Kettle went on. "He has not come with a forked tongue or with two hearts, but his words are straight and his heart single. Had he told us that he would give us peace, on the condition of our delivering to him the white prisoners, he would have told us a lie. For I know that he cannot give us peace, there is a greater Chief in the far off Camp of the White Soldiers."[34]

That was it. In a sudden turnabout, Black Kettle had defused the nerve-racking situation and ended the council. As the chiefs and warriors began to depart, Wynkoop, knowing they were going to meet to discuss his proposition, said he'd return to his camp and await their decision.[35] Black Kettle shook Wynkoop's hand, then Soule's, and, according to John Smith, assured Wynkoop that "he was still, as he always had been, a friend to the whites," and would do what he could to end the war.[36] Even if his people continued the war, Black Kettle told Wynkoop, he and his men would not be attacked when they returned to Fort Lyon.

It was time to leave. Unsure what would happen next, Wynkoop repeated that "it was not in his power to ensure them peace."

Wynkoop and his escort left the council ground, and finding his men's original camp deserted, followed the trail the troops had left to the bivouac they had set up on Hackberry Creek. There he discovered that he had another problem. His men demanded to return to Fort Lyon immediately. Wynkoop had come too far to leave now. Faced with the possibility of mutiny, he and Soule and the other officers spent a long night walking guard.

Dawn arrived without a single desertion. Still Wynkoop had a hard time preventing his men from leaving. The Indians did not attack, and no one shot Wynkoop in the back. Nothing happened until almost noon, when several Arapahos, including Neva (Nevah), appeared, and gave him a sixteen-year-old-girl who had been traded to him by the Cheyennes. Her name was Laura Roper, and she had not been abused. She had been captured on August 7, 1864, along with four members of the Ewbanks clan, when Southern Cheyennes raided along the Little Blue River in Nebraska Territory. Nine of the Ewbanks family, including all the men, died in the attack, scalped, their genitals hacked off.[37]

Black Kettle did not appear, and he did not send a message. Wynkoop spent another night wondering what would happen. Finally, on the second day, he heard that Black Kettle was on his way to talk. Excited, he rode out to meet the chief, bringing One-Eye and most likely John Smith to interpret. As he greeted Black Kettle, Wynkoop saw warriors, women, and three white children. "The feelings I then experienced I would be powerless to fully describe," he remembered. "Such happiness I never experienced before, never since, and do not expect to in this world."[38]

A white boy riding a pony rode up to Wynkoop. "Well my boy," he asked, "who are you?"

"My name[']s Dan . . . are you the Soldier man who has come to get me?" He was Daniel Marble, who had been captured when Bull Bear's Dog Soldiers and some Arapahos attacked a wagon train near the Plum Creek Ranch in Nebraska Territory on August 8, 1864. The warriors killed eleven people in the train, sparing only Daniel and the pregnant Mrs. Nancy Morton, who would not be freed until late January 1865, when two white men bought her. Daniel and Nancy had watched in horror as warriors mutilated the corpses. Warriors whipped Daniel whenever he cried. Treated harshly, Nancy miscarried five days after her capture.

Wynkoop met another boy, Ambrose Asher, whom he guessed to be younger than Marble. Ambrose must have suffered terribly during his ordeal, for he was uncommunicative. Then Wynkoop saw a mounted Cheyenne woman holding a child with blonde hair peeking from the folds of a blanket. "With quickened pulse I drew near," he remembered, "when out popped two little arms which were stretched toward me; while I caught sight of a pair of imploring blue eyes. In an instant I reached forward, drew the little girl from within the folds of the blanket, and seated her on the saddle in front of me." She wrapped her arms around Wynkoop and murmured "I want to see my Mamma." This was three-year-old Isabelle Ewbanks. "Poor child," Wynkoop remembered, "she never saw her Mamma [again] in this world." Afraid his emotions would overcome him and not wanting the others to see him cry, Wynkoop galloped back to camp with Isabelle.

Wynkoop had acted without orders, but he had also succeeded beyond his wildest imagination. Black Kettle and other chiefs agreed to go to Denver to discuss ending the war. Wynkoop had pulled off a coup. Although he did not have all the prisoners he had been promised, he had four. The prisoners Wynkoop did not receive were Lucinda and Willie

Ewbanks, Isabelle's mother and infant brother whom her mother still nursed, and Nancy Morton. Although Morton stated she was in the village at the time of Wynkoop's visit, Lucinda Ewbanks was not. On June 22, 1865, a month after her release from captivity, she said she had been separated from Isabelle "just after we were captured, and I never saw her after."[39] Her Cheyenne captors had traded her to a Sioux named Two Face.

An exuberant Wynkoop set out for Fort Lyon the next day. He thought he would be hailed in the streets of Denver as the man who ended the war.

CHAPTER NINE

Perfidy

A triumphant Ned Wynkoop returned to Fort Lyon on September 17, 1864.[1] Cheyennes Black Kettle, Bull Bear, and White Antelope and Arapahos No-ta-nee (Nattanee), Bosse (Borcee), Neva, and Heap of Buffalo, as well as twenty to thirty warriors, made the journey with him.[2] Edmund Guerrier, who had written one of Black Kettle's letters, may have been with Wynkoop at this time. George Bent, the scribe of the other letter, knew better than to put his life at risk. He joined a war party of Southern Cheyennes hunting Pawnees on the Republican River.[3] Shortly after Wynkoop's arrival at Fort Lyon, "large numbers of Arapahoes and Cheyennes came in and camped near the post."[4]

The next day Wynkoop sent off reports to General Samuel Curtis, who commanded the Department of Kansas, and Colonel James Ford, who commanded the District of the Upper Arkansas, which included Fort Lyon, and announced his plans to take the Cheyenne and Arapaho chiefs to Denver to meet the governor. He informed Evans that he was bringing Indian leaders whom he mistakenly called the "principal chiefs of the two tribes" to meet him.[5] He did not realize that the leaders with him spoke only for their own followers.

Wynkoop's efforts to end the war could not have been more poorly timed. Evans and Chivington, who were both supporters of statehood, saw their political aspirations destroyed when statehood received a resounding defeat at the polls during Wynkoop's absence, much to the chagrin of Byers.[6]

Although not yet an issue, the one-hundred-day enlistment limit of the Third Colorado hovered in the background. Poorly armed and inadequately trained, the "hundred-days-ers" yearned to kill Indians. Evans and Chivington also craved victory, but for different reasons. As part of his efforts to put a stop to Indian raiding, Evans had done everything within his power to end the war, and when he failed, he had petitioned for the enlistment of volunteer troops. Chivington saw the problem as a chance to become an Indian fighter. In addition, both needed vindication after the drubbing their push for statehood had taken in the September 13 election.

About the time Wynkoop returned to Fort Lyon with the Indian leaders, erroneous rumors reached Denver that he had departed "for the Big Timbers" on a punitive expedition. Without bothering to confirm the information, Byers rushed the story to print. "We may expect to hear of warm work in that direction soon."[7] When the real reason for Wynkoop's expedition became known, it did not garner much support in the press, which would have surprised Wynkoop had he known.

Thinking he was about to help bring peace between the territory's whites and Indian peoples, Wynkoop set out for Denver on the morning of September 20 with seven Indian chiefs, four children, John Smith, and Louise. Lieutenant Joseph Cramer commanded the escort of forty men. Captain Silas Soule, who Wynkoop now considered a friend, also made the trip. Seeing deserted farms all along the Arkansas and Fontaine Qui Bouille rivers, Wynkoop became anxious. He decided that he needed to speak with Evans before the Indians arrived. Feeling secure enough that he could complete the trip without his escort, at Booneville Wynkoop left the Indian leaders with Cramer. He took Louise and the children, and pushed on to Denver with Soule and a small escort.[8] According to his son, Edward, he hoped "to enlist the governor's aid in having the authorities at Washington make a peace treaty."[9]

As Wynkoop and his entourage approached Denver, Chivington worked at sabotaging any chance of a peace settlement. "Winter approaches," Chivington wrote General Curtis on September 26.[10] "Third Regiment is full, and [the Indians] know they will be chastised for their outrages and now want peace." He urged Curtis to authorize a campaign against the Cheyennes and Arapahos that Wynkoop had met, who were currently en route to Denver.

By the time Wynkoop reached Denver he was still unaware that his actions had angered Evans. That night when he knocked on the governor's door he was told that Evans was sick and had retired early. The next morning when the major descended the staircase in his hotel, he was pleasantly surprised to see Evans talking with Dexter Colley, the governor's illness apparently gone. Wynkoop introduced himself to Evans and said hello to Colley. Confident that he was about to end a war, Wynkoop described meeting the Indian leaders and explained how important it was for Evans to meet them.

Evans's reply surprised Wynkoop, perhaps even shocked him. The governor declared that he was not happy the chiefs were en route to Denver and that he wanted "nothing to do with them."[11] "They had declared war against the United States," Evans continued, and "he did not think, anyhow, it was policy to make peace with them until they were properly punished."

Wynkoop refused to give up. "I ha[ve] brought these Indians a distance of nearly four hundred miles from their village," he said, "and [I hoped you] would furnish them an audience."

Evans ended the meeting, saying "he was to start next day to visit the Ute agency on business." Pounding the point home, he added that "he did not want to see them, anyhow."

Wynkoop refused to be dismissed, later claiming "I endeavored to explain to him the position in which I was placed, and earnestly requested that he would await their arrival."

Tired of arguing, Evans told Wynkoop that the Third Regiment had been created at his insistence, and that "they had been raised to kill Indians, and they must kill Indians." More than once, Evans exclaimed "What shall I do with the third regiment, if I make peace?" As one historian summarized the situation, the governor had a major problem on his hands. "The external pressure of the military situation in 1864 was immense. From April through August Indian attacks along the Platte and the Arkansas, the Overland, Santa Fe, and Smoky Hill Trails, on ranches and settlements were vigorous and vicious. Immigrant trains, freight lines carrying essential supplies, passenger and mail coaches proceeded at great risk intermittently and were stopped altogether for varying periods."[12]

The meeting ended, and an extremely concerned Wynkoop watched Evans and Colley walk out of the hotel. He had risked his command in an attempt to end a war and now it looked as if all his efforts were for naught. The *Rocky Mountain News* added to his apprehension, for after reporting his arrival in Denver with the rescued children, it stated that the chiefs Wynkoop brought in had always opposed war and had "little if any influence over . . . the 'Dog Soldiers' . . . and it is not likely that a treaty with them would" bring about peace.[13] The *News* emphasized that blood needed to flow on the prairie.

After reading the article, on the morning of September 28 Wynkoop hurried to the newspaper office and told Byers he believed the chiefs wanted peace and would do all they could to control their warriors. Byers listened, and in the afternoon edition, he reported "Major Wynkoop has considerably changed our opinion respecting the pending council."[14] He went on: "They have unquestionably had great provocation for hostilities, and were not the first to violate friendly relations," concluding, "As he [Wynkoop] is very familiar with all the circumstances, and has given the matter his especial thought we are willing to defer to his judgment."

On September 28 Wynkoop and Soule sat on their horses and watched the Cheyenne and Arapaho leaders' arrival in Denver. Byers's opinion, combined with the Indians' arrival, gave Wynkoop hope that Evans could not ignore the chiefs. Adding more pressure on the governor, he had his father-in-law, George Wakely, photograph the Indians' arrival in Denver and made sure to have the wagons halt in front of Evans's residence. Wynkoop's gambit worked, and the governor found himself forced to meet with the chiefs at Camp Weld that day. Wynkoop had been a major player in the events, but now he stood back and quietly observed. Evans and Chivington, with John Smith translating, spoke with the chiefs. Wynkoop, Soule, Robbins, and Colonel George L. Shoup (Third Colorado) watched the proceedings.

Black Kettle gave a long, animated talk, speaking about the children he had given to Wynkoop and then about the prisoners still in captivity. The translation may have been off, for Black Kettle was heard to say "there are two women and one child yet in their camp, whom they will deliver up as soon as they can get them in"—two contradictory phrases.[15] Next, Black Kettle explained why he had traveled to Denver.

We have come with our eyes shut, following his [Wynkoop's] handful of men, like coming through the fire. All we ask is that we may have peace with the whites. We want to hold you by the hand. You are our father. We have been traveling through a cloud. The sky has been dark

The Southern Cheyenne and Arapaho leaders arrive in Denver on September 28, 1864, followed by a cavalcade of white civilians. The two soldiers on horseback watching the Indians' arrival at lower right are Maj. Edward Wynkoop, the taller of the two, and Capt. Silas Soule. Wynkoop asked George Wakely to document the arrival, and Wakely's efforts contributed to Governor John Evans's meeting with the Indians. Courtesy History Colorado (Scan #10025737).

ever since the war began. These braves who are with me are all willing do what I say. We want to take good tidings home to our people, that they may sleep in peace. I want you to give all these chiefs of the soldiers here to understand that we are for peace, and that we have made peace, that we may not be mistaken by them for enemies.

As he had told Wynkoop he would, Evans rejected the offer to end the war. "Your young men are on the war path. My soldiers are preparing for the fight," he said. "The time when you can make war best, is in the summer time; when I can make war best, is in the winter. You, so far, have had the advantage; my time is just coming." He then passed the Indians to Chivington, "the great war chief," saying they must help the soldiers win the war. "It is utterly out of the question for you to be at peace with us while living with our enemies."

"We will return with Major Wynkoop to Fort Lyon," Black Kettle replied. "[W]e will then proceed to our village, and take back word to my young men, every word you say." While the chief said he could not speak for all his warriors, he thought most would help the soldiers. Wishful thinking on Black Kettle's part—or perhaps he just wanted to placate Evans.

Wynkoop stepped forward and spoke for the first time. asking Black Kettle if the Dog Soldiers agreed "to do whatever you said, after you had been here?" Black Kettle said they did, but Evans ignored this conversation. He insisted that the Indians make "an arrangement with" the military or "they would be all treated as enemies."

Other Indians spoke, and Evans interrogated them about the current hostilities. The chiefs spoke openly about fights while also warning that Sioux were congregating on the Republican River in preparation for raiding along the Platte River. Byers heard Evans tell the Indians that "they must submit to [the military] authorities and lay down their arms before any peace can be declared."[16]

As Chivington waited his turn to speak, he knew something Wynkoop did not. Curtis had given him new instructions that day. "I shall require the bad Indians delivered up . . . I want no peace till the Indians suffer more. . . . No peace must be made without my directions."[17] Chivington realized that Wynkoop's newfound relationship with the Indians could work to his advantage.

According to Byers, when Evans passed the chiefs to him, Chivington told them they must make "an unconditional surrender."[18] Then, confusing the issue, he handed the Indians to Wynkoop, as he was closer to them "and more familiar with their disposition, wants and necessities." Ute Agent Simeon Whiteley, who officially documented the council, recorded Chivington's concluding statement differently. "I am not a big war chief," Chivington said, "but all the soldiers in the country are at my command. My rule of fighting white men or Indians is to fight them until they lay down their arms and submit to military authority."[19] He then seemingly placed Wynkoop in charge, telling the Indians, "You are nearer Major Wynkoop than any one else, and you can go to him when you get ready to do that."

The meeting ended. "Every one present seemed to be satisfied with the course taken in this most important and critical interview," the *Rocky Mountain News* proclaimed before echoing Black Kettle's words, that the chiefs would do their utmost "to induce their tribes to lay down their arms; a consummation devoutly to be wished for."[20]

And this is what Wynkoop thought. For he, like Byers, believed peace had returned to the land. Wynkoop understood Chivington to tell the Indian chiefs "that the whole matter was referred to myself, who would act toward them according to the best of my judgment, until such time as I could receive instructions from the proper authorities."[21]

John Smith also shared this impression, for he thought he heard Chivington and Evans tell the chiefs "to return with Major Wynkoop [to Fort Lyon], and whatever he agreed on doing with them would be recognized by them."[22]

But it would not be. Either Wynkoop closed his eyes to what he saw and heard at Camp Weld or he only heard what he wanted to hear. Up to now, Wynkoop had not played a leading role in events that would shape the future. This had all changed when he met the Indians and talked them into coming to Denver. Everything had gone well and the war appeared to have ended. Wynkoop thought his actions pleased his superiors.

But Wynkoop had misunderstood, for at no time did Evans say the war had ended. On September 29 the governor wrote Agent Colley, "The chiefs brought in by Major Wynkoop have been heard. I have declined to make any treaty with them."[23] Evans, unlike Wynkoop, understood what was happening. He must have guessed that the Indian leaders did not grasp his true meaning. Knowing that the Indians, as instructed, would congregate with Wynkoop near Fort Lyon, the governor insisted that Colley tell the leaders that his only purpose in speaking with them was to learn their thoughts. He also reminded Colley that the Indian Bureau must not care for Indians at war.

Like most people in the territory, Evans wanted an end to the hostilities, but he also wanted to save face. He had reported time and again an Indian terror. The military had authorized the creation of a volunteer regiment to confront the menace, but the Third Colorado had not yet drawn blood. The war could not end until the volunteers scored a major victory.

Unaware of the governor's or the military's views on the war, the Cheyenne and Arapaho leaders were as pleased as Wynkoop. When asked to have their image taken, they readily accepted. Set in front of a hastily hung curtain, Black Kettle, White Antelope, Bull Bear, and the Arapahos posed with Wynkoop, Silas Soule, John Smith, and Dexter Colley.[24]

On Monday, October 3, Wynkoop hurried back to Fort Lyon with Louise, Soule, Lieutenant Chauncey Cossitt, and J. P. Sears, Jr. The chiefs, accompanied by Lieutenant Cramer and a military escort (Company K), left at the same time but traveled at a slower pace. When Wynkoop arrived at the post on October 8, he wrote a report detailing the events in Denver and asking for instructions. As soon as he finished, he dispatched his adjutant, Lieutenant W. W. Denison, to deliver it to Curtis.[25]

On October 12, Cramer arrived at Fort Lyon with the chiefs, and whites and Indians alike were in "first rate spirits."[26] Ready to move forward, Wynkoop and his officers met with the chiefs who had visited Denver and with Arapahos Little Raven and Left Hand, who had come into the fort. Wynkoop told them "to bring in their villages" so he could watch them until he heard from headquarters.[27] A few days after he returned to Fort Lyon he began feeding the Arapahos who were already camped nearby. Even though Wynkoop had established himself as a man of peace with the Cheyennes and Arapahos, he could still think like a warrior. He wrote later "that I could at any moment, with the garrison I had, have annihilated them had they given any evidence of hostility."[28]

Unrest continued to haunt the territory, but to a much lesser degree. "Previously to the time that the armistice was granted to the Cheyennes and Arapahoes by Major Wynkoop," opined the *Rocky Mountain News* on October 20, "it was impossible for any person to pass over the road on

Participants at the Camp Weld council on September 28, 1864. Kneeling in the foreground are Maj. Edward Wynkoop (*left*) and Capt. Silas Soule. Sitting (*from left*) are White Antelope (Southern Cheyenne), Bull Bear (Dog Soldier), Black Kettle (Southern Cheyenne), Neva (Arapaho), and No-ta-nee (Arapaho). Standing (*from left*) are unidentified, Trader Dexter Colley, Trader/Interpreter John Smith, Heap of Buffalo (Arapaho), Bosse (Arapaho), Secretary of Colorado Territory Samuel Elbert, and an unidentified soldier. Note that Neva has sometimes been identified as One-Eye (Southern Cheyenne), Heap of Buffalo has sometimes been identified as White Wolf (Kiowa), and that Bull Bear has sometimes been identified as the fourth sitting from the left, which is incorrect as a close examination of the many images of him in later life conclusively proves. Courtesy History Colorado (Scan #10025492).

the Arkansas, unless in very large parties or attended by large escorts of troops, but since that time the [Indians] have [not] committed a single overt act on the said road."[29] The people of the Arkansas valley agreed. Believing that peace had returned, they signed a "Memorial" praising Wynkoop's efforts to bring the Indians to Denver and initiate a peace. "We the undersigned citizens of the Arkansas valley desire to further express our appreciation of your bravery, as well as your sense of right, and earnestly express the hope that the merrit [*sic*] which is justly your due

Detail of woodcut of Bull Bear and Black Kettle at the time of the Camp Weld council, Colorado Territory, on September 28, 1864. From Dr. Robert Brown, *The World: Its Cities and Peoples* (London: Cassell & Co., 1880). Author's collection.

may not go unrewarded, in official preferment, as well as the gratitude of private citizens."[30]

While Wynkoop waited for instructions from headquarters on how to handle the Indians, "various false rumors," as he later commented, "reached district headquarters in regard to my course."[31] Something was afoot and he sensed it. His son, Edward, later wrote that "strong, hidden forces—forces that lie in safe covert to avoid danger when the soldier is at the front, but often reach forth their slimy fingers to befoul his good record—demanded that Wynkoop be punished for leaving his post of duty with his hostages."[32]

On October 7, 1864, Curtis relieved Major Scott Anthony of command at Fort Larned, Kansas, and ordered him to "proceed to Fort Lyon, and take Command of that Post."[33] Anthony reached his new assignment on November 2.[34]

When Anthony arrived at Fort Lyon, he had orders to investigate "any officer leaving this post without orders."[35] He would also investigate "certain officers [who] have issued goods, stores or supplies to hostile Indians in direct violation of orders from the General Commanding the Department."[36] He knew exactly where to begin. Everyone from the commanding general down to the lowest second lieutenant had heard what had happened. Wynkoop had become a marked man and while questioning him about recent events, Anthony quickly confirmed what headquarters already knew: Wynkoop had assembled an escort and traveled to Denver with the chiefs, and after returning to Fort Lyon had issued supplies to the Indians.

It did not take Wynkoop long to realize his military career might be in jeopardy. Within days of Anthony's arrival at the post he had Special Orders No. 13 in hand, which relieved him "from the command of Fort Lyon," and "ordered [him] to report without delay to headquarters District of the Upper Arkansas, for orders."[37]

Anthony waited until November 5 before replacing Wynkoop as commandant of Fort Lyon. He then told Wynkoop "that he was under strict instructions to have nothing to do with the Indians, to make them no issue, and to keep them away from the post."[38] This would not do. Wynkoop made certain that Anthony understood the current situation. He must have been persuasive, as Anthony relented. According to Wynkoop, Anthony assured him "that, notwithstanding his stringent orders, he was obliged to follow the same course almost that I had adopted."

As a state of war existed, Anthony was not pleased with the location of the Arapaho village only a mile from Fort Lyon. Consisting of 113 lodges housing 652 people under the leadership of Left Hand and Little Raven, it posed a threat. Arapahos freely entered the post, and per Wynkoop's order, received rations from the commissary. In spite of what he had said to Wynkoop, Anthony lost no time in asserting his authority and immediately arrested all Indians inside the fort.

Maj. Scott Anthony replaced Wynkoop as commander of Fort Lyon in November 1864. Although ordered not to treat with the Indians, he listened to Wynkoop, and after meeting with Southern Cheyenne and Arapaho leaders decided that he would continue feeding the Indians. Courtesy History Colorado (Scan #10028280).

Even though he had been ordered to report immediately to head-quarters, Wynkoop remained at Fort Lyon to ensure that the command changed hands without incident. He arranged for a meeting with the Arapaho leaders halfway between their village and the fort. After in-troducing the chiefs to Anthony, Wynkoop informed them that he had been relieved of command. Anthony had contracted scurvy and his red eyes disturbed the Indians. The "Red-eyed Chief," as they called him, told them that he had orders not to deal with them because of raids near Fort Lyon that he had since learned were only rumors. Nevertheless he did not want them camped near the post. The Arapahos said they would move as soon as there was game to sustain them. Anthony told them that he regretted that his orders forbade his feeding them. He assured them that they could remain in their current camps while the warriors hunted buffalo.

Aware that the switch of commanders bothered the Arapahos, Wynkoop assured them that nothing had changed, that there would soon be peace. The Indians' condition had apparently affected Anthony. He promised he would continue the policy Wynkoop had established, and would feed them as prisoners of war.[39] This pleased Wynkoop, who claimed that Anthony supplied "a greater quantity" of food to the Arapahos than he had.[40]

But then Anthony got tough. No armed Indians would be allowed near the fort, and none could enter the post unless they were prisoners of war.[41] The Arapahos accepted this prohibition. Anthony also demanded that they deliver any arms and stock that had previously belonged to whites. Left Hand saw to the surrender of arms. He then said "he was willing to submit to anything; that the whites might place him in irons, or kill him, but that he would not fight them."[42]

While Wynkoop continued to work with Anthony, the Third Colorado had its first fight with Cheyennes on November 10. The dawn attack on two lodges at White Butte Creek, near Sterling, Colorado, became a problem for the governor when it became apparent that the Indians who were attacked might have been peaceful. Company D, Third Colorado, killed all the Cheyennes but one during the attack. Captain David H. Nichols allowed his men to mutilate the bodies (perhaps six warriors, three women, one boy, and two small children). After the fight, his men found a child under the body of its dead mother. One of Nichols's civilian guides quickly murdered the youngster.[43]

Back at Fort Lyon, the situation had changed. Anthony and Wynkoop, along with Soule, Cramer, and Lieutenant William Minton (First New Mexico Volunteers) spoke with Black Kettle and Left Hand at the commissary on the hill above Fort Lyon. Wynkoop and Anthony told the Indians that if they moved to Sand Creek they would be under the military's protection. Soon after the council ended, Left Hand and a small number of Arapahos moved to Sand Creek. Anthony later testified that the Cheyennes in Black Kettle's band joined Left Hand's people on Sand Creek by November 17, 1864.[45]

Unhappy at Wynkoop's removal and feeling he needed to express his opinion, Cramer drafted a letter to his commander. "I cannot let the opportunity pass without bearing testimony," he wrote, "to the fact that the course adopted and carried out by you, was the only proper one to pursue and has been the means of saving the lives of hundreds of men[,] women and children as well as thousands of dollars worth of property."[46] After commenting on the rescue of the children and bringing the chiefs to Denver, Cramer concluded, "Since that time no depredations have been committed by these tribes, the people have returned to their homes and farms, and are now living as quietly and peaceably as if the bloody scenes of the past summer had never been enacted."

Eight other officers, including Soule, signed Cramer's letter. The lieutenant then gave it to Anthony to endorse, and he did. "I think Major Wynkoop acted for the best in the matter," Anthony commented.[47] Before forwarding it to district headquarters, Anthony gave Wynkoop a copy.

The support of his subordinates must have boosted Wynkoop's spirits somewhat. Still, he worried; not only for himself, but also for Soule, Cramer, and other officers under his command. On November 26, 1864, headquarters announced that "Wyncoop [sic] has laid himself liable to arrest and dismissal for absence without leave, and the Officer[s] who went with him liable, for being absent without proper authority."[48] This dictum placed at risk all officers who accompanied Wynkoop to the Smoky Hill and Denver. Continuing, headquarters stated that Wynkoop's "looseness" of command in the "affairs at Fort Lyon . . . has passed many things, by attributing it more to ignorance than intentional insult, until the months September and October" when he left his post, jeopardizing his men's lives and government property while attempting "to make treaties between a hostile force, and parties that had no authority in the matter."

Taking an escort of twenty-eight men, Major Edward Wynkoop set out for Fort Riley, district headquarters in Kansas, on November 26. He was deeply concerned. He had made decisions based upon circumstances, decisions he thought right. With potential charges looming, the extent of what he might face must have been overwhelming.

On the day Wynkoop left for Kansas, Anthony gave John Smith permission to visit the Cheyenne encampment on Sand Creek to trade with the Indians. Smith took two men with him; Private David H. Louderback (First Colorado) and R. Watson Clarke, a civilian.[49]

No-ta-nee and two Arapahos overtook Wynkoop's column on November 28. According to Wynkoop, No-ta-nee, who had gone to Camp Weld in September, told him that Black Kettle had instructed him to find "me and warn me that some two hundred Sioux had left the headwaters of the Smoky Hill, and had gone down to strike the road between where I was and Fort Larned, for the purpose of making war on the whites."[50] No-ta-nee told Wynkoop that if he did not have enough men with him he should return to Fort Lyon.

Feeling safe, Wynkoop continued on to Fort Larned, which was on the way to Fort Riley. After arriving at the post he learned that a body of Sioux did appear as far south as the Arkansas, but he never saw any signs of them.

. . .

Colonel John Chivington was ambitious. Victory meant glory, the confirmation of his military career, and a chance of politics in his future. After the Camp Weld council, he knew time was short. Major General Patrick Connor, who commanded the Military District of Utah and had made a name for himself as an Indian fighter in 1863, had recently visited Denver to observe the Indian threat. Chivington feared he might have to report to Connor, so if he wanted to make a name for himself he needed to do so before Connor arrived. The Third Colorado's one-hundred-day limit on enlistment was nearly at an end, and the regiment was eager to fight, though they were not yet properly outfitted.[44] Many almost mutinied at Camp Evans when they heard that Wynkoop brought the Indian chiefs to Camp Weld. Reports of horrid depredations, combined with fear and racial hatred, guaranteed that these men wanted to annihilate their foe. Chivington wanted to take advantage of their anger.

Finally in October 1864 there were enough horses, saddles, and bridles to mount about half the Third Colorado. The men lucky enough to be assigned a horse began congregating in Bijou Basin. On November 14 five companies set out for the Arkansas (A, B, E, I, and M). Marching through snow, the regiment finally reached "Boon's" ranch on November 18. Companies C and D and the mounted portion of F arrived three days later. A detachment of the First Colorado (H) arrived, followed by Company G of the Third on November 23. Chivington arrived that night and assumed command. By this time his army also included portions of Companies K and M, as well as a battalion of the First Colorado (portions of Companies C, E, and H).

Chivington moved quickly, reaching Fort Lyon unannounced on November 28, two days after Wynkoop's departure. He immediately set up a picket around the post, preventing anyone from leaving.[51] After securing the post, Chivington assembled the officers of the First Colorado stationed at the fort and informed them what he intended to do. Lieutenant Joseph Cramer spoke up, telling Chivington "that I thought it murder to jump them friendly Indians."[52] "Damn any man or men who are in sympathy with them," Chivington exploded. "Such men as you and Major Wynkoop better leave the U.S. Service, so you can judge what a nice time we had on the trip." Cramer and Soule spoke up, angry at what Chivington proposed, but the colonel silenced them.

That night Chivington departed Fort Lyon at 8:00 P.M. with his command, which now included 450 troops of the Third Colorado (Colonel George Shoup commanding three battalions: Lieutenant Colonel Leavitt Bowen, Major Hal Sayre, and Captain Theodore Cree), and two battalions of First Colorado troops: 100–125 troops under Lieutenant Luther Wilson and 125 troops from Fort Lyon under Major Scott Anthony, for a total of 675–700 men and four howitzers. According to Cramer, he and Soule accompanied the command under protest. Chivington force-marched northeast. The night was frigid, and men and animals suffered. Contrary to later newspaper reports, there was little snow on the ground, and that only in hollows. After traveling about thirty-seven miles Chivington reached his target, the Cheyenne-Arapaho village on Sand Creek. The encampment consisted of approximately one hundred lodges and perhaps five hundred people, two-thirds of them women and children. It was just before dawn on November 29. With an army craving blood at his back, Chivington attacked.[53]

The volunteers were upon the village before most of the Indians realized they were under attack. Balls ripped into tents as half-naked people scrambled out into the freezing dawn. Abruptly awakened, Black Kettle and White Antelope emerged from their lodges; an American flag flew from a pole near Black Kettle's tipi. They yelled for their people not to run, that they were at peace, but this was in vain. White Antelope walked

John Chivington became colonel of the First Colorado Volunteer Regiment shortly after Union forces stopped the Confederate invasion of the Southwest in March 1862. He and Wynkoop became friends soon after they enlisted in the regiment in 1861. Courtesy History Colorado (Scan #10025590).

toward the soldiers and was struck down. A ball hit Medicine Woman Later (Voh-is-ta), Black Kettle's wife, and she fell. Thinking that she was dead, he left her and ran, hiding in a creek bed. After nightfall, he returned to where his wife fell and was surprised to find her still alive, although she had nine wounds.[54]

The attack changed Black Kettle's life forever. Like Wynkoop, to whom he had given his trust, he would now walk a lonely road. He had been influential with his people, but henceforth fewer and fewer would follow his lead. He had stood strongly for peace between the races. He still did, but from this day forward most refused to listen to him.

Lieutenant Wilson, with three companies of the First (C, E, and F), charged across Sand Creek, driving one of the pony herds toward the village to cut off escape. Successful, Wilson dismounted his men and attacked the village from the northeast. Meanwhile, Captain John McCannon, with Company I (Third Colorado), tried to capture another herd to the southwest of the village.

Anthony and his troops followed Wilson across the creek and took positions south of the village. He then dismounted his men and awaited orders. In the meantime, Chivington with the rest of his command reached the riverbed below the village and behind Anthony's battalion. He halted, dismounted his troops, and ordered them to remove their overcoats. He then exhorted his men, reminding them of the women and children the Indians had killed on the Platte.[55]

When Wilson's command opened fire, so did Anthony. Chivington ordered his command to remount and began firing through and over the heads of Anthony's men. Perhaps as many as one hundred warriors confronted the onslaught. But the number of Indians fighting differed depending on the location of the conflict and the person making the observation. "There seemed to be no organization among our troops," Cramer later testified, "every one on his own hook, and shots flying between our own ranks."[56]

Not all the soldiers wanted to kill. Soule, who was part of Anthony's battalion, saw women and children begging for their lives. "I refused to fire and swore that none but a coward would."[57] Cramer, who was also disgusted by what he saw during the attack, "got so mad I swore I would not burn powder, and I did not."[58] He claimed that "Col. A—— was going to have Soule hung for saying the[y] were all cowardly Sons of B[itche]s."

Whites hated mixed-bloods as much as they hated full-blooded Cheyennes and Arapahos. This put those with mixed blood in the village in great peril. Luckily for Charley Bent, William Bent's youngest son, was wounded and taken prisoner, Soule, who disgusted Chivington for refusing to take part in the fight, talked his commander into allowing him to take Bent on a wagon hauling wounded back to Fort Lyon.[59]

Edmund Guerrier escaped the attack unhurt. He traveled to the Smoky Hill camps, arriving on the second day after the fight.[60]

George Bent was wounded in the hip, but also survived the attack. He later wrote about the soldiers after they tired of chasing the fleeing Indians: "As they retired down the creek they killed all the wounded they could find and scalped and mutilated the dead bodies which lay strewn all along the two miles of dry creek bed." Bent later claimed that soldiers created "tobacco bags made of pieces of skin cut from the bodies of dead Cheyenne women."[61] Chivington had ordered Robert Bent, George and Charley's brother then employed at Fort Lyon as guide and interpreter, to accompany the soldiers to the village. Robert later stated he saw five women beg for mercy and expose themselves to the troops to show their sex, only to be shot down. "There were some thirty or forty squaws collected in a hole for protection," he said. "[T]hey sent out a little girl about six years old with a white flag on a stick; she had not proceeded but a few steps when she was shot and killed."[62]

There were more atrocities—many more.

But the attacking soldiers did not view their actions as heinous. Raiding Indians had butchered friends and neighbors, innocent people, hacking their bodies beyond recognition. Motivated by the horrific events of the spring and summer, the soldiers killed with a vengeance.

What happened on that bloody ground would have been even worse if Chivington's reports of the outcome were accurate. He wrote the first of two reports on November 29, 1864, stating that he surprised "one of the most powerful villages of the Cheyenne nation, and captured over five hundred animals; killing the celebrated chiefs One Eye, White Antelope, Knock Kno [sic], Black Kettle, and Little Robe [Ha-ke-hu-mah, Ha-ke-ho-mah], with about five hundred of their people, destroying all their lodges and equipage, making almost an annihilation of the entire tribe."[63] Chivington captured animals and destroyed the village, but much of the rest of the report consisted of braggadocio, mixing fiction and fact. Little Robe was not at Sand Creek and Black Kettle did not die. The actual death count ranged somewhere between 60 and 160. Finally, the village was not powerful, as most of the warriors who had been raiding were camped with the Dog Soldiers farther north.

On December 16 Chivington wrote a second report, which was more detailed, but still error laden. Continuing to maintain that the assault resulted in five to six hundred Indian dead, Chivington stated, "It may, perhaps, be unnecessary for me to state that I captured no prisoners," but even here he erred; Charley Bent survived as a prisoner—something

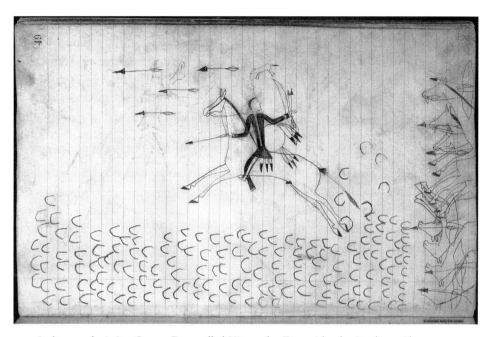

Ledger art depicting George Bent, called Hi-my-ike (Beaver) by the Southern Cheyennes, the mixed-blood Southern Cheyenne who walked between two worlds and eventually worked for Edward Wynkoop. This drawing is in a book of ledger art found in Tall Bull's Dog Soldier village after it was attacked and destroyed by soldiers on July 11, 1869. It shows Bent defying unseen traditional enemies as he races from their assault of arrows. Bent impressed Wynkoop; first when the major met Southern Cheyenne and Arapaho leaders in September 1864 and later at the Medicine Lodge peace council in fall 1867. Courtesy History Colorado (Scan #10036188).

Chivington knew.[64] The colonel claimed he suffered eight dead and forty wounded during the battle, with two wounded dying later.

Jack Smith, the half-Cheyenne son of John Smith, was in the village when the attack began. He ran about a mile but then returned to his father's lodge. The next day, November 30, Jack, now a prisoner, was in his father's tipi when a soldier called out to "Uncle John," as the elder Smith was sometimes known, and escorted him to see Chivington. As they walked toward the colonel the soldier said, "I am sorry to tell you, but they are going to kill your son Jack."[65] Smith knew there was nothing he could do and kept walking. A shot rang out, striking Jack "below his right breast."[66]

Anthony supported attacking the Cheyennes, but he had seen things during the battle and its aftermath that bothered him. Prior to

Chivington's arrival at Fort Lyon, Jack Smith had supplied him information on Indian movements. Knowing that Smith was on the military's payroll, Anthony struggled with his death. In an attempt to blot out the truth, when he wrote his brother, Anthony told a different story. "John Smith's son was . . . suddenly taken ill in the night and died before morning,"[67]

. . .

The outcast Wynkoop reached Fort Riley, his destination, by early December and reported to Colonel James Ford, the district commander. It was here that he learned of Chivington's attack. Although outraged over what he considered perfidy, he faced a more immediate problem. The military had not decided what to do with him, and when Major B. S. Henning, who commanded the post, contacted Curtis seeking guidance, Curtis replied, "The treaty operations at Lyon greatly embarrass matters, and I hope you have disposed of Major Wynkoop and directed a change for the better."[68] This information did not ease Wynkoop's concern over his future, and he sent a letter to Curtis asking permission to meet him and explain his side of the story in person.

Wynkoop sat and waited. Rumors swirled. One paper thought he had been arrested and sent to Fort Leavenworth to face a court-martial for rescuing the four children and stated that if Wynkoop did not speak up and tell the truth, "he is a fool, that's all."[69]

If Chivington's death count of five to six hundred was accurate, Wynkoop knew that just about everyone in the Cheyenne village had died. He was appalled. The U.S. Army did not wage war on women and children; the attack by Colorado Volunteers at Sand Creek was murder. The dead were people he had worked with to end the war. He felt that he had set the Cheyennes up to be exterminated, that he had led the sheep to the slaughter.

It would get worse.

In late December Wynkoop received a letter from his subordinate, friend, and former second in command at Fort Lyon, Silas Soule.

Dear Ned:
    . . . The massacre lasted six or eight hours, and a good many Indians escaped. I tell you Ned it was hard to see little children on their knees

have their brains beat out by men professing to be civilized. One squaw was wounded and a fellow took a hatchet to finish her, she held her arms up to defend her, and he cut one arm off, and held the other with one hand and dashed the hatchet through her brain.... I saw two Indians hold one of anothers hands, chased until they were exhausted, when they kneeled down, and clasped each other around the neck and were both shot together. They were all scalped, and as high as half a dozen taken from one head. They were all horribly mutilated. One woman was cut open and a child taken out of her, and scalped.

White Antelope, War Bonnet and ... others had Ears and Privates cut off. Squaws['] snatches were cut out for trophies. You would think it impossible for white men to butcher and mutilate human beings as they did there, but every word I have told you is the truth.[70]

A short while later Wynkoop received a second letter, confirming Soule's account. On December 19 Lieutenant Joseph Cramer wrote:

Bucks, women and children, were scalped, fingers cut off to get the rings on them, and this as much with Officers as men, and one of those officers a Major: and a Lt. Col. cut off Ears, of all he came across, a squaw ripped open and a child taken from her, little children shot, while begging for their lives (and all the indignities shown their bodies that ever was heard of) (women shot while on their knees, with their arms around soldiers a begging for their lives.) things that Indians would be ashamed to do.... Most of the Indians yielded 4 or 5 scalps. But enough! For I know you are disgusted already.[71]

Cramer told Wynkoop that "Col. C[hivington]—and [Maj. Jacob] Downing will do all in their power to have Soule, Cossitt and I dismissed.... If you are in Washington, for God's sake, Major, keep Chivington from being a Bri'g Genl. which he expects."

We can only imagine what went through Ned Wynkoop's mind as he read of the butchery. He must have been shattered. It mattered not that the dead were people he may or may not have met; they were people who thought they were safe—safe because he gave his word. After hearing of the butchery, Wynkoop must have thought of his own family—Louise, three-year-old Edward, and infant Emily. Did he imagine them too, torn and hacked and strewn about a barren ground? After the attack and its aftermath he would never be the same again. Edward W. Wynkoop had reached a crossroads and he knew it. "[W]ild with rage," he chose humanity and let the rest be damned.[72] The decision would change the course of his life.

CHAPTER TEN

A People Divided

Finally General Curtis granted Ned Wynkoop's request to speak in person, and after reaching Fort Leavenworth in late December, Wynkoop met with the general. At first Curtis was noncommittal, but Wynkoop was insistent. Using the endorsement of the officers at Fort Lyon, the memorial by the citizens of the Arkansas Valley, and Soule and Cramer's letters as ammunition, he demanded that Chivington and his cronies be tried and punished for their crimes. Surprisingly, Curtis listened to his diatribe; even more surprisingly, he agreed with Wynkoop, telling him that his mistake had been taking the Indians to Denver and not to him. Instead of being banished, Wynkoop assumed command of Fort Riley while the military investigated his actions.[1] He did not have long to wait, and, as his son Edward recalled, "he was exonerated from blame and officially praised."[2]

On the last day of December 1864, Colonel James Ford released Wynkoop from duty at Fort Riley and instructed him to return to Fort Lyon to assume command. His orders included investigating the "operations against the Indians" and submitting a detailed report to Ford "with as little delay as possible."[3] This sudden reversal not only confirmed everything Wynkoop had attempted to do when he tried to end the war but also gave his military career new life.

As Wynkoop realized the turnabout in his fortunes, whites in Colorado cheered Chivington's victory, as did most newspapers. When it reported that Lieutenant Colonel Leavitt Bowen, who commanded

Companies A, C, H, L, and M of the Third Colorado at Sand Creek, seized a "papoose" by the hair and killed it with his sword, the *Daily Mining Journal* lamented that Bowen did not reveal if his victim was male or female.[4]

Although they were in the minority, disgruntled and disgusted soldiers began to talk about what they had seen at Sand Creek. Others rode to the village site to see for themselves, and they, too, told a story that differed from the official reports. At first these stories were put down as facetious lies with no basis in truth, but they persisted, and soon politicians in the East began questioning Chivington's victory. Sensing an uprising and knowing it had to be nipped in the bud, in early January 1865 the *Rocky Mountain News* defended the Colorado volunteers. "Reports of 'high officials' say that a large proportion of the Indians killed were women and children. To those who were present, this would seem too base a fabrication to need contradiction, but fearing that many . . . hearing only the lie might be deceived by its apparent truth," Byers claimed he counted "two hundred and one dead bodies of Indians, among whom we do not think there were over a dozen women and children" at the battlefield.[5]

Although unsure what awaited him, Wynkoop set out for Fort Lyon and his new assignment. While he could not take full credit for the military and political change in attitude toward Chivington's attack on Black Kettle's village, his outrage was influential. Also influential was a letter that Agent Colley sent to Wisconsin Senator James Rood Doolittle. "All the chiefs and their families were in camp and doing all they could to protect the whites and keep the peace," Colley wrote, "when Colonel Chivington" attacked them.[6] Doolittle, who served as chairman of the Senate Committee on Indian Affairs, exclaimed that the accusation "made one's blood chill and freeze with horror," and demanded an inquiry.[7]

In December 1864, during the lull after Chivington's attack, Dog Men, Southern Cheyennes, and their allies amassed in the north near the Republican River. In early January 1865 they began targeting whites along the South Platte River. By January 7 more than a thousand warriors gathered near Julesburg and Fort Rankin in Colorado Territory, where they successfully lured sixty soldiers from the fort, killing over two-thirds of them in a running fight. The warriors then attacked and looted the town.[8]

Wynkoop had not yet reached Fort Lyon, when in Washington, D.C., on January 10, 1865, the Joint Committee on the Conduct of the War declared it would investigate Chivington's attack on Black Kettle's village. Chairman B. F. Wade and members C. R. Buckalew, D. W. Gooch, and Mr. Loan asked most of the questions when the hearings began two months later.[9] The small murmur of protest that had begun with Soule, Cramer, and others refused to go away. Instead of ending with the proposed inquiry in Washington, it continued to grow. A day after the Conduct of the War announcement, Major General H. W. Halleck, who served as Chief of Staff of the Army, ordered Curtis to "inquire into and report on [Chivington's attack], and . . . take measures to have preserved and accounted for all plunder taken from the Indians at Fort Lyons [sic] and other places."[10] Curtis immediately replied that Chivington had been removed from command, "and is probably out of the service."[11] By implying that Chivington was beyond the reach of military censure, Curtis hoped to forestall the possibility of an investigation.

With the verbal fireworks igniting in the East, a rejuvenated Major Wynkoop reached Fort Lyon on the night of January 14, 1865 and assumed command the next morning.[12] The war he had hoped to stop now raged. Whites again feared for their lives. This renewal of Indian attacks, combined with Chivington's victory, complicated Wynkoop's assignment.

Major Scott Anthony had relieved Wynkoop of command in November 1864 and now Wynkoop returned the favor, for the last time. When he was replaced, Wynkoop had supplied Anthony with information that might have been damaging had the military court-martialed him. Now, with the situation reversed, Wynkoop would have liked to be privy to Anthony's confidential comments, which he had written in letters to his brother. But Anthony intended to protect himself until his discharge. Wynkoop never learned that Anthony (1) did not know there was two feet of snow on the ground until he read about it in the Denver papers, (2) debunked the claim that a two-day-old scalp was found in the village, or (3) felt that Chivington had whipped peaceful Indians.[13]

Everyone at the fort was aware of the explosiveness of the situation, and already the other officers were distancing themselves from criticisms of the attack. Although he knew he was treading on dangerous ground, knew his stance would anger Coloradans, who considered his views close to heresy, Wynkoop refused to back away from what he felt right. Moving quickly, he began his investigation on January 15. As he reported, he "talked to every officer in Fort Lyon, and many enlisted men."[14] But did they speak openly with him? Certainly he agreed to grant anonymity to those he spoke with, except for Captain Booth, the district inspector, who had examined the battlefield on January 1 and reported his findings. Although Chivington claimed that some five to six hundred Indians had died at Sand Creek, Booth told Wynkoop he only saw "sixty-nine bodies," then said that battle participants swore that "few, if any, over that number were killed, and that two-thirds of them were women and children." Wynkoop doubted that the death count numbered much above Booth's estimate.

When Wynkoop finalized his report he did not gloss over the decision that had gotten him in trouble, taking the Indians to Denver instead of to Curtis, and admitted "making a mistake, of which I have since become painfully aware." He concluded that rather than ending Indian troubles, the attack at Sand Creek did just the opposite. "[T]he country presents a scene of desolation; all communication is cut off with the States except by sending large bodies of troops," Wynkoop wrote, "and already over 100 whites have fallen as victims to the fearful vengeance of these betrayed Indians."[15] He then surmised that only "the total annihilation of all the Indians on the plains" could restore peace.

Wynkoop's words came close to mimicking Evans's reasoning for the recruitment of the Third Colorado. Even though he had a full understanding of the events since his departure from Fort Lyon, his report was a rush to judgment. He had not examined the battlefield, and he could not have interviewed many battle participants. Nevertheless, he claimed that the officers and men he spoke with agreed with his findings. Wynkoop attached depositions given by Lieutenants Minton and Cossitt, John Smith, Lieutenant James Cannon and Captain R. A. Hill (First New Mexico Volunteers), and Private Louderback to his January 15 report.

Sometime after sending the report, Wynkoop rode to the battlefield to see it for himself. What he saw confirmed what he had already heard. "[It] was still covered with the ghastly remains of the victims," he stated. "Three fourths of them were women and children, among whom were many infants. There was not a single body but what had been scalped, while many, both male and female, had been mutilated in such a manner that decency will not permit recording here."

These grotesque remains were a harsh reminder of man's inhumanity to man. During his short time with Indians, Wynkoop had seen that, although different from him, they were human. He understood the pain and hatred that consumed the warriors as they extracted vengeance. He feared that he might be a target for revenge as he had brought the Indian leaders to Denver and had guaranteed the villagers' safety.

He also feared an Indian attack on the fort. A quick survey made him realize that he should focus his defensive efforts on the commissary and other outbuildings on the hill above Fort Lyon (Bent's New Fort). From prior experience Wynkoop knew that all the buildings of the fort proper except the sutler's store, mail station, and officers' quarters were at risk of being underwater when the Arkansas flooded. They offered little protection from attack as they were surrounded by hills and bordered by a ravine to the west. Nevertheless, he optimistically reported "that a comparatively small garrison can hold the fort against any attack by Indians."[16]

Knowing that he could not waste time, and eager to complete the project quickly, he made every soldier—except the officer of the day and those serving guard duty—available to build breastworks. He also enlisted the aid of civilians to beef up fortifications. Julia Lambert, who lived at the post at the time, remembered that "Major Wynkoop, in a blue flannel shirt, used pick or shovel as it was needed and everybody worked hard to complete the fortifications. I asked the Major if we women folks could help and he said 'yes, you might pass the whisky; that would leave us one more man.'"[17]

Wynkoop erected breastworks on the north and east boundaries and stationed cannons on the northeast and northwest corners of the commissary. Finally, he built a stone wall along the road that led to the Arkansas. If an attack came, he reasoned, he could safely evacuate civilians and soldiers to the stone-and-adobe fortress on the hill and outlast a siege.

Lambert echoed the sentiments of the other civilians at Fort Lyon when she stated, "We felt greatly relieved when the fortifications were completed. Reports of depredations were coming in from all sides and without these fortifications we had felt that we were not prepared for any trouble which might come. No one who had [sic] not had a similar experience can realize what this anxiety and sense of insecurity meant to us."

Wynkoop's fears of Indian reprisals were warranted. On January 18, 1865, a war party attacked wagons carrying supplies to James Streeter, the sutler at Fort Lyon.[18]

The forgotten man at Fort Lyon, Major Anthony, sat and waited, but not for long. As Wynkoop continued to prepare for an attack, on January 21 Anthony mustered out of the First Colorado at Fort Lyon.[19]

Seventeen days after Wynkoop's return to Fort Lyon, Colonel Thomas Moonlight (Eleventh Kansas Cavalry), who had replaced Chivington as commander of the Military District of Colorado, dashed all hope that the proposed Washington inquiry would remain in the East. On February 1, 1865, he ordered an investigation of his predecessor's actions. Lieutenant Colonel Samuel Tappan chaired the committee, which also included Captains E. A. Jacobs and G. H. Stilwell (First Colorado Cavalry).[20]

The inquiries initiated a backlash against the attack, followed by an explosion of controversy in Colorado Territory. Byers lashed out against the growing wave of negative publicity. But the Golden-based *Black Hawk Journal* angered him when it printed a February 2 editorial that stated "The *News* is unfair and wrong; it presents but one side of the question [of who is responsible for the Cheyenne war] to its readers; it pays no attention to facts or logic which is against [its views]."[21]

Initially the *Rocky Mountain News* had supported Wynkoop's efforts to end the Indian war. Now Byers claimed that he had only printed Wynkoop's reason for bringing the chiefs to Denver out of fairness. Wynkoop became the focus of Byers's ire, as he had during his failed bid to become marshal of Denver in 1861, and ultimately the scapegoat for the entire Cheyenne war. The *News* dismissed Wynkoop as little more than a "yes man" to the Indians. It attacked everything he said and everything he had done, from the number of white children he freed to the number of arms the Indians surrendered *after* Anthony relieved him of command at Fort Lyon. "The Major was fully infected with the Fort Lyon disease," the *News* said, "and the Indians hoodwinked him just as they pleased week after week and month after month." Byers pointed out that the Cheyennes and Arapahos Wynkoop brought to Denver admitted to murdering whites. "The fact is that the statements of the Indians themselves so utterly disagreed with the advanced story of Maj. Wynkoop [in September 1864] as to destroy all one['s] confidence in the latter."

As Byers pounded Wynkoop, Tappan's appointment shocked Chivington. The two had not gotten along since the latter gained control of the First Colorado in 1862, and Chivington rightly protested Tappan's appointment on the grounds that they were enemies. Tappan had spoken out against the attack at Sand Creek, and, in Chivington's opinion, could not separate himself from his prejudice. The Military Commission convened in Denver on February 11, 1865, fully a month before its Washington counterpart, and included testimony from both battle participants and nonparticipants who would not appear in the capital city. It rejected all Chivington's objections and began calling witnesses on February 15. Chivington, who did not testify, attended the proceedings and handled most of the cross-examination. Silas Soule was the first witness, and his testimony confirmed Wynkoop's account of the events. Others followed, including Lieutenant Joseph Cramer, who also confirmed Wynkoop; Lieutenant Charles Hawley (First Colorado); and Denver attorney Amos Steck, who was present at the Camp Weld meeting. The commission recalled Cramer on March 1, and beginning the next day Chivington cross-examined him for three days.[22]

Also on March 2, Wynkoop replaced Lieutenant J. L. Maynard (First Colorado) and became acting assistant inspector general. His appointment "authorized [him] to make inspections, condemn and recommend the disposition of public property in accordance with existing Orders and Regulations."[23]

By this time the Third had become national villains—except on the frontier, where they remained heroes. The Sand Creek controversy was no longer about who was right, who was innocent, or who had acted improperly. The *Rocky Mountain News* articulated the pro-Chivington view. "Our sympathies are upon the side of the white man, and between the two stories we incline to believe his. The [Black Hawk] *Journal* . . . favors the Indians, excuses the Indians, justifies the Indians, believes the Indians, and its editor probably expects to go to Black Kettle when he dies."[24] Byers and company stated that Wynkoop never had any right to negotiate peace. Without stating it in so many words, the *News* made it clear that at no time had it backed the end of war.

As the Denver inquiry dragged on and Byers relentlessly attacked anyone who spoke out against Sand Creek, Wynkoop enjoyed the remoteness of Fort Lyon. Although he was unaware of it, on March 3 Senator

James Doolittle, who wielded considerable power in Washington, became the driving force behind the creation of a Joint Special Committee
to investigate the treatment and condition of Indian tribes.[25] On March
7 and 8, Doolittle and his committee interrogated Samuel Colley, John
Smith, and John Evans in Washington before splitting into groups and
setting out for the frontier to continue their investigation.[26]

Back in Denver the inquiry continued. Naman D. Snyder, a trooper
in the First Colorado, had returned to the battlefield in January and
claimed he saw ninety-eight dead, half of them women and children. He
had seen soldiers scalping Indians during the fight, but his most damaging testimony came when he reported seeing an American flag flying in
"the lower end of the village. The west end."[27]

A few days later, on March 13, the Washington inquiry finally began.
Many witnesses to the events surrounding the Sand Creek controversy
did not appear, including Wynkoop, whose January 15 report sufficed.[28]

On that same March 13 Wynkoop received a brevet (honorary rank)
promotion to lieutenant colonel.[29] This would be the highest rank he
attained, and he was very proud of it. Thanks to an 1866 ruling that officers who served during the rebellion could use their highest brevet
rank when addressed, even if no longer a member of the military, and
could "wear the uniform of the highest grade they have held by brevet,"
Wynkoop was known from this day forward as Colonel E. W. Wynkoop,
and most often was addressed as such.[30]

The Sand Creek testimony in Denver ended on March 9 and the
commission moved to Fort Lyon. Wynkoop was the first to testify. When
he spoke on March 20 of his meeting with the Cheyennes near their
Smoky Hill village, Chivington objected that what the Indians said to
him was hearsay. This the court overruled, and Wynkoop answered questions about bringing the Indians to Denver to meet Governor Evans.
He continued his testimony for two more days, recounting when he set
out for the village, the Indians' desire for peace, the reports he submitted after his return to Fort Lyon, his meeting with Evans in Denver, the
meeting at Camp Weld, and his being relieved of command. The questions asked and the answers given related to Wynkoop's participation in
the events that led up to the attack.

After an adjournment on March 23, Wynkoop resumed his testimony
with Chivington cross-examining him. The colonel began by asking,
"What instructions had you received from the commanding officer of

the district, or department in which Fort Lyon was located, in regard to your intercourse with the Indians?"[31]

"I had never received any instructions in regard to what the question has reference to," Wynkoop answered. "I had received a letter from General Blunt, the effect that on account of the peculiar position of Fort Lyon, a great deal was left to my discretion, being so far removed from headquarters, and the opportunities for communicating being seldom."

"Prior to your expedition to the Smoky Hill, had not Field Order No. 2, headquarters department of Kansas, Major General Curtis commanding[,] been received at Fort Lyon?" Chivington asked.

"It had not, to my knowledge," Wynkoop replied.

Frustrated, Chivington moved away from this line of questioning, only to return, asking if Wynkoop had seen Field Order No. 2, to which Wynkoop answered: "I have."

"When did you see it?"

"I can't remember the date or time, but it was since my expedition to the Smoky Hill." Next, Chivington wanted to know when the order reached Fort Lyon, but Wynkoop did not know, stating "The first I heard of it being at Fort Lyon was when Major Anthony relieved me from the command on the 5th day of November, 1864. He brought some copies with him."

Chivington stopped trying to pin Wynkoop down for disobeying orders and turned his questioning to meeting the Indians. The day ended and Wynkoop resumed the stand on March 24 with the commission asking few questions. Chivington, in his short cross-examination, asked if Wynkoop allowed large numbers of Indians into Fort Lyon, to which Wynkoop said "Large numbers of Indians were not allowed to enter Fort Lyon as they pleased." This ended Wynkoop's testimony.

Government contractor John Prowers, who had married One-Eye's daughter, testified, as did Lieutenant James Cannon, who served as Anthony's adjutant at Sand Creek. James Combs, a resident of Denver, was the next witness (March 29). He had been at Fort Lyon on November 26, 1864, when Wynkoop set out for Kansas. While traveling to Pueblo he stopped in Spring Bottom, where he met Chivington, who bivouacked there with his army. Hearing that Combs had been at Fort Lyon, the colonel questioned him, particularly about Wynkoop. Combs claimed to have heard Chivington tell several officers, "I long to be wading in gore."[32] When Chivington cross-examined Combs he attempted to get him to admit that Left Hand commanded Fort Lyon and not Wynkoop, but Combs refused. Combs did state that both Wynkoop and Anthony allowed Indians inside the post, and that the Indians traded and begged.

April arrived, and while the inquiry droned on at Fort Lyon, the streets of Denver seethed. By this time many of the volunteers who had fought at Sand Creek had mustered out of the service and now resided in the city. Byers repeatedly referred to the Indians' mode of warfare to feed their fears while keeping them mindful that they had acted properly. He published this typically inflammatory view in mid-April: "In gathering up the dead, we found heads, lifeless trunks, feet and hands scattered in all directions . . . horribly mutilated, and marked with all the disgusting devices that savage ingenuity could invent."[33]

Captain Silas Soule remained in Denver after he testified before the committee. He commanded the provost guard, which patrolled the city and the surrounding neighborhoods. Although keeping the peace among former comrades was stressful, he found enjoyment at this time for on April 1, 1865, married Hersa A. Coberly.[34]

Back at Fort Lyon soldiers of the First Colorado testified, including David Louderback, who was in the Sand Creek village, George Roan, who spoke of mutilations, Sergeant Lucian Palmer, and Amos James. While the board attempted to confirm atrocities, Chivington fought to protect himself. When former Lieutenant William Minton (First New Mexico Volunteers) testified, his statements regarding the military offering Black Kettle and Left Hand protection while at Sand Creek did not help Chivington.[35]

After Minton stepped down other members of the First Colorado testified. Corporal James Adams and Lieutenant Chauncey Cossitt were the last witnesses, and the commission adjourned on April 8.

It had been a stressful time at Fort Lyon, especially for those who testified. For Wynkoop it had also been a time of closeness, support, and love. That month Louise conceived their third child.[36] With the next scheduled session of the committee set for April 17 in Denver, those involved with the inquiry left Fort Lyon.

During the break in the Colorado inquiry, on April 14, 1865, actor John Wilkes Booth assassinated President Abraham Lincoln.[37] Due to the murder of the president, the commission did not recommence until April 20. As the ongoing investigation into Sand Creek continued, Wynkoop

Capt. Silas Soule in Denver on the day of his wedding to Hersa A. Coberly (April 1, 1865). Anne E. Hemphill Collection (Des Moines, Iowa), Byron Strom custodian.

"deemed it policy to remain quiet" and not speak out in "Public Journals."[38] However, he was sickened when he read the sworn statement of Lieutenant James Olney (First Colorado), who took part in the attack. Olney stated "that during the massacre he saw three squaws and five children, prisoners in charge of some soldiers; that, while they were being conducted along, they were approached by Lieutenant Harry Richmond, of the Third Colorado cavalry; that Lieutenant Richmond thereupon immediately killed and scalped the three women and the five children while they were screaming for mercy: while the soldiers in whose charge these prisoners were shrank back, apparently aghast."[39]

Unable to keep his promise to himself, Wynkoop spoke out in the hope "that all honest men ... hound this cold blooded dastardly murderer through the world."[40]

That same April 20, when Soule learned that Chivington had accused him of collaborating with John Smith and receiving buffalo robes from the destroyed Sand Creek village, he wrote district headquarters. "I never was in partnership with [Smith] or any one else since I entered the service of the United States."[41] Unlike Wynkoop, who was luckily out of sight and far from the maelstrom in Denver, Soule was dead center. On April 23 he told Byers that he received frequent threats and expected "to be attacked."[42] Prophetic words, for at 10:30 that night when he investigated shots he came upon Charles Squiers (Second Colorado) and a man named Morrow sitting in the doorway of a building. They stood, Morrow behind Squiers. When Soule saw that Squiers held a revolver, he shot him in the hand. At almost the same instant, Morrow fired.[43] The ball hit Soule in the right cheek and lodged in the back of his head. It was the general consensus that the murder was "deliberately planned, and as systematically carried out."[44] The wounded Squiers escaped to Las Vegas, New Mexico Territory, while Morrow supposedly set out for the Platte. Wynkoop remained at Fort Lyon and did not attend Soule's memorial service on April 26.[45]

After a break for Soule's interment, the inquiry continued. When reports and affidavits relating to Wynkoop's meeting with the Cheyennes the previous September were introduced as evidence on April 28, Chivington objected, only to be overruled. The inquiry continued until May 30, 1865, when the committee finally adjourned.[46] Even though Wynkoop knew that the commission was "not intended for the trial of any person, but simply to investigate and accumulate facts," he had followed the committee's progress from afar.[47] Chivington had mustered out of the army in January 1865, which effectively eliminated any military prosecution before the process even began.

The inquiry, in combination with the eastern inquiry and Doolittle's investigation, had drawn a line in the sand. With battle lines set, Wynkoop refused to back away from what he considered right.

After taking depositions at Forts Riley and Larned at the end of May, Joint Special Committee members Doolittle, Foster, and Ross, along with Major General A. McDowell McCook traveled to Fort Lyon, where Wynkoop welcomed them with open arms and invited them to stay in his quarters.[48] Accepting the hospitality, Doolittle collected sworn statements from Cramer, Cossitt, and others before taking Wynkoop's on June 9. Wynkoop took his guests to Sand Creek and watched their "expressions of horror" when they saw "the bleaching bones of the slain," including "skulls of Infants, several of which Senator Doolittle collected that had bullet holes through the top of the head, showing conclusively the manner of their death."[49]

During Doolittle's visit to Fort Lyon he asked Wynkoop, "[W]hen your regiment is mustered out what do you intend doing?"[50] Before Wynkoop could answer, the senator continued, "I have a proposition to make, if you wish we will see that you have the appointment of major in a Cavalry regiment." Wynkoop thanked Doolittle, but declined the offer, saying "I went into service . . . to help my country in her time of trouble, not to play soldier." He was already toying with the idea of working with Indians; Louise remembered her husband telling the senator "he would rather become Indian agent."

Even though Ned Wynkoop's popularity had bottomed out, his military career thrived. On June 12, 1865, Colonel James Ford requested Wynkoop be named chief of cavalry, and two days later the assignment became official.[51]

At this time Thomas Murphy received an appointment as superintendent of Indian affairs. An ex–Kansas state senator and former owner of Massasoit House, a hotel in Atchison, Kansas, he would soon play a big part in Wynkoop's life.[52]

In early July 1865 Lieutenant James Cannon heard that Squiers had been apprehended in Las Vegas, New Mexico Territory. He traveled to Las Vegas, took Squiers into custody, and delivered him to Denver on July 11. Three days later Cannon's lifeless body was found in his room at the Tremont House. An incomplete autopsy concluded that Cannon, who had been vocal about what he saw at Sand Creek, died of a stroke and had not been murdered.[53]

In the meantime, Squiers escaped a second time and fled to California, never to be seen again.[54] Most likely Wynkoop did not hear of Squiers's capture, at least not immediately, as he was en route to Fort Riley, Kansas, where on July 12, 1865, he assumed command.[55] As Wynkoop's fortunes continued to improve, those held culpable for the attack at Sand Creek suffered the consequences. On July 18, 1865, John Evans, who probably knew which way the wind was blowing, received a letter from Secretary of State William H. Seward. "I am directed by the President [Andrew Johnson] to inform you that your resignation of the office of Governor of Colorado Territory would be acceptable."[56] Seward requested "that the resignation . . . reach [Washington] without delay."

As Evans's tenure as governor wound down, Doolittle spoke to a capacity crowd at the Denver Theatre about the Indians' lack of understanding of white-man ways and their raiding in desperation. After comparing atrocities committed by whites and Indians, he asked if the government should help the Indians or eliminate them. The crowd yelled for extermination.[57] While the controversy continued in Denver, a trooper in the First Colorado raised a question at Fort Lyon. He wanted to know "by what means a warrior may be distinguished from his squaw. I have been among Indians of different tribes, and I think it an impossibility to distinguish one sex from the other at gun-shot distance."[58]

Far from the war of words that raged in Colorado Territory, Fort Riley offered a respite for Wynkoop. One day he took his son, Edward, and the children of several other officers to play, leaving Louise alone in their quarters, which were isolated. While she was sitting by a window sewing, a movement caught her attention. An Indian was watching her through the window. When she did not react to his presence, he spoke, and looking at him, she pointed to the door. When she confronted him, he offered her beaded moccasins and made it clear he wanted something to eat. She motioned for him to sit and went into another room to prepare food. While the food cooked she tried on a moccasin, but then heard him move and hid the other. Soon after he had eaten the food she served him, he rose from the table and asked for the return of the moccasins. Louise understood his meaning, but refused to return them. He barged into the other room, found one, and demanded the other. Louise shook her head and backed to where a holster and Colt revolver hung on the wall. Whether he understood her intention or just tired of her refusals, he left.[59]

Less than a month after Wynkoop's arrival at the post, he learned that Soule's widow, Hersa, had traveled to Kansas. Upon hearing she wanted to return East, Wynkoop proved his loyalty to Soule's memory and obtained a leave of absence. In August he, along with Louise, Samuel Tappan, and a forty-man escort accompanied Hersa to Lawrence, Kansas. Here Wynkoop saw her safely enter the bosom of Silas's family.[60] He then continued on to Pennsylvania with Louise and the children to see his mother and siblings.

While Wynkoop and Louise relaxed with his family, Major General McCook returned to the East after escorting the Doolittle commission. Like Wynkoop, he found the Sand Creek affair heinous, calling it "the most *cold blooded*, revolting, diabolical atrocity ever conceived by man or devil . . . soldiers adorned their hats with portions of the bodies of both males and females; and the flag and uniform of the United States were disgraced by acts of fiendish barbarity."[61]

Enjoying himself, Wynkoop refused to let himself get upset at the government's proposal to meet with the warring tribes on the Little Arkansas River in Kansas to discuss peace. Knowing that the Southern Cheyennes and Arapahos blamed him for Sand Creek, he figured that he would be the last officer the military assigned to the treaty talks.

Wynkoop could not have been more wrong. The Commissioner of Indian Affairs, Dennis Cooley, had been apprised of Wynkoop's actions. Cooley understood "the intensely hostile attitude assumed by the people of Colorado against all Indians."[62] The war had been bloody and vicious and Cooley knew that not only did the commissioners need to be carefully selected, but the military escort must be "placed under command of a prudent and sagacious Officer, who is known to have the confidence of the Indians, and to be sincerely desirous of restoring friendly relations between them and the whites."

His leave cut short, Wynkoop drew the one assignment he did not want. In early October 1865 he returned to Kansas and escorted the peace commissioners to the Little Arkansas River. Upon arrival at the council grounds, he set up his camp about a mile from the Southern Cheyenne village. The next day he rode to the Indian encampment. As he feared, they recognized him immediately. However, instead of facing angry people, as Wynkoop remembered, "I was surrounded and greeted with the utmost kindness, but mournfully, while some of the old Squaws reminded by my presence of their affliction raised a most dismal wail."[63] When he dismounted, Black Kettle greeted him and they walked to his tipi. With other chiefs surrounding him, Black Kettle told Wynkoop "that not for one moment had any of them doubts of my good faith." The Cheyennes' respect for Wynkoop was real and they named him the Tall Chief, because of his height. At this time he also became known as the Man Who Will Not Tell a Lie.[64]

The peace conference on the Little Arkansas River began on October 12, 1865. The commissioners included Major General John B. Sanborn (president of the commission), Judge James Steele, General William S. Harney, Colonel Christopher "Kit" Carson, Trader William Bent, Superintendent of Indian Affairs Thomas Murphy, and Kiowa, Comanche, and Apache Indian Agent Jesse Leavenworth. James Harlan, secretary of the interior, also attended. Mrs. Margaret Wilmarth interpreted for the Arapahos and John Smith interpreted for the Southern Cheyennes.

Although Black Kettle had not seen the tall officer since he had been replaced at Fort Lyon, he, along with Arapaho Chief Little Raven, "urgently recommended" Wynkoop "as their Agent."[65] They were not the only ones requesting Wynkoop; the commissioners heard numerous requests by Cheyennes and Arapahos that he become their agent. The tribes had two other requests. They wanted to be transferred to the central superintendency under Thomas Murphy, headquartered at Atchison, Kansas, and they wanted Charles Rath and William Bent appointed their traders.[66]

Sanborn addressed the destruction of the Cheyenne and Arapaho village, telling the Indians that if they lived in peace the United States would

> restore all the property lost at Sand creek, or its value. So heartily do we repudiate the actions of our soldiers, that we are willing to the chiefs in their own right three hundred and twenty acres of land, to hold as his own forever, and to each of the children and squaws, who lost husbands or parent, we are also willing to give one hundred and sixty acres of land, as their own, to keep as long as they live. We are also willing that they receive all money and annuities that are due them, although they have been at war with the United States.[67]

Sanborn admitted shame for the murder of Indian people, but then hammered home that the United States wielded the power to kill again. Afterwards Sanborn named "Black Kettle chief of the Cheyenne nation," guaranteeing the chief's future. Regardless of what he did or said and regardless of what the Southern Cheyennes did or said, he now bore the responsibility for the all the People's actions, regardless of his input or lack thereof.

Wynkoop probably did not realize how ridiculous the proposition was, but Carson, Bent, and Harney knew. They should have pointed out that one man did not lead the Cheyenne people. If they did speak up, Sanborn and the other commissioners ignored them.

Sanborn next addressed the goal of the United States, saying that "it is better that the Indians should be located south of the Arkansas, or north of the North Platte, away from the lines of travel."

Wynkoop did not understand Plains Indians culture. At best, he was a novice. He heard the comments, but certainly did not comprehend the consequences. And even if he had, and if he had said something, his words would not have carried much weight.

The die had been cast. This was what the United States wanted, and this would be what it got. No one listened when Little Raven said "It will be better to wait until next spring and have all the tribes meet." When he said that most of his people were in the north, the commissioners told him they had five months to "come in." This did not please Little Raven, whose people's relatives were buried north of the Arkansas. It would be "a very hard thing to leave the country that God gave [my people]," he said, "and we hate to leave these grounds." Sanborn refused to bend. "We have all got to submit to the tide of emigration and civilization," he replied.

And so it would be.

On October 17, 1865, the Southern Cheyennes and Arapahos made their marks on the treaty. That day the Plains Apaches became associated with them. The Cheyennes and Arapahos had been granted the right to continue to "reside upon and range at pleasure throughout the unsettled portions of that part of the country they claim as originally theirs, which lies between the Arkansas and Platte Rivers" (this they understood) until they "have removed to the reservation provided for them" in southern Kansas and northern Indian Territory (something they did not want to do).[68] This total misrepresentation or total misunderstanding cannot be overemphasized. More damaging, the Indians expected to see the goods promised them within an acceptable amount of time. Although they would receive some annuities the following spring, it was never what they anticipated nor was it enough to sustain them, for Congress did not ratify the treaty until the following May, seven months later.

The Cheyennes, Arapahos, and Apaches departed the ground on October 17, and the Kiowas and Comanches signed their treaty the next day. Before Kit Carson departed on October 19, Wynkoop made a point of speaking with him. Carson, who bunked with William Bent at the council, had heard of the chiefs' respect for the young officer, which opened the door for a conversation. Wynkoop is very likely to have broached the possibility of becoming an Indian agent.[69]

Wynkoop did not return to Fort Riley until several hostages were released and an additional treaty signing took place on October 24. He may have departed on October 25. Since he had already been granted a leave of absence in September but had not been able to use all the time owed him, he applied a second time, and on November 17 his request was granted; he could use his unused time. By early December, Wynkoop, Louise, and their children were passing through St. Louis on their way to Washington.[70]

CHAPTER ELEVEN

Walking between the Races

In 1864, Ned Wynkoop had been ordered back to Kansas, possibly to face a court-martial, only to be returned to active duty. Now he was in a very different position. Trader William Bent had observed the warm greetings the Southern Cheyennes had bestowed upon him at the Little Arkansas council. On November 21, 1865, Bent told Superintendent of Indian Affairs Thomas Murphy that Wynkoop had the trust of the Indians and would make a good choice to deal with them. Although others supported Wynkoop's loan to the Interior Department, he remained unaware of what the future held. Then, in late November, while Wynkoop was still in Washington, Commissioner of Indian Affairs Dennis Cooley informed him that that he would become a "special agent." Knowing the destitute condition of the Indians, Wynkoop told Cooley that the victims of Sand Creek were in desperate need of "clothing and food" and that they should not be forced to wait until Congress acted.[1]

On December 5, 1865, the War Department ordered Wynkoop to "report to the Honorable Secretary of the Interior [James Harlan] for special duty."[2] He did, and a week later he accepted the assignment. After submitting his bond to Cooley in New York that day, he asked the Interior Department to purchase provisions in New York City for the Cheyennes and Arapahos. Aware that Indians had been attacking the Butterfield Overland Dispatch on the Smoky Hill, Wynkoop moved quickly.[3] As Louise neared her term and would soon deliver their child, he took his family to Pennsylvania to live with his mother before setting out for the frontier.[4]

The Treasury Department received Wynkoop's bond on December 21, 1865, making his appointment official.[5] That day Major General Grenville M. Dodge, who commanded the Department of the Missouri, issued orders that directed Wynkoop to report to Secretary of the Interior James Harlan.[6] Wynkoop's lone duty would be to interact with Indians. Or, as he put it, "I was selected . . . to submit the treaty as changed to the Indians for their signatures."[7] The directive instructed officers to render Wynkoop all the military assistance he required, including supplies, escorts, and transportation.

Major General John Pope, commander of the Military Division of the Missouri, was pleased with Wynkoop's assignment. In 1862 and 1864 charters had been granted to the Union Pacific Railroad to lay track across the plains, and now Pope oversaw the protection of the roads along the Arkansas and Platte rivers.[8] Wynkoop's efforts, if successful, would go a long way toward forestalling Indian attacks. Pope told Dodge to "give [Wynkoop] every assistance at your command to carry out his instructions."[9] Officially reporting to the Interior Department and no longer operating on his own hook, Wynkoop had an appointment to see Dodge. The general had been ordered to "harmonize" with his wishes, for as Pope put it, Wynkoop's "mission and experience among these Indians promise results satisfactory to the Government and to the quiet of the Department."

While Wynkoop hustled to begin his assignment, in mid-December 1865 Cheyenne-Arapaho Agent I. J. Taylor delivered Indian annuities to Fort Zarah, Kansas. He then traveled to Fort Larned, arriving on Christmas Eve. Instead of distributing goods to his wards, Taylor announced that he would not pass out additional supplies until the following spring but would hand out provisions if his wards traveled to Fort Zarah and asked for them. Unfortunately he did not bother to mention this to the Indians. Major Hiram Dryer (Thirteenth U.S. Infantry), who commanded Fort Larned, knew this development meant trouble with the Indians.[10]

Wynkoop reached St. Louis on December 23, two days later than anticipated, and checked into the Lindell House. The supplies had not yet arrived. During the delay he met with General Pope, who promised him full support. As it turned out, ice on the Missouri River had blocked the delivery. Tired of waiting, he set out for Fort Leavenworth, District of Kansas headquarters, arriving on December 30. By January 6, 1866,

General Dodge provided transportation for the Indian supplies to Fort Zarah. With eleven six-mule teams and wagons supplied at Fort Leavenworth, Special Indian Agent Wynkoop left for Lawrence, Kansas, where the supplies now awaited him, arriving on the evening of January 12.

While relishing his assignment, Wynkoop was concerned about Louise. He need not have worried, for that month she gave birth to their third child, Angeline Catherine.[11]

In Lawrence, Wynkoop met with Superintendent Thomas Murphy, with whom he would now interact closely. They discussed his immediate problem of paying the freight and storage fees for the provisions so that he could take delivery. Although Murphy had no instructions to cover the charges, he paid the bill of $736.34 from his $10,000 Cheyenne, Arapaho, Kiowa, Comanche, and Plains Apache budget.

Wynkoop loaded his wagons on January 14 and on January 16 set out for Fort Zarah, where an additional 221 boxes of provisions awaited him. While the special agent dealt with extreme weather conditions as he struggled to cross the prairie with the cumbersome wagons, the Dog Men and their allies raided along the Smoky Hill. At this time the southern bands that wanted peace kept their distance from their brethren in the north. As William Bent informed the military, he expected the Southern Cheyennes and Arapahos in the north to return to the Arkansas soon. Bent said that the Indians would be pleased when they heard that Wynkoop had returned to their land.

By late January 1866 news reached Fort Larned that raiding Dog Men, Southern Cheyennes, and Arapahos (approximately one hundred lodges) had crossed the Arkansas and camped seventy-five miles south of the river. They wanted to discuss peace. Major Dryer hoped that Wynkoop could meet with them for "the Indians seem to have a great deal of confidence in him."[12] With Indian agent I. C. Taylor's love of alcohol and his failure to deal with his wards, Wynkoop's anticipated arrival could not have been better timed.

When Wynkoop finally reached Fort Zarah, he found that some of the supplies intended for the Indians had been stolen and that others had been left outside and rotted. His brother George, who wanted to see Indians up close, lifted his spirits when he joined him at the fort. But right after the happy reunion, Wynkoop had an unpleasant encounter with expense reports. In St. Louis Murphy had given him $600, which the government deemed necessary to cover the expenses of his mission.

However, when Wynkoop totaled up what he really required, there was a huge disparity. He came up with $450 for clerks, $900 for interpreters, $1,800 for scouts and runners, and $250 for incidental expenses, which totaled $3,400. After deducting the $600 that Murphy had given him, he found himself short by $2,800, and asked Cooley to forward the additional funds to him at Fort Zarah.[13]

Taking the supplies that were still usable, Wynkoop set out for Fort Larned, reaching it by the middle of February. Upon his arrival, Dryer informed him that warring Southern Cheyennes were camped south of the Arkansas and that the village was growing in size. This presented a perfect opportunity for Wynkoop, whose orders dictated he discuss the treaty with the war faction. He sent out runners to announce his desire to meet.[14] The government had changed the treaty since the council on the Little Arkansas, and Wynkoop needed those who had already signed to sign the new document. Along with securing all the leaders' signatures, he hoped to resolve any problems bothering the Indians. Taking charge, he told Agent Taylor he wanted him present when he met the Indians and distributed annuities.

The village was forty miles southeast of Fort Dodge at a place called Bluff Creek, seventy-five miles from Fort Larned. Wynkoop completed his preparations by February 15. Although his new position and responsibilities invigorated him, he was nervous. Black Kettle had exonerated him from any wrongdoing, but that did not mean all Cheyennes felt this way about him. Not for one moment did he underestimate the war leaders. For safety, Wynkoop requested a military escort. Captain G. M. Gordon, commanding Company K (Second U.S. Cavalry), arrived at Fort Larned on February 16, and on February 18 Lieutenants Cahill and A. E. Bates led Company I (Second U.S. Cavalry) into the fort. This amounted to about sixty soldiers, and they became Wynkoop's escort. Heap of Bears, a Kiowa, acted as guide. Wynkoop wanted both Gordon and Dryer at the council as he thought they "should see these Indians, and talk with them."[15] Both agreed. George Wynkoop continued to accompany him, but Agent Taylor proved a different matter. Wynkoop was irked by Taylor's reluctance, which created an antagonistic relationship between them.

By the time Wynkoop led his caravan southward, William Bent and John Smith had already joined the Bluff Creek camp. Realizing the importance of having as many Southern Cheyennes present as possible when Wynkoop arrived, Smith gave Chief Little Robe a horse valued at eighty dollars so he could ride north and encourage others to attend the council.[16]

Wynkoop's journey to Bluff Creek halted fifteen miles below Fort Dodge when ice and bad weather prevented the crossing of the Arkansas for three days. He finally reached the opposite side on February 24 and the next day, after a twenty-mile march, reached the Bluff Creek village. As the whites began to make camp, Gordon reported that "Indians came out to meet us evincing signs of friendship."[17]

They included Cheyennes Black Kettle and Stone Forehead (a coup for Wynkoop as they almost never camped together), Plains Apache Poor Bear, and some Kiowas. The Arapahos, under Little Raven and Big Mouth (Pah-uf-pah-top), camped thirty to forty miles away. The Dog Soldiers had not yet arrived at the camp.

Stone Forehead (Hohonai´viuhk´tanuh, Nan-ne-sa-tah, Nan-ne-sat-tah, Rock Forehead, Man Who Walks With His Toes Turned Out, and by the white man, Medicine Arrow or Medicine Arrows), an Aorta Tsistsista chieftain, mystic, and medicine man, was Black Kettle's cousin.[18] He was also keeper of Maahótse, the Sacred Arrows, which symbolized the life of the tribe, embodying its soul.[19] Although the mystic has erroneously been referred to as a Dog Soldier, he was not one even though he often camped with them.

While Black Kettle would lean more and more toward peace, Stone Forehead stood for retaining the old ways at all costs.[20] As keeper of the arrows he was perhaps the most powerful Tsistsista on the southern and central plains.[21] Wanting nothing to do with the hated white man (*vi´ho´i*), he made it clear that those who associated with whites were no better than the spider that stood ready to devour the People, and this included Black Kettle.

On February 26 Wynkoop stepped from his tent. A line of Dog Soldiers waited for him: Bull Bear, Porcupine Bear, Big Head (Tangle Hair), Hairy Wolf, Bear Tongue, and Red Iron. "Many of them did not greet me very cordially and one particularly refused [my] hand," Wynkoop remembered, "covering his face with his blanket."[22] Wynkoop had just met Porcupine Bear. It was his father (also named Porcupine Bear) who had killed tribal member Little Creek during a drunken confrontation in winter 1837–38, turning the Dog Men into outlaws. The son hated whites; he had lost loved ones at Sand Creek and held Wynkoop responsible. Wynkoop had feared this encounter at the Little Arkansas but it never happened. Now he faced Porcupine Bear and the other Dog Soldiers head on.

By February 28 the Arapahos had still not arrived, and Wynkoop decided not to wait for them. That day he spoke with Cheyenne leaders. John Smith interpreted for him while George Bent, wearing a breech-clout with a trade blanket wrapped around his body, did the same for the Cheyennes. The meeting passed without incident, and afterwards when Big Mouth and his band of Arapahos had pulled into the encampment, Wynkoop decided to meet those present and distribute goods the next day.[23]

That night while Wynkoop sat in his tent with friends, Margaret McAdams entered and sat down. He had met the half-Arapaho half-white interpreter at the 1865 peace council when her last name was Wilmarth. She currently interpreted for him. According to Wynkoop, "she buried her face in her blanket" and bitterly wept.[24] When he asked her what was wrong, she said she feared they would die tomorrow, that if he insisted Porcupine Bear touch the treaty paper in council, the Bear would kill him. Suddenly Wynkoop realized just how deadly a foe he faced. He had a job to perform, but more importantly he had a life to preserve—his own.

Wynkoop made the distribution of the goods on March 1. Before holding the second council, he pulled his brother George aside and told him to hide in his tent with his Spencer carbine and shoot Porcupine Bear if the need arose. When it was time to meet, Wynkoop sat facing his tent, twenty yards away, forcing Porcupine Bear, Bull Bear, and George Bent to sit with their backs to it.

During the council, Wynkoop spoke of his earlier meetings with the People. He praised their past attempts to make peace, while pointing out what he considered "their evil" actions.[25] Wynkoop then read the current treaty terms, pointing out the "advantages of peace, and [the] disadvantages of war."[26] After telling the leaders that he had never lied to them, he said he had no intention of lying now. "Agree to and abide by the terms of the treaty," Wynkoop urged them, promising "it would result in their future happiness and welfare."[27] Needing signatures by leaders who had avoided the 1865 peace talks, he asked "them and their followers to abide by and keep the treaty made by their brethren at the mouth of the Little Arkansas."[28]

Wynkoop also had another objective: get the Indians, particularly the Dog Soldiers, to agree to move south of the Arkansas River. The Union Pacific Railroad, Eastern Division, intended to lay track between the Smoky Hill and Republican Rivers and wanted the tribes removed from the area. It paralleled the Union Pacific (a separate railroad) and was a southerly branch of the transcontinental railroad. Wynkoop knew that Stone Forehead and Big Mouth had been antagonistic since the signing of the Little Arkansas treaty and had no intention of giving up their land.

Along with the Dog Men, they absolutely refused to abandon their homeland between the Smoky Hill and Republican Rivers and did not want a railroad cutting through their land. Not in a negotiating mood, Dog Man Big Head vented his anger over being attacked while en route to the council. He then made Wynkoop a counterproposal. Instead of ceding his land to white invaders, Big Head wanted just the opposite: close all roads traveled by whites through Indian/buffalo land.

Objecting to the laying of railroad tracks along the Smoky Hill, Big Mouth said his people did not want to give up "their best hunting grounds" and live "south of the Arkansas."[29] They wanted to remain "where they were born and bred." Wynkoop said he understood and would present his views "to the proper authorities." He then cautioned Big Mouth that "he and his tribe had better stay peaceably where they were."

Black Kettle stood and backed Wynkoop's words, turning the discussion in the colonel's favor. Stone Forehead and Big Head agreed and touched the updated paper. George Bent claimed "Agent Wynkoop gave his best efforts towards gaining the consent of the Dog Soldiers to the building of this new road through their country."[30] Others also agreed to the terms. Only Porcupine Bear remained adamant in his refusal. Wynkoop crossed to him and asked him to reconsider. The war leader refused and Wynkoop sat down. George Bent quietly urged Porcupine Bear to change his mind, but still he refused. Then, as he had done to Wynkoop at Big Timbers, Bull Bear confronted the disgruntled Dog Man using "loud and emphatic language."[31] Other chiefs urged him in a less demanding way. Suddenly Porcupine Bear leaped to his feet. His action was so abrupt that a startled Wynkoop grabbed the butt of his revolver and had it halfway out of its holster before he realized that the other meant him no harm. Porcupine Bear stormed to the document next to Wynkoop and made his mark. Luckily George did not shoot, and luckily everyone watched the Bear and not Wynkoop. Relieved and pleased, the special agent had his signatures.

The stakes were high, perhaps as high as they had been in 1864 for Wynkoop, and a huge chasm separated the two points of view. Fortunately Black Kettle and Bull Bear helped him get the antagonistic leaders to agree to the altered treaty terms. Gordon reported that the Indians "all showed a desire for peace and friendship, and not a single unfriendly act occurred between them and the command."[32]

While at Bluff Creek, Wynkoop heard that a white girl had been captured by Cheyennes east of Fort Halleck on the North Platte the previous summer. Arapahos had traded for her, and she was now in Little Raven's Arapaho village. Two white traders had paid a high price for her. Wynkoop asked Captain Gordon to send a detail to retrieve her. Gordon sent Lieutenant Bates with Company K to accomplish the task, and they delivered her to Wynkoop.

Knowing that Wynkoop had the girl, Charles Hanger visited the special agent's camp and presented him with an inventory that listed exactly what he had traded for the girl. Totaling $1665 in goods, it included a bay horse, a mule, nine blankets, 100 pounds of coffee, 212 pounds of sugar, 100 pounds of flour, and six butcher knives, among other items. Wynkoop accepted Hanger's bill, writing, "I believe the said Morris & Hanger were governed entirely by motives of humanity in this trading for the said female and are deserving of credit for their philanthropy; and should be remunerated by the Government."[33] He signed the inventory, certifying that they indeed were owed the amount they requested. Then, writing on the inventory, Wynkoop expressed his disgust at the Cheyennes for not abiding by the Little Arkansas treaty terms. Hanger also obtained Agent Taylor's signed statement before sending the paperwork to Commissioner Cooley on April 17.

Little Raven and his band of Arapahos appeared at the encampment. Wynkoop spoke with them on March 2, then distributed the supplies designated for them. His first official mission completed, on March 3 he and Gordon's escort departed the campsite with the girl, who was English. They reached Fort Dodge the next day and Fort Larned by March 5.[34]

That day Wynkoop wrote to Colorado Governor Alexander Cummings, "I have just procured from the Dog Soldiers [sic] . . . a white girl, fifteen years of age, named Amanda Fletcher."[35] "Procured" seems an unfortunate word, but Wynkoop used it because he had authorized the payment to Hanger for her. He hoped that Cummings could locate surviving family members and learn if the girl's mother still lived. As it turned out, Amanda's mother had died when Southern Cheyenne Min-im-mie captured her and her three-year-old sister, Elizabeth, whom warriors from Southern Cheyenne Sand Hill's Aorta band took.

Next Wynkoop updated Commissioner Cooley on what he considered a successful mission. The Cheyennes had agreed to abide by the provisions of the 1865 treaty, and Amanda Fletcher had been freed. He mentioned that white men, most likely traders, moved among the Indians without authorization. He also updated General Pope on his success with the "hostile bands."[36]

Approximately 4,800 Cheyennes and Arapahos lived in the district of the Upper Arkansas. Using half rations for a soldier as his standard, Wynkoop calculated that the Indians needed 81,000 pounds of flour, 27,000 pounds of bacon, 11,100 pounds of sugar, 7,200 pounds of coffee, and 2,700 pounds of salt per month.[37] Then, realizing that the Cheyennes "are still prone to be suspicious of all white men with few exceptions," and trying to come up with a way to preserve the peace, he suggested "that I be [e]mpowered to select such *young* chiefs who have never visited the Capital and convey them thither."[38] He felt that the young leaders had more influence over their people than the old chiefs, and wanted them to see for themselves "the sincere desire of the Government to ameliorate their condition and in future act in good faith with them."

When Cooley heard of Wynkoop's "prompt and successful action," he thanked him, adding he had sent the newly signed agreement to Secretary of the Interior James Harlan to forward to the Senate.[39] Cooley then told Wynkoop something that pleased him: Agent Taylor would be notified that anyone not employed by the government could not remain among the Indians. This provided Wynkoop an opening to say he wanted to become a "real" Indian agent for the Cheyennes. "[T]he subject is looked upon with favor by this office," Cooley replied, "and you will be advised if such action is taken."

On March 13 the *Rocky Mountain News* reported that Wynkoop had "been entirely successful in removing all hostile Indians south of the Arkansas, and that he has received pledges from their chiefs of their future good behavior."[40] But he had not completed his mission. In early April

1866 Wynkoop returned to the field, traveling fifteen miles from Fort Larned to Wood Creek. On April 4 he met "a large portion of the fighting element of the [Southern Cheyennes] and although their head men signed the agreement [in March] . . . I deemed it my duty as well as very necessary for the public interest to see and talk with the warriors of that band as well as to have them proceed south of the Arkansas river."[41] The conversation must have been heated, for once again the Dog Soldiers' land along the Smoky Hill was at stake. Not only was it their best hunting grounds, but it also housed the remains of their ancestors. "They listened to me with great attention and exhibited a fervent desire for peace."[42] But this did not ease the tension, and Wynkoop understood the importance of their decision, for they discussed "the subject with much feeling."

As with his previous meetings, Wynkoop's persuasive words obtained the desired results, and the Dog Soldiers agreed to give up their land. No longer a novice, the special agent had gained confidence with each meeting. Proclaiming the "routes of travel across the Plains perfectly safe," he triumphantly announced, "I have now got all of the hostile bands in, and I can safely declare the Indians to be at peace."[43] Wynkoop concluded that he had negotiated "a 'strong peace,' as it has been consummated with the *warriors* in the field, rather than with the *old men* in council." Although thrilled with his success and looking forward to the future, Wynkoop made sure to include in his report a warning that the Dog Soldiers would only keep their agreement "so long as the government fulfils its promises to them."[44] But it is hard to be sure that Wynkoop and the Indians completely understood each other.

On April 9, Wynkoop met with the Oglala Sioux war leader Pawnee Killer (Sy tee-mah-wa), who had about one hundred people with him. The Oglalas often rode with the Dog Men on the central plains, and had taken part in the attack on Julesburg. Pawnee Killer was imposing. According to a contemporary description, his "face had a lean and hungry look; he was long and lank, and reminded one of a prowling wolf."[45] He spoke about his peaceful intentions and of his wish to return to his homeland in the north. Wynkoop believed him and wrote a safe-conduct letter for him. Byers commented on the report, "This is pretty good evidence that Maj. Wynkoop is accomplishing some good in his mission."

Byers, who had begun to vacillate between castigating and praising Wynkoop, reprinted praise originally published in the *Lawrence Journal*. "Maj. Wynkoop is thoroughly conversant with the Indian character. He is one of the most accomplished officers in the employ of the government. He is thorough and efficient in everything he does."[46] Wynkoop's future looked promising. Of course Byers could not refrain from commenting, "Ed. certainly does seem to succeed admirably with the beauties, *if* they stick to what they promise him."

Later in April 1866 Wynkoop sent Edmund Guerrier to Pond Creek (Fort Wallace), a military station two hundred miles east of Denver, with a message. Wynkoop believed "that there would be no more depredations committed [by Southern Cheyennes] on this route."[47] His mission accomplished, Special Agent Wynkoop set out for Washington to present his report on the state of affairs with the Cheyennes and Arapahos. By April 23 he had reached Atchison, Kansas. He remained convinced that the Indians would keep their word and that there would be no more violence.[48] Upon reaching Washington, Wynkoop met President Andrew Johnson, and with Senator James Doolittle's recommendation in hand, he told the president of his desire to become an Indian agent. Johnson had heard of Wynkoop's dealings with Indians, as had everyone else in Washington, but instead offered him a commission in the regular army. By this time Wynkoop wanted nothing more to do with the military, and he declined the president's offer. Johnson expressed appreciation for Wynkoop's sincerity and said he would consider the appointment.[49]

Even though Wynkoop pressed for the position he craved, he did not forget the people he wanted to serve. On May 8, 1866, he urged Commissioner Cooley to listen to him. "I recommend that measures be taken immediately to supply these Indians with subsistence," Wynkoop said, reminding the commissioner of the 1865 treaty.[50] More important, Wynkoop continued, the Indians "are compelled to leave their hunting grounds and occupy a certain tract of country below the Arkansas river, a country which is almost devoid of game, which has heretofore been their only means of subsistence." Wynkoop understood the situation clearly. Warriors performed two principal activities; they hunted and they rode the war trail, both of which provided for the family circle. Remove their ability to hunt and make war, and they would no longer be able to provide for their families. Wynkoop reiterated the truth as he saw it: "every sense of justice and humanity demands that they should be properly provided for and without delay."

But not everyone on the frontier agreed with Wynkoop. Major J. W. Davidson (Second U.S. Cavalry), who commanded Fort Riley, looked upon the Special Agent's efforts in a much darker way. "I have no confidence in the Wynkoop beauties & my opinion is shared by several officers."[51]

Ned Wynkoop's return to the East did not bode well for the Indian cause. Agent Taylor made a distribution of annuities on July 21, 1866, at Fort Zarah, and immediately heard a barrage of Cheyenne complaints. In Wynkoop's absence, he cared nothing for Cheyenne reactions, for he had his own agenda. Black Kettle spoke with Taylor and told him that he would soon meet with the Dog Men to "make medicine." The chief assured the agent that he would do what he could to get the Hotametaneo o to reopen negotiations regarding "their relinquishing the right of way to the Smoky Hill country." Black Kettle and Taylor placated each other, but neither believed the other. Certainly Taylor did not think Black Kettle could coax the militant division of his tribe into giving up their land. "I have not the least distant idea that they will ever give it up peaceably," Taylor reported, "as the Dog Indians say they will fight for it as long as there is one of them remaining. That being their determination, extermination of that portion of the Cheyenne nation, in my opinion, is the only ultimatum to a permanent peace."[52]

Unaware of Taylor's frightening take on the current state of affairs, Black Kettle "asked for a permit to hunt buffalo on the Smoky Hill." Taylor agreed, but instructed John Smith to continue living with the chief and report any "hostile demonstrations upon that road." The militant Dog Soldiers might have been the major threat to expansion, but all Cheyennes, regardless of their stance on peace, were now Taylor's targets.

The Southern Cheyennes and Dog Soldiers with whom Wynkoop had met in council were sincere in their promises to keep the peace, but peace was not on the horizon. In May 1866 there had been a few isolated attacks on whites on the Solomon River in Kansas.[53] Since that time unrest and the threat of more violence kept the frontier on edge. What Wynkoop had accomplished was not enough. It would never be enough.

W. H. Watson, an Interior Department agent, accused Wynkoop of misleading the Indians in order to secure their signatures on the altered treaty papers and then failing to inform his superiors how he had really obtained them. Watson knew that Taylor's chances of retaining his position were not good, and he did not want Wynkoop to replace him. Watson claimed that Superintendent Thomas Murphy, who had obtained his information from unnamed sources (and who did not criticize Wynkoop on this subject), told him Wynkoop had secured the Dog Soldier signatures "with the express understanding that the whites were to keep away from the Smoky Hill route westward through Kansas."[54] Watson revealed that his accusation was based on hearsay when he added, "If this is true, Major Wynkoop was greatly to blame for not stating these facts in his report." To drive the point home, Watson added, "Their concealment can only be ascribed to a great desire to magnify his sham in pacifying the Indians." A little over a week later Watson again criticized Wynkoop, claiming that he now heard from other sources that Wynkoop's misleading the Indians meant that the Dog Soldiers did not break the treaty by raiding but the United States did when it invaded their land. Watson then got to his real reason for attacking Wynkoop. Comanche and Kiowa agent Jesse Leavenworth should become agent to the Cheyennes and Arapahos because they desired "to be under his charge."[55]

The Southern Cheyennes and Dog Men understood what they had agreed to when they met Wynkoop in council. They wanted peace, but they found it hard to turn their backs and walk away from the land that was their home just because a stronger enemy demanded it. Wynkoop understood this. He also knew that when he had recently met the Indians in council "the time had come and passed wherein certain distributions had been promised to be made in accordance with the provisions of the treaty," and this had not happened.[56] According to Wynkoop, the Cheyennes "judge . . . good faith by performance," and the U.S. government had failed to deliver.

Wynkoop thrived on walking that precarious line between whites and Indians but he now knew that no matter what he accomplished in his current situation it would be contested by civilian, military, and government officials or rejected by Indians who refused to give up what they considered theirs. Wanting to separate himself from the entire Colorado situation, Wynkoop decided that his current position was tenuous at best and needed to end.[57]

On July 11, 1866, Brevet Lieutenant Colonel Edward W. Wynkoop, Major, First Colorado Cavalry, who still remained in Washington, mustered out and was honorably discharged, "his services being no longer required, he having been retained in service to this date by special authority from the War Department."[58] Wynkoop terminated his enlistment because he was fed up with the constant struggle and he wanted to pursue a position within the Interior Department.[59]

On July 25, 1866, fourteen days after Wynkoop ended his military career, he met with Commissioner Cooley in his office in Washington. He told the commissioner that the Cheyennes and Arapahos were restive as they still had not received the goods and other stipulations promised at the 1865 treaty talks.[60] Cooley directed Wynkoop to meet with the Cheyennes and Arapahos on the Smoky Hill. No longer on detached duty from the military, Wynkoop now held a special commission from, and reported directly to, the Interior Department. Cooley explained that Congress had finally passed the required appropriation bills the day before, but that it would still take time before the money became available for the Indians. After signing a bond, Wynkoop received $1,000.00 for travel expenses and to use as necessary to provide the Indians with temporary supplies. He prepared to leave for the West.

While Wynkoop was in Washington, his brother George, who had accompanied him to the Bluff Creek village, remained on the frontier. In July George decided to go back to the states. While en route he became sick. On July 29 he died thirty-five miles west of Kansas City, and was buried in that city the next day.[61]

This news hit Wynkoop hard. He had a challenging assignment and a sad heart. Instead of going directly to Fort Ellsworth, Kansas, Special Commissioner Wynkoop traveled to Denver, arriving August 2. He settled his brother's affairs before setting out for the Smoky Hill on August 4. As Wynkoop rode toward Fort Ellsworth, the Department of the Missouri issued orders concerning his mission. "The Commanding Officer at Fort Riley will on application of Col. E. W. Wynkoop furnish him with an ambulance & team and such transportation as may be necessary to enable him to comply with his instructions from the Secy. of the Interior. He will also on application be furnished with a suitable escort by the Comdg. Officer of any post to whom he may apply."[62] Wynkoop's commission, although not permanent, gave him confidence that the position he actively sought would eventually become his.

Wynkoop did not reach Fort Ellsworth until August 10, 1866. The post, on the north side of the Smoky Hill where the Fort Riley–Fort Larned Road crossed the river, was almost uninhabitable and would soon be abandoned. Officers lived in small huts and the soldiers lived in log huts without floors and in which they could not stand upright. Wynkoop explained why he was late in arriving and then apologized in a report to Commissioner Cooley.

As soon as possible after his arrival, Wynkoop met with Major General I. N. Palmer, who commanded the district, and found the general's information interesting to say the least. Agent Taylor, Palmer explained, is "at Fort Zarah where he remains constantly in a state of intoxication."[63] Indians and soldiers often got drunk in Taylor's office. But as the post was controlled by Kansas and not on Indian land, Palmer had no jurisdiction. Wynkoop used this information to his advantage. "I consider this a very serious matter, I have heard these same facts from numerous citizens who have passed Fort Zarah and are loud in their denunciations, and unless immediate action is had the result may be serious."

The next day Wynkoop sent a runner to Taylor at Fort Zarah with a letter, telling him he intended to meet the Indians and ask what they thought of his performance. Taylor reacted negatively, replying to Wynkoop that since the department did not bother to inform him of his mission, he had no intention of working with him.[64]

On August 13, John Smith brought Southern Cheyenne headmen into Fort Ellsworth to meet with Wynkoop, who already knew some of them: Black Kettle and Little Robe, Little Wolf, The Man That Shot The Ree, Big Head, Sitting Bear, Little Black Kettle, and the Ohméséheso leader Gray Head (White Head), who often traveled to the south. There was one other Tsistsista present, and this may have been the first time Wynkoop came in contact with him. Unusually large, Roman Nose (Wo´ o ke nih´, Woquini ["hook nose"], Sautie ["bat"]), was a member of the Crooked Lance (Himoiyoquis) society, and would soon become the most famed warrior on the southern and central plains.[65] Even though he often rode with the Dog Men, he never joined them.

Roman Nose stood firmly for the People, right or wrong, and considered any person or race that threatened their lifeway an enemy. For Roman Nose there were no exceptions, Wynkoop included. And he had a complaint, as did the rest of his people. The Great Father had forgotten them and had not delivered the goods they were promised on the Little Arkansas.[66]

The headmen told Wynkoop "that it was hard for them to give up the Smoky Hill country, but that they were satisfied now that it was useless" to fight the loss and "they would not trouble the road, but resign themselves to their fate, and they hoped . . . the Great Father would have pity upon them and . . . promises made to them would be fulfilled."[67] Wynkoop tried to make them understand that the U.S. government worked slowly and had just now appropriated the money to pay for the promised supplies.

The lack of cash would constantly hinder Wynkoop in his dealings with Indians. This was not just Wynkoop's problem. Special U.S. Indian agents W. R. Irwin and Charles Bogy, future Commissioner of Indian Affairs Lewis Bogy's brother, said, "An agent can not operate in this country without funds. . . . It is impossible to obtain proper couriers without paying good prices and an agent is compelled to act promptly in most cases in order to effect anything."[68]

The discussion continued, and the chiefs said that in addition to what the white man owed them, they wanted two children taken at Sand Creek returned. Roman Nose, who Wynkoop mistakenly thought a chief, insisted that this must happen. Wynkoop had not heard of these children but said he would do what he could to find them. The Cheyennes also wanted six hundred ponies to replace those lost at Sand Creek, and fancy gifts to be bought out of whatever remained of the funds owed them. They said that they had agreed to give up their homeland because they felt they could not possibly stand up to the white military power, but now regretted it.

Feeling secure that the government would make good on the annuities promised by the treaty, and thrilled that the Indians said they would not contest the Smoky Hill, Wynkoop set the date for the annuity distribution at the end of September. As the council ended he felt he had soothed the frayed tempers of the Indians. His mission complete, he received instructions to return to Washington. Before heading east, he traveled to Denver. The Colonel, as more and more people addressed Wynkoop, visited Byers at his office and recounted his latest dealings with the Indians.[69]

Unknown to Wynkoop, Agent Taylor was fuming over being ignored at Bluff Creek. He wrote to Cooley complaining "that the feeling existing between E. W. Wynkoop, and myself, are not of the most friendly nature, owing to the course he, and some of his unprincipled friends pursued toward me, when out here, as special Agent."[70]

On August 15 Kiowa Chief Satanta and twenty-three warriors attacked the James Box family in Montague County, Texas, killing and mutilating Box. Box's wife, Mary, and daughters Margaret, Josephine, Ida, and Laura, an infant, became captives. Soon after, Laura fell from her mother's arms and was abandoned.[71] By early September news circulated that Kiowas and Comanches held five white captives, whom they had "outrageously abused."[72] Margaret had been traded and raped numerous times. When Satanta met Taylor, the agent demanded he give up the white females. The Kiowa refused. He wanted payment for the hostages, but none was forthcoming; instead Taylor told him he had broken the treaty. Satanta then made a strange and telling statement. "[T]he Indians would give them up to Col. Wynkoop, their own agent, whenever he should demand them."

Wynkoop departed Denver and traveled to Fort Larned. Soon after his arrival, Lieutenant General William T. Sherman appeared. When Black Kettle and Little Raven, along with some Kiowas and Plains Apaches, visited the fort, even though he did not serve as their agent, Wynkoop set up a meeting between the general and the Indians with John Smith and Dick Curtis interpreting.

While the Kiowas and Apaches remained silent, Black Kettle and Little Raven told Sherman that they needed weapons to hunt buffalo and wanted him to get the weapons for them. Sherman acquiesced, but then turned sarcastic, saying that the Indians "would have something to fight his soldiers with when they went on warpath again."[73]

Unaware of Satanta's depredations, Wynkoop continued eastward, reaching Washington by the end of August. He reported to Cooley, who, he was pleased to hear, had lobbied for him to meet President Johnson again. While waiting for an appointment, he met with Cooley several times to discuss the horses the Cheyennes lost at Sand Creek. The reported losses had now shrunk to five hundred. On August 28 Wynkoop recommended buying at least three hundred horses by October 1, 1866, at a cost of no more than fifty dollars per animal. He told Cooley that he should order the Cheyenne agent to purchase the remaining two hundred horses from the "Semi-Civilized Tribes of Kansas."[74] Wynkoop thought he had been ordered to Washington to discuss the duties of an Indian agent, but this did not happen. Nothing happened. Days passed with no progress on his quest to become agent. All he did was sit around and wait.

On the frontier peace remained tenuous. At 2:00 A.M. on September 19, 1866, fifteen Cheyenne warriors invaded beef contractor H. P.

Wyatt's home at Pond Creek, Kansas, and demanded food and coffee. He served them and they left peacefully. A short while later they raided the Fort Wallace herd and captured twenty to thirty mules and horses.[75]

Finally on September 20 President Andrew Johnson appointed Wynkoop "Agent for the Indians of the Upper Arkansas Agency."[76] His wards included the Southern Cheyennes, Arapahos, and Plains Apaches. Six days later he submitted the bonds the government required, saying "I . . . respectfully request that I be notified of their acceptance and approval."[77]

Although he was undoubtedly thrilled, Wynkoop had no intention of leaving Washington until he dealt with money issues. On September 27 he met with Cooley and asked the government to pay for his return trip to the frontier. "It will also be necessary for me to have some funds to pay expenses incident to the distribution of Annuities."[78] He asked for $300.

Two days later Commissioner Cooley requested an accounting of the $1,000 Wynkoop had used during his last mission as special agent. An angry Wynkoop told Cooley that if he had been required to make as detailed a report as a regular agent, he should have been informed earlier.[79]

Wynkoop did not return to Kansas until the end of October. If he did not already know it, he would soon learn that during his absence the Indians' situation had not improved. At Fort Riley the new U.S. Indian agent met with Major J. W. Davidson, commander of the District of the Upper Arkansas, and told him that he had decided to distribute Indian annuities at Fort Ellsworth. When Davidson offered a military escort to the post, Wynkoop refused it, pointing out that it was "bad policy . . . that the Arapahoes & Cheyennes" lived in fear of another Sand Creek, and would be intimidated "to such a degree that they would fly before an approaching column of Troops."[80] Thinking of the past while looking to the future, Wynkoop hoped to keep the "well disposed Indians" separate from "the bad ones," in case of military action. He did not want to see "the recurrence of former fatal mistakes of punishing the innocent for the crimes of the guilty."

Wynkoop reached Junction City by October 26. Here he halted, and during the respite drafted a letter to Commissioner Cooley. Although he felt the military would do everything possible to maintain peace, he did not feel the same about the Indians. "I believe that there are some outlaws among the tribes who should be punished."[81] Eager to reach his destination, Wynkoop pressed on, arriving at Fort Ellsworth later that day. The next morning he informed Cooley that he had begun performing his duties as agent.[82]

On October 28 Wynkoop drafted a hefty requisition from the Indian Department. He wanted $2,000.00 to supply his agency, which also included furnishings and ongoing expenditures, as well as $3,000.00 to provide for his wards per the 1865 treaty stipulations. As he considered the Indians in an unsettled state, which would require long and frequent trips by him to ascertain their needs, he wanted the money in advance.[83]

About this time a dispatch from the military caught up to Wynkoop, ordering him to deduct from the Southern Cheyenne annuities the cost of the Chalk Bluff station on the Smoky Hill route. Cheyennes were said to have burned the station and driven off Fort Wallace's livestock.[84] The new commander of the Department of the Missouri, Major General Winfield Scott Hancock, who had gained fame during the Mexican war (1846–48), the Seminole Indian war (1855–58), and the Civil War, issued the order.

It must have seemed to Wynkoop that every time he turned around, someone deprived Indians of promised annuities. By this time he had a good idea what might happen if too much was withheld. Switching employers had not improved matters. The problems he had faced on detached duty as a special agent still existed.

Right after Wynkoop received orders to withhold money from Cheyenne annuities, he ran afoul of Hancock. In the past, Wynkoop had acted as he thought right regardless of the consequences. This time the consequences were daunting, and reminded Wynkoop of 1864. Hancock had sent him a list of charges against Cheyenne raiders. He wanted the names of the guilty Cheyennes. Wynkoop asked for additional time. Hancock declined, stating sarcastically that Wynkoop must have misunderstood the instructions forwarded to him.[85] He then told Wynkoop that he wanted to know "the extent of your authority over the Indians, and the names of the tribes you are Agent for, as it may be important for me to know this, in case of future communications from me to you." Hancock said he would "delay action against the Cheyennes" until Wynkoop learned the identities of the "guilty parties."

Wynkoop may have taken Hancock's tone as condescending. Since Wynkoop's knowledge of Indians had grown steadily over the past year and Hancock knew nothing of Indians, he was not pleased with the general's tone. He did not meet the Arapaho and Cheyenne leaders until early November. After a council at Walnut Creek, he fed them and passed out supplies, but he had no weapons to distribute. Angry chiefs demanded to know why the government issued arms and ammunition to the Comanches and Kiowas, but not them.[86] Clearly, the Cheyennes and Arapahos were desperate for guns. At the conclusion of the meeting Wynkoop hustled back to Fort Ellsworth, which was being rebuilt with stone, lumber, and logs a mile north of the Smoky Hill (it would be re-named Fort Harker on November 17, 1866). Upon his arrival Wynkoop telegraphed the new commissioner of Indian Affairs, Lewis V. Bogy. He wanted to know if he could issue weapons, and he wanted to know immediately. At this time Wynkoop must have wondered what the fu-ture held. Former Commissioner Dennis Cooley had promoted him and played the lead in securing his current position, but now he was gone.

Bogy wasted little time. Instead of answering the agent he forwarded the $5,000 request Cooley had received from Wynkoop to Thomas Murphy. Murphy, in turn, told Wynkoop to submit a detailed descrip-tion specifying how he intended to use the funds. Wynkoop told the new commissioner "it is impossible for me to make any closer estimate under the circumstances," and resubmitted his original estimate.[87] "I was particular in not asking for more than I deemed absolutely necessary," he said, "and would beg respectfully that I be furnished with the funds with as little delay as possible." Wynkoop asked special Indian agents Charles Bogy and W. R. Irwin to draft a letter backing up his proposal, and they did.

Nothing happened. Conscious that the supplies allotted to his wards were insufficient and that none might be forthcoming in the near future, Wynkoop again met with special agents Irwin and Bogy. They agreed with him that more staple items had to be added to his inventory, and Wynkoop purchased an additional $14,356.02 worth of goods on No-vember 23.[88]

Wynkoop distributed supplies to the Plains Apaches, Arapahos, and some Cheyennes, and found them "to be very well satisfied."[89] At the same time he was acutely aware of how nomadic the tribes were, mak-ing it difficult for him to keep in close contact with them unless he remained constantly "on the Plains far removed from civilization." He needed a remote location for his agency, one centrally located to the Indians' migration habits, and Fort Larned fit the bill.

But it would not be that simple. The Interior and War departments, currently in competition for control of the Indian situation, did not assist one another. To set up his headquarters Wynkoop needed living quarters, an office, and a storehouse for provisions. When he requested the military supply his needs, they refused. Wynkoop explained his dilemma to Commissioner Bogy, suggesting that since he lived at a military post, the commissioner should present his case to the secretary of war.

Wynkoop knew that a good portion of the white population on the frontier despised him. When he received a letter dated October 5, 1866, from William Byers, regarding the Chalk Bluff depredations, he decided to reply. Having already discussed the killings with Cheyenne leaders, Wynkoop had come to the conclusion that three Dog Soldiers were responsible. However, when he responded to Byers, he refused to mince words and addressed what bothered him. "I am called, in Colorado, an Indian lover and . . . d[amne]d by many for the policy which I have pursued," he wrote.[90] "I am not yet convinced that I have been wrong, and until I am, will continue [as I have in the past]."

As December 1866 arrived, Wynkoop decided to spend the cold months on the frontier. He expected that as soon as Southern Cheyennes in the north and south heard he had been appointed their agent they would appear at Fort Larned.[91] He had no intention of missing their arrival.

Although anxious to begin dealing with his wards Wynkoop faced two financial problems. He had been a U.S. Indian agent since September but had yet to receive a paycheck. At the same time, the money he requested to deal with the Indians had not been approved and setting up his headquarters at Fort Larned had bogged down.[92]

Weeks passed and it became obvious that his employers were dragging their feet. Wynkoop, like many at the post, lived in squalor, in a mud dugout cut from the bank above the river. He found the situation intolerable. In December he realized that neither the Department of War nor the Department of Interior cared where or how he lived. Feeling he had no recourse, Wynkoop queried Hancock about setting up his headquarters at Fort Larned, and asked if the military could supply his living quarters, office, and store house.[93] The request fell on deaf ears.

CHAPTER TWELVE

Hancock's War

At the end of 1866 violence on the prairie was diminishing, but race relations remained strained as white encroachment continued into the new year. As part of the national effort to secure the plains for white migration, the Union Pacific, Eastern Division, concentrated on laying track.

For Ned Wynkoop, 1867 began with the same financial difficulties that had plagued him in 1866. Superintendent Thomas Murphy rejected his budget for the first half of the year. On January 1 Wynkoop tried again, informing Murphy that what he listed was absolutely necessary and to date had not been provided (at least not completely). He required $750 for his salary, $200 for an interpreter based at Fort Larned (he also employed other interpreters in the field), and $100 for contingencies. He asked for advice on how to get the amount approved. "I have been very much cramped ever since I have been on duty for funds; and these have been expenses which have been absolutely necessary and which have not been provided for," he complained.[1]

Many Indian agents were on the take by the mid-1860s. A number of agents retired rich because of their lucrative weapons sales, and the military wanted it stopped. Traders, agents, and even interpreters more and more found themselves accused of amassing large amounts of money by defrauding Indians and the U.S. government. By January 1867 Lieutenant General William Sherman had had enough and ordered General Hancock to stop Indian agents from selling arms to warriors. Actually Sherman wanted to eliminate civilian traders and Indian agents and replace them with military personnel. He wanted officers commanding military posts in Indian districts to control the sale of weapons, and all other sales of weapons be made illegal. And he had a trump card; if sales did not stop, he would withdraw troops from the plains. President Andrew Johnson supported Sherman's proposals, setting the stage for more infighting between the War and Interior departments.

In February 1867 Major Henry Douglas (Third U.S. Infantry), who commanded Fort Dodge, Kansas, reported that the plains tribes "were never better armed than at the present time," and that warriors boasted they were ready to ride the war trail come spring.[2] "For a revolver an Indian will give ten, even twenty times its value in horses and furs," Douglas said.

This accusation fed the widespread distrust of Indian agents and became a problem for Colonel Wynkoop, one that undermined his ability to perform the duties of his office. He often found himself linked with his brethren, whose sole ambition was becoming rich. Frequently the accusations were accurate, but not when aimed at him.[3]

Even though President Johnson had appointed Wynkoop U.S. Indian agent on September 20, 1866, by February 1867 his appointment was still unofficial. On February 11 the Department of the Interior finally commissioned him agent, but the assignment would not become official until he filed his bond and took the oath of office. This exposed another shortcoming within the Interior Department, for Wynkoop had filed his bond before leaving Washington the previous September. Most likely he took the oath of office at that time. Wynkoop had still not received any salary since becoming Indian agent. On February 22 he tired of asking for the money owed him and complained to Commissioner Bogy.[4] He was given a blank bond from the commissioner with instructions to fill it out. Wynkoop politely replied. "Presuming that some mistake has been made I would respectfully inform you that my bond is now on file in your office and I have received my commission."[5]

While Wynkoop struggled with his financial predicament, Cheyenne warriors almost created an incident below Fort Larned when they insisted a rancher feed them on February 28. A week later Roman Nose rode into Fort Larned and met with Wynkoop. He camped with Dog Men seventy miles up the Pawnee Fork. All was quiet in the village, but runners from the north brought distressing news of a massive concentration of soldiers on the Platte.[6]

At this time Hancock was organizing a massive military force at Fort Leavenworth that consisted of the Seventh U.S. Cavalry (four companies), Thirty-Seventh U.S. Infantry (seven companies), and Fourth U.S. Artillery (one battery) to meet with the migrant tribes on the southern and central plains and impress them that the United States could annihilate them if they did not do as instructed.[7] On March 11, Hancock informed Wynkoop that he had completed his arrangements to march and only awaited decent weather. He intended to visit Wynkoop's wards and wanted the agent to join him so that they appeared to act in harmony. The general also told Wynkoop "that we are able to chastise any tribes who may molest people who are traveling across the plains."[8] He did not want to create a problem with the Indians, he said, and would "treat them with justice and according to our treaty stipulations." Hancock then assured Wynkoop, "I desire especially in my dealings with them to act through their Agents as far as possible."

Two days later Hancock restated his plans. To ensure that Wynkoop understood his meaning, he used the exact same phrases regarding chastising tribes, treating the tribes with justice, and working with the agents. However, he did have a change of plan. Now, instead of visiting the Southern Cheyennes, he wanted them to come to him and asked Wynkoop to set up a meeting with them at Fort Larned on April 10.[9]

Hancock's communications did not please Wynkoop. There were too many harsh words, including a disquieting phrase Hancock used in both letters: "and tell them also, if you please, that I go fully prepared for peace or war." A little over a week later Hancock wrote Wynkoop again. "I do not expect to make war against any of the Indians of your Agency, unless they commence hostilities against us."[10] Peace or war? Actions spoke louder than words to Indians. Wynkoop knew that a massive assembly of soldiers did not go hand-in-hand with peaceful negotiations, and feared what might happen.

As the route the Union Pacific, Eastern Division, proposed cut through the Southern Cheyennes' prime hunting ground, Wynkoop knew that trouble loomed dangerously close.[11] The Dog Men had been vocal about protecting their land between the Smoky Hill and Republican rivers. But Wynkoop failed to realize that Hancock had no intention of heeding his advice when dealing with the Cheyennes.

Most likely Wynkoop was not aware of Hancock's prejudicial view of Indian agents. The general considered agents little more than thieves out to get rich by stealing from Indians. To Hancock's credit, when directly asked for his opinions of agents, after discussing the rampant fraud he said: "I do not know about Wynkoop," meaning he had no proof that Wynkoop padded his pockets by robbing Indians.[12]

Wynkoop employed half-Cheyenne interpreter Edmund Guerrier, and on this occasion George Bent as a runner to deliver messages. Fred Jones, an interpreter operating out of Fort Dodge, also worked for him. Wynkoop sent his runners to invite the Southern Cheyenne and Dog Soldier leaders to meet Hancock at Fort Larned on April 10.[13]

Chief Bull Bear did not want war, nor did his people or the Sioux then camping with the Dog Men on the Pawnee Fork. Hoping to avoid trouble, he sent word that he and other headmen would attend the council with the soldier chief.[14] But on April 8 snow fell and wind raked the land, making travel impossible.[15] Hancock's army, camped a short distance from Fort Larned, waited out the storm on April 9, expecting the Indians to arrive at the fort the next day.[16] The chiefs did not appear. Instead, they sent runners to Wynkoop, informing him that their ponies were too weak to travel through the snow. Wynkoop updated Hancock on the situation and the council was postponed until better weather. The next day runners visited Wynkoop and told him that the chiefs were about to leave their village on Red Arm Creek (Pawnee Fork) and travel to Fort Larned, but had been sidetracked by a herd of buffalo, which they hunted. This update did not please Hancock. On April 12, the general announced that he would leave the next day for the Indian encampment.[17]

Late that afternoon perhaps twelve members of the "Dog band," as Wynkoop called the Dog Soldiers, rode into Fort Larned on jaded ponies. He named Tall Bull, Bull Bear, and White Horse. According to the Ohméséhesos leader Gray Head, who with his band had traveled to the south and camped with the Dog Men, he and Slim Face (a Tsistsista) also were present. Worn out and hungry, and anticipating meeting the soldier chief the next morning, the Dog Men asked if they could eat. Wynkoop informed Hancock of their request and he acquiesced, but insisted upon meeting that night. As soon as Wynkoop relayed the general's demand, the headmen became wary for peace councils always took place during daylight hours.[18]

Wynkoop and Guerrier ate with the Indian leaders in a tent. Finally, after two hours, Wynkoop led the chiefs to a large bonfire. Henry Stanley, the Welsh-born reporter who would become a celebrity when he found Scottish missionary David Livingston in Africa in 1871, was traveling with Hancock's army. On this night he wrote about Wynkoop for the first time. "The Colonel is an Indian agent par excellence, of whom a slight description will not suffice to convey any just idea. He is a Plains man, and the best handler of Indians that has been on the Arkansas. The Indians have every confidence in his integrity, and respect him for the 'heap fight' that he is known to be capable of making."[19] Wynkoop and Guerrier sat with the headmen while Hancock sat with his officers on the opposite side of the fire.

Lieutenant Colonel George Armstrong Custer (Seventh U.S. Cavalry) joined the council and saw Cheyennes up close for the first time. During the Civil War Custer had "exploded across the American scene like a skyrocket, . . . exhibit[ing] his desire for action while showing no fear against the enemy."[20] This new foe would challenge his capabilities.

One of the chiefs lit a pipe, inhaled four sacred mouthfuls, and passed the pipe on to the next person. Everyone shared the pipe before the council began.[21]

Just how much Wynkoop was privy to the struggle between the War and Interior departments for the control of the Indians is unknown. Lieutenant General Sherman told Hancock that the military must "respect the Indian treaties, because they are the law of the land."[22] Congress had mandated that the Interior Department manage the Indians. "We are bound also to respect the authority of Commissioners, or Agents, who are charged with the intercourse with, and control of the various tribes," Sherman continued, "and to leave them to manage all questions not amounting to actual war." He also said the military had a "duty . . . to protect our own people," that great numbers of Cheyennes, Arapahos, and Kiowas had appeared near the forts on the Arkansas and Smoky Hill and threatened to block the roads. "This cannot be tolerated for a moment. If not a state of war, it is [the] next thing to it, and will result in war unless checked." Sherman had given Hancock free rein to act as he thought best.

The smoking ritual complete, Hancock scolded the chiefs for not bringing more leaders with them and announced he would give them a Cheyenne boy, that there was a girl near Denver, and that he wanted all white and black prisoners freed. Without giving the chiefs a chance to reply, Hancock moved on to the reason for his tour of Indian lands.

"I have a great many soldiers—more than all the tribes put together. The Great Father has heard that some Indians have" white captives, that "many Indians are trying to get up war, to try to hurt the white man."[23]

Wynkoop had been concerned prior to the meeting, but now, as Guerrier translated for the Southern Cheyennes, he waited anxiously for what Hancock would say next. Speaking as if he were a conquering lord, Hancock continued. "I am going to visit you in your camp. The innocent and those who are truly our friends, we shall treat as brothers. If we find hereafter that any of you have lied to us, we will strike them." Regardless how well or poorly the words were translated, the Cheyennes understood the gist.

Hancock pressed on, stating that he had evidence of outrages and that once Wynkoop studied it and named the guilty parties, he would punish them. "I have heard that a great many Indians want to fight. Very well; we are here, and we come prepared for war. If you are for peace, you know the conditions. If you are for war, look out for its consequences." Pounding his point, he said: "If you go to war with the white man, you would lose."

Hancock then showed his ignorance of Cheyenne ways. Their leaders only spoke for themselves and those who followed them at that moment. "Every tribe ought to have a great chief," Hancock pronounced, "one that can command his men. For any depredation committed by any one of his tribe, I shall hold the chief and his tribe responsible." Wynkoop cringed at the last sentence, knowing what it meant to the innocent. Hancock plowed forward. The U.S. government seldom honored its own treaty requirements, but he warned the Indians not to break their portion of treaties.

"I have no more to say," Hancock concluded. "I will await the end of this council, to see whether you want war or peace."

This angered the slender Tall Bull (Hot u´a a ka´ash tait, Hotoa-qa-ihoois), who stood and faced Hancock. "You sent for us—we came here. We have made the treaty with our Agent, Colonel Wynkoop." After saying, "We never did the white man any harm," he addressed his people's concerns. Indians, like whites, should be able to travel on roads without being shot; his people wanted to be friends with the white man; no one recognized or wanted Hancock's "Cheyenne" boy; once plentiful, buffalo and antelope now vanished at an alarming rate; and finally, his people should not be shot when they traveled to forts to get food promised them. "You say you are going to the village tomorrow," Tall Bull said in conclusion. "If you go, I shall have no more to say to you there, than here. I have said all I want to say here."

Hancock refused to be dismissed and threatened the Indians with extermination. The general had stated his objectives, the Indians realized their danger, and Wynkoop found himself straddling the two positions. When the antagonists stepped away from the fading fire, Tall Bull pulled Wynkoop aside (and most likely Guerrier, too). As they walked into the night he told the agent that he must stop Hancock from moving toward the village, that his people feared another Sand Creek. Wynkoop said he would tell Hancock of the People's fear and do what he could to stop the soldiers. Satisfied, Tall Bull walked off.

Midnight passed. Finally Wynkoop gained an interview with the general. He repeated Tall Bull's request not to visit the village as he feared another massacre.[24] Hancock refused to listen. He had made his decision, and nothing would change it. He told Wynkoop that in the coming days he would do exactly what all his officers expected him to do, mainly "talk war or peace to them, as they may elect."[25] Finished with Wynkoop, Hancock said his army would march at 7:00 A.M.

At the specified time Wynkoop set out with Hancock's army. "I accompanied the column for the purpose of subserving the interests of my department by looking after the interests of the Indians of my agency as far as lay in my power."[26] Jesse Leavenworth, the Kiowa-Comanche agent, also joined the military advance.

During the day several Cheyennes approached the soldiers and sought out Wynkoop. They spoke of "their fear of the result of the expedition— not fearful of their own lives or liberty . . . but fearful of the panic which they expected to be created among their women and children upon the arrival of the troops."

Intent upon halting the soldiers' advance, warriors set the prairie on fire twenty-one miles from Fort Larned, filling the sky with black smoke. The ploy failed, for Hancock simply halted his command, crossed the Pawnee Fork, and resumed his march. That afternoon the general camped twenty-three miles from the fort.[27]

After the military set up camp, Pawnee Killer and several Oglala warriors rode into the bivouac. Announcing that he camped with the People, he sought out Wynkoop and said his band intended to join the Southern Cheyennes in seeking peace. Wynkoop believed him.[28] White

Horse and several Dog Soldiers also visited the soldier camp. Hancock invited the Indians to spend the night. They accepted, saying that the other headmen would arrive early next morning.[29]

But this was lip service and nothing more. Wynkoop knew the headmen would not come, as did Agent Leavenworth. The Indian headmen and their people feared the methodically advancing white juggernaut. Women and children whimpered in fear—would the soldier army rape them, hack them to pieces? The warriors were just as worried; everyone knew what had happened at Sand Creek. The soldier chief had threatened their headmen the previous night, a prairie fire had not stopped him, and now the soldiers were closing in on them.[30]

Early the morning of April 14 Pawnee Killer said he would hurry his brothers to the soldier camp to talk and rode out, never to return. When Cheyenne and Sioux leaders did not appear, tempers flared. However, before Hancock ordered an advance, Bull Bear rode into the camp at 9:30 A.M. and said that the Indian headmen were on their way.[31]

Reporter Stanley wanted to see a war and write about it. He quickly sided with the military. "In flagrant violation of treaties solemnly entered into in 1866 with the Government [meaning the signatures Wynkoop obtained on the updated 1865 treaty], the chiefs of the hostile tribes have commenced their depredations on the settlers in the Platte valley. . . . The Indians must be compelled to learn that treaties are not to be trampled upon with impunity."[32]

By midmorning Hancock had lost his patience. The general was not alone; Wynkoop's patience had also reached the breaking point. Hancock had told him that he would "defer to me certain matters connected with the Indians of my agency."[33] Wynkoop considered himself the expert on the Cheyennes and yet Hancock consistently refused to listen to him. Angry, concerned, and frustrated, Ned Wynkoop made no effort to hide his feelings. Reporter Stanley saw this and referring to both Wynkoop and Leavenworth, stated: "The General commanding has been very kind and courteous to the agents, but everything that he has done, so far, has been met by them with acrimonious censure."[34] By this time Wynkoop had long passed the point of caring what anyone thought. Knowing if he did not stop Hancock's advance the Indians would panic and run, he again told the general not to close on the village.

Hancock refused to listen. Shortly after 11:00 A.M. Wynkoop watched as the column resumed its march. A persistent wind whistled over the prairie. Battle-ready—something Wynkoop realized—the trains traveled in three columns, the infantry in-line, the cavalry covering the flanks. The army had only traveled a mile when it reached a small hill. It was just noon and the command slowly began to climb it. Hancock led the portion of the command that reached the crest first. Upon seeing what Custer called a "wild fantastic battle array, which extended far to our right and left and not more than half a mile in our front," the general halted.[35] Those following quickly clustered behind him.

Between three and four hundred Cheyenne and Sioux warriors halted their line of march in the valley below and shouted obscenities at the soldiers. Most of the warriors rode ponies, others walked. "[S]ome of them gaily dressed," Captain Albert Barnitz (Seventh U.S. Cavalry) wrote his wife Jennie, "with flaming red toggery and scarlet blankets, displaying their burnished lances &c. &c."[36] Custer, ever the warrior, wrote that "we witnessed one of the finest and most imposing military displays, prepared according to the Indian art of war, which it has ever been my lot to behold. It was nothing more nor less than an Indian line of battle drawn directly across our line of march; as if to say: thus far and no farther."[37]

As soon as the initial shock of the sudden confrontation passed, Hancock ordered his officers to form battle lines. The infantry and artillery hustled into position while the cavalry drew sabers and galloped forward. Wynkoop looked about. The soldiers surrounding him appeared nervous, anxious, eager. Looking down at the Indian battle line, he undoubtedly remembered Big Timbers in 1864 and his own confrontation, which had come within a heartbeat of combat. Black Kettle had ridden between the lines that day and prevented violence, but today the chief was not present. Hancock's army faced Bull Bear and Tall Bull as well as Roman Nose and Pawnee Killer. These men were not proponents of peace, and would fight to protect their families. An explosion seemed inevitable. Wynkoop knew what he saw: "The whole command presented such an appearance as I have seen just prior to the opening of an engagement."[38]

The warriors halted their advance, shocked at the massive size of the soldier army. While mounted warriors fought to control their nervous ponies, some of the warriors on foot retreated. Chiefs, fully expecting the white men to charge, rode before their warriors, yelling for them hold firm and prevent the hated white men from reaching the village and killing their families. Defying the soldiers, warriors shouted as they waved their weapons in defiance.[39]

Tension froze the scene into a tableau of hatred and fear. One spark could ignite it. Wynkoop understood the moment, knew he had to act. Instinctively he sensed that bloodshed might be avoided if his wards knew he was present. Yelling for Guerrier, he rode to Hancock and hastily explained the situation. This time, the general listened. Wynkoop asked permission to ride between the lines, saying he could calm the situation if given the chance to speak with the headmen. Hancock acquiesced.

Jerking his mount about, Wynkoop galloped into the valley toward the screaming line of warriors, Guerrier beside him. As they approached the Indians they slowed their pace. A group of leaders rode toward them, swallowing them up about two hundred yards from the soldier line. Heavily armed, the Indians had their bows strung and their arrows ready for use. Wynkoop knew he was putting himself at risk.[40] The Cheyennes were angry and suspicious, and he knew that memories of Sand Creek made them "bitter against the whites," even though most of the people in this village had not lost their homes and loved ones in 1864.[41] Black Kettle trusted Wynkoop, believed him, and made it known that the agent should not be blamed for 1864. Yet others held him responsible for that disaster, and must have wondered if he had brought the soldiers to destroy *their* homes.

Uncertain what would happen, Wynkoop felt a sense of relief when he realized that some of Indians surrounding him were happy to see him, "saying that now they knew everything was all right, and they would not be harmed."[42]

But he had not resolved anything.

As he talked to the chiefs through Guerrier, Wynkoop saw Roman Nose riding back and forth in front of the line of warriors screaming for them to fight. Knowing he had to defuse the war leader's antagonism before his men reached the point of no return, he took Guerrier and rode toward the warrior. Painted and ready to fight, Roman Nose wore an officer's uniform and a buffalo-skull cap with a lone horn and trailing feathers. Armed with his bow and arrows, a Spencer carbine, and four revolvers, he was a one-man arsenal. Wynkoop told him no one would be hurt if his warriors did not attack.

While Wynkoop and Guerrier spoke with Roman Nose, Bull Bear left the soldiers and joined the headmen who had spoken with the agent:

Dog Men White Horse and Medicine Wolf; Ohméséheso Gray Head; Oglalas Pawnee Killer, Little Bear, Bad Wound, Tall Bear, Little Bull, Left Hand, and The Bear That Walks Under The Ground. Bull Bear echoed Wynkoop's words that no one would be harmed. But the chiefs knew differently, telling Bull Bear that Roman Nose boasted that he would kill the soldier chief.

Wynkoop and Guerrier persuaded Roman Nose to listen to reason, and the three of them rode to the group of headmen. Upon their arrival the talk centered on what the Indians should do. Somehow Wynkoop convinced the headmen that the army meant them no harm, and they agreed to talk with the soldier chief. Roman Nose fashioned a makeshift white flag. Then Wynkoop led everyone toward the soldiers. Hancock and his officers, including Custer and Colonel A. J. Smith (Seventh U.S. Cavalry), who actually commanded the Seventh, rode down the hill, and the two sides met between the lines.[43]

Hancock did not waste time, saying if the Indians came to fight, he was ready to commence.[44] Roman Nose answered by saying that he would not have come this close to the soldier guns if he came to fight. He then reached out and touched Hancock's face, counting coup. Turning to Bull Bear, he told him to return to the warrior line. He intended to kill the soldier chief and did not want him to die when he did it. The coup must have been a light touch, for Hancock had no idea what had happened and Wynkoop did not comment on it. Nevertheless Bull Bear immediately grabbed the bridle from Roman Nose's hand and led him from the group. Surprisingly, Roman Nose did not argue. Bull Bear acted to protect the People, not to save his friend's life. He feared that if Roman Nose murdered the soldier chief the military would massacre the village.

Unexpectedly Hancock's main concern became the wind; he did not want to talk while exposed to it. He told the headmen he intended to move closer to their village, then insisted upon a second meeting after the army pitched camp. Wynkoop watched the Indians agree to the general's demand.

The meeting ended and the leaders rejoined their respective battle lines. While the Indians hustled toward their village, Hancock and his army followed them. With Roman Nose safely out of the way, Bull Bear chose not to return to the village. Instead he lagged behind and sought out Wynkoop, who fortunately traveled with perhaps his most important companion during the expedition, Edmund Guerrier. As they rode, Bull Bear told the agent he did not want the soldiers close to his village. Wynkoop said he understood and would do what he could. After Bull Bear left, Wynkoop waited for a halt in the march before approaching Hancock. He repeated Bull Bear's request, then added, "I [fear] the result [will] be the flight of the women and children."[45]

Hancock refused to change his plans or halt the advance. His goal was the village and he had every intention of reaching it. The command marched another seven miles before halting that afternoon. The military set up camp on the Pawnee Fork one mile from the village (Wynkoop placed it 300 yards off, but must have referred to its distance after the army moved closer). Barnitz described the pastoral setting: "On our left the wooded stream, beyond which at the distance of a mile or two are the bluffs—on our right a mile or two off, rolling swells of the prairie, and on our right front, by a little belt of timber, is the Indian (Cheyenne) encampment."[46] The village consisted of 132 Cheyenne lodges and 140 Sioux lodges.

The panic that had begun when the warriors brought news that soldiers came reached fever pitch when the *vi'ho'i* army appeared and set up camp. Frightened women frantically packed their ponies. Then, as Wynkoop expected, they grabbed their children and abandoned their homes.

Those in the soldier bivouac who watched could see the frenetic activity in the village, and it quickly became obvious that Indians were fleeing. As soon as Hancock heard of the exodus he exploded with anger. This concerned Wynkoop. Worried over what Hancock might do, he told the general that his actions "terrified the squaws and children."[47] Livid, Hancock threatened to destroy the village, to which Wynkoop responded with a warning that he would have an Indian war on his hands. With darkness closing in, Hancock needed to act and sent a runner (most likely Guerrier) to the village to insist that the chiefs explain why their families left.

Tall Bull, Roman Nose, and Bull Bear talked over their options before they rode with other leaders to the soldier camp. Night had fallen by the time they arrived and made their way to Hancock. As he had during the previous meetings, the general did not waste time with pleasantries. He wanted to know why the women and children ran. Ignoring the question, Roman Nose asked if white women and children were more timid

View from the south and above part of the Southern Cheyenne encampment at the
Cheyenne-Sioux village on the Pawnee Fork in Kansas. Along with trees, the cutbacks in
the river, combined with the erosion of the land from the flow of river that terraced it,
made the location a favorite Cheyenne campsite, even after Maj. Gen. Winfield Hancock
ignored Wynkoop's protests, burned the village on April 19, 1867, and ignited an Indian
war. The village site was blessed by Southern Cheyenne chiefs Lawrence Hart and Gordon
Yellowman on April 24, 1999. Thanks to Historian Leo Oliva's leadership the site was
added to the National Register of Historic Places on June 17, 2010. Photograph © 1999
by Louis Kraft.

than men. Hancock did not bother to answer, and Roman Nose pressed
on. He wanted to know why Sand Creek had happened. Instead of answering, Hancock demanded that Roman Nose and Bull Bear "bring
their women and children back," that "he considered [their leaving] an
act of treachery."[48] By this time the Sioux had also begun to abandon
the village. Their mounts too weak to travel, Bull Bear and Roman Nose
rode after their families on horses Hancock loaned them.

After the Indians left, Wynkoop spent several restless hours wondering
what might happen. Then, about 11:00 P.M., Guerrier, who had been in
the village but did not rush to return to the soldier camp, appeared with
the borrowed horses. He told Hancock that not only did the chiefs fail

to catch their families, but Cheyenne warriors were now fleeing the village.[49]

Hancock summoned Custer and ordered him to capture the village. With the camp alive as troops prepared for battle, the general sent for Wynkoop, and after updating him he asked the colonel what he thought of Custer's orders. "If there [a]re only two men found there," Wynkoop said, "when they s[ee] the cavalry they would have a fight," to which Hancock replied: "it matter[s] not."[50]

As ordered, Custer surrounded and then warily invaded what turned out to be an empty village. "Dogs half eaten up, untanned buffalo robes, axes, pots, kettles, and pans, beads and gaudy finery, lately killed buffalo, and stews . . . cooked in . . . kettles, [everything] scattered about promiscuously, strewing the ground," Henry Stanley wrote.[51] Although it was obvious to anyone who looked that the Indians had left as quickly as possible, reports varied. Custer found several people in the village; an old Sioux warrior with a broken leg, whose wife may have remained with him; White Horse's demented mother; and a girl who might have been as young as eight or as old as twelve and could have been blind in one eye. Her discovery initiated a controversy about her race. Was she white, mixed-blood, or Cheyenne? Hancock claimed that she told him she had been raped by a young Cheyenne warrior. Others claimed she was an idiot. All agreed she had been raped, and if she was violated as often as some claimed, it might account for her incomprehensible babbling.[52]

As soon as he heard that most of the reports stated the little girl was white and had been raped by Indians, Wynkoop spoke up. "That she was white is false, that she was ravished is correct. She was found after the camp was occupied by the troops, and the question in my mind is still, by whom was this outrage committed? If by her own race, it is the first instance I have any knowledge of."[53]

The situation now critical, Wynkoop refused to go to bed. Instead he kept after Hancock, as Jesse Leavenworth put it, "exerting himself all he can in the line of his duty."[54] Wynkoop tried to convince the general that the Cheyennes were innocent of any wrongdoing, but Hancock refused to listen, and at 2:00 A.M. said "that he intended to burn the village [the] next morning, as he considered [the Indians] had acted treacherously towards him, and they deserved punishment."[55]

Wynkoop told Hancock he believed the destruction of the village "would have a bad effect upon the Indians generally, . . . [and] would probably cause other tribes whom we wish to see to fly from us."[56] If he burned the village, Wynkoop told Hancock, "I am fully convinced that the result would be an Indian outbreak of the most serious nature, while at the same time there is no evidence in my judgment that this band of Cheyennes are deserving this severe punishment."[57] When Hancock did not reply, Wynkoop changed directions and told the general that the Cheyennes ran because of "fear alone. . . . Your movement toward the village terrified them."

Wynkoop had lost, and he knew it. With Hancock shutting him out and knowing he had to do something, he left the general and looked for Colonel A. J. Smith. When he found him, Wynkoop implored Smith to talk Hancock out of burning the village. After Wynkoop left, Smith found the general and told him he did not think he should burn the camp.[58]

Unwilling to give up, Wynkoop returned to his tent and wrote a letter of protest to Hancock. He outlined the day's events, told Hancock what he thought he should do, and then predicted war if the general ignored his advice.[59] Next, Wynkoop wrote to Nathaniel Taylor, who had replaced Lewis Bogy as commissioner of Indian Affairs, predicting that Hancock would ignite an Indian war.[60]

Wynkoop had become a thorn in Hancock's side, and although the general ignored him, Wynkoop initially won. Hancock did not burn the village the next morning.

As the Cheyennes and Sioux fled across the prairie they split into small groups, making pursuit almost impossible for Custer, whom Hancock ordered after them. Unable to catch his foe and frustrated with his initiation to Indian warfare, Custer agreed with Wynkoop. "The hasty flight of the Indians . . . convinces me that they are influenced by fear alone," he reported on the night of April 16, "and . . . that no council can be held with them in the presence of a large military force."[61]

Everyone in the military camp was waiting for Custer's next report. Wynkoop found this interval excruciating as he waited in vain for an answer from Hancock.

On April 17 Custer reached Lookout Station. After studying the burned ruins and the mutilated remains of the employees, he accused the Cheyennes of the murders.[62] This report would have dire consequences.

That day, Hancock sent Wynkoop's formal protest to Sherman, stating he had not replied to Wynkoop, "and probably will not make any

U.S. Indian Agent Ned Wynkoop with Dick Curtis, one of the interpreters traveling with
Maj. Gen. Winfield S. Hancock's army when it approached the Cheyenne-Sioux village on
the Pawnee Fork in Kansas in mid-April 1867. Theodore R. Davis artwork, *Harper's Weekly*
(May 11, 1867). Author's collection.

at all—certainly not before I leave this place."[63] Then, discussing the
problem of the deserted village, Hancock made a telling statement. "We
have evidently frightened these Indians badly," he said. Wynkoop's warnings had taken hold, and Hancock realized that the destruction of one
or both village circles would ignite war. Nevertheless, before he heard
from Custer, Hancock issued a special field order. "As a punishment for

the bad faith practiced by the Cheyennes and Sioux who occupied the village at this place, and as a chastisement for murders and depredations committed since the arrival of the command at this point by the people of these tribes, the village recently occupied by them, which is now in our hands, will be entirely destroyed."[64]

Hoping to prevent the destruction, Wynkoop hounded Hancock, but his words carried little weight when Custer's April 17 report arrived, causing Hancock to ignore Wynkoop, whom he now considered little more than a nuisance. Hancock concluded "that war has begun."[65] He now had justification for his premature April 17 order to destroy the village, and, without fully considering the consequences, issued a second order to destroy all the Indians' property. On April 19 Hancock refused to listen to Wynkoop and burned both villages.

While Hancock destroyed the Indians' property, Seventh Cavalry troops under the command of Major Wickliffe Cooper came upon six Cheyennes who were on foot and "skulking" near the Cimarron Crossing of the Arkansas River in Kansas. Reportedly they attempted to steal horses from a stage station near the crossing, but failed, and in a running fight were shot and killed. After examining the corpses, Cooper proclaimed that the dead rode the war path and were probably spies. The deceased had between them one carbine, one pistol, two bows, and arrows.[66]

Additional findings changed Custer's opinion. He now concluded that the murders at Lookout Station had been committed prior to the flight of the Cheyennes. But his April 19 report arrived too late to save the village.[67] War had returned to the prairie.

After the destruction of the Pawnee Fork village, as Hancock marched to Fort Dodge, a livid Wynkoop refused to back off. For him the fight had just begun. Convinced that Hancock had manufactured an Indian war, he refused to remain silent. "This whole matter is horrible in the extreme," Wynkoop yelled as soon as he heard news of the fight on the Cimarron Crossing.[68] And this was just the opening salvo.

After arriving at Fort Dodge, Wynkoop had his hair and mustache trimmed. On the night of April 22 it snowed, changing to rain April 23. That day Hancock met with Kiowa leaders Kicking Bird, The Man that Moves, and Stumbling Bear in a Sibley tent at his camp near Fort Dodge. Dressed in an officer's uniform, Wynkoop joined Kiowa Agent Jesse Leavenworth, Colonel A. J. Smith, two other officers, and Dick

Theodore R. Davis's woodcut of Maj. Gen. Winfield Hancock's meeting with the Kiowas near Fort Dodge, Kansas, on April 23, 1867 (*Harper's Weekly,* May 25, 1867). Interpreter Dick Curtis is standing at the lodgepole. To the right of Curtis, white-haired U.S. Indian Agent Jesse Leavenworth (wearing his colonel's uniform) sits on the ground. Hancock sits on a box at the far right. He is looking at Wynkoop, who sat across from him and glared at him during the entire meeting. Wynkoop, who had his hair cut at Fort Dodge, also wore his uniform per an 1866 army ruling that officers who served during the Civil War could wear the uniform of their highest brevet rank and be addressed by that rank after they left the military. *Harper's Weekly* erroneously stated the meeting occurred on April 24. Author's collection.

Curtis, who translated. Wynkoop sat on a folding stool across from Hancock who sat on a box. Although he did not take part in the council, he made his presence known by staring at Hancock and listening to everything the general said about the Cheyennes.[69] "We do not come here to make war upon the Indians," Hancock began, "but to confirm the good feelings of those who are friendly toward us."[70] Continuing, he said, "We come, however, to fight those who wish to have war with us." He then spent half the council telling the Kiowas how harshly he treated the Cheyennes and Sioux, and what he did to the Pawnee Fork village. Hancock told them to avoid the Cheyennes, then offered the Indians "the same pay as our soldiers, horses, guns, blankets, &c." to scout for the military.

Kicking Bird said his people wanted to remain at peace, but needed to speak with Satanta, Lone Wolf, and other Kiowa leaders before they could make a decision. The chief then asked about seeing Black Kettle, who was in the south, and Hancock warned him to stay away from all Cheyennes. Before the council ended, Kicking Bird attempted to secure clothing for his people, but Hancock declined, saying he could only supply clothes for warriors who "enlist as guides and scouts."

Next Hancock told Wynkoop that he wanted to speak with the Arapahos. Wynkoop sent runners to tell Little Raven that the soldier chief wanted to talk with him.[71] No longer able to deal with Hancock, he left abruptly for Fort Larned, arriving by April 24.

At this time Wynkoop wondered about Hancock's competency. Although the general claimed he could not tell one village from the other, his inspector general distributed an inventory that listed in detail the property in both villages.[72] On April 24 Wynkoop submitted his own inventory of everything destroyed in the Cheyenne and Sioux village sites.

While Hancock dominated his time, Wynkoop continued to be plagued by money problems. Finally a communication arrived that stated that his bond had been accepted and his commission approved. The farce had finally ended. Wynkoop updated Commissioner Taylor on the current state of affairs, then said that if the Interior Department moved quickly it could stop Hancock from forcing a war. He then dealt with an ongoing personal problem that had become unacceptable. "I have not received any funds since entering upon my duties as Indian Agent[,] that I am sadly in want of the same, and have made repeated applications."[73]

News of war spread quickly. Little Raven, fearing his people would become involved in it, jumped at Wynkoop's invitation. He arrived at Fort Dodge with several chiefs and warriors on April 28. With Wynkoop absent, he met with Hancock that day, professing his love of whites, his people's avoidance of the Cheyennes and Sioux, and his desire to remain at peace. Little Raven pleased Hancock when he said that commissioners in Washington had named him chief of all the Arapahos.[74] The general wanted to hold one chief, and only one, responsible for an entire tribe. Hancock offered to make him a scout for the military—the same offer he had made to the Kiowas—but Little Raven declined.

As the tragic days of April drew to a close, Thomas Murphy agreed with Wynkoop. "Hancock's expedition," he wrote Commissioner Taylor, "has resulted in no good . . . [and] has been productive of much evil."[75]

By May, Wynkoop had scouts scouring the countryside for information. James Morrison, who did not work for him, but wanted a job, moved freely among the Southern Cheyennes and Arapahos on the Washita River. Morrison reported that Arapaho Big Mouth claimed he would not go to war and would move his people anywhere Wynkoop wanted. Morrison also told the agent that the Indians were starving and feared what the whites would do to them. Wynkoop decided it would be best if the Indians traveled to Fort Larned to obtain supplies. When he told Murphy this, the superintendent instructed him to travel to the Washita and tell the Cheyennes and Arapahos that soldiers were warring against Indians between the Platte and the Arkansas rivers and that they would be safe as long as they kept their treaty pledges.[76]

In early June, Wynkoop, who had again been in the field, hurried back to Fort Larned. He claimed he needed to obtain annuities for his wards who remained at peace, but this was a half truth at best. History had repeated itself. He had guaranteed the safety of a village only to see it destroyed, and knew that he would once again be blamed. He returned to Fort Larned because the threat of violence was real, and it would have been foolhardy to remain in the land of the Cheyennes.[77]

Certain the military had fabricated a war, Wynkoop vented his anger in his reports to Washington. "General Hancock has declared war upon the Cheyennes, and ordered all to be shot who make their appearance north of the Arkansas or south of the Platte Rivers. The question is, what have these Indians done to cause such action?"[78] As he had done in 1865, Wynkoop pointed out every inconsistency in the emerging war. When Hancock used Custer's erroneous April 17 report that eight hundred Pawnees, Cheyennes, and Sioux crossed the Smoky Hill road on April 16, Wynkoop observed, "[It] is well known by every man who has the least knowledge of Indian affairs in this country, that the Pawnees are the hereditary enemies of the Cheyennes and Sioux, and war has always existed between them."[79]

Wynkoop likened Hancock's handling of the entire affair to Sand Creek, that is, igniting a war by destroying a peaceful village. Relentlessly, he criticized Hancock's burning of the village. Initially Hancock claimed he could not tell one village circle from the other, then allowed the release of what each campsite contained, belying his lack of knowledge of the village contents. "We then burned their village and destroyed every thing in it except some lodges," Hancock had bragged to the Kiowas on April 23. "We have 'Bull Bear's' tent and that of 'Roman Nose.'"[80] Not wanting this information buried, Wynkoop spoke up. Defending himself, Hancock said, "I can only say that the villages stood upon the same ground, and I was unable, after an inspection which I made in person, to distinguish with any certainty the lodges of the Cheyennes from those of the Sioux; nor could any of the officers who were with me say positively where the line of separation between the village commenced, although it was understood that the Sioux were on the north side, and the Cheyennes on the southern and eastern sides."[81] He failed to mention his trophies and inventory.

But Wynkoop's revelations had little effect. On June 20, 1867, Superintendent Murphy wrote Commissioner Taylor that the Cheyennes north of the Platte were guilty and deserved punishment while the Indians south of the Arkansas had tried to avoid war and should be protected.[82]

While holding firm to his beliefs and desperate to protect the people he considered innocent, Wynkoop faced a major roadblock. Military operations now cut him off from all communication with his wards. They also stopped him from investigating personal-loss claims against the Indians. This bothered Murphy, who insisted Wynkoop press the John Prather and Hugo Wedeles claims when he again distributed annuities.[83]

Although the growing war dominated Wynkoop's days, it was not his only concern. He had still not secured suitable housing, an office, and a storeroom, the necessities to function as agent at Fort Larned. Learning that he could rent dwellings from the post sutler, Wynkoop acted quickly and negotiated with trader Theodore Weichselbaum and his new partner John E. Tappan, who charged him $100 per month for his combined living quarters/office and the storeroom.[84] Tappan had been the assistant adjutant general Wynkoop communicated with two years earlier. Coming into close contact with each other at Fort Larned, they became friends, a friendship that grew as the years passed.

Weichselbaum, who became the post's trader in 1860, erected a stone-and-plaster sutler's store in 1863. Just outside the perimeter of the post, it stood behind (that is, southwest of) officer's row, near a bend in the

Pawnee River. Weichselbaum also built a wood-frame mess hall. Two years later he built a stone-and-plaster frame structure that served as a residence. Surrounded by a picket fence and garden, the sixteen-and-a-half-by-thirty-and-a-half-foot building also had a cellar with additional rooms, four doors, four windows, and a pantry.[85] Wynkoop moved from his dismal quarters into Weichselbaum's building. Captain Albert Barnitz, who would soon visit Wynkoop, described the agent's home: "His parlor is in a little building of board. . . . His library contains some valuable and entertaining books, and his walls are hung with photographs and Indian trophies."[86]

Although a stone blockhouse had been erected in 1864, and the re-building of Fort Larned had begun two years later, a good portion of the buildings were still dilapidated, insect-ridden adobe and wood-framed structures. Some soldiers lived in dugouts cut into the banks of the Paw-nee. By 1867 the rotting buildings were being torn down and replaced with sandstone structures.[87]

As July began, some of the Southern Cheyennes congregated south of the Arkansas River, but Wynkoop had no contact with them, for the war made travel dangerous. He knew that Southern Cheyennes blamed him for the destruction of their homes. Although he felt that many of his wards had not "engaged in hostilities," he knew that eventually they would be attacked and forced "to make war in self-defense."[88]

To defend themselves the Southern Cheyennes and their allies in-creased their raiding. The land between the Arkansas and Smoky Hill rivers all the way to the South Platte became a war zone.[89] As the con-flict increased, Wynkoop tried to find a way to protect the nonwarring Indians from the might of the American military. Preventing a repeat of Sand Creek remained his primary concern. "I therefore consider it of the utmost importance that these Indians should be separated," he proposed, "and those whom I can vouch for, as friendly[,] be brought under protection, while the campaign is . . . carried on against those who deserve punishment."[90]

Now Wynkoop had yet another problem to deal with, one just as pressing as securing lodging. He needed supplies for himself and his family. Isolated at Fort Larned, and unable "to procure necessaries of life" from the fort's commissary, he asked Thomas Murphy to ask the Secretary of the Interior "to procure me the said privilege from the War Department."[91] Murphy quickly forwarded Wynkoop's request.

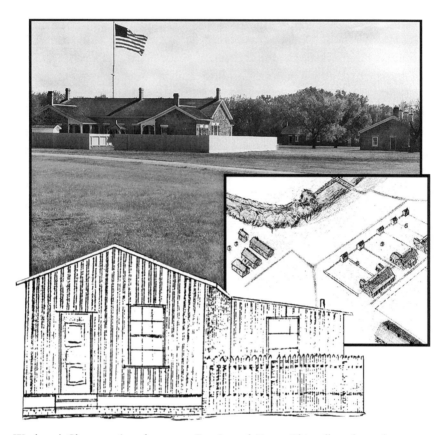

Wynkoop's Cheyenne-Arapaho agency, Fort Larned, Kansas. This collage shows the wooden sutler residence (foreground; drawing shows eastern side of building) that Wynkoop rented from Fort Larned post trader Theodore Weichselbaum, who charged him $100 per month (the price also included a storeroom); the location of the residence in relation to Officer's Row as seen in a detail of Bonita Oliva's sketch of the fort; and a photograph of the southernmost officer's residence. The three larger buildings on the left of Oliva's sketch represent the Sutler's residence (smallest building of the three), the Sutler's mess hall, and the Sutler's Store. The fence on the residence Wynkoop rented attached to the Sutler's mess hall. The Sutler's buildings were outside the western perimeter of the fort and just below a curve in the Pawnee River (as shown in Oliva's sketch). The Plans for Wynkoop's quarters still exist. Photograph © 2004 by Louis Kraft; drawing of Sutler's residence courtesy of Fort Larned National Historic Site (Kansas); detail of map of Fort Larned © Bonita Oliva 1982.

Wynkoop had first written to Murphy about his housing situation back in June but had received no reply. When he had moved into the residence and needed vouchers to pay the rental fees, he again contacted his superior. This time he submitted his budget for the third and fourth quarters of the year. Murphy agreed to most of what he required: $1,000 for annuities, $750 for his salary, $200 for an interpreter, and $100 for contingencies. However, Murphy bulked at paying $600 rent for the storehouse and office. The fight for the storehouse became an ongoing battle as Wynkoop continued to defend the rental fees.[92]

The problem of lodging went hand-in-hand with Wynkoop's effort to secure food for his family from the Fort Larned commissary. After another month passed with nothing happening, he again forwarded his request. This time his superiors sent it on to Secretary of the Interior O. H. Browning, who forwarded it to Edwin M. Stanton, the Secretary of War. Stanton rejected the request as Wynkoop was not a member of the military.[93]

Sensing that his fate was precariously linked with that of his wards, on August 13 Ned Wynkoop wrote to Thomas Murphy. His job entailed contact with the Indians, and to succeed he had to deal with them either in person or via people in his employ. "[T]he Arapahoes, Cheyennes, and Apaches, are in a nomadic state, which renders it impossible for the business of my agency to be carried on with the same regularity as those agents who have their Indians on reservations quietly settled down."[94] Although Wynkoop carefully avoided using the word "war," he admitted he had been "discouraged" when he assumed his current position in 1866, but "persevered." His wards "complained of the government not having fulfilled its promises to them, and of numerous impositions practiced upon them by the whites, which complaints I am compelled to admit were correct." In a rare admission, he confessed that "some of their young men, thinking they had been badly treated, started out and committed some depredations."

Wynkoop was good at what he did, and more important, liked doing it. But now, with the Cheyennes waging war, he knew his future hung in the balance. Needing to validate his existence and paycheck, Wynkoop clarified exactly what he did. "I remain constantly in the Indian country and will continue to do so, and exert myself to further the public interests as long as I hold the position I now occupy.

Louise Wynkoop with her first son, Edward Estill Wynkoop. The image dates to 1867 or 1868 when Wynkoop's Upper Arkansas Indian Agency was headquartered at Fort Larned, Kansas. Denver Public Library, Western History Collection, by E. E. Henry, Call Number F-11480.

CHAPTER THIRTEEN

Hope and Discontent

"I believe . . . all the Indians who have gone South of the Arkansas," Thomas Murphy said, did so to avoid war.[1] Murphy thought the Indians who chose to remain north of the Platte should be punished. Ned Wynkoop disagreed, fearing that war would again result in the slaughter of innocent people.[2] This time his fears were unjustified. Limping through most of the summer, Hancock's war cost the lives of approximately three hundred citizens and soldiers, "several millions of dollars in expenses, and an immense amount of public and private property."[3] It accomplished nothing.

Luckily for Hancock, on the evening of July 15, 1867, Custer, who found the Indians totally frustrating, began a forced march to see his wife, Elizabeth (Libbie). He found her at Fort Riley on July 19, and she called it that "one long, perfect day."[4] But it cost Custer dearly. Colonel A. J. Smith arrested him for "absence without leave from his command."[5] The charges would grow, eventually including, among others, shooting deserters. Hancock had a scapegoat for his ill-advised campaign. Still, he needed to defend himself, and decided that the best way to do it would be in print. Hancock assembled a number of reports by himself and others and manipulated them so that they justified his actions. The resulting article appeared in the September 7, 1867, issue of the *Army and Navy Journal*. Custer's court-martial began eight days later and resulted in a guilty verdict and his suspension from rank and command without pay for one year.[6]

As fall approached, the government called for another peace council, this time at Medicine Lodge Creek in Kansas. Wynkoop and Murphy left Fort Larned on September 11, 1867, and arrived at the council grounds three days later. Already fourteen hundred Indians had set up camp circles: Kiowas, Comanches, Arapahos, and Plains Apaches. The only Southern Cheyennes present were Black Kettle's band.[7]

Soon after their arrival, Wynkoop and Murphy heard that Stone Forehead had called for a gathering of the Tsistsistas thirty miles to the south on the Cimarron River. The old mystic had proclaimed that it was time to renew the Sacred Arrows. Wynkoop sent runners to invite Stone Forehead and the Cheyennes gathering on the Cimarron to attend the peace talks, but the mystic refused; the sacred ceremony had to be completed first. Stone Forehead may have been the most powerful influence on the central plains, but he did not control Cheyenne warriors. Against his wishes a large war party rode out of the Cimarron village, again accentuating the whites' failure to understand that chiefs only controlled those who followed them.[8]

Wynkoop saw Hancock's *Army and Navy Journal* article at the council grounds and complained bitterly to Murphy.[9] The general made him the villain of the Pawnee Fork fiasco, claiming he had misrepresented the Indians' actions. Over the years Wynkoop had suffered a lot of bad press, but this struck home. Hancock's words did not appear in a frontier newspaper spouting a prejudicial viewpoint but in a military publication.

Hancock had assembled a mix of errors and misstatements that combined effectively to justify his actions at Wynkoop's expense. Hancock began by stating that the reason he led the expedition was because Wynkoop's wards, the Kiowas (an intentional error), threatened whites if they did not vacate their land. The general then claimed Custer's conflicting reports influenced him to burn the village, failing to mention he wanted to burn the village the night the Indians fled. Even though Hancock sanctioned a detailed report of the contents of both villages before he burned them and later bragged that he kept Bull Bear's and Roman Nose's tipis, he continued to state emphatically that he could not tell which village circle belonged to which tribe. Hancock also stuck to his claim that Cheyennes and Sioux rode the war trail with Pawnees. And finally, he stated that at no point during the expedition did he threaten the Cheyennes with war, claiming that war was never his objective. Actions spoke louder than words, and Wynkoop knew that Hancock's actions belied his words. He decided to counterattack in print.

Aware of the lambasting that Hancock had given Wynkoop, William Byers reprinted a letter from the *Leavenworth Conservative* that claimed Wynkoop worked in collusion with Special U.S. Indian Agents W. R. Irwin and Charles Bogy, trader D. A. Butterworth, and the Kiowas to fleece the U.S. government. In the letter, J. Elliott Williams alleged that the Arapahos, Cheyennes, and Plains Apaches only received $1,000 of the $14,000 in goods Wynkoop had distributed to them the previous November. Williams stated that Butterworth sent his wagons loaded with inferior goods south, and Kiowas attacked the train at a prearranged location, took the goods, and sent the wagons back to Butterworth unharmed. The trader then submitted a claim against the loss, which "must bear the certificate of Wyncoop [*sic*]."[10] For his participation in the scam, Wynkoop supposedly received $4,000. Nothing came of the accusation.

Every day more Indians arrived at the meeting ground, as did a stream of wagons packed with supplies and gifts for them. Wynkoop had secured thirty-five wagons at a cost of fifteen dollars each per day to haul the necessities for his wards. He and Murphy watched and listened (particularly to events unfolding on the Cimarron), and although they felt safe, Murphy wrote Nathaniel Taylor that the peace commissioners might appreciate the security of a military escort "in number not exceeding two hundred."[11] Taylor heeded the advice. Along with an additional thirty wagons of supplies, the commissioners employed an escort of three troops (Seventh U.S. Cavalry) along with a battery of Gatling guns (Fourth U.S. Artillery).

Although concerned that most of the Southern Cheyennes might not attend the council, Wynkoop enjoyed seeing old friends, in particular Black Kettle. He spent the evenings with the chief along with George Bent, who impressed him, and Murphy.[12] While the four were at dinner on the night of October 9, Roman Nose and ten warriors raided the camp. Roman Nose blamed Wynkoop for the destruction of the Pawnee Fork village and intended to kill him. Arapahos heard of the war leader's intention and delayed him while a warrior ran to Black Kettle's tipi and warned Wynkoop of the danger. The surprised agent cautiously ducked out of the lodge and saw a "racing horse" tethered behind it. He quickly mounted the animal and "left the village at the very moment Roman

Nose had a revolver drawn on him."[13] Riding for his life, Wynkoop raced back to Fort Larned.

Shortly after Wynkoop's return to Fort Larned, the peace commissioners arrived on October 12. He found them a frightened bunch of men; Southern Cheyennes had burned the prairie in an attempt to stop their journey. Wynkoop, Murphy (who had followed him at a leisurely pace), and peace commissioner General John Sanborn greeted Jesse Leavenworth, John Smith, and three news correspondents, including Henry Stanley, at Wynkoop's residence behind officer's row. Wynkoop led everyone into the room that served as his office and pulled a bottle from his liquor cabinet. At first the talk centered around the efforts of Murphy, Leavenworth, and Wynkoop to get the Indians to the council, then moved to the colonel's escape from Roman Nose. Wynkoop's charm lifted everyone's spirit. Even Stanley, who continued to view him in a less than positive light, said, "The major is a genial soul and a polished gentleman. He is a skillful concoctor of drinkable beverages, and in his company we whiled away a social hour."[14]

In time the talk devolved to a discussion of Hohnecke's beer. Seeing an opportunity to interrupt the chitchat, Wynkoop and Sanborn told everyone that Murphy had arranged for Indian leaders who had come into Fort Larned to accompany the commissioners to Medicine Lodge. Minutes later Wynkoop opened the door and Chiefs Satanta, Little Raven, and Stumbling Bear joined his get-together. When introduced to Stanley, Satanta pulled him into a bear's hug, which impressed the reporter; he wrote that the war chief's "defiant and independent bearing . . . attracted all eyes."[15] Stanley described Little Raven as "a fat, good-natured sachem; one who loves to smoke his pipe peacefully in his lodge, surrounded by dusky concubines."

Charming and knowledgeable Wynkoop may have been. Unfortunately he had a knack for upsetting people. Indians and whites alike often wanted him banished. Just the day before, October 11, Kansas Governor Samuel J. Crawford had demanded that the Indian Bureau replace him. Shortly thereafter Stanley reported, "It is thought best to relieve the major from his agency, as he has lost the confidence of Sioux and Cheyennes, for whom he was agent."[16] To his credit, Commissioner of Indian Affairs Nathaniel Taylor refused to fire Wynkoop.

The next day, Wynkoop, Murphy, the commissioners, and the press left for Medicine Lodge. The group included Senators John B. Henderson

Arapaho chief Little Raven. Unfortunately the image isn't dated, but it appears to be from the reservation years—that is, 1869 or later. Courtesy of the Braun Research Library, Autry National Center of the American West, Los Angeles, A.79.28.

and Edmund G. Ross; Commission Secretary A. S. H. White; Generals Alfred H. Terry, James A. Hardie, and William S. Harney, retired; Commissioner Taylor (acting president of the commission); Samuel Crawford; Samuel Tappan; and, in addition to Henry Stanley, reporters John Howland, *Harper's Weekly,* S. F. Hall, *Chicago Tribune,* H. I. Budd, *Cincinnati*

Gazette, George Center Brown, *Cincinnati Commercial,* Solomon Bulkley, *New York Herald,* and William Fayel, *Missouri Republican,* among others. They reached Medicine Lodge on October 14. During the trip, after seeing bison indiscriminately killed for no reason other than sport, Satanta spoke up. "Have the white men become children," he said, "that they should kill meat and not eat? When the red men kill, they do so that they may live."[17]

By the time the caravan reached the encampment, the whites numbered six hundred, while the indigenous population had exploded to five thousand. Black Kettle told Wynkoop and the commissioners that he heard the Cheyennes might attack. Most of the commissioners and press struggled through a sleepless night.[18]

At twilight on October 15 fifty to eighty chanting and painted warriors appeared across from the commissioners' campsite. Nerves became frayed when the riders urged their mounts into the stream and rode toward the whites. General Harney recognized two of the riders, Tall Bull and Ohméséheso Gray Head, and greeted them. Rumors spread that the Dog Soldiers were fresh from the warpath and only rode into camp to size it up before attacking. Then Gray Head handed a ragged piece of paper to Harney, a letter of safe conduct Harney had written for him back in 1858. Gray Head came in peace. Having a good idea what Wynkoop might say when he testified in two days, Harney invited Tall Bull and Gray Head to attend so they could hear Wynkoop. They said they would return.[19]

Another day passed. Then, on the morning of October 17, the commissioners held an impromptu council. Wynkoop and Leavenworth attended, as did many reporters. About twenty-five chiefs, including Black Kettle and Satanta, and five hundred warriors observed the proceedings. Commissioner Taylor talked about gifts he had to distribute once the tribes signed their treaties. When he said he wanted to delay the start of the council until the Cheyennes arrived, Arapahos, Comanches, Kiowas, and Plains Apaches stated they did not want to wait. After placating the chiefs, Taylor invited them to speak. Satanta said he did not want to talk until the council. "What I say is law for the Comanches," Chief Ten Bears said, "but it takes half a dozen to speak for the Kiowas."[20] Tired of waiting and wanting his annuities, Apache Chief Poor Bear said he would wait four more days and no more. After Satanta spoke again, exciting the crowd but saying nothing, Black Kettle stood. "We were once friends with the whites, but you nudged us out of the way by your intrigues, and now when we are in council, you keep nudging each other. Why don't you talk and go straight, and let all be well?" Afterwards, when others spoke, both Indian and white, Senator Henderson urged Taylor to keep the talks as short as possible.

That afternoon, General Harney began gathering testimony about the causes of the Indian problem and the recent war. As promised Tall Bull and Gray Head reappeared at dusk, this time quietly and without warriors, and the general escorted them to the tent where the commissioners were listening to testimony.[21]

Agent Wynkoop appeared before the commissioners just before nightfall. Viewing his testimony as an opportunity, he began with 1864, pointing out that Governor Evans did not want to meet the Indians at Camp Weld even though they wanted peace. With wounds reopened, Wynkoop said the Indians moved to Sand Creek, and three days after he left Fort Lyon Chivington attacked the village. Knowing that Stanley recorded his words, Wynkoop stated that the massacre ignited a war that still continued.

When Senator Henderson asked about Chivington, Wynkoop replied that at the Camp Weld meeting Chivington said "his business was to kill Indians, and not to make peace with them."[22] He continued, "After Sand Creek the Indians were at war everywhere, mostly on the Platte. Property was destroyed, horses were stolen, and emigrants were killed."

Wynkoop next addressed how whites cheated Indians. "Some annuity goods which Commissioner Goodall bought in New York," he said, "three-point blankets which are used as wrappers, and which were charged in the bill at $13 per pair, were the most worthless things that I ever saw. The Indians told me that they would not have taken those goods from anybody but myself. It was a most shameless affair. They were not only killed, but the friendliest were cheated." Wynkoop's narration of fraud continued. Barrels of sugar were never full, and often less than half full. Other annuities included absolutely worthless articles of clothing, such as white women's bonnets, gaiters, and frilly dresses. The Indians received less than a third of the goods promised them.[23]

Continuing, Wynkoop spoke words no one wanted to hear. "Concerning the disposition of the Sioux, I will state that they were under the impression, previous to the destruction of that Cheyenne village by Hancock, that as the Cheyennes had made peace," they also wanted peace.[24]

When a drunk Cheyenne killed a Mexican near Fort Zarah, Hancock demanded Wynkoop identify the Indian, until General Sherman ordered him to back off. Still "the Indians, generally were satisfied with keeping the peace," Wynkoop said, "and save that murder at Zarah, they had kept it." After Indians ran off stock near Fort Wallace in fall 1866, officers could not fix the blame on "any particular band." Without conclusive proof Hancock blamed the Cheyennes.

Hancock's expedition became Wynkoop's next topic. He spoke about sending for the Cheyennes, the meeting at Fort Larned, the subsequent march to the Pawnee Fork camp, the Indians' flight. "Hancock stated in my presence [at 2:00 A.M.] that he intended to burn the village next morning, as he considered that they had acted treacherously towards him, and they deserved punishment." Wynkoop spoke of his protest to Hancock and the subsequent destruction of the village on April 19.

After mentioning the warriors killed at the Cimarron Crossing, he spoke about the old warrior and girl found in the deserted village, both of whom had died several days after arriving at Fort Dodge. When General Sanborn asked who raped the girl, Wynkoop replied, "I firmly believe that the soldiers ravished the child. It was the conclusion I arrived at when I heard that she was ravished. It is my belief now."

Since attending the council, Wynkoop had spoken with a number of Cheyennes regarding the Pawnee Fork village. "The Cheyennes I have seen lately gave me to understand that the war this summer was in retaliation for the destruction of their village by General Hancock," he said, ending his testimony.

Wynkoop stepped outside the tent and met briefly with Harney, Gray Head, and Tall Bull. He had to have known that the Indians listened to him as they sat next to Harney. Both chiefs had been bitter but were now satisfied with what they heard, and told Wynkoop they did not hold him responsible for the destruction of their homes. William Fayel, reporter for the *Missouri Republican,* watched the conversation, reporting that the Indians and Wynkoop shook hands with warmth and friendship.[25]

Henry Stanley listened to the agent's testimony intently that night. Taking offense at Wynkoop's statements, Stanley refuted what he considered inaccuracies. "War was already declared when Hancock appeared with his army," he wrote, and "the soldiers were not the persons who violated the young girl found at the Cheyenne village."[26]

Stanley's comments set off an avalanche of vitriolic prose in the western press. Quoting the *Kansas Tribune,* on October 29, 1867, the *Daily Colorado Tribune* printed the typical viewpoint of the day: "There seems to be a determination on the part of some men [meaning Wynkoop], who ought to know better, to saddle all the Indian war on the whites, and to ignore the fact of there being trouble long before the Chivington affair or Sand Creek."[27]

As soon as Byers heard of Wynkoop's testimony, he exploded. After exclaiming that everyone in Colorado, except Wynkoop, knew what really happened at Sand Creek, Byers declared that now Hancock had been "attacked by so consummate a thief and a scoundrel is astonishing."[28] Continuing, Byers predicted that reporter Stanley would tell the truth and expose Wynkoop as a liar. "We are able to expect almost any thing from Wynkoop," Byers wrote. "The words and oaths of some men are always worthless, and partially aware of the fact, they tell as large a falsehood as possible. Wynkoop is such a man, and whether he swear to much or little, it is all the same. No one who knows him will believe his word or his oath." Having demolished Wynkoop, Byers sarcastically stated that the Indian Commission would accomplish nothing. They would wine and dine at the government's expense, but when 1868 arrived, the "savages," as the *News* called the Indians, would use U.S.-issue "powder and lead" and once again ride the warpath.

Two weeks later the *News* again called Wynkoop a liar. "Wynkoop, if he wishes to give any more evidence must take care and not have it published, and then no one will know how great a liar he is. Stanley, of the *Democrat* contradicted him[,] General Smith contradicts him, and all Colorado contradicts him. Under such circumstances, Wynkoop will have to go to places where he is not known to be believed. Let the *whole* west spot him."[29]

Soon after shaking Wynkoop's hand, Tall Bull and Gray Head mounted, crossed the creek, and rode to Black Kettle's lodge. Tall Bull insisted Black Kettle ride to the Cimarron village and explain why the Tsistsistas should make another treaty. When Black Kettle hesitated, Tall Bull threatened to kill his ponies.[30]

Teenager Alfred A. Taylor accompanied his father, Commissioner Nathaniel Taylor, to the council. Young Taylor observed much of what happened from a privileged position, aware of his father's views on events and people. He claimed that Wynkoop "was very popular with these tribes [Cheyennes and Arapahos], as well as all neighboring tribes, and his services, from beginning to end, were immensely valuable."[31] Alfred Taylor's words leave little doubt why his father dismissed Kansas Governor Crawford's demand to fire Wynkoop.

After days of waiting for the Cheyennes on the Cimarron to arrive at Medicine Lodge, the council began officially on October 19, and Wynkoop observed the proceedings. "A vast amphitheater had been cleared in the center of a grove of all elms," Stanley recorded. "Logs had been arranged so as to seat the principal chiefs of the southern nations. Tables were erected for the accommodation of the various correspondents. Before these tables were the seats ranged in a semicircle for the commissioners. Facing the commissioners were a few of the most select chiefs of the different tribes.... Above the space allotted to the commissioners and the press were placed boughs to shelter them from the sun."[32] Wearing a general's coat that Hancock had given him, Satanta sat on a camp chair in front of the Kiowa chiefs. The Comanches sat next to the Kiowas, Ten Bears wearing his eyeglasses. Only two Cheyennes attended, Black Kettle and Gray Head. George Bent and brother Charlie sat behind them to interpret. Beside them, Little Raven sat on a stool, and next to him, Arapaho interpreter Margaret McAdams, who wore a crimson dress. Poor Bear, whom Stanley described as "a poor-looking, superannuated warrior," represented the Plains Apaches.[33] The warriors sat behind their chiefs, and behind them the rest of the tribal members.

Taylor introduced Senator Henderson, who spoke of wrongs committed by both sides. Before telling the Indians what the government planned for them, Henderson invited the leaders to speak. Gray Head said that neither he nor Black Kettle could speak for their people. Satanta spoke next. After proclaiming his innocence of any wrongdoing since the 1865 treaty, he said "when I go up to the river, I see a camp of soldiers, and they are cutting my wood down or killing my buffalo. I don't like that, and when I see it, my heart feels like bursting with sorrow."[34] Little Raven damned the Pawnees for stealing some Arapaho ponies (actually, Kaws stole the animals). Ten Bears questioned why his people had to attend the council, as they had not broken any treaties. He would do as told, wanted his annuities, and wanted to go home.

On October 20, 1867, the council continued. Ten Bears said he wanted to die as he had lived. Satanta said he wanted all that was his, then rode off in a huff only to return later. Henderson took center stage, telling the Comanches and Kiowas that the buffalo would soon be gone; they needed to learn how to use the plow and live in white-man houses. He threatened them with war if they refused to move to their new homeland on the Red River near the Wichita Mountains. Henderson concluded by announcing that the treaty would be signed the following morning.[35]

Even though the interpreters did not read the entire treaty, the Comanches and Kiowas touched the paper on October 21. They had given up 60,000 square miles of land in return for 48,000 square miles of land in southwest Indian Territory. The Plains Apaches asked to live with them on their new reservation. The treaty signed, the Indians wanted their gifts, especially the guns. The first guns they received were inferior revolvers that exploded upon firing, prompting the commissioners to replace them immediately with Colts. Hoping to keep matters peaceful, the commissioners distributed the annuities.

Under a black sky and braced against a howling wind, some of the Kiowas began to move off. That night, a driving rain fell. In the wee hours of morning, Little Robe, White Horse, and Gray Head, among others, rode into the encampment from the Cimarron village and woke Black Kettle. They then rode to the commissioners' bivouac and demanded a council with Harney. While waiting, they spoke with a nervous Black Kettle.[36]

Wynkoop joined the commissioners and reporters at the impromptu assembly, and found the Indians short-tempered. After Henderson vented his anger at being awakened, Little Robe snapped that the People also had important meetings. Black Kettle explained that his people still needed four days to complete their Sacred Arrows ceremony. "I give you my word I will not ask you to stay here six or seven or eight days," he promised, then asked both sides to shake hands.[37]

"Bah!" Henderson exploded. "This medicine is all humbug."

"Oh no, it ain't," General Augur replied. "It is life and death with them. It is their religion."

Wynkoop knew the general spoke the truth; he also knew the Cheyennes would not appear until they were good and ready. Aware of threats directed at Black Kettle by his own people, Wynkoop feared for his friend's life. Unfortunately he did not realize that when the chiefs from the Cimarron village left, they would take Black Kettle with them.

As days passed, tension built while Wynkoop and everyone else waited. Sensing the moment right, Little Raven said his people wanted to end their relationship with the Cheyennes, but this drew little response. The morning of October 27 arrived, "a real Indian summer's day... a filmy haze swam in the air," Stanley reported. "Out of the earth issued a vapor, in which distant objects seemed to float and assume monstrous proportions. It was a day which invited rest."[38]

Suddenly runners raced through the camp circles disrupting the calm of midmorning. Cheyennes were coming! Confusion reigned. Women and children shrieked in terror, running to get away from the impending attack.[39] Unsure just what the Tsistsistas intended, warriors retreated to their campsites and prepared for battle.

Fear gripped the white contingent. "[W]e got ready; loaded our rifles, our revolvers, and our derringers," Stanley wrote, "and then awaited their coming with what patience we could command."[40]

An hour passed.

Dust clouds billowed ominously to the south. A bugle call sounded as mounted riders emerged from the trees. Painted warriors shouted as they fired their weapons into the air and in large columns charged across the stream. Neither Stone Forehead nor Roman Nose appeared, but Black Kettle did, "dressed in a dingy shirt and dingier blanket, his long black hair floating behind him like a bashaw's tail."[41] Alive, much to Wynkoop's relief, he galloped toward the commissioners, "his horse covered with foam."[42]

As Cheyenne warriors formed a battle line, Captain Albert Barnitz instructed his men to arm themselves for the impending onslaught. "One portion of the tribe—about a squadron formed in line in front of my camp," Barnitz recorded, "on a little rise of ground about 150 yards distant, and behind them and on their left flank about 200 Arapahos sat on their ponies, with bows strung, and on the other side of camp the Comanches, and Kiowas, and Apaches were out in force."[43] But the Southern Cheyennes did not attack. It was the Moon of the Changing Season. They had completed their Sacred Arrows ceremony, and were ready to hear what the vi'ho' i had to say. Black Kettle spoke with the commissioners.

The day had begun with a haze only to turn clear and bright. Then as the afternoon drifted toward nightfall, clouds blew in and the sky darkened. Before evening arrived Sanborn, using John Smith to interpret, interviewed Gray Head about what happened on the Pawnee Fork. Gray Head described the fear and anxiety when Hancock came upon the Indian battle line, the panic that gripped the village when the military appeared, and the decision to go to war after Hancock destroyed their homes. Sanborn then brought up the subject of the raped Cheyenne girl. "Was she hurt by anyone before you left?" Gray Head said that he knew her as she grew up. "I was the last one that left the village, and she was not hurt then . . . She would not come with us, and we had to leave her there."[44] Although Stanley had constantly confirmed the military point of view on the raped girl, calling Wynkoop a liar, he now blamed the interpreters, whom he claimed "said that the girl captured by the village was either a white or a half-breed."

At 10:00 A.M. on October 28 Wynkoop found a spot at the Grand Council where he could hear. Arapahos (with Little Raven most prominent) and Southern Cheyennes (Black Kettle and Little Robe, among others) and the Dog Soldiers, among them Tall Bull, Bull Bear, White Horse, and Buffalo Chief, gathered at the council grounds dressed in their finest. Little Raven spoke first, saying he wanted to live near Fort Lyon and wanted an honest trader. Surprisingly, when it was the Cheyennes' turn, only little-known Buffalo Chief spoke. He did not waste words. His people would never give up their land between the South Platte and Arkansas rivers. Finally the moment arrived. It was time to touch the treaty paper. No Cheyenne leaders stepped forward to make their X, and the proceedings came to a halt.

Henderson could not conclude the negotiations without the chiefs' marks. The Indians had to move from the contested land. Thinking fast, he assured the leaders their people could hunt buffalo *north* of the Arkansas for as long as there were buffalo. Still not winning the day, he took John Smith and George Bent aside and reiterated the importance of completing the treaty negotiations. Bent understood the urgency and spoke with his brethren.[45]

And Wynkoop watched.

Henderson's promise to the Cheyennes was real, and it included the Arapahos. Everyone heard it, and all the reporters mentioned it in their dispatches. Sherman later issued a general order to the Division of the Missouri stating that Wynkoop's wards could hunt buffalo in the unsettled areas as far north as the South Platte so long as they remained ten miles from a public road or fort.[46]

The major points of the treaty called for the Indians to (1) cease their opposition to the building of a railroad along the Platte River, (2) drop all objections to the building of mail stations, railroads, or roads, (3) cease all aggressive actions against whites, including attacking, killing, scalping, or abducting, (4) leave their homeland and live like white men in Indian Territory, and (5) retain the right to hunt on their former land *south* of the Arkansas (the exact opposite of what Henderson told the Indians).

The Arapahos and Cheyennes made their marks on the treaty. Surprisingly, Wynkoop, who had attested the 1865 treaty, did not attest this treaty.[47] Barnitz, who, like Wynkoop, observed the proceedings, wrote, "*They have no idea that* they are giving up, or that they have ever given up the country which they claim as their own, the country north of the Arkansas."[48] The *New York Times* reported that the Indians agreed to a "voluntary abandonment of the country between the Arkansas and Platte rivers."[49] The agreement was another peace in word only.

Wynkoop had no clue that Henderson's promise would not make it into the ratified treaty. Realizing that George Bent had played a key role in convincing the chiefs to touch the paper, and knowing the importance of trustworthy intermediaries, Wynkoop offered Bent a job.[50]

Immediately after the chiefs touched the treaty paper, Cheyennes and Arapahos ran to two mounds of presents and goods worth $50,000. Chiefs uncovered the piles and their people shouted out in "guttural expressions of pleasure."[51] The chiefs began handing out gifts, which included revolvers and ammunition, beads, axes, camp kettles, bugles, and red blankets. The Indians treasured the blankets and beads, but the guns were their priority. The piles also included frilly dresses, which Wynkoop had already complained about. "Nothing had changed. Many of the gifts would prove useless to the Indians. They might delight in touching them and displaying them, but they would never use them."[52] As soon as the warriors received the revolvers, they loaded them and shot them into the air.

Day dissolved into evening and still the Cheyennes and Arapahos celebrated, firing their guns into the night sky, misting it with smoke as they sang and danced. The celebration lasted until rain pounded the earth. By morning the storm had passed. Black Kettle, Bull Bear, and the other chiefs met one last time with the commissioners before the Indians began to leave for their winter camps, and the commissioners and soldiers prepared to depart.

Before Taylor and Murphy left, Wynkoop walked with them. They had shared an exhilarating and eventful time together, but Wynkoop also ran a business—the Indian agency. Getting what he needed remained an endless challenge. After chatting about the council and what the future might hold, Wynkoop went to work. Ignoring the Indian Bureau's stinginess with funds, he made two requests. He presented Murphy with the estimated cost for four mules ($700), a wagon ($150), and harness ($80) for the agency. He then asked Taylor if he could employ James Morrison as scout, and the commissioner gave his assent.[53] After his employers departed, Wynkoop returned to Fort Larned.

Soon no humans remained at the treaty ground, only piles of trash. The stink of rotting food lured wolves and other predators, who tore into the choicest parts and snarled when a subservient member of the pack or an interloper ventured into forbidden territory. The remnants of what the press proclaimed the "Grand Council" had become a feast for wolves, ruled by survival of the fittest.

. . .

An era had been marked for extinction, although many of the participants did not yet know it. As the days passed the treaty negotiations elicited a variety of reactions, some negative, others positive. "The treaty . . . amounts to nothing, and we will certainly have another war sooner or later with the Cheyennes," Barnitz wrote.[54] *Harper's Weekly* proclaimed the treaty a success, repeating the erroneous promise that the Cheyennes could "hunt on the old reservation, south of Arkansas."[55] Even the white do-gooders in the East sanctioned the agreement. "Thank God!" abolitionist Lydia Maria Child exclaimed. "We have, at last, an Official Document, which manifests something like a right spirit toward the poor Indians."[56] But she and others who praised the treaty did not consider the Indians' culture or religion, their feelings for their homeland, their lifeway.

During this time attacks continued to come Wynkoop's way. Colonel A. J. Smith heard of Wynkoop's testimony before the commissioners and wrote to Commissioner Taylor. The dead raped girl, he claimed, was

white and had been molested by Cheyennes. Although he did not say it
in so many words, he implied that Wynkoop had not done his job, that
he had lied and should be fired.[57]

Back at Fort Larned by October 31, 1867, Wynkoop drafted three
letters to Superintendent Murphy. All required funds that he considered
necessary. Wynkoop followed up on Commissioner Taylor's permission
to hire James Morrison, interchanging "scout" with "interpreter" as both
positions entailed the same duties (living with Indians and reporting
to him). He requested only two mules or horses (dropping the cost to
$400), one wagon ($150), and a harness (reduced to $45) for Morrison's
use. Next, Wynkoop submitted an estimated cost of $3,000 to bring a
delegation of his wards to Washington, a project of his for some time, and
one which Taylor had given permission at the council to explore. Finally,
he submitted the cost of renting thirty-five wagons for fourteen days to
transport the goods for the Indians to Medicine Lodge ($7,350).[58]

December arrived, and the buffalo below the Arkansas remained
plentiful; the Cheyennes and Arapahos had ample food.[59] Kansas settlers again felt secure as peace returned to the land. Governor Crawford,
who eased his demands to have Wynkoop fired, happily anticipated the
new year, proclaiming: "Peace reigned on the borders and throughout
the State."[60] By the beginning of winter many of the Cheyennes and
Arapahos pitched their village circles on the Cimarron and Arkansas
rivers south of Fort Dodge, while the Kiowas, Comanches, and some
Cheyennes camped on the Pawnee Fork west of Fort Larned. As they
prepared for the cold moons, the winter of 1867–68 seemed likely to be
mild. "There was frost during the nights," a pioneer wrote, "and the air
during the early morning would be cold, but each day would dawn the
same, and nearly all winter [the] Kansas prairie was blessed with clear
balmy days. It seemed that Indian summer had come to take the place
of winter."[61]

Beneath the apparent tranquility, the seeds of disruption were germi-
nating. As in the past, the tribal leaders who had made their marks on the
treaty would become little more than pawns whites could blame when
the next outbreak occurred. Not familiar with the pace of Washington
bureaucracy, the Indians waited patiently for the goods promised them.
As in the past, white officials failed to realize that once Indians came
to the conclusion that they had again been duped, they would want to
avenge what they considered a wrong.

Wynkoop's relationship with the Cheyennes remained good, but all was not peaceful. On November 21, 1867, Kaws attacked Southern Cheyennes near Fort Zarah, and his wards suffered five dead and seven wounded to only one Kaw death. As soon as Wynkoop heard of the attack, he warned his superiors that the war between the tribes could escalate as Cheyennes would seek vengeance.

At this time Wynkoop employed a handful of people—some white, others half-white—as his eyes and ears. Without them he could not function, and he fought to retain them. Birth or marriage allowed them to cross the boundaries of two cultures. Fluent in the native dialects, they had access to the world Wynkoop managed but could not totally enter. If Ned Wynkoop possessed any genius in race relations, it was that he knew and trusted people who bridged the gap between whites and Indians.

Edmund Guerrier had proven his worth, and Wynkoop fought to secure a fair wage for his services. Not only did he have to budget for future services, he had to fight for payment of services already performed. He employed Guerrier as "scout &c," a term that could cover a variety of jobs.

Only duplicates of the paperwork detailing Guerrier's services in convincing the Dog Soldiers to attend the Medicine Lodge council existed. Wynkoop was required either to provide a third copy or to certify that he had requested the payment in duplicate and not triplicate before Guerrier received his pay.[62] Wynkoop struggled with the absurdity of such paperwork, which never seemed to end, especially when it came to securing the monies owed his employees.

Feeding his wards was also an ongoing fight. Winter had arrived, and the Indians needed subsistence. Murphy had proposed feeding only the needy ones. But Wynkoop told him no. They all needed food, and if only a portion received supplies, the others would feel slighted, which would cause bad feelings. To ease his job, he asked Murphy to deliver the annuities to where the Indians currently camped, southwest of the head of Bluff Creek.[63]

Timing his journey to coincide with the arrival of the supplies, in early January 1868 Wynkoop visited the Indian camps. When he met them in council, he proposed that they travel to Washington with him to meet the Great Father. During the talks, Wynkoop and the leaders decided that two chiefs from each band should make the trip. But because they were at war with Kaws and Osages in the spring, the chiefs said they could not leave their people.

When Wynkoop returned to Fort Larned on January 7, 1868, he found Thomas Murphy at the post. Addressing Indian-white relations and not tribal relations, Wynkoop shared his optimism with Murphy. "Never has there been a better feeling among the different wild tribes through this section of the country than now exists," he said. "[A]nd I have heard of no instance of the slightest difficulty having taken place since the signing of the treaty."[64]

Although Agent Wynkoop painted a rosy picture, he was uneasy. The Indians did not understand the 1867 treaty. Only portions had been read to them, and what they understood had not happened. They had not been forced to live in white-man houses in a foreign land. More important, they had not received arms and ammunition, which to them were key to the negotiations. Far away, Wynkoop knew the U.S. Senate was still arguing over the treaty wording. Their failure to ratify it in a timely manner was holding up all funding and boded ill for the future.

Wynkoop did not ignore the problem of intertribal relations, which was now interfering with his desire to introduce his wards to President Johnson. The Indians' willingness to visit Washington pleased Murphy; he saw it as "strong evidence of their intention to remain at peace" and avoid war with "whites in the coming Spring as is prophesied by certain parties."[65] But for this to happen, the antagonistic tribes needed to solve their grievances. Wynkoop and Murphy discussed setting up a meeting between Cheyennes, Arapahos, Osages, Kaws, and U.S. officers in the spring. But this did not become high priority for anyone—not Wynkoop, not Murphy, not their superiors. No one realized how much tribal warfare would matter in the not-too-distant future.

Wynkoop and Murphy were not alone in their belief that Southern Cheyennes would not break the peace. If whites "can precipitate a war with the Indians next spring," E. B. Tuttle, post chaplain at Fort Sedgwick (Colorado Territory), forewarned, "they will do it."[66]

As had been true in the past, the government short-changed Wynkoop's wards when it came to distributing promised annuities. On January 21 he spoke to Murphy about buffalo. Plentiful in November and early December, the animals had migrated beyond the land of his wards. He told Murphy that what he said earlier no longer remained true. Now "all the Indians [under his control] required subsistence."[67] He explained that his previous reports were correct when he wrote them, but that buffalo did not stay in one place. He stressed that "the Indians had established their winter camps" and even though they currently had enough "meat, flour, sugar, and coffee," as the buffalo became scarcer, the distribution of weapons, as Wynkoop put it, "if not absolutely necessary to sustain life, is at least necessary for their comfort; and will go a long ways toward healing up the wounds inflicted upon them by our race in the past and has a strong tendency to make them better satisfied in the future." Forever conscious that someone might misconstrue his words, Wynkoop also said, "I made no misrepresentations or had no desire to do so."

The whereabouts of the migrant bands presented constant problems for Wynkoop. Since his duties, including paperwork, kept him close to Fort Larned for long stretches of time, he had to rely on scouts. With Murphy at Fort Larned, Wynkoop again made his case. After reminding the superintendent that Commissioner Taylor authorized him to employ Morrison, Wynkoop said he "considered the necessity great as it enables me to be kept constantly advised of the movements of the Indians and to communicate with them at any time." He handed Murphy an estimate for expenses for the first two quarters of 1868, which included the scout he currently employed. Continuing his pitch, he said, "I consider it necessary in the future in consequence of there being so many bands of the Indians of this agency to have at least two Scouts [as] the different bands [are] scattered over a large extent of territory."[68]

Murphy sometimes supported Wynkoop, but not this time. After considering everything, he agreed to the amount required to pay the scout for services until January 1 ($305), along with paying him for the month of January ($155), but he wanted the scout discharged at the end of the month. Murphy directed Wynkoop "to employ no more Scouts permanently."[69] The government already employed three interpreters in the field, he pointed out, two for the Cheyennes and one for the Arapahos, and they could report the Indians' movements. Wynkoop argued that he had no control over them as they did not report to him. "I cannot see the necessity of keeping Scouts employed at such a large expense to the government," Murphy said, refusing to budge. He then pointed out that once fed, the bands would remain together. Wynkoop disagreed, reminding Murphy that the Indians were nomadic, but to no avail; his opinion would again be ignored. Now even his immediate supervisor turned a deaf ear to what he considered an important matter.

Commissioner Taylor also balked at Wynkoop's requests. In addition to not liking the agent's budget for the first two quarters of 1868, Taylor frowned on the purchase of mules, a harness, and the rental of wagons to transport goods to Medicine Lodge Creek the previous fall. Nevertheless, Taylor issued a requisition for the goods Wynkoop requested amounting to $3,335.10, but this only covered the current year. Securing peace obviously meant nothing now that the treaty had been signed. "Any indebtedness that may have been created on account of such transportation will be adjusted and settled on presentation at this office."[70] Taylor held Wynkoop accountable for the cost. Further, on Murphy's recommendation, Taylor reduced the pay for scouts. Interpreters living with the Indians also saw a reduction of pay. Taylor even reduced the $600 for Wynkoop's living quarters/office and storeroom to $300 for six months. Murphy jumped in, and questioned the $1,000 for "pay of annuity." Making it clear that he wanted to rein Wynkoop in, Murphy now required that the agent explain why he did not file any returns for the fourth quarter of 1866 and the entire year of 1867.

In Wynkoop's view, his superiors were denying him the freedom to perform his duties as he saw fit, and casting aspersions on his honesty and good name. Since his initiation to Indian affairs in 1864, he had always dealt fairly with the Indians. With creditors in Colorado Territory demanding payment of past bills, Taylor and Murphy's dictum did not sit well with him, and again raised the question of his continued employment.[71]

Ever since Wynkoop had become agent to the Cheyennes, he had been periodically queried about Indian depredations. At the beginning of February 1868, Murphy again broached the subject. He was interested in the fate of a Mrs. Ward, who had disappeared during the White Rock massacre on the Republican River in April 1867. Wynkoop denied that she had ever been held captive by his wards, "who are south, nor have they had . . . any such personage a prisoner." He told Murphy that "if the outrage was committed by any portion of the wild tribes, it in all probability has been done by Pawnee Killer's band of Sioux who fled north when driven from their village" on the Pawnee Fork.[72] However, Wynkoop, who also felt that one of the semicivilized tribes might have

committed the abduction, admitted he had discussed the matter numerous times and always received negative responses except once when he
heard that Arapahos and Cheyennes were responsible.

The failure to deliver annuities had not yet caused trouble, and Murphy specified exactly what Wynkoop could dispense to the Indians. Since
the distribution would not be what the Indians expected, Murphy's direction angered Wynkoop and he became sarcastic. "I have not yet seen
Mr. Banks or the contractor," he snapped.[73] In other words, he did not
yet have any annuities to distribute.

Wynkoop told Murphy that Cheyenne warriors, after seeing a surveying party south of the Arkansas River, vented their anger at him. The
warriors felt these white men had one purpose, "laying out roads." Even
though Wynkoop had seen his wards react violently to a similar occur-
rence in the past, he remained optimistic. "I have endeavored to make
the necessary explanations *and presume* I will be able to satisfy them."

But, as Wynkoop knew, this could spark an outbreak, as could the annuities. As far as warriors were concerned, distributions always included
weapons. Although the lack of guns had not caused too much unrest,
Wynkoop knew it would only be a matter of time. The Indians' understanding of the Medicine Lodge treaty included weapons, a necessity
for their survival. From their point of view, there was no after-the-fact
renegotiation. The white man promised them guns, and they expected
to get guns.

At the beginning of February, Wynkoop prepared his report for the
month of January 1868. During February many Southern Cheyennes
congregated sixty miles south of Fort Dodge. As in the past, his wards
began to sense they would not receive what the U.S. government had
promised them, and began to grumble. Wynkoop knew their suspicions
were correct. Although promised "a large quantity of arms and ammunition," he knew the amount purchased was "comparatively a trifle taking
with consideration their numbers" and that they expected "an immense
quantity of arms and ammunition would be issued to them."[74] While
the question of weapons dominated Wynkoop's report, it also succinctly
reiterated his need for the additional scout.

The Interpreters employed to remain with the different tribes have so
far been of no service to me whatever, they being with the exception

of George Bent employed by different trading establishment[s], and consequently attending more to the private interests of the Traders than looking out for the interests of the Government; I never receive any reports from any of them; the only way in which I am able to gain any information in regard to the Indians is in person or keeping a Scout constantly running between them and the Agency.

In the absence of such a scout, on February 4, 1868, Wynkoop set out for the Cheyenne camps. He hoped to soothe tempers before anything happened, return "property captured by Gen. Hancock," and give the Cheyennes the "few arms I have still in my possession."

The day Wynkoop left, Philip McCusker, an interpreter who had been living among the Comanches, Kiowas, Southern Cheyennes, and Apaches since late October or early November 1867, claimed in a letter to Murphy that the Cheyennes professed themselves "friendly to the whites north of the Arkansas," and that "Roman Nose the chief [how many plainsmen made this mistake?] told me that his people had made peace with the whites & that the Cheyennes would not be the first to break it."[75] If Wynkoop saw McCusker at one of the villages, McCusker, who knew of Wynkoop's earlier run-in with Roman Nose, would have shared the war leader's current disposition with him.

In February 1868 John Smith was living in a Southern Cheyenne village sixty miles south of Fort Dodge. Unaware that Wynkoop moved among the Cheyennes for the second time that year, he made a complaint about the agent. Wynkoop had employed Smith off and on over the years, but they did not get along. Smith, angered over pay long owed him, blamed the agent, and complained to Thomas Murphy that Wynkoop had not been with his wards since Medicine Lodge. Murphy ignored the bogus accusation.

Smith then described a problem that Wynkoop had not addressed—perhaps because he was not yet aware of it. The Cheyennes "have been getting all of the whiskey that they wanted which is certainly a dangerous thing for them to tamper with at this time."[76] Smith did not overstate the problem, nor was he alone in his observation. Cheyenne and Arapaho Trader J. L. Butterfield claimed that soon after a Cheyenne warrior rode into his village with five gallons of whiskey he had bought at Fort Dodge, "nearly the whole camp was drunk."[77] Butterfield found himself in a similar situation after Big Mouth rode into an Arapaho village with eighteen bottles and one keg of whiskey, stating, "You know what effect whiskey has on Indians and what danger white men are in while in their camp."

The alcohol problem perturbed Thomas Murphy. He wanted the law breakers punished and requested the commander of Fort Dodge "assist the agent [Wynkoop] in finding out who it is that is engaged in this unlawful traffic . . . [for] if permitted to continue may lead to fresh trouble from the Indians in the coming summer."[78]

After Wynkoop returned to Fort Larned in mid-February, he continued his ongoing struggle to get his employees paid. They had performed for him, and he had every intention of obtaining the monies owed them. He had still not secured Guerrier's pay for getting the Dog Soldiers to Medicine Lodge Creek, and Wynkoop refused to back off until he was paid. Although Taylor's demands to improve his bookkeeping had angered Wynkoop, he also began working on this task, submitting a list of the scouts and interpreters he had used during the last three quarters of 1867.[79]

While Wynkoop satisfied Taylor, he struggled with Murphy. Even though he had convinced the superintendent he needed to know where his wards were at all times, Murphy remained adamant; Wynkoop could not hire a scout/interpreter. Instead, Murphy recommended to Commissioner Taylor that government-employed interpreters in Wynkoop's agency "report fully the movements of the respective tribes with whom they are stationed" and "are required to obey all instructions given them by Agent Wynkoop."[80]

Finally realizing the importance of Wynkoop's warning of Cheyenne anger at the beginning of February, Taylor responded on February 25. He informed Wynkoop that weapons would be purchased for the spring distribution. "Telegraph immediately amount and kind of arms and ammunition needed for your Indians."[81] Murphy had orders to support Wynkoop on the problem he had with interpreters in the field ignoring his requests for updates on Indian movements. If employed by the Upper Arkansas District, they would do as Wynkoop directed. If they did not, Wynkoop could remove them.

According to John Smith, although "peaceably disposed," the Southern Cheyennes found themselves "somewhat at a loss to know what to do to keep out of trouble."[82] Nervous that whites would blame them for recent depredations, they wanted to distance their villages from the Kiowas, who remained aggressive during the cold months. Fueled by trader-supplied liquor, what again appeared to be false white-man promises combined with a growing hunger kept the Cheyennes and Arapahos in a constant state of agitation. Spring approached, and soon Wynkoop would once again venture into an atmosphere of stifled anger.

CHAPTER FOURTEEN

A Matter of Conscience

Thrilled with Commissioner Taylor's support for purchasing weapons for the Indians, Colonel Wynkoop assembled the requested list on March 5, 1868. It included 250 Lancaster rifles, 500 Colt or Remington pistols, 1,500 pounds of lead, 1,000 pounds of powder, 35,000 pistol caps, and 17,000 rifle caps, some of which he could purchase locally.[1]

In early March 1868 General Philip H. Sheridan visited Fort Larned, and Wynkoop saw him as soon as possible. The general, who had recently served on a board that revised the Articles of War, had resumed command of the Department of the Missouri in late February.[2] When Sheridan traveled to Fort Dodge, Wynkoop accompanied him in order to be present at his meeting with tribal leaders. Soon after their arrival, chiefs began to appear. Impromptu meetings lasted several weeks. Kansas governor Crawford claimed the Indians "demand[ed] guns, pistols, and ammunition as a condition precedent to their remaining at peace."[3] When Sheridan refused to deliver weapons, a simmering anger began to permeate the meetings.

At the end of March Wynkoop issued supplies to his wards, for which he received receipts from the chiefs.[4] His delivery did not include weapons, as he had none, which again infuriated the Indians. The agent quickly returned to his oft-repeated request that the Cheyennes and Arapahos speak with the Kaws and Osages. This generated more anger; they had been hurt and put upon, and until they revenged themselves on their enemies, peace was out of the question. Wynkoop took a firm stance.

Another shipment of annuities was en route. If they attacked *anyone,* he would not distribute supplies. Wynkoop asked them which they wanted more, revenge or the goods. The threat initiated a change in attitude. Wynkoop reported finding his wards in a "quiet state." The "rumors sent East lately in regard to the Indians showing evidence of hostility in this neighborhood," Wynkoop told Thomas Murphy, "are absolutely false."[5]

By early April the annuities Wynkoop had said were en route in March arrived at Fort Dodge, and he made the distribution. Although he handed out 13,875 quarts of salt, 10,356 pounds of coffee, 166,500 pounds of beef, 124,875 pounds of flour, 41,625 pounds of bacon, and 20,705 pounds of brown sugar, he still had no weapons to distribute.[6]

Without consulting Agent Wynkoop, in late April 1868 Black Kettle and Little Raven sent George Bent to meet the Mohauche Utes and Jicarilla Apaches to set up a council to discuss peace between the tribes. Ute and Apache Agent B. Dennison attended the meeting and, unlike Wynkoop, asked his superiors for instructions before acting.[7]

His wards' desire to meet their enemies pleased Wynkoop. Although he had returned to Fort Larned, he did not reply to Dennison immediately. As usual, submitting budgets and reports consumed his time. Whenever he thought he was caught up, he faced another deadline and confrontation with Thomas Murphy. Wynkoop had ignored instructions not to hire more scout-interpreters. In April 1868 he hired Margaret McAdams to translate Arapaho for him. About thirty-four years old, she, like many interpreters, appeared and then disappeared from government payrolls. She impressed Wynkoop, and he had authorized a high salary for her. As soon as Murphy saw the pay voucher for McAdams for "services as U.S. Interpretress up to April 30th 1868," he sent two reports to Commissioner Taylor complaining about Wynkoop's free use of funds.[8] From now on, Wynkoop would be required to submit quarterly estimates for pay due his interpreters.

Near the end of April many Southern Cheyennes and Arapahos camped at the Pawnee Fork, where deep cutbacks in the river's flow and a profusion of trees provided protection from the wind. The Indians were waiting to receive their annuities. When Wynkoop arrived at the grounds in early May and met in council, he accepted his wards' determination regarding the Osages and Kaws. "I am perfectly satisfied, that until the contending parties come together and have a good fight, 'tis useless to try to have them make peace."[9] Past wrongs had to be avenged; Wynkoop knew the Indians would let him know when this happened, and flippantly informed Thomas Murphy that as soon as he heard they were ready to discuss peace, he would "immediately" notify him.

Wynkoop felt that two things had to happen before peace became a reality. The government had to supply all expected annuities on a regular basis to "wean" the Indians from the necessity of obtaining subsistence by hunting and raiding, and had to reinstill the Indians' confidence through kindness and fairness, which would make "them more peaceable."[10] Wynkoop viewed consistency as the key. Hopeful, and perhaps naïve, he strongly believed that the government and its representatives could convert the Indians to the white man's ways if it dealt with them ethically.

Wynkoop delivered annuities to Cheyennes Black Kettle, Stone Forehead, Big Jake, and Little Robe; Arapahos Little Raven, Yellow Bear, Storm, Big Mouth, and Spotted Wolf; and also continued to supply Plains Apaches Iron Shirt, Cut Nose, Young Chief. Although large (166,500 pounds of beef; 124,875 pounds of flour; 41,625 pounds of bacon; 20,705 pounds of sugar; 10,356 pounds of coffee; 8,880 quarts of salt), the distribution again did not include weapons, but this time it did not initiate an outburst.[11] Wynkoop later reported, "there has been no single instance that I am aware of, of any act of depredation being committed by these Indians, since the signing of the [1867] Treaty."[12] Taking a position that seems unrealistically positive, he found his wards "satisfied and more peaceably disposed then they have been for years," and pronounced that "the issuing of subsistence to them has the effect of making them feel well satisfied with the Government, and proves which heretofore has been hard to make them believe that it is our desire to do what we can for their comfort and welfare." Optimism aside, Wynkoop walked away from the April distribution with another concern. Due to the limited area in which to hunt the drastically reduced number of buffalo, he found his wards "almost [in] a state of starvation."[13]

After returning to Fort Larned on May 12, 1868, Wynkoop again issued food. (This distribution had not been announced, and he consented to it only because Tall Bull's band had missed the April delivery.) During the distribution a number of Kiowas from Satanta's band, approximately twenty lodges, appeared. Camped sixty miles below Fort Larned on Bluff Creek, they told Wynkoop their people were destitute.

Recognizing the need for an immediate decision, Wynkoop acted. "I took the responsibility of issuing some provisions to them," he reported, "governed by what I considered best for the public interests."[14] He knew that starving people become desperate people. "I hope that my action in this matter may meet with the approval of the Department."

Since 1864 Wynkoop had met, dealt with, and became friendly with many Cheyennes. Even though he felt that peace reigned on the plains, he knew that much was at stake and feared a spark could ignite yet another war. He also knew that a number of the chieftains, especially those who spoke out strongly for keeping their land and lifeway, were at risk. Before Tall Bull left Fort Larned, Wynkoop spent time with him. Feeling the chief wanted peace but had no qualms about going to war, Wynkoop wrote a letter for him to carry, stating Tall Bull "is peaceably disposed, and will do nothing that is wrong, unless forced to do so by imprudent acts of white men."[15]

Wynkoop had no time to catch his breath that May. No sooner did he claim that his wards were innocent of committing depredations than news arrived that Cheyennes had burned a ranch near Fort Zarah. He immediately set out to investigate, reaching the scene while it was still smoking. He walked the grounds and interviewed witnesses.

Messrs. Tappan & Weichselbaum (the Fort Larned traders), whom Wynkoop described as "two distinguished gentlemen," were at the ranch when the attack occurred, and both denounced as absurd the idea that Indians were responsible. Wynkoop located a warrior from the band of Cheyennes reported to have committed the outrage, and the warrior proclaimed his people's innocence. Wynkoop learned that Edmund Guerrier currently resided with the accused Southern Cheyenne band. Trying not to leave anything unexplored, he sent word to the interpreter asking him what he knew of the incident. Guerrier wrote Wynkoop stating "positively that none of the Indians that he was with committed any act of the kind mentioned."[16] Finally, Wynkoop visited the officer then commanding Fort Zarah to discuss the matter, and he came to the same conclusion: Cheyennes had not committed the depredation. Back at Fort Larned, Wynkoop put pen to paper. "[A]lready this [purported] outrage on the part of the Indians has been [well circulated] and much capital is being made out of it by [those] desirous of bringing on an Indian War," he wrote Thomas Murphy. "I can state most positively that no single act of outrage or depredation has been committed by the Indians

Edmund Guerrier, a mixed-blood of French and Southern Cheyenne parentage, became one of Wynkoop's most trusted interpreters. This image dates to the early 1870s. Courtesy of the Braun Research Library, Autry National Center of the American West, Los Angeles, A.152.34.

of my agency against the whites, since the signing of the Treaty at Medicine Lodge Creek."

As government issue was never enough, Wynkoop continued pushing to receive much needed annuities, and everything moved forward smoothly. By the end of the third full week of May most of what he expected had shipped. Unfortunately the government delivered most of the annuity goods to Fort Harker and stored them at the Chick & Co. warehouse. Wynkoop told his wards that he would soon deliver supplies to them, but the wagons to transport the goods never arrived. This boded ill, as Wynkoop well knew. On May 23 he wrote Murphy that "much delay in this matter is apt to be prejudicial to the public interests."[17] The superintendent understood Wynkoop to mean that something might happen if he did not distribute the goods in a timely manner. "I coincide in opinion with the agent," Murphy wrote Acting Commissioner Charles Mix twelve days later, "and recommend that the contractor for transportation of Indian goods be directed to send teams to Ellsworth [sic] at once, and take these goods to their destination."[18]

In the meantime, Wynkoop supported Agent Dennison's request for a peace council between the Cheyennes, Arapahos, Utes, and Jicarilla Apaches—one of the rare instances in which he agreed with his peers and followed the chain of command, forwarding the request to Murphy.[19]

Anticipating the next distribution of goods, the bands gathered on the Pawnee Fork. With the safe arrival of the annuities at Fort Larned near the end of May, Wynkoop set out for the assembled villages with a caravan of supplies. Interpreter John Smith and special agent Alex Banks accompanied him. Wynkoop found Cheyenne (Black Kettle, Big Jake, Stone Forehead, Little Robe), Arapaho (Little Raven, Yellow Bear, Spotted Wolf, Storm, Big Mouth), and Plains Apache (Cut Nose, Young Chief, Iron Shirt) leaders camped along the cuts of the river. Over the next five days he distributed the same quantity of annuities he had passed out in April. During the distribution he visited with Black Kettle, Little Robe, Stone Forehead, and others he had come to know, and began to hear a growing murmur of dissatisfaction over the failure to receive weapons and ammunition promised at Medicine Lodge.[20]

Surprisingly, Murphy acted quickly on the Dennison/Wynkoop proposal to set up a meeting with the tribes. But there was a catch. Per Murphy, Wynkoop and Dennison could move forward with their idea as long as "it can be done without any expense to the Government."[21] This was not workable. Wynkoop had already opined that "the Department should deem the conference of sufficient importance as to authorize a trifling expense for presents."

· · ·

June 1868 was very rainy in Kansas. The Solomon River rose rapidly and the Saline River flooded.[22] The early seasonal storms provided cover for Tall Bull and Little Robe to raid the Kaws. But instead of striking the enemies' village, they confronted the Kaws near Council Grove, Kansas. Three Southern Cheyennes and one Kaw suffered wounds. Returning to their villages, the warriors dissolved into smaller groups. Twenty raiders struck farms, killing livestock, destroying crops, and stealing.[23]

These events influenced Murphy, who had just given his blessing to the proposed council between the Cheyennes and their enemies, to change his mind. On a copy of his report that approved the council, he wrote: "Suggests that no action be had upon this at present."[24]

Ten days after the raid, Wynkoop met with Little Robe and asked him to explain what had happened. Little Robe said that his warriors were hungry, but every time they approached a farmstead, the inhabitants ran. He admitted that they did kill eleven cattle to survive, but according to Wynkoop, Little Robe and those with him "did not interfere with any person or thing."[25]

The missed opportunity to improve relations between the tribes, combined with a sudden reversal of the weather, set the tone for a long hot summer. The rains that pounded Kansas in June vanished, replaced by relentless winds from the south that raked the dry land. An unrelenting sun baked the earth and killed the crops. The hostile activity by Little Robe's warriors did not go unnoticed. Standing up for the people he represented, Kansas Senator Edmund Ross contacted Commissioner Taylor. Ross wanted the Indians to pay for their thefts and destruction with the monies designated for them by the government.[26]

Knowing he still would not be allowed to distribute weapons, Wynkoop invited the tribes to Fort Larned to receive their next annuity delivery. By the second week of July "many thousands of Indians" congregated at Fort Larned: Southern Cheyennes, Arapahos, Kiowas, Comanches, and Plains Apaches. "All the Indians carry revolvers," Barnitz wrote his wife, "and look formidable enough, but they appear to be very friendly, with perhaps the exception of a small number of disaffected ones from each tribe."[27]

At times Wynkoop must have felt he stood alone, but he had allies who had read about him in the eastern press. On July 14, 1868, Peter Cooper hosted a meeting at his Cooper Union in New York City to protest corruption within the Bureau of Indian Affairs.[28] Cooper, an industrialist, inventor, and philanthropist who became interested in the Indian reform movement when he read Lydia Child's writings, privately

funded the United States Indian Commission, whose goal was to protect and elevate Indians. Nothing came of the meeting, and accusations
that Indian agents and traders worked in collaboration to fleece Indians
would continue to proliferate until the corruption generated headlines
in the 1870s.[29]

Congress had still not ratified the Medicine Lodge treaty. This kept
Wynkoop's wards in limbo, disgruntled and unsure of their future. As
Wynkoop had proved a thorn in the government's side, now Lieutenant
General William Sherman returned the compliment. Aware that Senator
Henderson's promise that the Indians could hunt buffalo north of the
Arkansas had never made it into the 1867 treaty, the general stated that
the Indians did not have permission to hunt buffalo off the reservation.
Then, on June 24, he went one step further. Claiming that bows and
arrows were better suited for hunting buffalo, he informed Secretary of
the Interior O. H. Browning that the distribution of weapons was not
part of the treaty provisions. Since Cheyennes and Arapahos had used
guns given them in the past on "other Indians and whites," Sherman felt
justified in cutting off the supply of weapons.[30]

On July 15 Captain Henry Asbury (Third U.S. Infantry), who commanded Fort Larned, hosted a dance. All the officers received invita-
tions, including officers from several companies of the Seventh Cavalry
camped a mile above the post on the south side of the Pawnee. As was
often the case at frontier posts, only a handful of women, mostly wives,
were available, making them very popular. Louise attended the dance
with Wynkoop, who must have enjoyed the respite.[31]

Under a blazing sun, and again without weapons, on July 20 Agent
Wynkoop issued supplies to his wards. The Arapahos and Plains Apaches
readily accepted what the government offered them. Even though they
expressed their unhappiness at not receiving any guns, the transfer proceeded without incident. But as soon as the Cheyennes realized they
would not receive the promised weapons, the distribution ended abruptly.
The chiefs told Wynkoop "they thought that their white brothers were
pulling away from them the hand they had given to them at Medicine
Lodge Creek."[32] Although they refused their entire annuity issue, they
told Wynkoop they "would wait with patience for the Great Father to
take pity upon them and let them have the arms and ammunition which
had been promised them." After the Cheyennes left, Wynkoop stored the

goods designated for them. In his report to Murphy he asked to distribute arms and ammunition "as soon as possible."

The following day the temperature soared, but with a humidity that threatened rain. That evening Wynkoop, who took pride in his stable, raced one of his horses with a horse owned by Captain Frederick Benteen (Seventh U.S. Cavalry).[33]

The next day a thunderstorm sporadically pounded Fort Larned, and that evening it rained steadily for an hour. Braving the night's downpour, Louise and several officers' wives visited the Seventh Cavalry camp. "Some of them sing very well," Barnitz wrote, "and it is really a pleasure to hear female voices in our camp on quiet evenings."[34]

Wynkoop's report could not have been better timed. On July 23 Murphy, who had been in Washington since June, discussed Wynkoop's dilemma with Taylor. The commissioner acted quickly and dictated a wire to Wynkoop, directing him to exercise discretion when issuing weapons. He then ordered Murphy to leave for Fort Larned to discuss with Wynkoop the best course to maintain peace. If the agent convinced Murphy that giving weapons to the Indians would keep them peaceful and "no evil will result from such delivery," he should authorize the distribution.[35]

Finally on July 25, 1868, Congress ratified the Medicine Lodge treaty, nine months after the signing. It was almost another month until the treaty was proclaimed on August 19.[36]

That day Comanches (Ten Bears, Iron Mountain) and Kiowas (Satanta, Lone Wolf, Timber Mountain, Satank) camped near Fort Larned. When Wynkoop visited their village and spoke with them, he found them short on food and asking for additional guns to hunt game. Apparently Wynkoop had not yet heard Sherman's dictum. He told them that as soon as the Senate ratified the Medicine Lodge treaty, they would receive the guns promised them.[37]

During the council Wynkoop saw that the tribes held at least one white captive. There were many abductions on the central and southern plains during the 1860s. Some of the names crossed Wynkoop's desk. Usually he did not know who they were until he became involved with their release. One captive was Melinda Ann Caudle. She was eight or nine years old when Comanches abducted her at the Friend family homestead in Llano County, Texas, on February 5, 1868. Melinda's sister and her child, two female cousins, and another woman were brutally killed, some before her eyes. A young boy named Lee Temple Friend, whom Melinda called "Temple," also became a prisoner.

Guessing the Indians probably held others in captivity, Wynkoop told them there would be no more annuities until the captives were freed. He demanded they give him the white girl he had seen. This angered the Indians, who had planned to trade her. Wynkoop refused to budge, and they gave him the girl without further argument.[38]

Bringing Melinda, or "Minnie," as she called herself, into his home for Louise to care for until he could locate her family, Wynkoop quickly discovered that she was bright and talkative. Melinda told him that her mother and father were not killed when the Indians captured her.[39]

Barnitz claimed that Wynkoop freed two girls without paying a ransom. "One is very pleasing, modest looking girl about 14 years of age, I should think—she is soon to become a mother."[40]

Soon after, probably by July 27 or 28, or about a week after the council, Thomas Murphy reached Fort Larned. When Wynkoop convinced him that his wards would use the weapons to hunt, Murphy allowed him to send out runners to ask the Indians to come into the agency to discuss the frozen annuities. Barnitz, who had been camped a mile above Fort Larned since at least July 12, heard rumors of the upcoming distributions. On the morning of July 29, in a letter to his wife, he wrote: "Col. Wyncoop [sic], Indian Agent, commences, to day, to issue arms to the Indians. Is to issue 350 or 375 rifles to them, by order of the Secretary of the Interior, I believe—maybe they will feel very brave when they get those arms, and will begin to turn their thoughts to war again! Who knows. It is certainly very foolish to fight Indians with one hand, and to make presents, and give them arms with the other!"[41] He had not commented on the July 20 distribution, was not privy to the Wynkoop-Murphy meeting, and was repeating inaccurate information that was thirdhand at best.

The Arapahos and Apaches, camped closer to Fort Larned than the Southern Cheyennes, arrived first, in large numbers. On August 1 Wynkoop and Murphy met with the leaders in council. Referring to the failed June raid, Murphy told them that war parties could not cross lands occupied by settlers; doing so would lead to trouble. He insisted that they live in peace with the Osages and the Kaws.

Little Raven replied that Colonel Wynkoop and Murphy had been at the Medicine Lodge council "when the Kaws began the trouble, and wished to know if he and his people were to blame."[42] He promised to speak with the Cheyennes and said that if they made peace with the Osages and Kaws, the Arapahos would, too. According to Murphy, "Raven and the other chiefs then promised that these arms should never be used against the whites." Murphy agreed with Wynkoop's belief that his wards were sincere, and allowed him to distribute the weapons. Wynkoop gave "the Arapahos 160 pistols, 80 Lancaster rifles, 12 kegs of powder, 1½ kegs of lead, and 15,000 caps." He gave the Apaches "40 pistols, 20 Lancaster rifles, 3 kegs of powder, ½ keg of lead, and 5,000 caps." He did not hand out any other annuities, having made that distribution on July 20.

Murphy did not see the Cheyennes before he left for Atchison the next day as they had not yet arrived at the Upper Arkansas Agency. His parting orders to Wynkoop were to "explain to them why their arms were retained, to issue them now, and to counsel with them relative to making peace with the Osages and Kaws."

By early August Wynkoop's fight for pay for his interpreters and scouts had not been resolved. Superintendent Murphy finally recommended paying Margaret McAdams, per Wynkoop's request during the first quarter of the year.[43] With pay withheld for months it is a wonder that Wynkoop was able to retain the people who performed well.

At 10:00 P.M. on the evening of August 5, 1868, Wynkoop relaxed on the porch of the sutler residence he rented at Fort Larned with Louise, several officers, and their wives. The oppressive heat and humidity of the day eased to a cooler temperature after dark, and on this night Wynkoop wore a fur cap. The conversation probably centered around Wynkoop's boldness in demanding the release of the Caudle girl without paying ransom.

Suddenly, a gray wolf rushed up the steps and bit Lieutenant Thompson (Third U.S. Infantry) several times on the leg. The rabid animal then raced east. Wynkoop and James Morrison, whom he employed as clerk, scout, and Arapaho interpreter, grabbed their weapons and gave chase.

As the wolf approached the guardhouse with Wynkoop and Morrison in pursuit, the sentinel on duty saw the canine. He fired at it but missed, and the wolf attacked and bit him. Almost immediately the wolf changed direction, charging north across the parade ground, and entered an open doorway of the hospital on the northern perimeter of the compound. Before anyone inside realized the danger, the wolf attacked a corporal who was lying on one of the beds, gnawing his arm and fingers. The attack continued. The wolf assaulted a Tenth Cavalry trooper, then a laundress lying in bed in her quarters; she was lucky and not harmed. Next the wolf charged a guard who stood near a haystack north of the barracks and hospital. Alert, the sentinel shot and killed the animal.[44]

As the excitement of the ominous wolf attack faded, Wynkoop prepared to meet the Cheyennes, who had finally arrived at Fort Larned. On August 9 he dispensed the annuities, including guns, balls, and powder. This event was a major success that greatly improved the Cheyennes' disposition. Now they had the wherewithal to feed their families and could overlook previous slights. "They were delighted at receiving the goods particularly the arms and ammunition and never before have I known them to be better satisfied and express themselves as being so well contented," Wynkoop reported. "I am perfectly satisfied that there will be no trouble with them this season."[45]

On that same day, August 9, Lieutenant General Sherman decided that he wanted the Cheyennes, Arapahos, Comanches, and Kiowas living south of the Arkansas River in a military district commanded by Lieutenant Colonel William Hazen. The next day he issued orders that read in part: "When Indians are on reservations with civilian agents actually present with them, no interferences will be made, but military commanders may note any neglects or irregularities on the part of said Indians or their agents."[46] Sherman's orders bothered Commissioner Taylor, who felt that Sherman wanted to force the southern tribes to live at Fort Cobb in Indian Territory so the military could seize "control over issues or disbursements to Indians" from the civilian agents.[47] The struggle to control the Indians' destiny included a problem that neither the War Department nor the Indian Bureau addressed properly: the cost of providing for the Indians once they arrived at their new reservation. Acting Commissioner Charles Mix claimed that few funds had been set aside, and Sherman stated that only a small amount of money was available.

On August 10 Wynkoop submitted an expense estimate for the third and fourth quarters of 1868. His pay for this period amounted to $750 and the rent of his office/home $100/month. He listed $200 for an interpreter. The total expense estimate amounted to $4,175.[48] A week later Wynkoop submitted a payroll estimate for his three named interpreters (George Bent, John Smith, and Margaret McAdams). For the period from May 1 until December 31, 1868, at the rate of $5.00 each per day, the cost amounted to $3,675.[49]

On the day that Wynkoop submitted his expense request, August 10, over two hundred Tsistsistas and Dog Men from the villages of Black Kettle, Stone Forehead, Little Rock, and Bull Bear who had not participated in the previous day's annuity distribution appeared on the Saline River in north-central Kansas. Among the warriors were Edmund Guerrier and George Bent, Wynkoop's trusted interpreters. Four Arapahos and twenty Sioux had joined the war party on the Smoky Hill. They intended to strike the hated Pawnees in Nebraska. But, as traveling warriors often did, they swooped down upon a homestead to demand food. When frightened settlers shot at the war party, they captured a white woman, whom they set free the next day. By August 12 the raiders reached the north fork of the Solomon River and settlers again shot at them. Moving on, they attacked settlements, raping and killing. At this point, some of the warriors returned to their villages in the south while others continued their raid northward. Panic gripped the settlements, and people fled their homes. After leaving the rolling land of the Saline and the Solomon, the warriors returned to the Saline three days later and resumed their rampage. According to Guerrier, Man Who Breaks The Marrow Bones, from Black Kettle's band, and Red Nose, a Dog Man, "were the two leaders in this massacre."[50] Guerrier claimed that he and Bent did not take part in the killing."

For Wynkoop the raid was a devastating betrayal. For the Southern Cheyennes it changed everything. There would be no more excuses, no more second chances, no more treaties. From this day forward, the Cheyenne way of life would never be the same again, and neither would Wynkoop's.

On the evening of August 13 Ned Wynkoop met with Little Rock at Fort Larned. The agent knew the chief well, for Little Rock often traveled with Black Kettle's band. They spoke about the recent raids on the Saline River. Wynkoop asked Little Rock to find out who had committed the depredations. Since Black Kettle's village camped a short distance from his agency on the Pawnee Fork, Wynkoop knew the chief had not taken part in the raids, though he assumed some of his young men rode the war trail.[51]

It remained hot. Clouds hovered but the lack of rain kept the weather sultry. Race relations could have been described in much the same language. Wynkoop feared the future. Three days later, on August 16, a courier galloped into Fort Larned from Fort Harker to report that Captain Frederick Benteen had confronted the warring Indians on the Saline and was driven from the field.[52]

Kansas governor Crawford expressed outrage that two young women and two girls had been abducted. He wrote to President Johnson on August 17 with well-founded complaints. "If the Government cannot control these uncivilized barbarians while they are under its fostering care and protection, it certainly can put a stop to the unbearable policy of supplying them with arms and ammunition, especially while they are waging war notoriously against the frontier settlements. . . . The savage devils have become intolerable, and must and shall be driven out of this State."[53]

On August 19, Wynkoop again spoke with Little Rock at Fort Larned. According to the interpreter the chief said the Dog Man war party left their camp on a fork of Walnut Creek on August 2 or 3, but there is a strong possibility that the translation was wrong and the warriors set out two or three days before the Saline attacks began on August 10. It seems odd that a war party would take seven or eight days to travel sixty-plus miles. Little Rock named Little Raven's son and Stone Forehead as members of the raid. Some of the warriors belonged to Black Kettle's village, a reflection of a chief's lack of power over his band.

Little Rock's words distressed Wynkoop. Carrying the weight of peace on his shoulders, he had again fallen short. Everything he had attempted to do to prevent war had failed. On this dreadful day of August 19, Wynkoop knew what the future held. There was no stopping the collision of cultures, and no doubt which culture would emerge victorious. "Will you," Wynkoop asked, "deliver up the men whom you have named as being the leaders" of the raid?[54] He knew the answer before asking the question, but he had to ask. Little Rock said he would deliver them, but both knew this would not happen. Wynkoop did not want his friend harmed. "Bring your lodge and family here," he told Little Rock, "and I will protect you."

That day Wynkoop wrote to Murphy that the Cheyennes, "I am sorry to admit," had started a war. As far as he was concerned, the guilty had set in motion their own fate. His main concern now centered on protecting the people who remained at peace, to "save the innocent from being punished for the acts of the guilty." Wynkoop knew the Cheyennes who wanted peace would "be powerless to restrain their young men." Desirous of saving lives, he wanted to locate those "I know to be guiltless and desirous of remaining at peace" in a safe place. He wanted U.S. troops to protect the peaceful Indians from their people, who he knew would attempt to force them to join the war.

Murphy wasted little time in replying. He was pleased with Wynkoop's course of action. At the same time he made it clear that the Indians wishing to remain at peace must hand over the guilty parties. If not, they would be held responsible, considered hostile, and would not be protected. Murphy demanded that Wynkoop's interpreters and scouts deliver this message to the Indians.[55]

Murphy's response left Wynkoop unsure what to do. With many of his wards riding the war trail, he had reached another crossroads. He had long stood for peace, and now he found himself in a quandary.

Although he did not name Wynkoop, Governor Crawford clearly alluded to him when he wrote, "having run out of ammunition, [the warring Indians] returned to Fort Larned with the scalps of their victims dangling from their belts. There they made loud professions of friendship, and begged for more ammunition with which to *kill game* for food, while *en route* to their reservations."[56]

Even though Arapahos Little Raven, Standing Bear, Spotted Wolf Bull, Powder Bull, and Storm surrendered to Sheridan at Fort Dodge at the beginning of September 1868, only Stone Forehead dared approach Fort Larned. Wynkoop told the mystic what he had told Little Rock: the People must surrender the guilty parties.

By early September most of the Southern Cheyennes had moved south of the Arkansas and assembled near the Cimarron River; others, hoping to avoid the white man's wrath, had moved even farther south. And the war continued. Cheyennes attacked a wagon train south of the Cimarron Crossing of the Arkansas, killing everyone and burning the bodies. Soon after, Cheyennes attacked another wagon train, but only two people died.

Thomas Murphy, who had held that all the Cheyennes had to be punished, changed his mind. Most likely Wynkoop influenced his decision. The superintendent now felt the innocent should be protected.

Sherman had had enough. On September 8 he ordered Sheridan to "treat all friendly bands with kindness and forbearance but to the hostile, their families and adherents, to show no mercy as they show none. We should now settle these Indians forever one way or the other."[57] The previous day, September 7, Lieutenant Colonel Alfred Sully, who commanded the District of the Upper Arkansas, had set out from Fort Dodge in pursuit of the Southern Cheyennes with one company of Third U.S. Infantry and nine companies of Seventh Cavalry. On September 10 Dog Soldiers began attacking vulnerable points of Sully's command. When he failed to strike back, they harassed him at will.

Unaware of the volatility of the situation, or perhaps still hoping for a peaceful ending to the war, on September 13 Wynkoop prepared his budget for the coming year, prefacing it with a statement that he continued to learn from past experience. He filled four and one-half pages of lined paper listing what his wards needed. He did not make frivolous selections and only requested items the Indians would use.[58] But Wynkoop was ignoring the political climate. War existed. No matter what the Indians needed (or had been promised), they would receive no goods until Sheridan's army had defeated them. His budget was useless. His ally Thomas Murphy no longer backed him. Changing his mind once again, Murphy felt the Cheyennes had to pay for their unprovoked attacks on whites; until they complied they should not receive annuities.[59]

In the middle of September large numbers of Kiowas and Comanches approached Fort Larned and met Wynkoop. He found the Indians "in a very destitute condition . . . peaceably disposed . . . [and] humble."[60] Satanta told Wynkoop "that he and his people were willing and anxious to go upon their Reservation to live in houses and raise corn . . . that such must be their ultimate destiny."

Wynkoop feared the future, a dark future he could not handle. Whites across the frontier cried out for extermination. Knowing his every effort to prevent more bloodshed had failed, and unsure what to do, he knew he had to do something. His plans in place, he rose early on September 17. Unknown to him, just before dawn on that same day, Dog Men had attacked a force of fifty hand-picked frontiersmen under the command of Major George Forsyth on the Arickaree Fork of the

Republican River in Colorado Territory. Forsyth had been ordered to locate the tribal faction that led the war effort and do as much damage as possible. However, when the whites unknowingly approached a large Dog Soldier–Sioux village, they became the hunted.

Dog Men Chiefs Tall Bull and White Horse initiated the attack, and later that day they asked the Sioux to join them. Wynkoop would not learn of the attack until much later. However, when he did it would attract his interest, for his nemesis Roman Nose rode with the Dog Men on this day which saw the whites retreat to an island under heavy fire at the beginning of the attack. Here, using repeating carbines, they broke two charges, forcing the warriors to veer off before riding over them. Roman Nose's fame preceded him, and late that afternoon his companions asked him to lead a third charge. He was in the process of cleansing himself, for metal had touched his lips when he ate. Tall Bull had told him to complete his ceremony but instead Roman Nose heeded the requests and led a third change. When he rode over unseen scouts hidden in the grass he received a fatal wound.[61] Although the fight has been described as a heroic ordeal of survival, it proved tragic for the Southern Cheyennes, who lost their most renowned war leader, a person Wynkoop both feared and respected.

On that same September 17 Wynkoop placed Melinda Ann Caudle, who still lived with him, under the care of another family at Fort Larned and set out for Fort Harker with Louise and the children. He did not know that Sherman had declared the Southern Cheyennes and Arapahos at war. The general wanted Wynkoop's and Leavenworth's agencies shut down and the agents transferred to Indian Territory, where Hazen had a small amount of money to feed peaceable Indians.

While en route, Wynkoop met Sheridan and Hazen. Sheridan said he intended to send the Kiowas and Comanches back to Texas. Resuming his journey, Wynkoop reached Fort Harker without incident. Continuing on, he reached Leavenworth City by September 20. Only here did he put pen to paper and make known his intentions. After stating he had been in "Indian country" for the last two years without time off, he requested a leave of absence for twenty days. "I am cut off from all communication with the Indians of my Agency, they being in the hands of the military, and in consequence my hands tied for some time." He said he wanted to return to his mother's home in Philadelphia "to attend to some important private business," but this was a cover, a diversion.[62]

The following day Thomas Murphy approved the time off providing his absence "will not be detrimental to the public service or to the interests of the Indians under your charge."[63]

By now Wynkoop had heard Sherman's statement about the Cheyennes and Arapahos, "that it will be impossible for our troops to discriminate between the well-disposed and the warlike parts of those Bands, unless an absolute separation be made."[64] Even though Wynkoop had proposed such a separation not that long ago, a safe zone near Fort Cobb in Indian Territory would not be the same as a safe zone near Fort Larned. The separation of peaceful from warlike suddenly sounded ominous. Fearful of the military, Wynkoop continued eastward, but Philadelphia was not his destination and he did not appear at his mother's home. When acting Commissioner of Indian Affairs Charles Mix tried to contact him in Philadelphia, his mother telegrammed Mix on September 26 that her son had not yet arrived.[65]

Wynkoop did not advertise his destination, but most likely headed for New York seeking support to end the war. Certainly he talked to anyone who would listen. On October 5 he wrote to Samuel Tappan, a fellow supporter of Indian rights who over the years had drifted in and out of Wynkoop's life. He updated Tappan on the problems that had led to the current war, then wrote about the Kiowas and Comanches. Both tribes lived in a state of starvation and had been ordered south. As whites had difficulty telling Indians apart, he worried that they might be attacked when passing through land controlled by soldiers, forcing them into the war.[66] A day later, on October 6, dispatches confirmed Wynkoop's fear. The Kiowas, Comanches, and Plains Apaches had joined the conflict.[67]

Wynkoop finally appeared at his mother's home in Philadelphia. On October 7, he ended his silence and wrote to Acting Commissioner Mix. He blamed the inefficiency of the Indian Bureau for the war. The Indians' game had dwindled, the government did not provide weapons for them to secure enough food to survive properly, and at the same time did not provide enough annuities (as promised) to see his wards through times of hunger. These failures had led directly to discontent, anger, and desperation.[68]

Wynkoop never completed his twenty days of vacation. On October 8 he received orders to return to the frontier and take control of his wards. The Interior Department ordered both him and new Comanche and Kiowa agent Albert Boone to report to Fort Cobb on the Washita River in Indian Territory, assemble their wards, and "keep them out of the war."[69]

As October passed, Sheridan's plans for a winter campaign took shape. Per Sherman's order to force the Indians to bow down to white supremacy, Sheridan plotted to enclose and strike the tribal bands where they wintered along the Washita River in Indian Territory.[70] He requested Custer's early recall from his one-year suspension from active duty, as he wanted a field commander more capable than Sully, one who would carry fire and sword to the enemy. "Custer, I rely on you in everything," Sheridan told his protégé.[71]

Continuing to lash out at military operations, Wynkoop wrote a letter that saw print and became general knowledge. It ignited the ire of Custer's second in command, Major Joel Elliott. Sitting in camp near Fort Dodge, Kansas, Elliott wrote to correspondent and artist Theodore Davis: "Ed. Wyncoop [sic] is out in a letter defending the Indians. If he were not so insignificant I would like to see him 'Touched up' in good style."[72] Elliott liked to pound his chest and proclaim his bravura. But the two men never met again, and Wynkoop never heard the threat.

In early November Wynkoop reached St. Joseph, Missouri, en route to his first destination, Lawrence, Kansas, where Murphy would hand him additional orders. After meeting with the superintendent he obtained a wagon, a harness, two horses, and a small tent, and continued his journey to Fort Cobb.[73]

But times had changed. He learned that five columns of troops were converging on the Washita River. As recently as two months earlier, Wynkoop had believed that innocent people could be protected if assembled in one place, but now he feared disaster. On November 29, 1868, while still en route to Fort Cobb, he wrote to Commissioner Taylor. "[Volunteer troops] have expressed their determination to kill under all circumstances the Indians of my agency. . . . [The Cheyennes and Arapahos] will readily respond to my call [to congregate at Fort Cobb], but I most certainly refuse to again be the instrument of the murder of innocent women and children. . . . All left me under the circumstances, with the present state of feelings I have in this matter, is now to respectfully tender my resignation."[74]

Two days before Wynkoop resigned his commission, on November 27, Lieutenant Colonel George Armstrong Custer and the Seventh U.S.

Cavalry had attacked and destroyed Black Kettle's Cheyenne village on the Washita River. Custer's official report stated, "The Indians left on the ground and in our possession [include] the bodies of one hundred and three of their warriors, including Black Kettle himself, whose scalp is now in possession of one of our Osage guides. . . . In the excitement of the fight, as well as in self-defense, it so happened that some of the squaws and a few children were killed and wounded."[75]

Unaware of Black Kettle's fate, Ned Wynkoop set out for the East. Over the years his views on war and race relations had been published many times. By now he knew that much of what he said and did was controversial. Knowing that he would set off another controversy, Wynkoop released his resignation letter to the press. A wide range of papers printed it, from the *Leavenworth Commercial* (December 9) to the *New York Times* (December 19), and, as he anticipated, it generated a maelstrom of comment. No longer would Wynkoop play the Judas goat. He was finally taking a stand.

At Atchison, Kansas, Wynkoop returned the government property in his possession to Thomas Murphy. He then set out for Washington, where he settled his account with the Interior Department. Then, on December 17, the Senate Committee on Indian Affairs, which was weighing the benefits of transferring the Indian Bureau to the War Department, questioned him about the Washita attack. He accused the military of forcing the Indians into war.[76]

After testifying before the Senate committee, Wynkoop traveled to New York. By now those offended by his reason for resigning were speaking out. He had stood up to the military for four years, and during that time high-ranking officers—Hancock, A. J. Smith, Sheridan—had struck back at him. Nothing had changed; again officers lined up to engage him in a battle of words. Unexpectedly, however, some eastern papers praised Custer's victory. After citing all Wynkoop's reasons for protesting, the *Brooklyn Daily Eagle* (December 14, 1868) stated, "It is well to accept Wynkoop's assertions with caution." Another paper, the *Chicago Post*, gave the former agent a backhanded compliment. "Col. Wynkoop has signalized himself by resigning. . . . Hence we trust he will be retained in service. Any man whom Johnson would be likely to nominate in his place would not be so willing to resign. Johnson's appointees never resign so long as there is anything left to steal."[77]

Wynkoop soon acquired new evidence to back up his accusations. James Morrison supplied him with an account of the attack on Black Kettle's village from two mixed-blood Arapahos, John Poysell, Jr. (or Poisal) and Jack Fitzpatrick, scouts who fought at the Washita with Custer. These men disagreed with the official report of casualties. They told Morrison at Fort Dodge "that there were not over twenty Bucks killed[;] the rest, about forty, were women & children."[78] They agreed with the official count of Indian captives: one Arapaho boy and fifty-two Cheyennes, including Mrs. Crocker, who was full-blooded. With Custer back in the field and Sheridan with him, Morrison reported, "the officers [at Fort Dodge] say that he [Custer] is going direct to Fort Cobb swearing vengeance on Indians and Indian Agents indiscriminately."

Ned Wynkoop had been a hero and a villain, and now his appearance in New York generated a stir. His views made him a "cause célèbre." Soon after his arrival in Manhattan, Peter Cooper invited him to meet with members of the General Committee of the United States Indian Commission. On December 21, 1868, Wynkoop met Cooper and five committee members in one of the Geographical and Statistical Society's rooms at the Cooper Union. After a few minutes of casual talk the committee got to the point. They wanted to know why Wynkoop had resigned his commission, what had led to the recent conflict, how it could have been avoided, and Black Kettle's background.

Wynkoop agreed to speak at 7:30 P.M. on December 23, and the conversation quickly turned to how best to excite "public sympathy and attention."[79] Having only two days to prepare did not give Wynkoop pause. He had been speaking out for four years and yearned for an opportunity such as this.

On the appointed evening Wynkoop arrived at the Cooper Union and patiently awaited his turn to speak. After being introduced, he took the podium in the cavernous hall and read from a letter he had written that day. He explained clearly why he had resigned his position as U.S. Indian agent, making explicit his fears that "I was only acting as a decoy to induce these Indians [those at peace] to present themselves in a locality where they were liable to be fallen upon at any moment and murdered."[80] He refused to again be "an accessory to the crime" of systematic slaughter. Wynkoop placed the blame for the continued hostilities on Chivington and Hancock. He then summarized the situation as

A rally for Democrats in favor of the Grant and Colfax platform at the Cooper Union in New York City on October 21, 1868, two months before Wynkoop appeared in the same hall at Peter Cooper's request and damned the attack on Black Kettle's Washita village. *Frank Leslie's Illustrated Newspaper* (November 7, 1868). Author's collection.

the "withholding of arms and ammunition disabling [the Indians] from procuring game for subsisting their families, which game was becoming more scarce every day, and the neglect to supply them with the absolute necessities of life drove some to desperation."

After Wynkoop finished his speech, he took questions. One, by the chair, got right to the point: how best to solve the Indian problem? Wynkoop said that the best way to end the difficulties would be "to extend American citizenship to the Indians, and allow their representatives seats in Congress."[81]

Strong words, words that set the stage for Wynkoop's next career move. His ability to continue walking between the races hinged upon the outcome of the forthcoming battle for control of the future of the Plains Indians. Wynkoop's stance piqued Peter Cooper's interest in protesting "the transfer of the Indian Bureau to the War Department." With this powerful advocate behind him, Wynkoop hustled to Philadelphia to enlist the support of influential Quakers.[82]

Back in Denver, Byers remained on the offensive. Over the years he had repeatedly used his paper to damn Wynkoop. He had never gotten over his anger at the accusation that the volunteers who attacked the Sand Creek village "were murderers." Now the *News* criticized Wynkoop again. "In the ardor of his friendship for the 'Noble Red man,'" it proclaimed, "[Wynkoop] threw up his commission; relinquished his nice berth, with all its perquisites. Of course, that step was for effect. He expected to overslaugh Custar [*sic*] and Sheridan, and plunge them into disgrace."[83]

The fight was beginning to take a toll on Wynkoop. From Philadelphia, where he now lived at 648 North 17th Street, on January 2, 1869, he wrote Samuel Tappan, enclosing a copy of Morrison's letter, which he asked him to share with the commissioners. In the letter he rhetorically asked which Indian leaders would next be put to death. Satanta? Little Raven? According to Wynkoop, more murders would unleash "another chapter of horrors to add to the damnable infamy." After lamenting that "this caps the climax of infernal atrocity," he wrote, "I will be damned if I don[']t desert my country[,] forswear Christianity and become a Mahometan if this state of affairs continue and is endorsed by the Government."[84] As he was a religious man, this comment shows how distraught he was.

Wynkoop had made a stand, and there would be no turning back. By January 5 he had returned to Washington, where he hoped to gain more support. He changed his resignation from the Interior Department to "unconditional." At this time the Indian Suffrage Party was formed in Texas. The *Rocky Mountain News* wasted no time proclaiming: "That's the outfit for Sam. Tappan, Ned. Wynkoop, and the *Omaha Herald*."[85] Not missing a chance to lash out at Wynkoop, the paper again reported that Hancock claimed that everything Wynkoop said in regards to the Pawnee Fork debacle was false.

Other frontier papers also attacked Wynkoop. On January 6, 1869, the *Colorado Transcript* wrote: "We regret our inability to lay before our readers in this issue a graphic account of General Custar's [*sic*] first fight with the Indians. . . . The battle of Wachita [*sic*] was regarded by Western men as a valiant conflict, and all honor will be bestowed upon the gallant officers and men who braved the inclemency of winter and storm to avenge the wanton outrages upon the frontier settlers."[86] In general the western press staunchly upheld their notions of right and wrong. And, as in the past, Wynkoop's stance placed him decidedly in the enemy camp. The *Transcript,* after praising the enlightenment of the East, added: "Yet it is astonishing, in the face of all that has occurred during the last few months, that an intelligent audience, headed by such an ordinarily practical man as Peter Cooper can swallow the falsehood and misrepresentation of such a person as Ned Wynkoop. The officer reports of Sheridan and Custar [*sic*], endorsed by General Sherman, give the lie to the twaddle of this *friend* of the Indian."

Try as it would, the western press failed to silence Wynkoop, who once again became a thorn in the government's side. Along with Thomas Murphy and agent Albert Boone, he sent letters to Nathaniel Taylor, who in turn forwarded them to Secretary of the Interior O. H. Browning. Taylor also included Sherman's correspondence, which supported the attack. Browning, in accordance with the December 14, 1868, U.S. Senate resolution that the Interior Department "communicate to the Senate all reports, papers, and other information in the department connected with the late battle of the Washita river," sent the package to the Honorable B. F. Wade, president pro tempore of the U.S. Senate.[87]

By the end of January, Wynkoop had returned to Philadelphia. Aware that newspapers continued to ridicule his insistence that Black Kettle and those with him remained peaceful, on January 26 he supplied Taylor with what he considered proof of his friend's innocence. Wynkoop knew that Black Kettle had not personally taken part in the Saline River raids. He included Morrison's December 14, 1868, letter that denied Custer's official report of 103 warriors killed and stated that Samuel Tappan had another letter that confirmed Morrison's statement. "There have been Indians deserving of punishment, but, unfortunately," Wynkoop wrote, "they have not been those who received it at the hands of the troops at the battle of the Washita."[88] After pointing out that the military justified the attack with alleged "evidence" of hostilities found in the village after the attack, he asked, "how did they know that those evidences existed previous to the assault?" Wynkoop concluded, "Mr. Morrison states that there were forty women and *children* killed, that fact needs no comment, it speaks for itself. I do not know whether the government desires to look at this affair in a *humane* light or not, and if it only desires to know whether it was *right* or *wrong* to attack the village refer[r]ed to; I must emphatically pronounce it wrong and disgraceful."

Wynkoop had gained a powerful ally in Peter Cooper. Certainly they discussed the continuing war and what needed to be done to prevent the continued extermination of Wynkoop's former wards. As the early days of 1869 passed, Ned Wynkoop tentatively began to set his sights on a position within the Interior Department. While unsure of his future, he wanted to continue working with Indians if possible. Although the position of U.S. Indian agent for the Navajos was not his first choice, it would soon become available. Wynkoop had heard that Colonel Frank Chaves, who was well known in the Southwest, would have a say in who became the next agent.[89]

On January 27, Wynkoop received a letter from Sam Tappan. Although the two were not close early in their careers, their similar views on Indian management now made them allies. We don't know what Tappan wrote to Wynkoop, but it evidently influenced him, for he immediately left for New York and then Washington.[90]

Realizing that Tappan counted Chaves as a friend, Wynkoop wrote to him on February 10. He fulfilled Tappan's request for information and assured him that Louise would gladly answer any questions regarding her experiences with Indians. Although he desired another position within the Interior Department, he could not ignore the job opening. Choosing his words carefully, Wynkoop asked Tappan if he would promote him as Navajo agent with Chaves.[91]

Southern Cheyenne women and children captured when Lt. Col. George Armstrong Custer and the Seventh U.S. Cavalry attacked and destroyed Black Kettle's Southern Cheyenne village on the Washita River, Indian Territory, on November 27, 1868. The image was most likely taken at Camp Supply, Indian Territory, in 1870. The woman holding the child (fourth from the left) may be Mo-nahs-e-tah, who gave birth to her first child on January 12, 1869, at Fort Cobb (on Medicine Bluff Creek) in Indian Territory. Courtesy of Little Bighorn Battlefield National Monument (Elizabeth B. Custer Collection, Catalog Number 391).

Although Wynkoop knew that his stance for Indian rights was unpopular, he naïvely thought his outrage over what he considered the wanton murder of innocent people would win the day. With characteristic optimism, he applied for a position that not only appealed to him but that he was qualified to perform. Most certainly Peter Cooper discussed the matter with him and probably even prompted him to apply. In March 1869 Cooper wrote to President Ulysses Grant on Wynkoop's behalf:

Having heard that Mr. E. Wynkoop is a candidate for the position of Superintendent of Indian Affairs and from the strong and earnest manner in which he is recommended by men to whom the welfare of our country is a consideration paramount to every other and from what I have known of himself personally and of his services among the Indians I consider him eminently fitted for the post of Superintendent of Indian Affairs and have no hesitation in commending him to your favorable notice.[92]

High praise, but without a future. Wynkoop waited, and waited, . . . and waited.

Almost alone, he had stood firm on his beliefs that Indians were human beings and should not be punished for the actions of a few. He understood the people he worked with, and would have made an exceptional superintendent of Indian affairs. But a confirmation never materialized. The people living on the frontier emphatically opposed him, the military constantly disagreed with him, and Andrew Johnson's lame-duck presidency lacked the strength to override powerful opposition.

Grant's ascendancy in Washington played a pivotal and final role in Wynkoop's future, but not in the way he expected. Wynkoop owed his commission to Johnson, and Grant had every intention of purging the old in favor of the new. The incoming president initiated massive change. Enoch Hoag soon replaced Thomas Murphy as superintendent and Eli Parker supplanted Nathaniel Taylor as commissioner. But not everything changed. Interpreters, lacking Wynkoop's support, struggled to obtain pay long owed them while the new Cheyenne and Arapaho agent, Brinton Darlington, echoed his predecessor as he fought to employ an interpreter.[93] Although the peaceful hand that Ulysses Grant's incoming administration held out to the Indians sounded good, the tribes were no longer considered independent nations. There would be no more treaties. The Cheyennes and Arapahos would live where they were told and do as they were told. Little more than prisoners of war, they would walk the white man's road or face the consequences.

Epilogue

Sometime in 1869—most likely after realizing he would not become superintendent of Indian affairs—Edward W. Wynkoop returned to Louise and their three children in Pennsylvania. Turning his back on the past, he joined his brother John in taking over the unsuccessful Anthracite Furnace from the Starr Iron Company to engage in the manufacturing of pig iron. Using "Wynkoop Bros." on their stationery, they operated the Stanhope Furnace. A one-hundred-horsepower engine powered two hot ovens and provided the steam that issued from the forty-foot furnace stack. It took thirty-two hundred pounds of coal to produce one ton of iron. John lived in Pottsville; Ned lived at the furnace, which was near Pinegrove, about one hundred miles from Philadelphia.

Ned learned the business quickly, and by September 1869 he considered himself an "ironmaster." It took two years to upgrade the furnace to almost new condition. Then, and only then, did they begin to show a profit.

"We have a beautiful place and a large house capable of accommodating any number of visitors," Wynkoop wrote John Tappan.[1] "I have horses, dogs, and guns, good fishing and hunting." After inviting Tappan and his family to visit, he asked his friend to "take an old fashioned toddy with me for the sake of 'Auld Lang Syne.'" And sometime after returning to Pennsylvania in 1869 the Wynkoops' fourth child, Francis (Frank) Murray Wynkoop was born.[2]

Although engaged in a new career, Wynkoop stayed abreast of the Indian rights movement from afar, owing in part to his acquaintance with Peter Cooper. In 1870 he traveled to New York to attend a United States Indian Commission convention at the Cooper Union on May 18. Opening the proceedings, Cooper spoke about the continued abuse of Indians by the U.S. government. Next, letters were read that espoused a number of diverse opinions, including one from Lieutenant General William T. Sherman inviting the attendees to travel to the frontier and see *real* Indians up close; the general's unstated implication was clear.

The assembly formed committees. After a lengthy debate Wynkoop joined the group that wrote resolutions while Cooper and Samuel Tappan's group recommended action. The assembly praised President Grant's peace policy, then called for Grant and both houses of Congress to act in a Christian and humane manner toward the Indians and end the government's violent practices.[3]

This marked the beginning of the end of Wynkoop's active participation in the Indian movement. As his involvement decreased, slipping into memory, the next few years passed uneventfully. Wynkoop continued working with John, entertained friends from his past, and enjoyed his family, which increased in size. With the arrival of Charles Wanshaer (January 6, 1871, Stanhope, Pennsylvania) and Harman Henry (December 6, 1872, Harrisburg, Pennsylvania), Mr. and Mrs. E. W. Wynkoop now had six children.[4] Times were good, but they would not remain so.

In September 1873 banker Jay Cooke's financial woes resulted in the bankruptcy of the Northern Pacific Railroad, leading to a panic that swept over Wall Street, part of a worldwide financial downturn. According to a modern historian, "Stocks and bonds began falling, and many banks simply shut their doors. The panic, a desperate run to find cash, reverberated from city to city. Tens of thousands lost everything," including Ned Wynkoop and his brother John.[5] Their iron plant in Stanhope became one of the casualties. From this point forward Wynkoop's primary concern became providing for his family. Luckily the firm that took over the Wynkoop business retained him to oversee it.

Working at his family's defunct business proved less than ideal, and it did not take Wynkoop long to sour on the new company. In early May 1875, perhaps hoping to recapture his youth on the frontier, he solicited support for a return to Indian duty. Benjamin Martin, a former member of the U.S. Indian Commission who had been impressed with Wynkoop years before, contacted President Grant and recommended Wynkoop be appointed Indian agent. H. B. Whipple, the Episcopal Bishop of Minnesota, respected what Wynkoop had done in the 1860s, and even though he did not know him, he presented Wynkoop's application as Indian agent to the Executive Committee.[6] There would be other recommendations, but, as in 1869, Wynkoop's reputation as one who stood firm in his beliefs quickly smashed his chances.

His early career had been marred with wanderlust and continual false starts until he became involved with Indians; now he found himself casting about and struggling with setbacks once again. Even though he had failed to land an Indian position, he looked to the West for opportunity. Leaving his family in Pennsylvania, Wynkoop headed for the frontier. Gold fever had motivated him in 1858, and in 1875 it was also the driving force behind his migration. Wynkoop reached the Black Hills, Dakota Territory, in early summer, hoping to recoup everything he had lost during the panic of 1873. Originally he used Custer City and Hill City on Spring Creek as his base of operations, but he had little luck and drifted thirty miles northward to White Wood and Deadwood gulches, which he felt were "rich in quartz and placer deposits."[7] In spite of his experience as a miner, the venture fizzled.

Wynkoop did not return home in December 1875 when Louise gave birth to their seventh child, Thomas Atwood.[8] Instead he clung to the hope of finding the Mother Lode. As the new year approached, he remained on the frontier even though the demanding physical labor drained him. By this time Deadwood, Dakota Territory, had become his home. Men bent upon striking it rich mined, drank, gambled, whored, begged, and fought. And as he had in Denver in the late 1850s, Wynkoop learned how to survive in a new boomtown.

. . .

In December 1875 the Commissioner of Indian Affairs ordered the Sioux living off the reservation to return to it by January 31, 1876, or face war. A harsh winter made travel almost impossible, and the deadline came and passed. At dawn on a frigid March 17, 1876, the military attacked an Oglala village on the Powder River in Montana Territory. Although the strike failed, the Sioux and their allies became the hunted as the military set in motion a three-pronged pincer movement designed to find and attack them in the spring.[9]

As the days warmed, more and more warriors left the reservations and joined the resistance, and as their numbers grew they became more aggressive. By late April 1876 whites living in Dakota Territory were starting to panic. When citizens in Custer City decided to form a militia called the Black Hills Rangers for protection, it reminded Wynkoop of another time, long gone, giving him a chance to relive his youth, if for only a fleeting moment. He knew soldiering, he knew how to command, and he knew Indians. Why not again?

Wynkoop took a leading role even though the West he once knew no longer existed. With his celebrity paving the way, he became captain of the Rangers. He held a recruiting meeting at the Metropolitan Hotel in Custer City on May 6, 1876.[10] The gathering proved a success. Between two and three hundred men enlisted to serve under Wynkoop. Captain Jack Crawford, the self-proclaimed poet scout, became his chief of scouts, initiating a long-lasting friendship.

If Wynkoop longed for action, he soon found it. In May he heard that Sioux warriors had attacked a wagon. With twenty Rangers he set out to rescue the beleaguered people, who were supposed to be near Red Canyon. While camped in Pleasant Valley, six whites, who had departed Custer City six hours before Wynkoop, stumbled into his camp at 2:00 A.M. and described the fight with the Sioux.[11] As in the past, Wynkoop saw no action. Most of the patrols amounted to little more than hard marches and deprivation. During one near Deadwood City, Wynkoop saw the barrel of a rifle sticking out of the mud. He stopped to investigate. When he pulled the stock from the goop, Wynkoop realized he held a "needle" rifle—a high-powered long-distance weapon.[12]

For Wynkoop the exhilaration of the Indian war would be short-lived. The spinal injury he had suffered in 1863, which for years had only caused him sporadic discomfort, had become chronic with the passage of time, limiting his physical activity. By 1876 the jarring motion of riding a horse shot spasms of pain up his spine. "At times he could not ride on horseback without very great suffering," Crawford observed, "and often walked while on marches on account of the pain caused by riding. He complained of urinary trouble, and I often observed that it was difficult for him pass urine."[13]

Ned Wynkoop returned to the frontier in 1875. This portrait was taken in 1876, when he was in Dakota Territory. Courtesy History Colorado (Scan #10040353).

When he spoke to the press, Wynkoop always presented his best face to the public, refusing to talk about health problems. In stark contrast to Crawford's assessment of his health, a local paper described him as "a fine specimen of a mountaineer."[14] Realizing that the Rangers were too few to function offensively or offer much protection, Wynkoop left for Washington on June 21, 1876, to solicit backing to organize a regiment of volunteer soldiers. Forever the optimist, he hoped to see Sheridan and the secretary of war, but nothing came of the trip.

The deterioration of Wynkoop's health frightened him. His short-lived adventure on the frontier had not resurrected his youth, and the days of walking with Indians had vanished, never to return. When he finished in the capital city, instead of going back to Deadwood Wynkoop hustled back to Pennsylvania and his family.

Wynkoop brought the needle rifle to Pennsylvania with him and displayed it. One day while he sat on his porch at Stanhope, curious fiends asked about the rifle. Wynkoop nonchalantly told them he could kill any living thing within a mile. When they scoffed, he smiled. Loading the weapon, Wynkoop took careful aim at a schoolhouse roof a little more than a mile away. Confident, he squeezed the trigger twice, and placed two bullets through the roof pitches of the building.[15]

With his family his only concern, Wynkoop spent the rest of his life making career moves in an effort to provide for them. There would be ups and downs, as he struggled to put food on the table. But he never turned his back on the 1860s, a time whose memory he cherished. In 1876 Wynkoop attempted to record his experiences on the frontier, a project he never came close to completing.[16]

April 1877 brought sadness and joy. On April 13 his mother, Angeline, died, and fifteen days later, on April 28, Louise gave birth to their last child, Rose M., in Pennsylvania.[17] Sometime after Rose's birth Wynkoop moved his family to Santa Fe, New Mexico. The wanderlust continued and he soon moved back to Pennsylvania, where he found employment at the Dauphin furnace. Again, the job did not last, and in 1881 he moved his family to Harrisburg, Pennsylvania.

In March 1882 Wynkoop became a Special U.S. Timber Agent in the General Land Office at a salary of $1200 annually plus expenses.[18] His duties were extensive, focusing on protecting timber on government land in New Mexico, Arizona, and part of Colorado. Again employed by the Department of the Interior, he moved back to Denver in April. As had happened with the Cheyennes when first he reunited with them in 1865, so it would be with Coloradans. "Ned Wynkoop, as he is known to all old settlers, is hourly greeted with open hands by all his old friends and associates, who are more than pleased to welcome him once more to the scenes of his early ventures and undertakings, and who are now glad to learn he has returned to remain and to devote his ability and energy in the city which he helped to form."[19] Times had changed, for the *Rocky Mountain News,* his old nemesis, concluded their story by saying "The News, in common with his many friends, join in a hearty welcome with best wishes for his success in the future." The reason for this reversal of editorial viewpoint was simple. William Byers, Wynkoop's most vocal critic, had sold the newspaper in May 1878.

Pueblo, Colorado, initially served as Wynkoop's headquarters, but within a year he moved to Santa Fe, New Mexico Territory, the town that would remain his home for his remaining years. In March 1883, soon after he set up his headquarters close to the plaza on San Francisco Street, Louise and the children joined him from Pennsylvania.

A short while after moving to Santa Fe, Wynkoop learned that a saw-mill operator named Joseph Rutledge had been illegally cutting timber on government land and ordered him to stop. As though on cue, Rutledge appeared at Wynkoop's office. Instead of apologizing or stating he had stopped cutting timber, he offered a bribe so he could continue breaking the law. According to his son, Frank, Wynkoop "leaped to his feet with a deep growl and an oath, seized his visitor and bodily pitched him through the office doorway into San Francisco street."[20]

The Southwest suited Wynkoop. At the same time, it reminded him of the man who more than any other represented the opening of the western frontier, Kit Carson. Although Carson had died in 1868, Wynkoop had not forgotten their brief encounter at the time of the Little Arkansas treaty talks. Since moving to Santa Fe, Wynkoop had become district commander of the Department of New Mexico Grand Army of the Republic (G.A.R.). He campaigned to secure funds for a proper marker for Carson's grave in Taos, New Mexico.[21]

Whatever he did, one thing remained a constant for Wynkoop—his struggle to provide for his family. Toward the end of 1884, he sensed that a change of political parties in the White House might end his tenure as timber agent and sought employment as warden of the New Mexico State Penitentiary. His friend from Dakota Territory, Jack Crawford, heard of his application and on his own wrote New Mexico Governor Lionel Allen Sheldon, but nothing came of the high praise the poet scout heaped upon him.[22]

Wynkoop's fears were well-founded. When Grover Cleveland became president in 1886, W. S. Fletcher replaced him as U.S. timber agent.[23] Unemployed, Wynkoop again became a miner, and in March he "located a well of illuminating oil at a point about four miles from Santa Fe."[24] But his discovery did not pan out, and the aimless move from job to job continued.

Although his Indian years were long gone, Wynkoop found himself in demand. People wanted to hear about what he had seen. His name preceded him, and at times he found himself bombarded with questions. Longing for the limelight, whenever asked he gladly talked about the old days. But now his words began to take on a life of their own, and with each retelling the stories grew. Most were based on fact, but some were not. He claimed he had met Custer in 1876 and warned him about the "foolhardy venture" of going after the Sioux. He even played cards with James Butler "Wild Bill" Hickok in Deadwood when the famed pistoleer held his infamous "dead man's hand."[25] While recounting his earlier exploits, he created his own set of tales, his own legend, which often garnered him praise in the press. In May 1886 the *Santa Fe Daily New Mexican* made a suggestion. "If Col. Wynkoop had the leisure and the opportunity he ought to utilize his fine literary powers in writing a history of the Indian campaigns in the far west. Such a book would be worth reading."[26] Wynkoop had begun such a project ten years before, but he would never return to it.

After a few lean months Wynkoop used his mining expertise and Santa Fe connections to land an appointment as mining agent. When the articles of association were filed in July 1886, the Toltec Mining Company of Santa Fe, New Mexico Territory, listed its capital stock at $100,000. Looking to the future, the company quickly expanded into Colorado. In August, after the articles became official, Wynkoop set up an office in Navajo City, Colorado.[27] The appointment meant additional separations from his family, who remained in Santa Fe. By October 1886 Wynkoop became convinced that the "Navajo river mining district" would pay dividends.[28] But again it proved to be a false lead.

Never one to walk away from a cause he cared about, for four years Wynkoop, with the G.A.R., pushed for a tribute to Kit Carson. When explorer John C. Frémont saw an article about their efforts, he wrote Wynkoop on June 7, 1888, asking about the memorial's progress. Wynkoop had good news, for he and the G.A.R. had succeeded. A column honoring Kit's memory had been erected in front of the building that became the United States Courthouse in Santa Fe.[29]

Another year passed, and in 1889 Wynkoop actively sought a new position, as U.S. timber inspector. Upon Governor L. Bradford Prince's submission of Wynkoop's name, William Stone forwarded the request to the secretary of the interior, who had the final say on the appointment. "I should be glad to have him appointed, because you recommend him," Stone wrote Prince.[30] "I have no doubt of his qualifications and of his merits." Certainly Wynkoop was a good choice as he had already served as timber agent.

However, before Wynkoop secured the position, Prince, who held him in high regard and placed "special trust and confidence in [his] ability and patriotism," offered him the position of Adjutant General of the Volunteer Militia of the Territory of New Mexico.[31] Wynkoop liked the idea and withdrew his application for timber inspector, becoming Adjutant General on December 2, 1889.[32]

Wynkoop's appointment coincided with an interesting episode in New Mexico's history. A secret organization of small ranchers and farmers, predominantly Hispanic, banded together in 1889 to protect land grants in San Miguel County, New Mexico. Known as Las Gorras Blancas (the White Caps), they began terrorizing ranchers who obtained and fenced off property that was part of the Las Vegas Land Grant. Beginning in April they rode at night, cut fences, destroyed crops, burned ranches, and shot people who opposed them. By the time Wynkoop had been sworn into office and paid a $5,000 bond, they had killed three men and wounded several others. Adjutant General Wynkoop boxed up fifty rifles and one thousand cartridges and set out for Las Vegas, New Mexico, arriving the night of December 11, 1889. Two days later local authorities arrested ten of the raiders, and although growing crowds who supported the White Caps posed a threat to the Las Vegas courthouse and jail, their presence did not erupt in violence and Wynkoop returned to Santa Fe.[33]

Even though the position of adjutant general appealed to Wynkoop, it did not last, as his health continued to deteriorate. The once slender and athletic man had put on a great deal of weight and now had difficulty walking. Less than four months after accepting the position, Wynkoop resigned (effective April 1, 1890) to become warden of the New Mexico Penitentiary, a position he had been interested in years earlier. Governor Prince made it clear that Wynkoop had not been forced to resign. "While gratified at his elevation to a more important position," Prince wrote, "we regret the loss which his resignation occasions to the Militia of the Territory.[34] Among the attractions of the position of warden were a pay increase and a second salary for Louise as matron for the female inmates.

Col. E.W.Wynkoop   "Capt. Jack"

Ned Wynkoop near the end of his life with his friend the self-proclaimed "Poet Scout" Capt. Jack Crawford. At this time Wynkoop was warden of the New Mexico State Prison. Ben Wittick, Courtesy Palace of the Governors Photo Archives (NMHM/DCA), Neg. No. 15714.

As he had in the past, Ned Wynkoop quickly made his mark. Within two months of assuming control of the penitentiary he secured permission to build a hospital for the inmates as well a four-acre garden that would provide the prisoners with vegetables year round. Wynkoop designed the hospital, erected by the inmates using stone they quarried and bricks they made at a zero cost to the government.[35] Wynkoop reduced

operating costs by more than half what they had been under his predecessor, Thomas P. Gable, while maintaining discipline "better than it was
at any time" previous to his tenure.[36]

Although it looked as if Colonel Wynkoop had discovered another
position to which he was well-suited, his luck did not last. His predecessor as warden, now a "gambling and whiskey saloon" owner, won election to the House of Representatives of New Mexico Territory and, still
seething over having had been forced to resign his position as warden
due to sexual misconduct, decided to attack his successor's administration.[37] By the arrival of summer 1890 Wynkoop had no clue that trouble
loomed on the horizon. At the same time his health continued to deteriorate. Unsure how long he would be able to function as warden,
on June 7 the man who had always appeared so robust applied for an
invalid's pension. His failing health a concern, he filed another request
on July 29. The second claim read in part: "That he is totally unable to
earn a support by reason of affection of the kidneys and bladder; also
from injury to the spine, by horse falling on him."[38] The application met
with approval, and he received a pension of twelve dollars per month.[39]

His pension in place, Wynkoop concentrated on administering the
prison. His tenure saw over 350,000 bricks produced (many of which
were used to construct the hospital), a new sewer installed, an ice pond
credit of $462.90, no reports of brutality by the guards, and, other than
one eruption at the dinner table, no misconduct by the inmates.[40] Louise
also received a glowing review. "We found Mrs. Wynkoop, the matron
of the institution, attending to her duties with the diligence of a trained
and thorough housekeeper," one newspaper reported, also commenting
on "her kindly, motherly eye."[41]

In spite of his exemplary record, Wynkoop was again attacked. Gable
claimed that he misused funds and added the totally unexpected charge
that Assistant Superintendent José Manuel Montoya engaged in illicit
sexual activity with an inmate (Ada Hulmes). Wynkoop immediately
contacted General Edward L. Bartlett in January 1891. "I have a favor
to ask of you," he wrote. "I am sick and cannot leave the building [he
failed to state he had trouble walking]. But I must see you on a matter
of importance connected with the institution; very great importance."[42]
Gable's attack boiled down to Warden Wynkoop being a Republican.
The colonel had no intention of ignoring what he considered an insult
and wrote Gable a scathing letter. When L. Bradford Prince questioned

his actions, Wynkoop vented his anger at the governor. "I must state that the letter I wrote Gable although impolite and hasty was not unjust," Wynkoop fumed. "In his speech on the floor of the 'House' he [Gable] indirectly charged my wife with cruelty to the female convicts in her charge, by stating there were six poor native women crowded into one room while Ada Hulmes had two rooms and a piano."[43]

Refusing to ignore the charge of corruption, Wynkoop instigated an investigation. In addition to Wynkoop, witnesses included Assistant Superintendent Montoya, guards, prisoners (including Hulmes), civilians, the territorial treasurer, members of the legislative council of New Mexico, and a district attorney for two New Mexico counties.[44]

The result was unanimous. The Special Committee reported to the Legislative Council of the Territory of New Mexico "that the charges preferred against the Officers [Wynkoop and his subordinates] are unfounded, perjured and malicious." After criticizing Gable, a Democrat, for attempting to drag the Republican party through the mud, the committee stated: "The record and facts prove that robbery, rascality, extravagance and sensuality characterized the administration of T. P. Gable while honesty, economy and the best interests of the public characterized the present administration."[45]

As in the past, the press had a field day. Divided and politically motivated, newspapers either attacked Wynkoop's administration or stood behind it. "We are convinced and we bel[i]eve anyone who will take the trouble to investigate the matter will be satisfied that the criticisms were unjust and wholly undeserved," one paper claimed.[46] "The territorial penitentiary is a well regulated prison, and those in charge of it deserve praise rather than censure."

Having been there before, Wynkoop knew what was coming: the end of yet another career. A political power play, backed by an upcoming board vote, forced Wynkoop to resign before "the cabal of unprincipled conspirators that controlled the last legislature" met "and went through the farce of appointing a Warden."[47] Even though public opinion supported him, reflecting the view of the *Las Vegas Optic* that he was not "culpable in any degree for the alleged shortcomings in the management of that institution," Wynkoop, who had already resigned, lost a politically motivated vote and was replaced.[48]

Barely able to walk, his weight now a robust 247 pounds, and with his ailments growing, Wynkoop knew the end was near. In August 1891, a sick man traveled to Ojo Caliente, New Mexico, to see if the hot waters would ease the pain that wracked his body.[49] The treatment did not help, and he returned to his home in Santa Fe.

The last year had played hell with Wynkoop's health, "an attack of la grippe having brought on muscular rheumatism which, about January last, resulted in inflam[m]ation of the bladder."[50] He died of kidney disease at his home on the evening of September 11, 1891. The *Santa Fe New Mexican* praised him the following day. "The death of Col. 'Ned' Wynkoop, as he was familiarly known throughout the entire Rocky mountain region, will cause sadness all over the west. He was a man of many superior characteristics. Brave as a lion, he made a model soldier and military officer. Honest, big-hearted, chivalrous, as true as steel, he had the faculty of making friends readily and keeping them." Bishop J. Mills Kendrick officiated over Wynkoop's funeral at the Episcopal Church on September 13.

. . .

Louise needed additional funds to survive and applied for a pension shortly after her husband's death, listing only her youngest daughter, Rose, as a dependent on the application.[51] She eventually returned to Denver with Rose and moved into a residence on Stout Street. John Chivington lived five doors away.

Shortly after Louise's move to Denver, son Harman landed a job as a compositor for the *Rocky Mountain Herald*. One day a tall white-haired man entered the shop and owner Halsey Rhodes introduced him. "Mr. Wynkoop," Rhodes said, "this is Colonel John M. Chivington." Chivington shook Harman's hand and looked at him for a while. "I did not know I would ever have the pleasure of meeting one of Major Ned Wynkoop's boys," Chivington said. "Your father was an excellent soldier, brave, honest and always a gentleman." Harman, like his father, refused to bend from what he thought correct. "Colonel Chivington," he replied, "I want to thank you for what you have just said of my father. I appreciate it very much. But, sir, I will always have the same feeling toward you and your men for the Sand Creek Massacre that my father had to his dying day."[52]

Chivington and Wynkoop had kept their distance from each other ever since Sand Creek. But now, stung by Harman's words, probably aware of Louise's struggle to survive, and perhaps hoping to mend the past, Chivington signed an affidavit in support of her bid for a pension. With others also signing affidavits, Louise eventually secured the pension. It increased to $25.00 per month in 1906, and ultimately reached $30.00.[53]

In 1905 Louise moved to San Francisco, where she joined two of her daughters' families.[54] The following year she survived the San Francisco earthquake. Sixteen years later, in December 1922, she became ill with bronchial pneumonia, and was already suffering from "arteriosclerosis with senility," and "general debility." The pneumonia, along with a clot on her brain, finally ended Louise's life. Having outlived her husband by over a quarter century, she died at Franklin Hospital in San Francisco on November 4, 1923.[55]

· · ·

Edward W. Wynkoop's years of walking between the races show that he was both a man of his times, capable of following a career path wherever it led, and at the same time willing to stand up for what was right and speak out against what he thought was wrong. Like many of his pre–Civil War contemporaries, he went "a-westering" to make his fortune in the late 1850s, harboring the prejudice against Indians that was widespread on the frontier. When presented with an opportunity to end war he chose to act without orders and risk his command regardless of the consequences. This decision set in motion a string of events that saw his life change from avowed Indian hater to someone who accepted people of another race as human beings, a metamorphosis that would cause a major upheaval in his life. Wynkoop had been a popular personality in Colorado Territory, and his popularity grew with the Civil War victory at Glorieta Pass. It soared when his mediation with warring Indians appeared to end war in 1864, only to plummet when he spoke out against the attack on the Sand Creek village. The stance he took turned him into an outsider while it set him on course to work with Indians, first on detached duty from the military, then as special Indian agent, and finally as U.S. Indian agent.

The West into which he ventured was rife with seekers after riches, land, and power. The nation would expand at the cost of an earlier lifeway. Wynkoop stood out in this environment for his refusal to allow his quest for riches to trump his conscience. At times the stance he took put him at odds with everyone—civilians, military personnel, government officials, the press, and even the Indians under his charge. Many of his decisions were controversial and not in tune with the accepted culture of western expansion. People spoke vehemently, publicly, and repeatedly against his actions, which had an enormous impact upon his life and career, an impact that cannot be overstated. Wynkoop walked a lonely road that allowed him to develop into a true westerner, a man who was not afraid to break the rules and who lived by a combination of intelligence, ethics, and courage.

Throughout Wynkoop's life, he repeatedly found himself in the presence of decision makers. During the 1860s he was party or witness to most of the major events involving the Southern Cheyennes on the central and southern plains. Never one to shy away from controversy, he always made his views clear, which in turn kept his name before the frontier public. And although some backed his views, most took exception to his efforts. His decision to meet the Indians in 1864, brave or foolish, changed his life forever. It also drew the line from which the public has since viewed him. The chance he took to speak with the enemy eventually ended his military career, damned his career as Indian agent, and ultimately relegated him to minor player when historians documented the Indian wars.

Until he stood up against the attack at Sand Creek, he had been regarded as a reckless and charming Denver pioneer. By 1865 he had become persona non grata—even a pariah. He remained an outsider, encountering varying degrees of hatred, until he quit working with Indians at the end of 1868. These two sides of his image, which made him a lightning rod for controversy during the 1860s, have still not been resolved even after a century and a half. The reason is simple: racial prejudice. As recently as the early twenty-first century, he has been blamed for the massacre at Sand Creek he had tried so desperately to prevent.[56]

The stance Wynkoop took in 1865 changed his image forever, and whenever he became newsworthy, the frontier press wasted little time criticizing him. Already evident after the events at the Pawnee Fork in 1867, this tendency continued until the press did little but call him a liar.

Wynkoop dared to speak up and point out that the "other side" had a viewpoint. For the most part this was not acceptable during the 1860s.

Many frontier vocabularies did not include the term "humanity," especially with reference to American Indians. According to this worldview, the other side—Roman Nose, Black Kettle, and Stone Forehead of the Cheyennes, or Geronimo and Naiche of the Apaches—can never have an opinion that is valid. It does not matter that they fought for their freedom, their land, their religion, and their loved ones for they are damned. And anyone who dares to speak up for them is also damned. Speaking out destroyed reputations in the 1860s and continues to do so well into the twenty-first century.

Looking at Wynkoop's Indian years it is easy to appreciate his humanitarian stance. At the same time, we do him a disservice if we do not give him credit for standing up to everyone who disagreed with him. If we can compare him to a film persona, he fought injustice with all the moral fortitude of the characters Errol Flynn portrayed during the golden age of cinema. Of course Flynn's humanity and his stand for justice always won out by the final reel of the film, whereas Wynkoop walked away from the pinnacle of his life knowing he had failed. During the 1860s human beings on both sides of the conflict suffered atrocities, starvation, rape, death, mutilation, and he could not stop the onslaught. For someone who stepped into the fray body and soul, this defeat was monstrous.

And Wynkoop never recovered.

For the remainder of his life, another twenty-three years, he forever found himself on the fringe as he struggled to support his family, whom he loved dearly. He had dared to reach out and grasp at the heroic image we now recognize as the Flynn persona, only to miss and recede into the life of an ordinary man.

Wynkoop was outraged by the perfidy of butchering people who thought peace had returned to their lives. That brutality pushed him over a line from which there would be no return. He crossed that line knowing full well what the future held. This was a brave act of conscience. To this day many people refuse to cross this line. Wynkoop dared, and was depicted as a villain, or even a traitor.

Wynkoop dared to step beyond the accepted mores of his day and dared to say no to what he knew was wrong. He did not care what others called him, for he chose to live by a dictum that would benefit all of us: "Whatever you do in this life, make sure you can live with it."[57]

Wynkoop did, and by so-doing reached into a future that still has not arrived. If only we could dare to reach out as Edward Wanshaer Wynkoop did during the 1860s, our world would be a better place today.

It is appropriate to end this book by quoting George Bent's straightforward characterization of the man he once knew. "[Ned] Wynkoop," he said, "was the best friend [the] Cheyennes and Arapahos ever had."[58]

Notes

CHS   Colorado Historical Society
NA   National Archives
NMSRC&A   New Mexico State Records Center and Archives
OR   War of the Rebellion: A Compilation of the Official Records of the
            Union and Confederate Armies
RMN   *Rocky Mountain News*

PREFACE AND ACKNOWLEDGMENTS

1. Bent's errors are more egregious than Gatewood's or Wynkoop's, for he was much further removed from the events when he recorded them and had far less material available to assist him.

2. Wynkoop, "Unfinished Colorado History" (manuscript), 1, Wynkoop Papers, MSS 695, Colorado Historical Society, Denver (hereafter referred to as CHS). Edward W. Wynkoop Collection (AC 247), Chávez History Library, houses a readable typescript of Wynkoop's manuscript by W. Charles Bennett, Jr. Wynkoop's manuscript saw print as Gerboth, ed., *The Tall Chief*. Gerboth correctly comments that Wynkoop's manuscript is poorly named as its scope encompasses much more than just Colorado history (vii). Unfortunately the publication has numerous errors. For example, Gerboth states that Wynkoop was an old thirty-nine when he returned to Pennsylvania in 1868 (vi), that Wynkoop resigned his commission as U.S. Indian agent on November 27, 1868 (30, 138n58), and that Lieutenant Colonel George Armstrong Custer and the Seventh U.S. Cavalry attacked Black Kettle's Southern Cheyenne village on the Washita River (present-day Oklahoma) on November 28, 1868 (30). Wynkoop was thirty-two when he returned to Pennsylvania, Custer attacked on November 27, and Wynkoop resigned on November 29. Other information in Gerboth's short biography of Wynkoop is also of questionable value.

PROLOGUE. FORMATIVE YEARS

1. Wynkoop, *Genealogy* (1904), 146. "Wanshaer" is the correct spelling of "Wanshear."

2. Christopher H. Wynkoop to author (July 30, 2007), Wynkoop manuscript review, Louis Kraft Collection (AC 402), Fray Angélico Chávez History Library.

3. Christopher H. Wynkoop to author (July 30, 2007); Wynkoop, *Genealogy* (1904), 146. Wynkoop to author (May 22 and July 16, 1999; July 30, 2007), and Wynkoop, "Descendants of Edward Wanshaer Wynkoop," 1, Kraft Collection. Angeline's father was Britton Estill.

4. Wynkoop to author (July 30, 2007). Spring Garden appears in written records for the first time in 1808.

5. Wynkoop, *Genealogy* (1904), 146.

6. Wynkoop, *Genealogy* (1904), 146; Kraft, "Wynkoop's Early Years," 21.

7. Wynkoop to author (May 22 and July 16, 1999), and Wynkoop, "Descendants of EWW," 1. The owner of the other half of the Spring Garden properties was Charles Shippen.

8. *Philadelphia Public Ledger* (July 6, 1837).

9. A great many printed and handwritten primary sources call Wynkoop "Ned," and, sometimes, "Ed." "Local Affairs, The Remains of Colonel Francis M. Wynkoop," *The Miners' Journal and Pottsville General Advertiser* (March 1, 1862), 2.

10. "Local Affairs, The Remains of Colonel Francis M. Wynkoop," *The Miners' Journal and Pottsville General Advertiser* (March 1, 1862), 2; Hackenburg, *War with Mexico*, 95–96; Roberts, *Mexican War Veterans*, 69. No stranger to the poetic word, Francis Wynkoop also published poetry. See F. M. Wynkoop, "The Baron's Ride," *Graham's Magazine* (February 1844), 74–75, for an example of his verse.

11. Frank Wynkoop, "Reminiscences," 2, mistakenly states his Uncle Francis was a general.

12. U.S. Department of Commerce and Labor Bureau of the Census, 1850 United States Census, Population, Hempfield Township (Westmoreland County, Pennsylvania), M432, Roll 837, 215.

13. Wynkoop daguerreotype, author's collection (photograph of daguerreotype in Kraft Collection).

14. Wynkoop's composition and handwriting in the multitude of reports and letters he wrote during his adult years clearly demonstrate his command of the English language.

15. Wynkoop to author (July 30, 2007).

16. Wynkoop, *Genealogy* (1904), 146.

17. Roberts, *Mexican War Veterans*, 70.

18. Greene, "Land-offices," 1–2.

19. Greene, "Land-offices," 4–5, 9; Bennett, "Reminiscences," 46n3. Brindle held the position of receiver until March 1861. Ely Moore of New York became the first register of the land office when it opened. The land office relocated to Topeka, Kansas, in September 1861.

CHAPTER 1. GONE A-WESTERING

1. Frank Wynkoop, "Intimate Notes," 1. Harman H. Wynkoop claimed his father's height was six feet, three and a half inches. HHW to Dorothy Gardiner (April 20, 1949), Wynkoop Papers, MSS 695, CHS.

2. Frank Wynkoop, "Reminiscences," 3. Also see Edward Estill Wynkoop, "Wynkoop," 71. Edward Estill's document is also available in manuscript form in the Wynkoop Collection, Chávez History Library.

3. Wynkoop, "Unfinished Colorado History," 1. Bennett, "Reminiscences," 46n1. The side-wheeler was named after St. Louis–Santa Fe–Chihuahua merchant Francois Xavier Aubry. The vessel is incorrectly called *F. F. Aubrey* in Gerboth, *Tall Chief*, 37.

4. Edward Estill Wynkoop, "Wynkoop," 71; Greene, "Land-offices," 6.

5. Author tour of the building which is now known as Constitution Hall, a national landmark, with site administrator Tim Rues, Kansas State Historical Society (May 29, 2008). At an unknown later date an entry into the south side of the structure was added.

6. Wynkoop, "Unfinished Colorado History," 3.

7. Crawford, "Candle-box," 200–201; Greene, "Land-offices," 6. Crawford called Henry "Harry." Hardman Petrikin was killed at Antietam. Although some spelled Petrikin as

"Peterkin" or "Petriken," Petrikin is the correct spelling. See Wynkoop/Petrikin ad in *Kansas National Democrat* on January 13, 1859, 3, and subsequent issues.

8. Wynkoop, "Unfinished Colorado History," 2.

9. Crawford, "Candle-box," 200.

10. Wynkoop, "Unfinished Colorado History," 3. Also see "Duelists and Dueling in Colorado," *Denver Inter-Ocean* (March 11, 1882), 136.

11. Wynkoop, "Unfinished Colorado History," 4 (also see 3), for the entire exchange with the Quaker.

12. Johannsen, "Lecompton Constitutional Convention," 226, and n2; Wynkoop, "Unfinished Colorado History," 4.

13. Gihon, *Geary and Kansas*, 293–99; Johannsen, "Lecompton Constitutional Convention," 226–27; Bennett, "Reminiscences," 46n4.

14. Bennett, "Reminiscences," 47n8. Walker served as governor until November 16, 1857.

15. Wynkoop, "Unfinished Colorado History," 4–5; Bennett, "Reminiscences," 46n7; Greene, "Land-offices," 3. Wynkoop mistakenly placed Paola in southwestern Kansas. Other Indian tribes that experienced a forced removal from their homelands in the East only to suffer a reduction of their reservations included the Sacs and Foxes, Kickapoos, Delawares, Shawnees, Chippewas, and Wyandottes, among others.

16. Wynkoop, "Unfinished Colorado History," 6–9, through Wynkoop's quotes that end the meeting. Also see Bennett, "Reminisces," 47n9–n11.

17. Wynkoop, "Unfinished Colorado History," 10–11. This section is crossed out in Wynkoop's draft, which presumably means if there were a second draft it would not have been included.

18. Wynkoop, "Unfinished Colorado History," 11–13. Again, this incident has been crossed out.

19. Wynkoop, "Unfinished Colorado History," 13–15. Wynkoop made an error here. He said that the gold caravan made a right turn away from the road and traveled in a westerly direction. He could not have traveled in a westerly direction unless the train made a left turn.

20. West, *Contested Plains*, 6–7. West erroneously called Kansas a state; it did not become a state until 1861.

21. Wynkoop, "Unfinished Colorado History," 19; Frank Wynkoop, "Reminiscences," 3; Christopher H. Wynkoop to author (July 30, 2007), Kraft Collection.

22. Wm. O'Donnall to *Lawrence Republican* (September 27, 1858), 88, and W. O'Donnall to *Lawrence Republican* (November 18, 1858), 163, in Hafen, *Gold Rush*; J. W. Denver to William H. H. Larimer (November 19, 1890), in Davis, *Larimer*, 90–91, 97; Wynkoop, "Unfinished Colorado History," 20; Bennett, "Reminiscences," 47n12, 48n18. O'Donnall was one of the members of the Smith/Wynkoop party, but would not be listed as a member of the Denver City Town Company. At this time the land that would eventually become Colorado was part of Kansas Territory. The 1855 Kansas legislature created the boundaries of Arapahoe County that year. Edward Estill Wynkoop, "Wynkoop," 71, 72n3, erroneously lists "John" Larimer treasurer; the Denver City Town Company did not have a member named John Larimer. For additional references of Wynkoop named as sheriff see letters dated December 2 and 14, 1858, in Hafen, *Gold Rush*, 177, 182.

23. Wynkoop, "Uncompleted Colorado History," 21, and 20. Wm. O'Donnall to *Lawrence Republican* (September 27, 1858), 88. Also see Bennett, "Reminiscences," 48n18; West, *Contested Plains*, 154. As has since been proved, the Republican River did not come close to the gold fields.

24. Wynkoop, "Unfinished Colorado History," 24–25. Also see 21–23.

25. Bennett, "Reminiscences," 48n19 and n20; Gerboth, *Tall Chief*, notes on 51–53; Wynkoop, "Unfinished Colorado History," 29–31. Wynkoop mistakenly thought Puebla was an old Spanish fort. The city of Pueblo, Colorado, now occupies the land where the adobe ruins once stood. Palmer Divide is approximately twenty miles north of Colorado Springs, Colorado.

26. W. O'Donnall to *Lawrence Republican* (November 18, 1858), in Hafen, *Gold Rush,* 163, and n206; Davis, *Larimer,* 77–78; Bennett, "Reminiscences," 48n21.

27. H. C. Rogers to Col. N. C. Claiborne (November 2, 1858), in Hafen, *Gold Rush,* 148. Here controversy appears. Larimer's entry in the Denver City Town Company record book (November 24, 1858), in Smiley, *Denver,* 212, placed the arrival at Cherry Creek on November 12, and on the South Platte on November 16; also see William H. H. Larimer, in Davis, *Larimer,* 78–82. The disparity in the dates is difficult to explain, and leads this writer to question when the entry to the record book was made, for Rogers's letter is quite clear, stating, "We arrived on Cherry creek on the evening of the 30th of last month, and on this stream to-day." Also, Larimer's math is faulty.

CHAPTER 2. TO CIVILIZATION AND BACK

1. "Latest Intelligence From the Gold Mines of Western Kansas," *Lawrence Republican* (December 30, 1858), in Hafen, *Gold Rush,* 131–32.

2. McGaa "Statement," 126–27; Hoig, *Smith,* 110.

3. "Latest Intelligence From the Gold Mines of Western Kansas," *Lawrence Republican* (December 30, 1858).

4. McGaa "Statement," 127. Also see Hoig, *Smith,* 112; Leonard and Noel, *Denver,* 8. There may have been forty-two members. Larimer never admitted that he threatened anyone.

5. Davis, *Larimer,* 89–90, 97–99; Frank Wynkoop, "Intimate Notes," 1; Wynkoop, "Unfinished Colorado History," 32–33; *Field and Farm* (August 31, 1889), 5; McGaa, "Statement," 128; West, *Contested Plains,* 112; Hoig, *Smith,* 112; Bennett, "Frontiersman," 19–20; Zamonski, *'59ers,* endpaper map, 17; Smiley, *Denver,* 213, 219; Bennett, "Reminiscences," 48n17; Bromwell, *Colorado Argonauts,* 2:307–308; "The New Eldorado," *Agitator* (February 10, 1859), 2; Wharton, *Denver,* 71–73. Moore, "Lecompton Party," 448–49, was confused. He claimed the Smith/Wynkoop outfit arrived at Cherry Creek on June 17, 1858. The outfit he accompanied to the gold fields set out in May 1858, had no connection with Governor Denver, and did not name the new town site Denver.

6. Hill letter (November 28, 1858), in Hafen, *Gold Rush,* 173–74.

7. Larimer to Rachel (November 23, 1858), Davis, *Larimer,* 100.

8. Wynkoop, "Unfinished Colorado History," 31, CHS. Also see G. N. Hill letter in Kansas City *Journal of Commerce* (January 15, 1859).

9. Noel Lajeunesse to father (December 2, 1858), Hafen, *Gold Rush,* 178.

10. Wynkoop, "Unfinished Colorado History," 33; Lajeunesse to father (December 2, 1858), J. B. Wisenall letter (December 3, 1858), Hafen, *Gold Rush,* 177 and n232, 178; Larimer to Rachel (November 23, 1858), Davis, *Larimer,* 102, also see 105; "Latest From the Gold Region," *Missouri Republican* (February 8, 1859); "The New Eldorado," *Agitator* (February 10, 1859), 2; and Isern, "Controversial Career," 2. Although based upon memory, another report claimed that Wynkoop and Steinberger set out on December 1 and departed the region on December 11, 1858.

11. Wynkoop, "Unfinished Colorado History," 34–36. It seems logical that they obtained the pony from the Arapahos, as this was the only "wild" tribe that Wynkoop singled out during the trip.

Eleven days after Wynkoop and Steinberger set out for Lecompton, another disgruntled Auraria resident complained about Governor Denver's officials. "Men sent out among people like we are, to administer the laws, should be men of good character. I am sorry to say there is considerable drinking and humbugging going on." Even though he called out Sheriff "Wynecoop" [sic] along with H. P. A. Smith and Larimer, there is a possibility that he included Wynkoop as he had heard the name. A. F. B. to *Council Bluffs Bugle* (December 14, 1858; published February 23, 1859), Hafen, *Gold Rush,* 182.

12. Wynkoop, "Unfinished Colorado History," 39–41, for the entire ice/river incident.

13. Wynkoop, "Unfinished Colorado History," 42–45, for the entire encounter with the Pawnees.

14. Wynkoop, "Unfinished Colorado History," 42. Also see 41.

15. Wynkoop, "Unfinished Colorado History," 45–46, including "somewhat reliable" quote. Byers and Kellom, *Gold Fields,* 86; Hafen, *Gold Rush,* 177n232.

16. Wynkoop spelled Herndon as "Hernden."

17. Wynkoop, "Unfinished Colorado History," 46.

18. Mac letter (January 10, 1859), in White, *Plains and Rockies,* 7:379, including Steinberger's gold quote.

19. Byers and Kellom, *Gold Fields,* 85–92.

20. "Ho! For the Gold Region" ad, *Kansas National Democrat* (January 27, 1859), 2. This long and detailed publicity advertisement contained an interesting assortment of facts and errors. It stated that Wynkoop and Steinberger completed their journey to Lecompton in thirty-two days, arriving on January 23, 1859. January 23 is an obvious error. They arrived in Omaha after twenty-eight or twenty-nine days of travel, and adding to this total, it is safe to say it took them another three or four days on the trail to complete the trip to Lecompton which would place the arrival date near January 10. This is important as Wynkoop arrived in Lecompton before the Territorial Legislature met on January 11.

21. Wynkoop, "Unfinished Colorado History," 46–47.

22. Petrikin/Wynkoop ad in *Kansas National Democrat* (January 13, 1859), 3. The ad also appeared in subsequent issues.

23. Smiley, *Denver,* 219. For an example of a Denver City Town Company stock certificate, see Edward Estill Wynkoop, "Wynkoop," 73. The *Wynkoop Scrapbook* was assembled using Denver City Town Company stock certificates.

24. During the territorial years of Kansas (1854–61) eleven men served as governor or acting governor.

25. "Important Trial," *Weekly RMN* (April 18, 1861), 2; Cobb, "Lawrence Party of Pike's Peakers," 196 (John Smith is missing from Cobb's list); Smiley, *Denver,* 219–20, 328; "Latest From the Gold Region," *Missouri Republican* (February 8, 1859); Wharton, *Denver,* 71–73.

26. Smiley, *Denver,* 220. At this time (January 17, 1859) a journal placed Wynkoop in a very confusing and undocumented "Arapahoe Village" in the Cherry Creek gold region. See Hafen, "George A. Jackson's Diary, 1858–1859," 207. Wynkoop's presence in Lecompton in early January 1859 totally discounts this entry and questions the validity of Jackson's journal.

27. "Latest From the Gold Region!" *Kansas National Democrat* (January 27, 1859), 2, through Wynkoop leading another party to the gold fields.

28. The Colorado River had been discovered as early as 1540 and became known as the Río Colorado by 1620. When the Grand and Green rivers were discovered (about 1776), it became known as the Grand and the Colorado, among other names, until May 25, 1921, when the House of Representatives (67th Cong., 1st Sess., Rep. 97, 1) officially named the river that "is formed by the junction of the Grand and Green Rivers" the Colorado River.

29. "Ho! For the Gold Region" ad, *Kansas National Democrat* (January 27, 1859), 2.

30. Smiley, *Denver*, 220.

31. "Ho! For the Gold Region" ad (January 27, 1859), 2; Rowena Hotel ad (September 1, 1859), 3, *Kansas National Democrat*.

32. "Cheap and Expeditious Passage to Pike's Peak," *Herald of Freedom*, cited in Hafen, *Gold Rush*, 271–72.

33. "The Reception of Governor Denver's Officers," *Kansas National Democrat* (February 3, 1859), 2.

34. Cobb, "Lawrence Party of Pike's Peakers," 196–97. The Territorial Legislature repealed the incorporation of the St. Charles Town Company on February 24, 1860.

35. "Pike's Peak Meeting," *Kansas National Democrat* (April 14, 1859), 3, for the entire meeting.

36. At this point we run into a problem. Apparently no issues of the *Kansas National Democrat* exist for April 21 and 28, 1859, and subsequent issues say nothing about a Wynkoop-led departure for the gold fields. Wynkoop, in "Unfinished Colorado History," 47, stated that he did not set out for the gold fields until summer 1859 (actually it was late summer 1859). This conclusively undermines Gower's understanding of the events (*Gold Fever*, 62). Even though Gower's documentation does not substantiate a spring departure for the gold fields, he concludes that Wynkoop set out in April 1859.

37. Gerboth, *Tall Chief*, 64fn.

38. "Off for Pike's Peak," *Kansas National Democrat* (September 1, 1859), 3; Wynkoop, "Unfinished Colorado History," 47. Wynkoop mistakenly thought the departure date was late August.

39. Wynkoop, "Unfinished Colorado History," 47–48, through the "deceived the public" quote.

40. Dial, *Saloons*, 10, 12.

41. Louise Wynkoop Certificate of Death (November 27, 1923), Wynkoop Pension File; Christopher H. Wynkoop to author (July 30, 2007); Christopher H. Wynkoop, "Brown-Wakely Family Descendants," Kraft Collection; Frank Wynkoop, "Data Concerning . . . Wynkoop," Colorado College, 1.

42. Dorset, *Eldorado*, 62–63.

43. "Local Items" and "Theatre at the Apollo Hall," *Weekly RMN* (September 28, 1859), 3; De La Torre, "Theatre Comes to Denver," 291; Dorset, *Eldorado*, 63.

CHAPTER 3. THE STREETS OF DENVER

1. *Wynkoop Scrapbook*, 4–6; Kraft, "Wynkoop's Early Years," 28–29; J. N. Hill letter, *K.C. Journal of Commerce* (January 15, 1859).

2. "Correspondence, Departure of Governor Steele," *Weekly RMN* (December 14, 1859), 2. Also see "Apollo Theatre," *Weekly RMN* (December 1, 1859), 3; Schoberlin, *Footlights*, 29–30.

3. "Meeting of the Arapahoe County Claim Club—Adoption of Revised Constitution—Election of Officers," *Weekly RMN* (February 15, 1860), 2.

4. Cherry Creek Settlements, CHS,; De La Torre, "Haydee Star Company," 201; Christopher H. Wynkoop to author (July 30, 2007), Kraft Collection.

5. "The Late Duel," *Weekly RMN* (March 14, 1860), 2, through all the quotes to the end of the duel. Also see Wynkoop, "Unfinished Colorado History," 54 (which includes an unnamed and undated newspaper account pasted into the draft). See Smiley, *Denver,* 326, for background on the Broadwell House.

6. See programs where an unnamed Rose Wakely appeared as M'lle Haydee that emphasized her dancing capabilities and not her acting ability, such as the "Cross of Gold." Also see De La Torre, "Theatre Comes to Denver," 291.

7. "Colorado Theatrics," *Daily Central City Register* (February 8, 1876), 3. Central City did not have a newspaper until July 1862.

8. Sayre, "Early Central City Theatricals," 47–48, through "displayed a preference" quote. Sayre appears to be the lone primary source for Mountain City's first theatrical season. Sayre, whose name was often spelled "Sayr" during the 1860s, served with the Third Colorado Cavalry in 1864, and knew Wynkoop in 1860.

9. Mountain City (August 1860) and Denver (August 23, 1860), Arapahoe County, Kansas Territory Census. The censuses are important as they infer that a relationship existed prior to the August 1860 date.

10. Gerboth, *Tall Chief,* 54n.

11. Frank Wynkoop, "Reminiscences," 1, Wynkoop Papers, MSS 695, CHS; Christopher H. Wynkoop to author (July 30, 2007), Kraft Collection.

12. "Emigration and a Newspaper Press," *New York Tribune* (March 19, 1859), Hafen, *Gold Rush,* 274-75; Anonymous, *Biographical Record,* 45; West, *Uncontested Plains,* 179. West missed on Byers's middle initial; it was N and not M.

13. Frank Wynkoop, "Reminiscences," 1; Wynkoop to author (July 30, 2007), Kraft Collection. Also see "An Armed Neutrality," woodcut by C. H. Hayes, image F-2389, CHS.

14. "Important Trial," *Weekly RMN* (April 18, 1860), 2.

15. "Rocky Mountain News," *Western Mountaineer* (July 19, 1860), 2.

16. "Throat-Cutting, *Western Mountaineer* (November 1, 1860), 4. The competition in this case was the *Herald,* another Denver paper.

17. "Murderous Assault Upon the Editor of the *News,*" 6; The *News* Office Attacked," 6–7; and "Resistance—Flight—One of the Gamblers Killed, 7, *Western Mountaineer* (August 2, 1860). Although charged with attempted murder, Wood was set free. Dial, *Saloons,* 13–17, is not close to matching the primary sources. See Kraft, "When Wynkoop Was Sheriff," 60, for a woodcut of the interior of the *Rocky Mountain News.* Notice the weapons scattered about.

18. Wynkoop Quit Claim Deed to Wadsworth, Kansas Territory (August 15, 1860), Cherry Creek Settlements, CHS.

19. West, *Contested Plains,* 239.

20. Mountain City (August 1860) and Denver (August 23, 1860), Arapahoe County, Kansas Territory Census; Wynkoop to author (July 30, 2007).

21. August 1860, Mountain City, Arapahoe County, Kansas Territory Census. La Torre, "Actress and the Gambling Man," 6, 9n9, citing Rose's obituary in the *Daily Denver Gazette* (June 21, 1865), 3, claims Rose was 25 in 1860.

22. "The Stub-Tailed Cow," *Field and Farm* (August 8, 1891), 6. Could the incident have taken place near Mountain City? Rule out Camp Weld, as construction did not begin on it until September 1861 (Whitlock, *Bugles,* 73).

23. "Criterion Saloon," *RMN* (November 22, 1860), 1; Edward Estill Wynkoop, "Wynkoop," 73; "The Trial of Charles Harrison," *RMN* (December 6, 1860), 2; Dial, *Saloons,* 13–14; Gower, "Vigilantes," 96. The number of people Harrison killed is questionable.

24. Lambert, "Plain Tales," Chapter 2, 11. Lambert mistakenly placed Harrison's Criterion Saloon on Blake Street.

25. "Reminiscences," *Field and Farm* (January 9, 1892), 6.

26. "Duelists and Dueling in Colorado," *Denver Inter-Ocean* (March 11, 1882), 136.

27. "The Governor's Proclamation," (September 27, 1860), 4; "Delegate Convention at Golden City" (October 11, 1860), 6, *Western Mountaineer.*

28. "The Territorial Convention," *Western Mountaineer* (October 18, 1860), 4. Also see "Delegate Convention at Golden City," 2–3.

29. "The Election Next Monday," (October 18, 1860), 2, "The Election," (October 25, 1860), 3, and "City Government," (October 18, 1860), 6, *Western Mountaineer;* "The City Marshall," *RMN* (April 4, 1861), 2, which documents Wynkoop's opposition to the new territory in the fall of 1860.

30. Smiley, *Denver,* 537; "Constitution," *RMN* (October 23, 1860), 2.

31. "The City Marshall," *RMN* (April 4, 1861), 2. This article details Byers's unhappiness with Wynkoop in fall 1860.

CHAPTER 4. A BAD MAN FROM KANSAS

1. Davis, *Larimer,* 178. Even though modern historians have spelled McLure's name as "McClure," during his lifetime the press almost always spelled his name "McLure."

2. Richardson, *Mississippi,* 305; Perkin, *Hundred Years,* 149–50.

3. "The McLure Case," *RMN* (November 3, 1860), 2.

4. "The Disgraceful Scene of Yesterday," *RMN* (November 5, 1860), 2.

5. Kraft, "Wynkoop's Early Years," 26. See Kraft, "When Wynkoop Was Sheriff," 58, for artwork showing what Wynkoop looked like in 1860.

6. "To-day's Proceedings," *RMN* (November 5, 1860), 2. Ki Harrison and Charles Harrison are sometimes thought to be the same person. They were both saloon owners in Denver in 1860–61, but there the similarity ended. Oftentimes Charlie "Ki" Harrison is listed as riding with Quantrill's Raiders but it was Charles Harrison who rode with Quantrill. See the December 13, 1860, issue of the *RMN,* 4, for advertisements of both saloons.

7. Wynkoop, "Unfinished Colorado History," 55–56. See Wynkoop to Democratic convention in Denver, *Weekly Commonwealth and Republican* (February 26, 1863), 1, wherein he authored a resolution on February 20 that was signed by all the Democratic officers of the First Colorado Volunteer Cavalry.

8. "Threats of Disunion," *Western Mountaineer* (November 15, 1860), 2. Also see "The Election," 2; "Recapitulation," 7, which listed the results as known on November 13. The only northern state the proslavers carried at this time was Delaware, and that by 1,000 votes.

9. "Rejoicing," *Western Mountaineer* (November 15, 1860), 2.

10. *Western Mountaineer* (November 15, 1860), 4.

11. "The Warfare of Peace Is Ended," *Western Mountaineer* (November 15, 1860), 2.

12. "Legislative Proceedings," *RMN* (November 23, 1860), 2.

13. "Brought Back" and "The Storm," *RMN* (November 20, 1860), 2. Also see Clark, "Good Show Town," 48–49; Zamonski, *'59ers,* 189. Kraft, in "Wynkoop's Early Years," 28, mistakenly thought Wynkoop brought back Louise and Evans. Kraft, "When Wynkoop Was Sheriff," 61, includes what is believed to be an image of Thomas Evans.

14. "The Abduction Case," *RMN* (November 23, 1860), 3.

15. "Married," *Western Mountaineer* (December 6, 1860), 3.

16. "Fatal Affray in Denver," *Western Mountaineer* (December 5, 1860), 7.

17. Wynkoop testimony, "Trial of Charles Harrison," *RMN* (December 6, 1860), 2. Also see Thomas testimony; and Smiley, *Denver,* 537. The woman was not named.

18. C. H. McLaughlin testimony, "Trial of Charles Harrison," *RMN* (December 5, 1860), 2. Also see John Covell testimony.

19. Wynkoop testimony, "Trial of Charles Harrison," *RMN* (December 6, 1860), 2, including clubbing his gun.

20. Thomas testimony, "Trial of Charles Harrison," *RMN* (December 6, 1860), 2. Also see Greer and J. T. Rice testimony. Rice testimony in "Fatal Affray in Denver," *Western Mountaineer* (December 6, 1860), 7, is slightly different.

21. Harrison, "A Card," *RMN* (December 11, 1860), 2. Also see C. H. McLaughlin testimony, "Trial of Charles Harrison," *RMN* (December 5, 1860), 2; and Thomas testimony, "Fatal Affray in Denver," *Western Mountaineer* (December 5, 1860), 7. Harrison may have fired as few as three or as many as five shots.

22. C. A. Crowell testimony, "Trial of Charles Harrison," *RMN* (December 7, 1860), 2. Also see Peck testimony.

23. "Trial of Charles Harrison," *Western Mountaineer* (December 13, 1860), 7. Also see "The Harrison Trial," *RMN* (December 8, 1860), 2.

24. "Reflections," *RMN* (December 10, 1860), 2.

25. "The Panic in the East," *Western Mountaineer* (December 13, 1860), 2. Also see "Secession," 2.

26. Williams, "People's Courts," 301.

27. "Capture of Waters," *RMN* (December 17, 1860), 3; "Capture of Pat Waters," *Western Mountaineer* (December 20, 1860), 7.

28. "Masonic Meetings," *RMN* (December 19, 1860), 2.

29. Wynkoop, Harrison, and John Wanless testimony, "Trial of Patrick Waters," *Weekly RMN* (December 26, 1860), 1; "The Recovery of the Body of Thomas Freeman," *RMN* (December 18, 1860), 2; Williams, "People's Courts," 302.

30. Zamonski, *'59ers,* 229. Also see "Duelists and Dueling in Colorado," *Denver Inter-Ocean* (March 11, 1882), 136.

31. Raine, "Fields of Honor," 134.

32. Masonic secretary A. Sagendorf letter (December 18, 1860), *RMN* (December 19, 1860), 2; "Trial of Patrick Waters," *Weekly RMN* (December 20, 1860), 1; "Capture of Pat Waters," *Western Mountaineer* (November 20, 1860), 7.

33. "The Waters Trial," *RMN* (December 19, 1860), 2.

34. "Trial of Patrick Waters," *Weekly RMN* (December 20, 1860), 1; "Capture of Pat Waters," *Western Mountaineer* (November 20, 1860), 7.

35. "The Execution of Waters," *Weekly RMN* (December 26, 1860), 1. Williams, "People's Courts," 302, claimed that Waters was hung "a little before three o'clock."

36. "Duelists and Dueling in Colorado," *Denver Inter-Ocean* (March 11, 1882), 136. Also see "Affair of Honor," *RMN* (December 31, 1860), 3; "Reminiscences," *Field and Farm* (January 9, 1892), 6. Zamonski, *'59ers,* 231, named the weapons as revolvers and not rifles, as reported in the articles based on Wynkoop's memory.

37. Kraft, "Wynkoop's Early Years," 25–26.

38. "Affair of Honor," *RMN* (December 31, 1860), 3. "Reminiscences," *Field and Farm* (January 9, 1892), 6, and Isern, "Dueling in Denver," 11, placed the date of the duel at ten

days after the challenge, but the *RMN* articles pinpoint the actual date. Also see "The Duel," *RMN* (January 2, 1861), 3.

39. Raine, "Fields of Honor," 134, for McLure's quote and Wynkoop's reply.

40. "Duelists and Dueling in Colorado," *Denver Inter-Ocean* (March 11, 1882), 136. "Reminiscences," *Field and Farm* (January 9, 1892), 6; Kraft, "When Wynkoop Was Sheriff," 58. Zamonski, *'59ers*, 231, and Raine, "Fields of Honor," 134, claimed that Wynkoop shot silver dollars that were thrown into the air, but this has a false ring to it as he was short of cash and would not have destroyed silver dollars.

41. "Duelists and Dueling in Colorado," *Denver Inter-Ocean* (March 11, 1882), 136. Isern, in "Dueling in Denver," 11, claimed Mrs. Cody was the future "Buffalo Bill's" aunt.

42. "The Duel," *RMN* (January 2, 1861), 3; "Duelists and Dueling in Colorado," *Denver Inter-Ocean* (March 11, 1882), 136; *Field and Farm* (January 9, 1892), 6; Zamonski, *'59ers*, 231; Kraft, "When Wynkoop Was Sheriff," 59. Lambert, "Plain Tales," Chapter 2, 8; Raine, "Western Fields of Honor," 134; and Isern, "Dueling in Denver," 11, claim that Mrs. Cody may have calmed the antagonists on the field of honor while the *Denver Inter-Ocean* (March 11, 1882), 136, claimed that when Mrs. Cody told McLure of Wynkoop's shooting prowess, the postmaster made the decision not to fight. Wynkoop may have only received his mail for six months.

43. "Settled," *Wynkoop Scrapbook.*

44. Wynkoop, "Unfinished Colorado History," 55.

45. "Probable Suicide," *Weekly RMN* (January 9, 1861), 2.

46. Justice, "Dueling," and "The Dueling Question," *Weekly RMN* (January 9, 1861), 1.

47. "The Letter List," *Weekly RMN* (January 9, 1861), 2.

48. "Military," *RMN* (January 30, 1861), 3.

49. "The Amatuer [*sic*] Performance," *RMN* (February 2, 1861), 3. Also see Kraft, "Wynkoop's Early Years," 29.

50. "Amateur Dramatic Association," *RMN* (February 5, 1861), 3.

51. Anonymous letter to *RMN* Editor (February 14, 1861) printed in *RMN* (February 20, 1961), 2. Italics in original. "Death of Dr. Stone," *RMN* (October 11, 1860), 3.

52. "Who is Gov. Gilpin?," *RMN* (April 23, 1861), 2; West, Contested Plains, 237–38; Whitford, *Glorieta,* 36. The boundaries of Colorado Territory included acreage from Kansas, Utah, Nebraska, and New Mexico territories. These would be the boundaries of Colorado when it became a state in 1876.

53. Frank Wynkoop, "Intimate Notes," 1.

54. "The Ameteur [*sic*] Exhibition," *Weekly RMN* (March 6, 1861), 3.

55. Isern, "Controversial Career," 5.

56. Zamonski, *'59ers*, 225, 228–29, 231; Smiley, *Denver,* 377.

57. "City Marshal," *RMN* (March 20, 1861), 1.

58. "Meanness," *Wynkoop Scrapbook,* including the accusation against Shaffer and the quote praising Wynkoop. As this story specifically mentions Coleman's *Mountaineer* and the Sunday issue prior to the election, it is obvious that Byers printed it.

59. "A Card" and "Election Frauds," *RMN* (April 3, 1861), 2.

60. "The City Marshall," *RMN* (April 4, 1861), 2. Also see "A Card" signed by C. H. Blake, Wm. Graham, S. S. Curtis, and others, 2.

61. "The Marshalship," [*sic*] *Wynkoop Scrapbook.* The focus of this story leaves little doubt that it was published in the *Daily Denver Mountaineer.*

62. "Good Enough!" *RMN* (April 6, 1861), 2. Also see "Election Day," and "Official Election Returns," 2, in the same edition of the paper; "Workingman's Independent Tickets

Candidate's Flyer" in *Wynkoop Scrapbook*; Denver *Daily Evening News* (April 6, 1861); and Isern "Controversial Career," 4.

CHAPTER 5. CIVIL WAR

1. Beauregard to L. P. Walker, Secretary of War (April 12 and 14, 1861), 305, 314; Beauregard to CSA President Jeff Davis (April 13, 1861), 309, *OR*, Series I, Vol. I/1.

2. Zamonski, *'59ers,* 261.

3. "Dramatic Association," *RMN* (May 10, 1861), 3. Also see "Another Entertainment," *RMN* (May 21, 1861), 3.

4. "Theatre To-morrow Night" (May 28, 1861), 3; "Postponement" (May 22, 1861), 3; "Amateur Entertainment" (May 27, 1861), 3, *RMN*; West, *Contested Plains,* 238.

5. Chivington, "The Pet Lambs," *Denver Republican* (April 20, 1890), 24. Chivington's article appeared in five consecutive Sunday editions of the paper. Also see "History of the Reverends John M. & Isaac Chivington," John M. Chivington Papers, M1594, Western History Collection, Denver Public Library, 2.

6. Wynkoop, "Unfinished Colorado History," 56.

7. Hollister, *Boldly,* 185–90, lists the officers of the First Colorado and when they obtained their grades of rank.

8. Company Muster Roll (July 29–August 31, 1861), Wynkoop Military File. It has been reported that he received his commission on July 21, but this is incorrect.

9. Louise Wynkoop to her son, Frank (May 20, 1920), Wynkoop Collection, Chávez History Library.

10. Tappan to Editors (August 12, 1861) (Denver) *Daily Colorado Republican and Rocky Mountain Herald* (August 14, 1861), 3.

11. Marriages, John H. Kehler Collection, MSS 721, FF2, 1864, CHS; "Married," *Daily Colorado Republican and Rocky Mountain Herald* (August 22, 1861), 3; Bromwell, *Colorado Argonauts,* 1:159–60.

12. Commission Certificate: Appointment of Edward W. Wynkoop as Captain of Company A, First Regiment of Colorado Volunteers, Wynkoop Collection, Chávez History Library. Also see Company Muster Roll (July 29-August 31, 1861), Wynkoop Military File; Transcripts of the records of the Colorado Volunteers, State of Colorado, Division of Archives and Public Records, Denver; Wynkoop, "Unfinished Colorado History," 56. Captain John Slough was promoted to colonel on August 26, 1861, and now commanded the First Regiment of Colorado Volunteers.

13. "Promotions," *Weekly RMN* (September 4, 1861), 4.

14. "First Regiment Colorado Volunteers," (Denver) *Daily Colorado Republican and Rocky Mountain Herald* (August 30, 1861), 3.

15. Whitlock, *Bugles,* 64–65. Chivington's size is in question. Edrington, *Glorieta,* 38, lists him as six feet four and a half inches and 260 pounds.

16. "Messrs. Editors," *Weekly RMN* (September 18, 1861), 2.

17. Wynkoop, "Descendants of EWW," 4; Christopher H. Wynkoop to author (June 5, 1999), Kraft Collection. Frank Wynkoop, "Commemoration," 2, placed his parent's marriage in January 1861 and Edward Estill's birth exactly one year after the actual date.

18. For an example of an advertisement see "Recruits Wanted for Company A," *Daily Colorado Republican and Rocky Mountain Herald* (November 22, 1861), 2.

19. Whitlock, *Bugles,* 23, 60, 81; Edrington, *Glorieta,* 9–11, 13–14; Whitford, *Glorieta,* 148.

20. Privates Co. D. to Editor (February 11, 1862), 3; and "Reply to 'Union,'" 4, *Weekly RMN* (February 15, 1862).

21. "On the Death of Lieut. Buell," *Weekly RMN* (February 15, 1862), 3.

22. "Local Matters," *RMN* (February 7, 1862), 3.

23. Chivington, "The Pet Lambs," *Denver Republican* (April 20, 1890), 24.

24. Chivington, "The Pet Lambs," *Denver Republican* (April 20, 1890), 24, for the entire incident. Italics in original. Also see Whitlock, *Bugles*, 146–47.

25. Hollister, *Boldly*, 45; Chivington, "The Pet Lambs," *Denver Republican* (April 20, 1890), 24.

26. Chivington, "The Pet Lambs," *Denver Republican* (April 20, 1890), 24.

27. Chivington, "The Pet Lambs," *Denver Republican* (April 20, 1890), 24; Hollister, *Boldly*, 45–48.

28. Hollister, *Boldly*, 48–49, 52; Chivington, "The Pet Lambs," *Denver Republican* (April 20, 1890), 24.

29. Whitlock, *Bugles*, 157, 160, 168–69; Hollister, *Boldly*, 54–56, 58–59; Edrington, *Glorieta*, 39, 44. Hollister called Bernal Springs "Ojo de Vernal" and "Vernal Springs."

30. Chivington to Brig. Gen. E. R. S. Canby (March 26, 1862), *OR*, Series I, Vol. IX, 530. Also see Alberts, *Glorieta*, 48. Alberts' total is larger than Chivington's March 26 total.

31. Walker to Lt. N. M. MacRae, AAAG, Fourth New Mexico Volunteers (May 20, 1862), *OR*, Series I, Vol. IX, 531.

32. Whitlock, *Bugles*, 172–73.

33. Walker to Lt. N. M. MacRae, AAAG, Fourth New Mexico Volunteers (May 20, 1862), *OR*, Series I, Vol. IX, 531. Also see Edrington, *Glorieta*, 46 (map). The engagement may have began at 2:45 P.M. Walker called Kozlowski's Ranch "Gray's Ranch."

34. Chivington to Canby (March 26, 1862), *OR*, Series I, Vol. IX, 530–31. Also see Edrington, *Glorieta*, 48 (map).

35. Walker to MacRae (May 20, 1862), *OR*, Series I, Vol. IX, 532.

36. Slough to Canby (March 29, 1862), 533; Slough to A.G. U.S. Army (March 30, 1862), 534, *OR*, Series I, Vol. IX.

37. Chivington report (March 28, 1862), *OR*, Series I, Vol. IX, 538. Chivington called the Union encampment at Kozlowski's Ranch "Camp Lewis."

38. Slough to Canby (March 29, 1862), 533; Slough to A.G. U.S. Army (March 30, 1862), 534, *OR*, Series I, Vol. IX. I have accepted Slough's times on March 30. Also, it follows that Chivington's force would have set out first. For details about this fight, see Sam. F. Tappan to Capt. G. Chapin, A.A.A.G, Dept. Hdqrs., Santa Fe, N. Mex. (May 21, 1862), 536–38; John F. Ritter to Capt. G. Chapin (May 16, 1862), 539–40; and W. R. Scurry to Maj. A. M. Jackson, A.G., Army of New Mexico (March 30 and March 31, 1862), 541–45, *OR*, Series I, Vol. IX. Scurry claimed the fight began at 11:00 and ended at 5:30 P.M., when the Confederates drove the Union soldiers from the field.

39. Chivington report (March 28, 1862), *OR*, Series I, Vol. IX, 538–39.

40. Chivington report (March 28, 1862), *OR*, Series I, Vol. IX, 539, including his quote about his command performing well. Also see 538.

41. Scurry to Maj. A. M. Jackson (March 30, 1862), 541–42; Chivington report (March 28, 1862), *OR*, Series I, Vol. IX, 539.

42. Whitford, *Glorieta*, 130; Hollister, *Boldly*, 86.

43. Alberts, *Glorieta*, 163.

44. Hollister, *Boldly*, 89; "Later From New Mexico," *RMN* (May 28, 1862), 2; Alberts, *Glorieta*, 163; Whitlock, *Bugles*, 229.

45. Company Muster Roll (March and April, 1862), Wynkoop Military File. This change from infantry to cavalry may have happened as late as November. Also see Cramer, "Anthony Calendar," MSS 14, 3, CHS.

46. Company Muster Roll (March and April, 1862), Wynkoop Military File. The Office Muster-in (A.G.O. April 1, 1884), Wynkoop Military File, states that Chivington promoted Wynkoop on April 14. Also see Edward Estill Wynkoop, "Wynkoop," 75.

47. Hollister, *Boldly,* 186.

48. Hollister, *Boldly,* 91; Whitlock, *Bugles,* 229–30.

49. Hollister, *Boldly,* 94. Italics in original.

50. Chivington, "The Pet Lambs," *Denver Republican* (April 27, 1890), 24, including Paul's complaint to Chivington.

51. Hollister, *Boldly,* 94.

52. Chivington, "The Pet Lambs," *Denver Republican* (April 27, 1890), 24.

53. Whitlock, *Bugles,* 232; Whitford, *Glorieta,* 132.

54. Tappan to Lewis Tappan (May 15, 1862), Tappan Collection, MSS 617, Box 1, ff 3, CHS. Also see Whitlock, *Bugles,* 232, who states that Tappan left for Denver after Chivington became colonel. This seems to be an error, unless Tappan lied, for Tappan in his letter claimed that he waited in reserve during the battle. It does not appear that Tappan's view of Wynkoop's actions at Peralta became general knowledge, for Wynkoop never commented.

CHAPTER 6. THE WINDS OF CHANGE

1. Whitlock, *Bugles,* 243.

2. Wynkoop, "Descendants of EWW," 1.

3. Wynkoop to H. Raguet (June 2, 1862), Alberts, *Glorieta,* 154.

4. Frank Wynkoop, "Commemoration," 2–3, Wynkoop Collection, Chávez History Library.

5. Wynkoop to H. Raguet (June 2, 1862), Alberts, *Glorieta,* 154. Raguet was later reburied at Nacogdoches. See Edrington, *Glorieta,* 86, for Raguet's death.

6. Military Returns (July & August, September 25, and October 1, 1862), Wynkoop Military File; Brig. Gen. James H. Carleton to John Evans (October 9, 1862), NA RG393, M1072 Roll 3. Polvadera was spelled "Polvodera" in the returns. Edward Estill Wynkoop, "Wynkoop," 75, thought Wynkoop commanded at Camp Valverde at this time.

7. Special Order No. 38 (October 24, 1862), Wynkoop Military File. Edward Estill Wynkoop, "Wynkoop," 75, mistakenly thought the journey northward went directly to Denver.

8. Wynkoop to Carleton (October 14, 1862), Wynkoop Military File.

9. Special Orders No. 38 (October 24, 1862). Also see Field and Staff Muster Roll (September & October 1862), Wynkoop Military File; Carleton to John Evans (October 9, 1862), NA RG393, M1072 Roll 3; September and October 1862 Fort Garland Post Returns.

10. Department of the Missouri, District of Colorado assignments for December 1862, *OR,* Series I, Vol. XXII/1, 891.

11. Frank Wynkoop "Reminiscences," 5.

12. Frank Wynkoop, "Commemoration," 3.

13. Military Return (January 21 to 31, 1863), Wynkoop Military File; Wynkoop, "Descendants of EWW," 1.

14. "Accident to Major Wynkoop," *Weekly Commonwealth and Republican* (February 5, 1863), 3; "The Tragedy of Monday Night," 3. "Accident," *RMN* (February 5, 1863), 3.

15. John (Jack) W. Crawford statement on "Neighbor's Affidavit, Condition of Soldier Since Discharge" (1895), Wynkoop Pension File.

16. "The Convention," *Weekly Commonwealth and Republican* (February 26, 1863), 1.

17. "Presentation," *Weekly Commonwealth and Republican* (March 5, 1863), 2; "Presentation to Major Wynkoop," *Weekly RMN* (March 5, 1863), 3.

18. Ivory calendar presented to Wynkoop (author's collection). A photo of the calendar is in the Kraft Collection.

19. "Presentation," *Weekly Commonwealth and Republican* (March 5, 1863), 2, including the rest of Wynkoop's quotes from the ceremony. Italics in text. Also see "Presentation to Major Wynkoop," *Weekly RMN* (March 5, 1863), 3.

20. Grinnell, *Cheyennes,* 97.

21. George Bent to George E. Hyde (November 16, 1904), Bent Papers, MSS 54, CHS.

22. Military Returns (April 30 and May 31, 1863), Wynkoop Military File.

23. Department of the Interior, Bureau of Pensions No. 749091 (June 7, 1890), Wynkoop Pension File.

24. Bartles, "Massacre of Confederates," 66; Zamonski, "Colorado Gold," 286, 292.

25. P. P. Elder to Maj. Gen. James G. Blunt (May 17, 1863), *OR,* Series I, Vol. XXII/2, 286; Bartles, "Massacre of Confederates," 62-65; Zamonski, "Colorado Gold," 292, 297–99. When Harrison left Denver, he first rode with William Quantrill's raiders on the Missouri border. The fight did not happen on May 22, 1863, as sometimes reported.

26. Decker, *Utes,* 29.

27. Wynkoop to Chivington (August 13, 1863), Harold B. Lee Library. See Allen to Chivington (July 10, 1863), 351; Allen to Capt. Frank Eno, AAG (July 7, 1963), 44; J. H. Jones to D. Johns (July 7, 1863), 370, *OR,* Series I, Vol. XXII/2, for raids at this time. Fort Halleck is southwest of Elk Mountain on the Overland Trail.

28. Soule to Wynkoop (June 30, 1863), *OR,* Series I, Vol. XXII/2, 368–69.

29. Wynkoop to Chivington (August 13, 1863), Harold B. Lee Library; "On Indian Expedition," 421, Soule to Wynkoop (June 30, 1863), 368–69, *OR,* Series I, Vol. XXII/2. Even though Wynkoop states that he commanded five companies on the expedition, he may have had only four companies.

30. Soule to Wynkoop (July 10, 1863), 370. Also see Soule to Wynkoop (June 30, 1863), 369. *OR,* Series I, Vol. XXII/2.

31. Soule to Wynkoop (July 11, 1863), *OR,* Series I, Vol. XXII/2, 370–71.

32. Ewing to Lt. Col. C. W. Marsh (July 26, 1863), *OR,* Series I, Vol. XXII/2, 400. Also see Fort Larned National Historic Site Chief Historian George Elmore to author (August 15, 2007), Kraft Collection, for the incident.

33. Chivington to AAG, Saint Louis, Mo. (August 7, 1863), *OR,* Series I, Vol. XXII/1, 443.

34. Wynkoop to Chivington (August 13, 1863), Harold B. Lee Library.

35. Chivington to AAG, Saint Louis, Mo. (August 8, 1863), 443; Chivington to Maj. Gen. John M. Schofield (July 13, 1863), 368, *OR,* Series I, Vol. XXII/1. Also see "An Indian Campaign," *Wynkoop Scrapbook,* 57.

36. "An Indian Campaign," *Wynkoop Scrapbook,* 57.

37. Wynkoop to Chivington (August 13, 1863), Harold B. Lee Library. Wynkoop stated that part of the pursuit took place in Nebraska. Consulting maps to track his line of march makes it obvious that part of what was then Nebraska Territory is now present-day Wyoming. He also stated that he traveled northward for thirty miles after leaving Fort Halleck before he came upon the Overland Mail Route. This appears to be an error. The mail route passes by

Fort Halleck and then turns to the west. If indeed Wynkoop followed the mail route before changing direction and moving south, he would have traveled west and not north.

38. "An Indian Campaign," "Return of the Indian Expedition," and "The Ute Expedition," *Wynkoop Scrapbook,* 57. Camp Collins seems the logical location, as his force did not return to Camp Weld before beginning its countermarch. The number of men Wynkoop took with him when he divided his command at North Park may have been as low as 150 or as high as 200. There is confusion as to whether Wynkoop left his wagons at Fort Meade on the North Platte. Finally, the author of "An Indian Campaign," commenting on Wynkoop believing he was near where the Eagle River and the Río Virgin merged when he called off the hunt, concluded that Wynkoop could not have camped at this junction and reached Georgia Gulch within three days' journey as the distance was some three hundred miles.

39. Military Returns (September 30, October 30, and November 30, 1863), Wynkoop Military file.

40. Kappler, *Treaties,* 2:857. Also see 856, 858–59. Decker, *Utes,* 30, stated the treaty created a confederate Ute Nation, and named Ouray (Arrow, U-ray) of the Uncompahgre band their head chief. The treaty did not say this.

41. Anonymous, *Biographical Record,* 1381–82; Hatch, *Black Kettle,* 97.

42. Evans to Dole (November 10, 1863), cited in Williams, *War,* 3–4. Emphasis in original.

43. "The Celebration," (Denver) *Daily News* (December 3, 1863), including the reference to Stuart's cavalry.

44. Wynkoop to Stanton (December 8, 1863), Wynkoop Military File.

45. Special Orders, No. 3 (January 4, 1864), Wynkoop Military File.

46. Field and Staff Muster Roll (January and February 1864), Wynkoop Military File. This document states that Wynkoop had been in command of Camp Weld since October 30, 1863.

47. Military Returns (February 20, March 31, 1864), Field and Staff Muster Roll (March 1864), Wynkoop Military File. See "Daily News," *RMN* (April 27, 1864), 3, which allows pinpointing the date his leave began.

CHAPTER 7. PRELUDE TO INFAMY

1. Hoebel, *Cheyennes,* 1–2.

2. Southern Cheyenne Minoma Littlehawk used her contacts Southern Cheyenne chief Lawrence Hart, Carol Joyce Bullcoming (Littlehawk's Cheyenne-language professor at the Cheyenne-Arapaho College, Weatherford, Okla.), and Christine Starr of Hammon, Okla., to confirm the Cheyenne words used in the text.

3. Kraft, "Wynkoop Confronts Hancock," 41. Also see George E. Hyde to George Bird Grinnell (December 13, 1916), Hyde Research, Grinnell Collection, MS.5, Folder 51E, Braun Research Library; Hyde, Bent, 3. Glenda F. Torres, a Northern Cheyenne, spoke with the author after a performance of his play, *Cheyenne Blood,* in Oxnard, California (May 22, 2009). The conversation focused on Cheyenne words and their pronunciation. Ms. Torres said that Tsistsistas also meant "beautiful people." Note of conversation in Kraft Collection.

4. Per author's request to Minoma Littlehawk, Chief Lawrence Hart confirmed that the Cheyennes never called their warrior society Dog Soldiers, that this was a white term; instead, they called them Dog Men. See notes of conversations between Littlehawk and author (December 31, 2008, and May 17, 2009), Kraft Collection.

5. Sanborn to Chivington (April 12, 1864), 883, Dunn report (April 18, 1864), 884–85, *OR,* Series I, Vol. XXXIV/1; Cramer testimony (February 23, 1865), 32, Dunn testimony

(April 27, 1865), 181, "Sand Creek Massacre"; Hyde, *Bent,* 122–23; Powell, *People,* 1:258; Of Dunn's four wounded, two later died.

6. "Daily News," *RMN* (April 27, 1864), 3.

7. Special Orders, No. 27 (April 26, 1864); Field and Staff Muster Roll (March and April 1864); Wynkoop issue of General Order No. 38 (April 27, 1864), Wynkoop Military File.

8. "Exciting News! War With the Indians, a Battle Fought," *The Commonwealth* (April 14, 1864), in Williams, *Wars,* 11. Also see 10. *The Commonwealth's* list of casualties varied from Dunn's; here the whites had two dead and four wounded while the Indians had several wounded, killed, and captured. Also see "Indian Depredations," *The Commonwealth* (April 9, 1864), 7.

9. Wynkoop, "Unfinished Colorado History," 47.

10. "Daily News," *RMN* (April 29, 1864), 3

11. Eayre to Chivington (April 23, 1864), *OR,* Series I, Vol. XXXIV/1, 880-81; Hyde, *Bent,* 124–26.

12. Special Orders No. 29 (May 2, 1864), Wynkoop Military File.

13. Greene, *Sand Creek,* 190n13, erroneously substituted Leadville for Oro City as the location of Anthony's store; Leadville was not founded until 1877.

14. Wynkoop to Chivington (May 9, 1864) and Maj. Gen. S. R. Curtis to John Evans (May 9, 1864), *OR,* Series I, Vol. XXXIV/3, 531; Military Returns (May 10 and 31, 1864), Wynkoop Military File. Also see Hyde, *Bent,* 108; and Thrapp, *Biography,* I:100.

15. Wynkoop to Chivington (May 9, 1864), *OR,* Series I, Vol. XXXIV/3, 531.

16. Curtis to Evans (May 9, 1864), *OR,* Series I, Vol. XXXIV/3, 531.

17. Chivington to Wynkoop (May 12, 1864), *OR,* Series I, Vol. XXXIV/3, 565. Also see Chivington to Maj. C. S. Charlot, AAG, Department of Kansas (May 29, 1864), 115; J. S. Maynard, AAAG, District of Colorado, to Wynkoop (May 29, 1864), 116, *OR,* Series I, Vol. XXXIV/4; Curtis to Brig. Gen. T. J. McKean (May 9, 1864), *OR,* Series I, Vol. XXXIV/3, 529.

18. Wynkoop to Maynard, AAAG (May 16, 1864), *OR,* Series I, Vol. XXXIV/3, 630; George L. Shoup to Maynard, AAAG (May 28, 1864), *OR,* Series I, Vol. XXXIV/4, 102.

19. Hyde, *Bent,* 132; also see 131, 133. Ash Creek is thirty miles below the Smoky Hill. Grinnell, *Cheyennes,* 144–46, supports George Bent's retelling of the fight, but places the fight twenty miles north of the Pawnee Fork. Perhaps as many as six hundred warriors were in the village.

20. Eayre to Chivington (May 19, 1864), *OR,* Series I, Vol. XXXIV/1, 935; Shoup to Chivington (May 30, 1864), *OR,* Series I, Vol. XXXIV/4, 207–208. Eayre claimed the fight took place three miles from the Smoky Hill.

21. Maynard, AAAG, to Wynkoop (May 16, 1864), *OR,* Series I, Vol. XXXIV/3, 630, for this and the quote regarding the Cheyennes.

22. Wynkoop to Maynard, AAAG (May 21, 1864), *OR,* Series I, Vol. XXXIV/3, 712.

23. Halaas, "Camp Was Weeping," 50, 52. Hatch, *Black Kettle,* 97.

24. Grinnell, *Cheyennes,* 146–47.

25. Wynkoop to Maynard, AAAG (May 21, 1864), *OR,* Series I, Vol. XXXIV/3, 712.

26. Wynkoop to Maynard, AAAG (May 27, 1864), *OR,* Series I, Vol. XXXIV/1, 935.

27. Fosdick to John Evans (May 29, 1864), *OR,* Series No. I, XXXIV/4, 206–207.

28. Chivington to Wynkoop (May 31, 1864), 151. Also see Maynard, AAAG, to Wynkoop (May 23, 1864), 14. *OR,* Series I, Vol. XXXIV/4.

29. Chivington to Wynkoop (May 29, 1864), 115–16; Maynard, AAAG, to Wynkoop (May 29, 1864), 116, *OR,* Series I, Vol. XXXIV/4.

30. Evans to Curtis (June 3, 1864), *OR,* Series No. I, XXXIV/4, 206.

31. Wynkoop to Maynard, AAAG (June 3, 1864), *OR,* Series I, XXXIV/4, 208.

32. Soule Military Returns (January & February, March & April, May & June, and June, 1864), Soule Papers, MSS 982, CHS; Edward Estill Wynkoop, "Wynkoop," 75.

33. Wynkoop to Maynard, AAAG (June 8, 1864), 273–74; Tappan to Chivington (June 6, 1864), 252, *OR,* Series I, Vol. XXXIV/4.

34. Chivington to Wynkoop (May 29, 1864), *OR,* Series I, Vol. XXXIV/4, 115–16. It is assumed that Wynkoop followed Chivington's instructions.

35. Wynkoop to Maynard, AAAG (June 8, 1864), 273–74; Tappan to Chivington (June 6, 1864), 252; Chivington to Curtis (June 8, 1864), *OR,* 273, Series I, Vol. XXXIV/4.

36. Grinnell, *Cheyennes,* 150–51, 153; Berthrong, *Cheyennes,* 191. According to Grinnell another man died with the Hungates.

37. "Fort Lyon Correspondence," *Weekly Commonwealth* (June 22, 1864), 4.

38. Wynkoop to Lt. H. L. Rockwell, AAAG, Military Dist. of Colorado (June 27, 1864), *OR,* Series I, Vol. XXXIV/4, 576.

39. Evans to Indians (June 27, 1864), 61; Evans to Colley (June 29, 1864), "Massacre of Cheyenne Indians," 60–61.

40. Samuel Colley testimony (March 14, 1865), "Massacre of Cheyenne Indians," 32.

41. Curtis to Chivington (July 30, 1864), *OR,* Series I, Vol. XLI/2, 483–84.

42. Wynkoop to Maynard, AAAG (August 9, 1864), *OR* Series I, Vol. XLI/1, 232. Also see 231.

43. Carey, "Chivington," 115; Roberts, *Sand Creek,* 1:324.

44. Evans to Dole (August 10, 1864), *OR,* Series I, Vol. XLI/2, 644.

45. Evans to Curtis (August 11, 1864), *OR,* Series I, Vol. XLI/2, 661.

46. Cramer to Wynkoop (August 12, 1864), *OR,* Series I, Vol. XLI/1, 238–39.

47. Wynkoop to Maynard, AAAG (August 13, 1864), *OR,* Series I, Vol. XLI/1, 238, for this and the following quote. Also see 237, and Cramer to Wynkoop (August 12, 1864), 239. Wynkoop also called the Big Sandy "Sand Creek."

48. "Local and Miscellaneous" (August 12, 1864), 3; "Proclamation" (August 13, 1864), 2, *RMN.*

49. Evans to Stanton (August 18, 1864), *OR,* Series I, Vol. XLI/2, 765.

50. Evans to Curtis (August 18, 1864), *OR,* Series I, Vol. XLI/2, 41, Part 2, 766.

51. Lambert, "Plain Tales," Chapter 4, 5.

52. Wynkoop, "Unfinished Colorado History," 78.

CHAPTER 8. WYNKOOP'S GAMBLE

1. Wynkoop, "Unfinished Colorado History," 84.

2. Colley testimony (March 14, 1865), "Massacre of Cheyenne Indians," 32. Also see 14. Wynkoop to J. E. Tappan, AAAG, District of Upper Arkansas (January 15, 1865), *OR,* Series I, Vol. XLI/1, 959. Wynkoop never once hinted or implied that he had met One-Eye prior to September 4. There is no evidence that Wynkoop was intimate to Agent Colley's dealings with the Cheyennes prior to September 4, or that he was present when Chivington wrote a safe conduct pass for One-Eye. A complete study of Wynkoop's reports, letters, and writing confirms this.

3. Wynkoop, "Unfinished Colorado History," 84–85; which includes the sergeant's response. Also see Wynkoop to J. E. Tappan, AAAG, District of Upper Arkansas (January 15, 1865), *OR,* Series I, Vol. XLI/1, 959; Wynkoop to J. E. Tappan (September 18, 1864), *OR,*

Series I, Vol. XLI/3, 242. John Smith sworn statement (January 15, 1865), Senate Ex. Doc. 26, 39th Congress, 2d Sess., 125; and Edward Estill Wynkoop, "Wynkoop," 75–76. Another version claimed a squad of soldiers "captured" the Indians, while yet another had Wynkoop preventing sentries from shooting the Indians upon their arrival at Fort Lyon.

4. Hyde, *Bent,* 142. Also see Wynkoop testimony (March 20, 1865), "Sand Creek Massacre," 84. Wynkoop claimed that the letters were addressed to William Bent and Colley while George Bent said they were addressed to Colley and the commander of Fort Lyon. Both had direct contact with the letters and should have known to whom they were addressed.

5. Photograph of Black Kettle's letter to Colley, in Hatch, *Black Kettle,* 186. This letter, with missing words added, and with spelling and punctuation corrected, is in "Sand Creek Massacre," 169. Note that in the senate document, "*some* prisoners" has replaced "*seven* prisoners."

6. Hoig, *Smith,* 41–43.

7. William Bent sworn statement (undated), "Chivington Massacre," 95.

8. Robert Bent sworn statement (undated), "Chivington Massacre," 96.

9. Wynkoop, "Unfinished Colorado History," 88. Also see 86.

10. John Smith sworn statement (January 15, 1865), "Massacre of Cheyenne Indians," 84.

11. Wynkoop, "Unfinished Colorado History," 88–89.

12. Wynkoop testimony (March 20, 1965), "Sand Creek Massacre," 84; Wynkoop to J. E. Tappan, AAAG, District of Upper Arkansas (September 18, 1864), *OR,* Series I, Vol. XLI/3, 242. Wynkoop to Tappan, AAAG (January 15, 1865), 959, John Smith sworn statement (January 15, 1865), 965, *OR,* Series I, Vol. XLI/1; Greene, *Sand Creek,* 12; Lee, *Smoky Hill,* 3, 69.

13. Wynkoop testimony (March 20, 1965), "Sand Creek Massacre," 84; Wynkoop to Tappan, AAAG (September 18, 1864), *OR,* Series I, Vol. XLI/3, 242; Wynkoop to Tappan, AAAG (January 15, 1865), 959; and John Smith sworn statement (January 15, 1865), 965, *OR,* Series I, Vol. XLI/1.

14. Wynkoop testimony (March 20, 1865), "Sand Creek Massacre," 84; Wynkoop, "Unfinished Colorado History," 89; Wynkoop to Tappan, AAAG (January 15, 1865), 959; John Smith sworn statement (January 15, 1865), *OR,* Series I, Vol. XLI/1, 965.

15. Wynkoop testimony (March 20, 1865), 84; B. N. Forbes testimony (May 11, 1865), 205, "Sand Creek Massacre." Forbes mistakenly thought Wynkoop sent One-Eye to meet the Cheyennes before camping on the night of September 9.

16. Schultz, *Freezing Moon,* 98.

17. Wynkoop testimony (March 20, 1865), "Sand Creek Massacre," 84.

18. Soule testimony (February 17, 1865), "Sand Creek Massacre," 16, through Wynkoop's quote of defending himself. Also see Forbes testimony (May 11, 1865), 205.

19. Joseph Cramer testimony (February 23, 1865), "Sand Creek Massacre," 31, 29–30, through Wynkoop's second request for the prisoners. Also see Wynkoop, "Unfinished Colorado History," 91.

20. Forbes testimony (May 11, 1865), "Sand Creek Massacre," 205.

21. Joseph Cramer testimony (February 23, 1865), "Sand Creek Massacre," 30. Also see Halaas, *Bent,* 117–18; Grinnell, "Southern Cheyennes, November 1901," MS.5, Folder 69, Item 334, 17, 32, and "Names of Noted Cheyennes and the Approximate Dates of Birth and Death," MS.5, Folder 119, Grinnell Collection, Braun Research Library; Hoig, *Peace,* 86, 96.

22. Wynkoop, "Unfinished Colorado History," 93–94.

23. Joseph Cramer testimony (March 2, 1865), "Sand Creek Massacre," 56, including Wynkoop using Bent as an interpreter. Also see Wynkoop, "Unfinished Colorado History," 93.

24. Wynkoop, "Unfinished Colorado History," 93.

25. Grinnell interview of Wolf Chief, "Life of Black Kettle" and "Lame Deer, 1913," both MS.5, Folder 69, Grinnell Collection, Braun Research Library; "Indian Affairs," *New York Times,* December 24, 1868; Wynkoop to N. G. Taylor (January 11, 1869), NA RG75, M234, Roll 880; George Bent to Samuel Tappan (March 16, 1889) in Hoig, *Peace,* 105; and Wynkoop, "Unfinished Colorado History," 79. There is a lot of confusion over Black Kettle's birth, which has been listed as early as 1797. Three people, Wind Woman, his sister who lived until 1915, George Bent, and Wynkoop placed his birth in 1814–15, 1807, and 1812, respectively. I have accepted Wynkoop's date, as he was conscious of specific dating at the time of Black Kettle's death.

26. Wynkoop, "Unfinished Colorado History," 93.

27. "Indian Affairs," *New York Times* (December 24, 1868), 1.

28. Szasz, *Cultural Brokers,* 16; also see 17.

29. Wynkoop, "Unfinished Colorado History," 93.

30. Col. James Ford sworn statement (May 31, 1865), "Chivington Massacre," 65.

31. Cramer testimony (February 23, 1865), "Sand Creek Massacre," 30.

32. Cramer testimony (March 2, 1985), "Sand Creek Massacre," 56. Also see Wynkoop, "Unfinished Colorado History," 95.

33. Cramer testimony (February 23, 1865), "Sand Creek Massacre," 30–31. Also see Wynkoop, "Unfinished Colorado History," 95.

34. Wynkoop, "Unfinished Colorado History," 96–97. Also see 95.

35. Wynkoop to Tappan, AAAG (September 18, 1864), *OR,* Series I, Vol. XLI/3, 243. Wynkoop erred in his report, for he did not know his men left the first camp until he returned to it after the council.

36. John Smith sworn statement (January 15, 1865). *O.R.,* Series I, Vol. XLI/1, 967, for Black Kettle's quote and Wynkoop's repeated statement regarding his authority.

37. Wynkoop, "Unfinished Colorado History," 99; Forbes testimony (May 11, 1865), "Sand Creek Massacre," 206; Wynkoop to Tappan, AAAG (September 18, 1864), *OR,* Series I, Vol. XLI/3, 243; Michno, *Fate,* 298, 301; Thrapp, *Biography,* 3:1239. Ewbanks is sometimes spelled "Eubank," "Eubanks," and "Ubanks."

38. Wynkoop, "Unfinished Colorado History," 100–102, for all prisoner quotes. Also see Thrapp, *Biography,* 3:1239; Broome, *Justice,* 130–32. Halaas, *Halfbreed,* 378n53, claims Sioux released Morton, and Michno, *Fate,* 141–42, confirms the date, but neither Michno nor Broome, who are as specific as possible, name the Indians who *ransomed* Morton. Morton claimed Daniel was nine. See Michno, *Fate,* 302, for Isabelle's death in Denver on March 18, 1865.

39. Lucinda Ewbanks statement (June 22, 1865), "Chivington Massacre," 91. Also see 90; Michno, *Fate,* 139; "New Light on Mrs. Lucinda Ewbanks' Experiences," 20–21, which documents her speaking with Mrs. Noble Wade after her release, but again making no mention of Isabelle's rescue. September 13 is the logical departure date, as Wynkoop had to await the arrival of the Indian leaders.

CHAPTER 9. PERFIDY

1. Military Return (September 30, 1864), Wynkoop Military File.

2. Samuel Colley testimony (March 14, 1865), "Massacre of Cheyenne Indians," 31; John Smith sworn statement (January 15, 1865). *OR,* Series I, Vol. XLI/1, 967.

3. George Bent to Joseph Thoburn (May 20, 1912), Thoburn Collection.

4. Samuel Colley sworn statement (January 27, 1865), "Massacre of Cheyenne Indians," 91.

5. Wynkoop to Evans (September 18, 1864), "Chivington Massacre," 80; Wynkoop to Lt. J. E. Tappan, AAAG, District of the Upper Arkansas (September 18, 1864), OR, Series I, Vol. XLI/3, 243; Wynkoop testimony (March 21, 1865), "Sand Creek Massacre," 89.

6. "Anti-State Arguments" (September 9, 1864), 2; "State" and "Election Returns" (September 15, 1864), 2, RMN. Also see Carey, "Chivington," 115; and RMN (September 6, 1864).

7. "The Indian War," RMN (September 19, 1864), 2.

8. Wynkoop testimony (March 21, 1865), "Sand Creek Massacre," 89–90; Wynkoop sworn statement (June 9, 1865), "Chivington Massacre," 77. Wynkoop called the Fontaine Qui Bouille the "Fountain-qui-bouit." He stated that he left for Denver a few days after returning to Fort Lyon; however, he may have left as early as September 19.

9. Edward Estill Wynkoop, "Wynkoop," 76. Also see Military Return (September 30, 1864), Wynkoop Military File.

10. Chivington to Maj. C. S. Charlot (September 26, 1864), OR, Series I, Vol. XLI/3, 399.

11. Wynkoop sworn statement (June 9, 1865), "Chivington Massacre," 77. Wynkoop/ Evans interview printed in "The Indian Commission on Sand Creek," RMN (January 18, 1868), 2.

12. Carey, "Another View," 6.

13. "Indian Treaty," RMN (September 27, 1864), 2.

14. "Indian Treaty," RMN (September 28, 1864), 2.

15. Camp Weld meeting (September 28, 1864), "Sand Creek Massacre," 213-15, including all quotes through "treated as enemies." Also see Hyde, Bent, 143; "Report," (September 13, 1865), 2, "Indian Council," (September 29, 1864), RMN, 1; and Christopher H. Wynkoop to author (February 25 and July 30, 2007), Kraft Collection.

16. "Indian Council," (September 29, 1864), RMN, 1.

17. Curtis to Chivington (September 28, 1868), OR, Series I, Vol. 41/3, 462.

18. "Indian Council," (September 29, 1864), RMN, 1.

19. Camp Weld meeting (September 28, 1864), "Sand Creek Massacre," 217.

20. "Indian Council," (September 29, 1864), RMN, 1.

21. Wynkoop to Tappan, AAAG (January 15, 1865), "Massacre of Cheyenne Indians," 82.

22. Smith testimony (March 14, 1865), "Massacre of Cheyenne Indians," 7.

23. Evans to Colley (September 29, 1864), OR, Series I, Vol. XLI/3, 495.

24. Hoig, Smith, 147n12.

25. Wynkoop to Tappan, AAAG (January 15, 1865), "Massacre of Cheyenne Indians," 82. Also see "A Party of the P. L.'s," Weekly RMN (October 5, 1864), 3; Anthony to AAG, District of Upper Arkansas (November 7, 1864), Wynkoop Military File.

26. "From the Arkansas," RMN (October 20, 1864), 2.

27. Wynkoop testimony (March 21, 1865), "Sand Creek Massacre," 91.

28. Wynkoop to Tappan, AAAG (January 15, 1865), "Massacre of Cheyenne Indians," 82.

29. "From the Arkansas," RMN (October 20, 1864), 2.

30. "Memorial" to Wynkoop, RMN (October 20, 1864), 2. The undated memorial is also in NA RG75, M234, Roll 879.

31. Wynkoop to Tappan, AAAG (January 15, 1865), "Massacre of Cheyenne Indians," 82.

32. Edward Estill Wynkoop, "Wynkoop," 77.

33. Special Orders No. 4 (October 7, 1864), Anthony Collection, MSS 14, CHS.

34. Anthony to AAAG, District of Upper Arkansas (November 6, 1864), "Massacre of Cheyenne Indians," 70.

35. Anthony to AAG, District of Upper Arkansas (November 7, 1864), Wynkoop Military File.

36. Special Orders No. 4 (October 7, 1864), Anthony Collection, MSS 14, CHS.

37. Special Orders No. 13 issued (November 4, 1864), OR, Series I, Vol. XLI/4, 433.

38. Wynkoop testimony (March 20, 1865), "Sand Creek Massacre," 87, including Anthony's assurance to Wynkoop.

39. Anthony testimony (March 14, 1865), "Massacre of Cheyenne Indians," 17–19.

40. Wynkoop testimony (March 20, 1865), "Sand Creek Massacre," 87. Also see John Smith sworn statement (January 15, 1865), OR, Series I, Vol. XLI/1, 968; and Anthony testimony (March 14, 1865), "Massacre of Cheyenne Indians," 28.

41. Anthony to AAAG, District of Upper Arkansas (November 6, 1864), OR, Series I, Vol. XLI/1, 912.

42. Wynkoop testimony (March 20, 1865), "Sand Creek Massacre," 87.

43. Nichols to Chivington (October 11, 1864), OR, Series I, Vol. XLI/3, 798–99. Also see Michno, Encyclopedia, 154.

44. "Notice to Militia," RMN (November 16, 1864).

45. Anthony Testimony (March 14, 1865) "Massacre of Cheyenne Indians," 21. In answer to a question as to how long Black Kettle and the Cheyennes were at Sand Creek before Chivington attacked, Anthony answered: "I should think about twelve days." Anthony, like Wynkoop, referred to the Big Sandy as Sand Creek. Also see Minton testimony (April 3, 1865), "Sand Creek Massacre," 146.

46. Cramer to Wynkoop (November 25, 1964), NA RG75, M234, Roll 879.

47. Anthony to District Headquarters (November 26, 1864), NA RG75, M234, Roll 879.

48. Tappan, AAAG, to Commanding Officer, Fort Lyon (November 26, 1865), Wynkoop Papers, MSS 695, CHS.

49. John Smith sworn statement (January 15, 1865), OR, Series I, Vol. XLI/1, 968. Smith also called the Big Sandy "Sand Creek."

50. Wynkoop testimony (March 20, 1865), "Sand Creek Massacre," 87. In "Unfinished Colorado History," 112, Wynkoop made two errors; the date he set out for Kansas and the date Chivington arrived at Fort Lyon.

51. Carey, "Another View," 6–7; Carey, "Puzzle of Sand Creek," 288, 292–93. Also see Soule to Wynkoop (December 14, 1864). This letter made national news when it was discovered in an attic in 2000 and printed in "The Sand Creek Massacre Letters," RMN (September 15, 2000), 7A. There were 400–500 horses for over 1040 recruits.

52. Cramer to Wynkoop (December 19, 1864) also made national news when discovered and printed in "The Sand Creek Massacre Letters," RMN (September 15, 2000), 7A, including Chivington's reply and "under protest."

53. John Smith sworn statement (January 15, 1865), OR, Series I, Vol. XLI/1, 968; George Bent to George E. Hyde (June 9, 1905), Bent Papers, MSS 54, CHS; Cramer to Wynkoop (September 15, 2000), RMN, 7A; Hoig, Sand Creek, 143–44; Greene, Sand Creek, 17.

54. Hyde, Bent, 151–55. See Wynkoop to Samuel Tappan (February 10, 1869), Samuel Tappan Collection, MSS 617, Box 2, Reel 1, CHS, for Medicine Woman Later's Cheyenne name.

55. Cramer sworn statement (July 27, 1865), "Chivington Massacre," 73; Hoig, Sand Creek, 146–47.

56. Cramer sworn statement (July 27, 1865), "Chivington Massacre," 73. Also see Maj. Jacob Downing sworn statement (July 21, 1865), 70.

57. Soule to Wynkoop (September 15, 2000) in *RMN* (September 15, 2000), 7A.

58. Cramer to Wynkoop (September 15, 2000), *RMN*, 7A. Col. A? Did Anthony have a brevet, or is this a transcription error and Cramer meant Chivington?

59. Soule to Wynkoop (September 15, 2000), *RMN*, 7A.

60. Halaas, *Halfbreed*, 155.

61. Hyde, *Bent*, 156, 162.

62. Robert Bent sworn statement (undated), "Chivington Massacre," 96.

63. Chivington to Chas. Wheeler, AAAG, Headquarters District of Colorado (November 29, 1864), "Massacre of Cheyenne Indians," 48.

64. Chivington to Headquarters District of Colorado (December 16, 1864), "Massacre of Cheyenne Indians," 49.

65. John Smith testimony (March 14, 1865), "Massacre of Cheyenne Indians," 10.

66. James P. Beckwith [*sic*] testimony (March 6, 1865), "Sand Creek Massacre," 71.

67. Anthony to Web Anthony (December 1, 1864), printed in *RMN* (December 8, 1864), 2. Also see Anthony Testimony (March 14, 1865), "Massacre of Cheyenne Indians," 21.

68. Curtis to Henning (December 2, 1864), *OR*, Series I, Volume XLI/4, 751; Wynkoop testimony (March 21, 1865), "Sand Creek Massacre," 92.

69. *Daily Mining Journal* (December 29, 1864), 3.

70. Soule to Wynkoop (September 15, 2000), *RMN*, 7A.

71. Cramer to Wynkoop (September 15, 2000), *RMN*, 7A. Lt. Col. Leavitt Bowen, and Majors Hal Sayre, Samuel Logan, Scott Anthony, William F. Wilder, and Jacob Downing all fought at Sand Creek; Cramer implies two of them committed atrocities.

72. Edward Estill Wynkoop, "Wynkoop," 77.

CHAPTER 10. A PEOPLE DIVIDED

1. Wynkoop testimony (March 21, 1865), "Sand Creek Massacre," 92. It is this author's opinion that Wynkoop needed more than two letters of praise to change Curtis's opinion; he had to have had Soule and Cramer's letters.

2. Edward Estill Wynkoop, "Wynkoop," 77.

3. Ford (December 31, 1864), *OR*, Series I, Vol. XLI/4, 971. Special Orders No. 43 (January 2, 1865), Anthony Papers, MSS 14, FF7, CHS, states basically the same, but has a different date.

4. *Daily Mining Journal* (December 29, 1864), 3.

5. "The Sand Creek Battle—'High Officials' Checkmated," *RMN* (January 4, 1865), 1.

6. Curtis to Thomas Moonlight (January 13, 1865), which included Colley to Doolittle (December 20, 1864) as an enclosure, in *Intelligencer* (January 7, 1865). *OR*, Series I, Vol. XLVIII/1, 511.

7. Doolittle quoted in Greene, *Sand Creek*, 21.

8. Grinnell, *Cheyennes*, 190–91; Berthrong, *Cheyennes*, 225–27.

9. "Massacre of Cheyenne Indians," I, VI, 3.

10. Halleck to Curtis (January 11, 1865), "Massacre of Cheyenne Indians," 74.

11. Curtis to Halleck (January 12, 1865), "Massacre of Cheyenne Indians," 75.

12. S.O. No. 43 Hd Qts Dist of Up Arkansas (January 5, 1865), Military Return (January 31, 1865), Wynkoop General Orders No. 3 (January 15, 1865), Wynkoop Military File;

Wynkoop to Lt. J. E. Tappan, AAAG, District of Upper Arkansas (January 15, 1865), "Massacre of Cheyenne Indians," 82.

13. Anthony to brother (December 23 and 30, 1864), Anthony Papers, Correspondence, MSS 14, CHS.

14. Wynkoop to Tappan, AAAG (January 15, 1865), "Massacre of Cheyenne Indians," 81–84, through "total annihilation." Also see Roberts, *Sand Creek,* 2:463.

15. Col. E. W. Wynkoop, "The Sand Creek Massacre," *Wynkoop Scrapbook,* 239, through Wynkoop's quote on "ghastly remains." Also see "Sand Creek Massacre," 125–31; Wynkoop, "Unfinished Colorado History," 115.

16. Wynkoop to Tappan, AAAG (January 15, 1865), "Massacre of Cheyenne Indians," 82.

17. Lambert, "Plain Tales," Chapter 5, 16, including Lambert's following quote.

18. R. M. Bratney (Streeter's attorney) to N. G. Taylor (January 4, 1868), NA RG75, M234, Roll 880. Streeter would eventually receive $4,500 for his losses. The United States as Trustee of Cheyenne Indians, NA RG75, M234, Roll 880.

19. Scott Anthony "Declaration for an Original Invalid Pension," Anthony Papers, MSS 14, CHS.

20. Special Order No. 23 (February 1, 1865), Senate Ex. Doc. 26, 39th Cong. 2d Sess., 2.

21. In "The Journal," *RMN* (February 8, 1865), 2, including Byers's quotes in the following paragraph.

22. "Sand Creek Massacre," 268. Cramer completed his testimony on March 4.

23. Special Order No. 60 by Command of Maj. Gen. Dodge (March 2, 1865), Wynkoop Military File.

24. "The Responsibility of the Indian War," *RMN* (March 2, 1865), 2.

25. Prucha, *Great Father,* 1:485–86, including n3. The congressional committee included Doolittle, Senators Lafayette S. Foster (Connecticut) and James W. Nesmith (Oregon), and Representatives Lewis W. Ross (Illinois), William Windom (Minnesota), William Higby (California), and Asahel W. Hubbard (Iowa).

26. "Chivington Massacre," 26–49.

27. Snyder testimony (March 8, 1865), "Sand Creek Massacre," 77; also see 78–81.

28. "Massacre of Cheyenne Indians," 3, 81–84.

29. Edward Estill Wynkoop, "Wynkoop," 77.

30. Army Regulations (July 28, 1866), NA RG94, M619, Roll 563.

31. Wynkoop testimony, "Sand Creek Massacre," 83–103.

32. Combs testimony, "Sand Creek Massacre," 117; also see 115–16, 118.

33. "One Eastern Man's Opinion of 'Friendly Indians,'" *RMN* (April 15, 1865), 2.

34. Hersa A. Coberly Widow's Declaration (Pension Claim), Soule Papers, MSS 982, CHS.

35. Minton testimony (April 3, 1865), "Sand Creek Massacre," 146. Also see 147–59.

36. Wynkoop, "Descendants of EWW," 1.

37. "Assassination of President Lincoln" (April 15, 1865), *RMN,* 2.

38. Wynkoop to Hollister & Hall (April 20, 1865), Wynkoop Papers, MSS 695, FF6, CHS.

39. Olney sworn statement (April 20, 1865), "Chivington Massacre," 61.

40. Wynkoop to Hollister & Hall (April 20, 1865), Wynkoop Papers, MSS 695, FF6, CHS.

41. Soule to Dist Hd Qts (April 20, 1865), Soule Papers, MSS 982, CHS.

42. "The Homicide Last Night," *RMN* (April 24, 1865), 2.

43. Squiers statement, *RMN* (June 13, 1865), 2.

44. "The Homicide Last Night," *RMN* (April 24, 1865), 2, including the next quote. Hersa Soule applied for a widow's pension twice (September 30 and November 25, 1865). On November 28, 1900, Emma S. Soule (Emma S. Bright) applied for a widow's pension, claiming she lived with Soule as his wife until she left for Iowa on April 3, 1865, but never knew he married Hersa Coberly. Hersa A. Coberly Widow's Declarations (Pension Claims) and Emma S. Soule Widow's Declaration (Pension Claim), Soule Papers, MSS 982, CHS. Milavec, "Alias Emma S. Soule," 3–23, conclusively proved Bright's claim fraudulent.

45. "Captain Soule's Funeral," *RMN* (April 27, 1865), 2; Field and Staff Muster Roll (April 1865), Wynkoop Military File.

46. "Sand Creek Massacre," 161, 163–228.

47. Col. T. Moonlight to Lt. Col. S. F. Tappan (February 12, 1865), "Sand Creek Massacre," 4.

48. "Chivington Massacre," 64–65.

49. Wynkoop, "The Sand Creek Massacre," *Wynkoop Scrapbook,* 239; "Chivington Massacre," 73–77; Company Muster Roll (May and June, 1865), Wynkoop Military File. There is confusion over McCook's first name; Wynkoop thought it was Alex but it has also been listed as Alan.

50. Louise Wynkoop to Frank Wynkoop (May 28, 1920), Wynkoop Collection, Chávez History Library.

51. Ford to J. W. Barnes, AAG, Dept. of the Missouri (June 12, 1865); Special Orders No. 162 (June 14, 1865), Wynkoop Military File; "Daily News," *RMN* (July 12, 1865), 4.

52. "New Indian Superintendent," *RMN* (July 12, 1865), 4.

53. "Daily News" (July 14, 1865), 4; "Mysterious Death of Lt. Cannon—Evidence Before the Coroner's Inquest," 1; "The Death of Lieut. Cannon, Further Evidence Before the Coroners Inquest—Sheriff O. O. Kent, Acting Coroner," 4, "Cannon funeral" (July 17, 1865), 4, *RMN*. Cannon was buried on July 15.

54. Edward Estill Wynkoop, "Wynkoop," 77; Hoig, *Sand Creek,* 172. Wynkoop's son has many errors in his article, including naming Cannon as Connor, and Cannon's regiment as the First Colorado.

55. Military Returns (July and August, August 31, and September 6, 1865), Wynkoop Military File.

56. Seward to Evans (July 18, 1865), Evans Personal Correspondence Collection, Colorado State Archives. "The Ute Difficulty—Return of Gov. Evans," *RMN* (July 20, 1865), 1.

57. "Speaking Last Night" (July 22, 1865), 1, and "Public Reception" (July 20, 1865), 4, *RMN*; Utley, *Indian Frontier,* 102. Utley, citing other sources, stated the event took place at the Opera House. The cry for extermination is in Utley but not the *RMN*.

58. "From Fort Lyon," *RMN* (July 19, 1865), 2.

59. Frank Wynkoop, "Commemoration," 3, Wynkoop Collection, Chávez History Library.

60. Hersa Coberly Soule to Annie J. Soule (August 6, 1865), Anne E. Hemphill Collection: Byron Strom custodian; Christopher H. Wynkoop to author (July 30, 2007), Kraft Collection; Military Returns (September and October, 1865), Wynkoop Military File.

61. "Chivington Massacre," *Saint Louis Dispatch* 1, No 220 (August 15, 1865), 1. The story was originally printed in the Atchison *Champion.* Emphasis in original.

62. Cooley to James Harlan (November. 22, 1865), Wynkoop Collection, Chávez History Library.

63. Wynkoop, "Unfinished Colorado History," 138-39, including "good faith."

64. Frank Wynkoop, "Intimate Notes," 2; Isern, "Controversial Career," 12; Kraft, "Wynkoop & Black Kettle," 8.

65. Cooley to James Harlan (November. 22, 1865), Wynkoop Collection, Chávez History Library.

66. "Report of the Commissioner of Indian Affairs," in *Message of the President of the United States* (1865), 700.

67. "Report of the Commissioner of Indian Affairs" (1865), 701–702, including all of Sanborn's and Little Raven's quotes in section.

68. Kappler, *Treaties,* 2:888. Also see 2:887, 889–92; Hatch, *Black Kettle,* 80, 203 (maps); "Treaties Made in 1865 and Previous Thereto," in *Report of the Commissioner of Indian Affairs for the Year 1866,* 2–3. Congress ratified the treaty on May 22, 1866.

69. Kappler, *Treaties,* 2:892–95; Kingman, "Diary of Samuel A. Kingman," 448. Much has been made of the Ned Wynkoop–Kit Carson relationship and of their traveling to St. Louis together. According to Frank Wynkoop, "He Led the Way," 37, the trip happened in December 1864 (also see Frank Wynkoop, "Data Concerning . . . Wynkoop," Colorado College, 4). As this author's book documents where Wynkoop was in December 1864 and debunks a trip that month, he and Carson Historian Lee Burke have shared research and discussed the Wynkoop-Carson connection, and came up with zero until the Little Arkansas peace council in 1865. We have found no occasion during the Civil War when both men were in the same location at the same time. Further research shows that the only time both could have traveled to St. Louis together would have been in late 1865, but we are sure this did not happen because we know Carson had orders dated October 11, 1865, to report to Gen. Pope in St. Louis after the peace council. On October 30, 1865, Carson had new orders sending him back to New Mexico Territory. See multiple correspondence between Burke and author (August 15–18, 2010), Kraft Collection, Chávez History Library.

70. Special Orders, No. 605 (November 17, 1865), extends leave granted Wynkoop on September 22, 1865 (Special Orders, No. 55) by thirty days. Wynkoop Military File. Also see Burke to author (August 17, 2010), Kraft Collection.

CHAPTER 11. WALKING BETWEEN THE RACES

1. Wynkoop to Cooley (November 22, 1865), NA RG75, M234, Roll 879. Also see Bent to Murphy (November 21, 1865) in Zwink, "Bluff Creek Council," 223.

2. War Department Special Orders No. 628 (December 5, 1865), Wynkoop Military File.

3. Wynkoop submits bond to Cooley (December 12, 1865); Wynkoop to Cooley (December 15, 1865), NA RG75, M234, Roll 879.

4. Wynkoop, "Descendants of EWW," 1.

5. Wynkoop bond (December 21, 1865), NA RG75, M234, Roll 879.

6. Special Orders No. 109 (December 21, 1865), Wynkoop Military File, and Wynkoop Collection, Chávez History Library. Also see Harlan to Cooley (December 6, 1965), NA RG75, M234, Roll 879.

7. Wynkoop, "Unfinished Colorado History," 140.

8. Berthrong, *Cheyennes,* 231.

9. Jos. W. C. Bell, AAG, to Dodge (December 27, 1865), Wynkoop Collection (AC 247), Chávez History Library. Also see "New Indian 'Policy,'" *RMN* (January 22, 1866), 2.

10. Dryer to Bvt. Maj. Smith, AAAG, Dist. of Kansas (December 26, 1865), NA RG75, M234, Roll 879.

11. Wynkoop, "Descendants of EWW Wynkoop," 1.

12. Dryer to AG, District of Kansas (January 26, 1866), NA RG75, M234, Roll 879.

13. Wynkoop to Cooley (January 15, 1866); Wynkoop to Murphy (January 12, 1866); paid bill (January 12, 1866), NA RG75, M234, Roll 879. "Death of Col. Geo. Wynkoop," *RMN* (August 9, 1866), 4.

14. Zwink, "Bluff Creek Council," 228–29.

15. Gordon to AAG, Dist. of Kansas (March 5, 1866), NA RG75, M234, Roll 879. George Bent claimed that Wynkoop's escort consisted of four companies of cavalry (Hyde, *Bent,* 251).

16. William Bent statement (March 10, 1866), Wynkoop Collection, Chávez History Library.

17. Gordon to AAG, Dist. of Kansas (March 5, 1866), NA RG75, 234, Roll 879. Also see Halaas, *Halfbreed,* 208.

18. See Grinnell, "Southern Cheyennes, November 1901," MS.5, Folder 69, Item 334, and "Noted Cheyennes and Cheyenne Chronology," MS.5, Folder 119, Grinnell Collection, Braun Research Library; Powell, *People,* 2:779, 1331, 1418; and Kraft, *Custer,* 3–4.

19. Hoebel, *Cheyennes,* 7.

20. For another view of Stone Forehead, see Hardorff, *Washita Memories,* 362n16. "The Cheyennes regarded him as a man of wisdom and peace, whose advice was respected in tribal affairs," implying that Stone Forehead more often than not agreed with Black Kettle, a conclusion this author has not made.

21. Kraft, *Custer,* 4n12.

22. Wynkoop, "Unfinished Colorado History," 141. See Hoig, *Peace,* 85; Halaas, *Halfbreed,* 30, for Dog Soldier background.

23. Gordon to AAG, Dist. of Kansas (March 5, 1866), NA RG75, M234, Roll 879.

24. Wynkoop, "Unfinished Colorado History," 142. Also see 141.

25. Wynkoop, "Unfinished Colorado History," 144. Also see Halaas, *Halfbreed,* 204, 208–209.

26. Gordon to AAG, Dist. of Kansas (March 5, 1866), NA RG75, M234, Roll 879.

27. Wynkoop, "Unfinished Colorado History," 144. Also see Halaas, *Halfbreed,* 209; Berthrong, *Cheyennes,* 258.

28. Gordon to AAG, Dist. of Kansas (March 5, 1866), NA RG75, M234, Roll 879.

29. J. G. Gordon to AAG, Dist. of Kansas (March 5, 1866), NA RG75, M234, Roll 879, including Wynkoop's reply.

30. Hyde, *Bent,* 251, erroneously implies Wynkoop met only Cheyenne leaders who did not attend the 1865 treaty talks on March 1.

31. Wynkoop, "Unfinished Colorado History," 144; also see 143, 145–46.

32. Gordon to AAG, Dist. of Kansas (March 5, 1866), NA RG75, M234, Roll 879. Includes Bates retrieving the white girl.

33. Charles Hanger to D. N. Cooley (April 17, 1866); Wynkoop certification on Morris & Hanger February 16, 1866, statement; Taylor certification, NA RG75, M234, Roll 879.

34. Zwink, "Bluff Creek Council," 233.

35. Wynkoop to Cummings (March 5, 1866), in *RMN* (March 20, 1866), 4. Wynkoop correctly called her Amanda; Gordon and George Bent (Hyde, *Bent,* 251) called her Mary. The memories Bent shared with Hyde dated to the twentieth century and are not close to being accurate. Also see Michno, *Fate,* 144–50, 168n115 and n120 for background on Fletcher, her family, the capture (when she was apparently thirteen), and depredation claims. Much of the information in the claims was based on memories long after the fact, including Charles Hanger's, who thought he traded for the girl on February 28 or March 1, 1866. The contradictory claims were denied as the Court of Claims thought them fraudulent.

36. Wynkoop to John Pope (March 12, 1866), NA RG75, M234, Roll 879.

37. Wynkoop to Cooley (March 5, 1866), NA RG75, M234, Roll 879.

38. Wynkoop to Cooley (March 12, 1866), NA RG75, M234, Roll 879, including "good faith" (emphasis in original).

39. Cooley to Wynkoop (March 19, 1866), Wynkoop Collection, Chávez History Library.

40. "Maj. Wynkoop's Mission," *RMN* (March 13, 1866), 4.

41. Wynkoop to Cooley (April 8, 1866), NA NG75, M234, Roll 879.

42. Wynkoop to John Pope (April 5, 1866), NA RG75, M234, Roll 879.

43. Wynkoop to Cooley (April 8, 1866), NA RG75, M234, Roll 879. Emphasis in report. It is this author's view that we must judge the past in its time and place—twenty-first-century assessments are not applicable (for example, Chalfant, *Hancock's War,* 41). This author also disagrees with Hoebel, *Cheyennes,* 37–48, regarding the Cheyenne council of forty-four chiefs, for it implies a structured hierarchy with wise elders directing the entire Cheyenne nation. This may have been true at one time, but by the 1860s this was no longer the case, as the chiefs themselves repeatedly stated.

44. Wynkoop to John Pope (April 5, 1866), NA RG75, M234, Roll 879. Also see Chalfant, *Hancock's War,* 42.

45. Capt. David C. Poole quoted in Broome, *Justice,* 55. Also see "From the Smoky Hill," *RMN* (April 23, 1866), 4, including "accomplishing goals" quote.

46. "Maj. Wynkoop," *RMN* (April 28, 1866), 4. Includes Byers's comment on the compliment (italics in quote).

47. "From the Plains," *RMN* (April 30, 1866), 2.

48. "Daily News," *RMN* (May 1, 1866), 4.

49. Frank Wynkoop, "Data Concerning . . . Wynkoop," Colorado College, 4.

50. Wynkoop to Cooley (May 8, 1866), NA RG75, M234, Roll 879.

51. Davidson report (May 16, 1866), NA RG75, M234, Roll 879.

52. Taylor to Thomas Murphy (September 30, 1866) No. 143, *Report of the Commissioner of Indian Affairs for the Year 1866,* 280, for all quotes in section.

53. Leckie, *Conquest,* 31.

54. Watson to Cooley (June 26, 1866), NA RG75, M234, Roll 879.

55. Watson to Cooley (July 5, 1866), NA RG75, M234, Roll 879.

56. Wynkoop, "Unfinished Colorado History," 140.

57. Edward Estill Wynkoop, "Wynkoop," 77.

58. Special Orders, No. 330 (July 11, 1866), Wynkoop Military File.

59. Department of the Interior, Bureau of Pensions No. 749091 (June 7, 1890), Wynkoop Pension File.

60. Cooley to Wynkoop in person (July 25, 1866), No. 141, *Report of the Commissioner of Indian Affairs for the Year 1866,* 278–79.

61. Wynkoop, *Genealogy* (1878), 114; "Death of Col. Geo. Wynkoop," *RMN* (August 9, 1866), 4.

62. Special Orders No. 182 (August 4, 1866), Wynkoop Collection, Chávez History Library. "Council on the Smoky Hill" (August 31, 1866), 2; "From Washington" (August 2, 1866), 1, *RMN*; J. S. Rice & Co. to D. N. Cooley (August 11, 1866); Wynkoop to Cooley (August 11, 1866), NA RG75, M234, Roll 879.

63. Wynkoop to Cooley (August 11, 1866), NA RG75, M234, Roll 879, including Wynkoop's apology to Cooley. For background on Fort Ellsworth, see Oliva, *Fort Harker,* ii, vii, 23, 27–28, 31.

64. Taylor to Wynkoop (August 13, 1866), NA, RG75, M234, Roll 879.

65. Grinnell, "Noted Cheyennes and Cheyenne Chronology," MS.5, Folder 119, Braun Research Library; George Bent to Joseph Thoburn (September 29, 1910), Thoburn Papers; Thrapp, *Biography,* 3:1236.

66. "Council on the Smoky Hill," *RMN* (August 31, 1866), 2. Also see John Smith statement (December 29, 1866), House of Representatives Ex. Doc. 240, 41st Congress, 2d Session, 137; Wynkoop to Cooley (August 14, 1866), NA RG75, M234, Roll 879.

67. Wynkoop to Cooley (August 14, 1866), *Report of the Commissioner of Indian Affairs* (1866), 279.

68. Irwin and Charles Bogy to Lewis Bogy (November 12, 1866), NA RG75, M234, Roll 879.

69. "Council on the Smoky Hill," *RMN* (August 31, 1866), 2; Wynkoop to Cooley (August 14, 1866), *Report of the Commissioner of Indian Affairs* (1866), 279; Wynkoop to Cooley (September 27, 1866), NA RG75, M234, Roll 879. Many whites erroneously called Roman Nose a chief.

70. Taylor to Cooley (August 15, 1866), NA, RG75, M234, Roll 879.

71. Irwin and Charles Bogy to Lewis Bogy (November 12, 1866), NA RG75, M234, Roll 879; Michno, *Fate,* 352–53.

72. Maj. C. Grover to AAG, District of the Upper Arkansas (September 20, 1866), NA RG75, M234, Roll 879, including Satanta's quote. Also see Michno, *Fate,* 354.

73. George Bent to Joseph Thoburn (January 19, 1912), Thoburn Papers.

74. Wynkoop to Cooley (August 28, 1866), NA RG75, M234, Roll 879.

75. Wyatt to Capt. Keogh (December 19, 1866), NA RG75, M234, Roll 879.

76. Certificate, Andrew Johnson appointment (September 20, 1866), Wynkoop Collection, Chávez History Library. Also see Wynkoop to Cooley (September 27, 1866), NA RG75, M234, Roll 879.

77. Wynkoop to Cooley (September 26, 1866), NA RG75, M234, Roll 879.

78. Wynkoop to Cooley (September 27, 1866), NA RG75, M234, Roll 879.

79. Wynkoop to Cooley (September 29, 1866), NA RG75, M234, Roll 879.

80. Wynkoop to Davidson (October 25, 1866), NA RG75, M234, Roll 879.

81. Wynkoop to Cooley (October 26, 1866). Also see Wynkoop to Cooley (October 27, 1866), NA RG75, M234, Roll 879.

82. Wynkoop to Cooley (October 27, 1866), NA RG75, M234, Roll 879.

83. Wynkoop to Cooley (October 28, 1866), NA RG75, M234, Roll 879.

84. Lt. W. H. Harrison to Wynkoop (October 25, 1866), Wynkoop Collection, Chávez History Library.

85. Hancock to Wynkoop (October 30, 1866), Wynkoop Collection, Chávez History Library.

86. Wynkoop to Commissioner of Indian Affairs (November 3, 1866), Charles Bogy to Lewis Bogy (November 3 & 6, 1866), NA RG75, M234, Roll 879; Oliva, *Fort Harker,* ii, 23, 31.

87. Wynkoop to Lewis Bogy (November 12, 1866), NA RG75, M234, Roll 879. Also see Charles Bogy and Irwin to Lewis Bogy (November 13, 1866), included with Wynkoop's missive.

88. Irwin and Charles Bogy to Lewis Bogy; Wynkoop's signature on the voucher (both November 23, 1866), NA RG75, M234, Roll 879.

89. Wynkoop to Lewis Bogy (November 26, 1866), NA RG75, M234, Roll 879, through the military/Fort Larned problem.

90. "A Letter from Colonel E. W. Wynkoop," RMN (November 24, 1866), 2.

91. Wynkoop to Murphy (December 2, 1866), NA RG75, M234, Roll 879.

92. Wynkoop to Murphy (December 9, 1866), NA RG75, M234, Roll 879.

93. Wynkoop to Hancock (December 26, 1866), NA RG75, M234, Roll 879.

CHAPTER 12. HANCOCK'S WAR

1. Wynkoop to Murphy (January 1, 1867), NA RG75, M234, Roll 879.

2. Garfield, "Defense of Kansas Frontier," 452, for Douglas's quotes and Sherman on illegal sales.

3. There is no evidence that Wynkoop made money by defrauding the government or the Indians although Craig, Fighting Parson, concocts a conspiracy theory in regards to the lead-up to, attack at, and aftermath of the Sand Creek tragedy. Others have echoed Craig's theory, notably Michno, Sand Creek.

4. John C. Cox, Department of the Interior, to Lewis Bogy (February 11, 1867); Wynkoop to Cooley (September 26, 1866); Wynkoop to Bogy (February 22, 1867), NA RG75, M234, Roll 879.

5. Wynkoop to Bogy (February 24, 1867), NA RG75, M234, Roll 879.

6. Capt. Henry Asbury to AAG, District of the Upper Arkansas (March 6, 1867), NA RG75, M234, Roll 879.

7. Hancock to W. A. Nichols, AAG (May 22, 1867), House of Representatives, 41st Cong., 2d Sess., Ex. Doc. 240, 78–79.

8. Hancock to Wynkoop (March 11, 1867), NA RG94, M619, Roll 563.

9. Hancock to Wynkoop (March 13, 1867), House of Representatives, 41st Cong., 2d Sess., Ex. Doc. 240, 125.

10. Hancock to Wynkoop (March 22, 1867), NA RG94, M619, Roll 563.

11. Hyde, Bent, 254.

12. "General Hancock's Testimony before the Indian Commission," RMN (September 9, 1867), 2.

13. Bent to George Hyde (June 9, 1905), Bent Papers, MSS 54, CHS.

14. Powell, People, 1:464.

15. Barnitz to Jennie Barnitz (April 9, 1867), in Utley, Life, 27.

16. Hancock to Nichols, AAG (May 22, 1867), House of Representatives, 41st Cong., 2d Sess., Ex. Doc. 240, 79.

17. Wynkoop to Murphy (June 11, 1867), 31; Hancock to Nichols, AAG (May 22, 1867) 80; House of Representatives, 41st Cong., 2d Sess., Ex. Doc. 240.

18. Stanley, "Medicine Lodge Peace Council," 88, 111; "Wynkoop on the Indian War," RMN (October 29, 1867), 2; Wynkoop to Murphy (June 11 and September 14, 1867), NA RG75, M234, Roll 879; Davis, "Summer on the Plains," 294; Hancock to Nichols, AAG (May 22, 1867), House of Representatives, 41st Cong., 2d Sess., Ex. Doc. 240, 80; Powell, People, 1:464–65. Utley, Life, 31. Chalfant, Hancock's War, 131, makes a good case that Little Robe and Pawnee Killer were not at the meeting.

19. "Kansas," New York Herald (April 22, 1867), 3. Henry Stanley attended the meeting at Fort Larned.

20. Kraft, "Custer, the Little Bighorn & History," 47–48.

21. Kennedy, On the Plains, 54; Powell, People, 1:465.

22. Sherman to Hancock (March 14, 1867), NA RG94, M619, Roll 563.

23. Hancock report (April 12, 1867), NA RG94, M619, Roll 563, for all the quotes during the council. Also see Hancock to Nichols, AAG (May 22, 1867), House of Representatives, 41st Cong., 2d Sess., Ex. Doc. 240, 80.

24. Wynkoop to Murphy (June 11, 1867), NA RG75, M234, Roll 879; Utley, *Life,* 31.

25. Barnitz to Jennie Barnitz (April 12, 1867), in Utley, *Life,* 30–31.

26. Wynkoop to Murphy (September 14, 1867), *Report on Indian Affairs by the Acting Commissioner for the Year 1867,* 311, including quote in following paragraph.

27. Hancock to Nichols, AAG (May 22, 1867), House of Representatives, 41st Cong., 2d Sess., Ex. Doc. 240, 80–81; "Wynkoop on the Indian War," *RMN* (October 29, 1867), 2. Custer, *My Life,* 25, placed this campsite twenty-one miles from Fort Larned.

28. "The Peace Commission: Indian Talks," *Missouri Democrat* (October 23, 1867), 2; "Wynkoop on the Indian War," *RMN* (October 29, 1867), 2.

29. Hancock to Nichols, AAG (May 22, 1867), House of Representatives, 41st Cong., 2d Sess., Ex. Doc. 240, 81; Utley, *Life,* 32.

30. Jesse Leavenworth to N. G. Taylor (April 15, 1867), NA RG75, M234, Roll 879.

31. Kennedy, *On the Plains,* 62.

32. Stanley, *Early Travels,* 1:132.

33. Wynkoop to Murphy (September 14, 1967), House of Representatives, 41st Cong., 2d Sess., Ex. Doc. 240, 38. Also see Kraft, "Wynkoop Confronts Hancock," 44.

34. Stanley, *Early Travels,* 1:46–47.

35. Custer, *My Life,* 27.

36. Barnitz to Jennie (April 14, 1867), in Utley, *Life,* 32. Also see Hyde, *Bent,* 258.

37. Custer, *My Life,* 26; also see 27; and Powell, *People,* 1:469.

38. Wynkoop to Murphy (September 14, 1867), *Report on Indian Affairs by the Acting Commissioner for the Year 1867,* 311.

39. Stanley, *Early Travels,* 1:36.

40. Hoig, *Peace,* 88.

41. Hyde, *Bent,* 245.

42. Wynkoop to Murphy (September 14, 1867), *Report on Indian Affairs by the Acting Commissioner for the Year 1867,* 312; also see Powell, *People,* 1:469; and Kennedy, *On the Plains,* 63.

43. Hancock to Nichols, AAG (May 22, 1867), House of Representatives, 41st Cong., 2d Sess., Ex. Doc. 240, 81; Powell, *People,* 1:469–70; Kennedy, *On the Plains,* 63; George Bent to Joseph Thoburn (September 29, 1910), Thoburn Papers; Halaas, *Halfbreed,* 231.

44. Hancock to Nichols, AAG (May 22, 1867), House of Representatives, 41st Cong., 2d Sess., Ex. Doc. 240, 81. Also see Hoig, *Peace,* 99–100; Grinnell, *Cheyennes,* 250; Powell, *People,* 1:470, 668n24. Hancock placed this meeting twenty-one and a half miles from Fort Larned, which does coincide with the previous day's mileage. Powell and Grinnell placed the Roman Nose/Hancock incident at the first meeting; George Bent (Hyde, *Bent,* 259–60) erroneously thought it happened at the second meeting. Wynkoop and Hancock confirm the second meeting, but it did not take place on horseback, and neither mention any aggressive action by Roman Nose. The incident happened during the first meeting. Also see George Bent to Joseph Thoburn (September 29, 1910), Thoburn Papers.

45. Wynkoop to Murphy (September 14, 1867), *Report on Indian Affairs by the Acting Commissioner for the Year 1867,* 312.

46. Barnitz to Jennie Barnitz (April 14, 1867), in Utley, *Life,* 33. See A. J. Smith to Taylor (October 30, 1867), in *RMN* (November 12, 1867), 2; Chief engineer's maps of the Hancock

expedition, Fort Larned National Historic Site, Kansas; Wynkoop to Murphy (June 11, 1867), NA RG75, M234, Roll 879; George Bent (Hyde, *Bent,* 259) placed the tipi count at three hundred.

47. Wynkoop to Hancock (April 13, 1867), NA RG75, M234, Roll 879. This archive houses Wynkoop's letter in his hand. He misdated it, for he discusses events that happened on April 14. Also see Powell, *People,* 1:470.

48. Wynkoop to Murphy (June 11, 1867), NA RG75, M234, Roll 879 and Wynkoop to Murphy (September 14, 1867), *Report on Indian Affairs by the Acting Commissioner for the Year 1867,* 312, for the split quote. Also see Jesse Leavenworth to Taylor (April 15, 1867), NA RG75 M234, Roll 879; Hyde, *Bent,* 260; and Powell, *People,* 1:471, for three unidentified headmen going after their loved ones.

49. 1908 Guerrier recollection, in Grinnell, *Cheyennes,* 253. Also see Wynkoop to Murphy (September 14, 1867), *Report on Indian Affairs by the Acting Commissioner for the Year 1867,* 312; "Wynkoop on the Indian War," *RMN* (October 29, 1867), 2.

50. "Wynkoop on the Indian War," *RMN* (October 29, 1867), 2.

51. Stanley, *Early Travels,* 1:39.

52. Wynkoop to Murphy (September 14, 1867), *Report on Indian Affairs by the Acting Commissioner for the Year 1867,* 312; Wynkoop to Murphy (June 11, 1867) and Jesse Leavenworth to Taylor (April 15, 1867), NA RG75, M234, Roll 879; Grinnell, *Cheyennes,* 253; Powell, *People,* 1:471–72; Hyde, *Bent,* 261; Hancock to W. T. Sherman (April 17, 1867), House of Representatives, 41st Congress, 2d Session, Ex. Doc. 240, 65; Stanley, *Early Travels,* 1:39–40; Custer, *My Life,* 38; "General A. J. Smith on Colonel Wynkoop's Testimony—Letter to Hon. N. G. Taylor, Superintendent of Indian Affairs" (October 30, 1867), in *RMN* (November 12, 1867); Barnitz to Jennie Barnitz (April 17, 1867), in Utley, *Life,* 35.

53. Wynkoop to Murphy (June 11, 1867), House of Representatives, 41st Cong., 2d Sess., Ex. Doc. 240, 31.

54. Leavenworth to Taylor (April 15, 1867), NA RG75, M234, Roll 879.

55. "Wynkoop on the Indian War," *RMN* (October 29, 1867), 2. Also see Wynkoop to Taylor (April 15, 1867), NA RG94, M619, Roll 565; Wynkoop to Murphy (September 14, 1867), *Report on Indian Affairs by the Acting Commissioner for the Year 1867,* 312–13.

56. Hancock to A. J. Smith (April 17, 1867), House of Representatives, 41st Cong., 2d Sess., Ex. Doc. 240, 66.

57. Wynkoop to Hancock (April 13, 1867), NA RG75, M234, Roll 879.

58. "Wynkoop on the Indian War," *RMN* (October 29, 1867), 2; Hancock to W. T. Sherman (April 17, 1867), House of Representatives, 41st Cong., 2d Sess., Ex. Doc. No. 240, 65.

59. "Wynkoop on the Indian War," *RMN* (October 29, 1867), 2.

60. Wynkoop to Taylor (April 15, 1867), House of Representatives, 41st Cong., 2d Sess., Ex. Doc. 240, 28.

61. Custer to Lt. Thomas B. Weir, AAAG, District of the Upper Arkansas (April 16, 1867), House of Representatives, 41st Cong., 2d Sess., Ex. Doc. 240, 69.

62. Custer to Weir (April 17, 1867), House of Representatives, 41st Cong., 2d Sess., Ex. Doc. 240, 69–70. Also see Stanley, *Early Travels,* 1:40.

63. Hancock to Sherman (April 17, 1867), House of Representatives, 41st Cong., 2d Sess., Ex. Doc. 240, 65.

64. W. G. Mitchell, AAAG, to Headquarters Dep't of the Missouri, in the Field (April 17, 1867), House of Representatives, 41st Cong., 2d Sess., Ex. Doc. 240, 66. This was Special Field Order, No. 12.

65. Hancock to Sherman (April 18, 1867), 67. Also see Mitchell, AAAG, to Headq'rs Dep't of the Missouri (April 18, 1867), 96; Hancock to Sherman (April 19, 1867), House of Representatives, 41st Cong., 2d Sess., Ex. Doc. 240, 70.

66. Cooper to Maj. Henry Douglas (April 19, 1867) and Lt. Geo. Wallace, Fort Dodge Post Adjutant, to Wickliffe Cooper (April 17, 1867), NA RG94, M619, Roll 563. Also see Michno, *Encyclopedia,* 196. Michno's text suggests that some of the Indians escaped.

67. Custer to Weir (April 17 and 19, 1867), House of Representatives, 41st Cong., 2d Sess., Ex. Doc. 240, 69–70, 72–74; Stanley, *Early Travels,* 1:40.

68. Wynkoop to Taylor (April 21, 1867), House of Representatives, 41st Cong., 2d Sess., Ex. Doc. 240, 26.

69. "The Indian War," *Harper's Weekly* (May 25, 1867), 328. See Theodore R. Davis's etching in this volume. *Harper's* erred on the date of the meeting.

70. Hancock meeting with Kiowas (April 23, 1867), 101–103, for the entire council. Also see Hancock to Sherman (April 24, 1867), 103–104. Both in House of Representatives, 41st Cong., 2d Sess., Ex. Doc. 240.

71. Wynkoop to Taylor (April 24, 1867), House of Representatives, 41st Cong., 2d Sess., Ex. Doc. 240, 28–29.

72. Wynkoop to Murphy (September 14, 1867), *Report on Indian Affairs by the Acting Commissioner for the Year 1867,* 313; Hancock to Sherman (April 19, 1867), 70–71, which included the village inventory, and Hancock to Maj. George K. Leet, AAG, Army of the United States, Washington, D.C. (July 31, 1867), House of Representatives, 41st Cong., 2d Sess., Ex. Doc. 240, 115.

73. Wynkoop to Taylor (April 24, 1867), House of Representatives, 41st Cong., 2d Sess., Ex. Doc. 240, 29.

74. Hancock meeting with Little Raven (April 28, 1867), NA RG94, M619, Roll 563.

75. Murphy to Taylor (May 13, 1867), NA RG75, M234, Roll 879.

76. Morrison to Wynkoop (May 29, 1867), Wynkoop to Murphy (June 8, 1867), Murphy to Taylor (June 20, 1867), NA RG75, M234, Roll 879.

77. Wynkoop to Murphy (June 8 and 13, 1867), NA RG75, M234, Roll 879.

78. Wynkoop to Murphy (June 11, 1867), House of Representatives, 41st Cong., 2d Sess., Ex. Doc. 240, 32.

79. Wynkoop to Murphy (September 14, 1967), *Report on Indian Affairs by the Acting Commissioner for the Year 1867,* 313. Also see Hancock to Leet, AAG (July 31, 1867), 114, and Custer to Weir, AAAG (April 19, 1867), House of Representatives, 41st Cong., 2d Sess., Ex. Doc. 240, 72.

80. Hancock meeting with Kiowas (April 23, 1867), NA RG94, M619, Roll 563.

81. Hancock to Leet, AAG (July 31, 1867), House of Representatives, 41st Cong., 2d Sess., Ex. Doc. 240, 115.

82. Murphy to Taylor (June 20, 1867), NA RG75, M234, Roll 879.

83. Wynkoop to Murphy (June 13, 1867) and Murphy to Taylor (June 24, 1867), NA RG75, M234, Roll 879.

84. Wynkoop to Murphy (June 24, 1867), NA RG75, M234, Roll 879.

85. "Fort Larned Post Sutlers and Traders," and "Sutler's Residence (HB 25)," Sutler's Store Folder, Fort Larned National Historic Site.

86. Albert Barnitz Journal, 1867–68, Memorandum No. 4 (November 1, 1867), 15. Barnitz Papers, Beinecke Library.

87. Stanley, *Early Travels,* 1:222–23; Oliva, *Fort Larned,* 25–31.

88. Wynkoop to Murphy (July 1, 1867), NA RG75, M234, Roll 879.

89. Bent to Hyde (June 9, 1905), Bent Papers, MSS 54, CHS.

90. Wynkoop to Murphy (July 1, 1967), NA RG75, M234, Roll 879.

91. Wynkoop to Murphy (July 6, 1967) and Murphy to Taylor (July 27, 1867), NA RG75, M234, Roll 879.

92. Wynkoop to Murphy (June 24, 1867); Wynkoop's estimate (July 1, 1867); Murphy to Taylor (July 10, 1867); Murphy to Taylor (July 24, 1867), NA RG75, M234, Roll 879. Also see Wynkoop estimate for storehouse and habitation (August 9, 1867); Wynkoop to Murphy (August 9, 1867), Fort Larned National Historic Site.

93. Stanton to Secretary of the Interior (August 9, 1867), NA RG75, M234, Roll 879.

94. Wynkoop to Murphy (August 13, 1867), House of Representatives, 41st Cong., 2d Sess., Ex. Doc. 240, 36.

CHAPTER 13. HOPE AND DISCONTENT

1. Murphy to Taylor (June 20, 1867), NA RG75, M234, Roll 879.

2. Wynkoop to Murphy (July 1, 1967), NA RG75, M234, Roll 879.

3. Taylor to O. H. Browning, Secretary of the Interior (November 23, 1868), *Report of the Commissioner of Indian Affairs for the Year 1868,* 9.

4. Elizabeth Custer, *Tenting,* 403. Also see Kraft, *Custer,* 19–20.

5. Smith initial charge against Custer, Elizabeth B. Custer Collection, Roll 2, Little Bighorn Battlefield National Monument.

6. Kraft, *Custer,* 20.

7. Powell, *People,* 1:506, 508; Hoig, *Peace,* 10, 115; Jones, *Treaty,* 44-45, 74, 76.

8. Powell, *People,* 1:508–10; Hoebel, *Cheyennes,* 7.

9. Wynkoop to Murphy (September 14, 1867), NA RG75, M234, Roll 879. For Hancock's article, see "The Indians," 18–28.

10. "How Indians Are Swindled By Traders," *RMN* (September 24, 1867), 3.

11. Murphy to Taylor (October 5, 1867), in Stanley, *Early Travels,* 1:217. Also see 1:216; and Wynkoop to Murphy (October 31, 1867), NA RG75, M234, Roll 879.

12. Halaas, *Halfbreed,* 243.

13. Stanley, *Missouri Democrat* (October 21, 1867), 2. Also see "Escape of Major Wyncoop" [*sic*], *Colorado Transcript* (October 30, 1867), 3; Jones, *Treaty,* 49; Hoig, *Peace,* 100; *Chicago Times* (October 22, 1867); Hyde, *Bent,* 284; Powell, *People,* 1:509. Roman Nose's raid might have happened on the tenth, although this is doubtful for Murphy also needed time to return to Fort Larned.

14. Stanley, *Missouri Democrat* (October 21, 1867), 2. Also see Jones, *Treaty,* 45–50.

15. Stanley, *Early Travels,* 1:223. Also see 225.

16. Stanley, *Missouri Democrat* (October 21, 1867), 2. Also see Jones, *Treaty,* 60–61, 63.

17. Stanley, *Early Travels,* 1:228–29.

18. Powell, *People,* 1:510–11; Jones, *Treaty,* 38–39, 49–50, 52, 66, 70, 73, 79; Grinnell, *Cheyennes,* 273–74.

19. Jones, *Treaty,* 84–85, citing the *Missouri Republican* (October 24, 1867); Hoig, *Washita,* 28–29; "The Peace Commission: Indian Talks," *Missouri Democrat* (October 23, 1867), 2. Stanley did not witness Tall Bull and Gray Head's first visit to the council grounds on October 17.

20. "The Peace Commission: Indian Talks," *Missouri Democrat* (October 23, 1867), 2, through Black Kettle's quote.

21. *Missouri Republican* (October 24, 1867) and *Chicago Tribune* (October 24, 1867), in Jones, *Treaty*, 94–95; Hoig, *Washita*, 28–29; "The Peace Commission: Indian Talks," *Missouri Democrat* (October 23, 1867), 2.

22. "The Peace Commission: Indian Talks," *Missouri Democrat* (October 23, 1867), 2, for all quotes through "the friendliest were cheated." Also see "Indian Council," *Daily Colorado Tribune* (October 29, 1867), 2, and "Wynkoop on the Indian War," *RMN* (October 29, 1867), 2, for examples of frontier newspapers that picked up quotes from the *Missouri Democrat*. For Hancock's list of depredations see Hancock, "The Indians," 26.

23. *Chicago Times* (October 29, 1867) in Hoig, *Washita*, 28.

24. "The Peace Commission: Indian Talks," *Missouri Democrat* (October 23, 1867), 2, for quotes through "destruction of their village." Stone Forehead's youngest son, Fox Tail, killed the Mexican herder. Hardorff, *Washita Memories*, 362n16.

25. *Missouri Republican* (October 24, 1867) in Jones, *Treaty*, 98; Hoig, *Washita*, 29; Powell, *People*, 1:514. Jones and Hoig mistakenly thought Gray Head spoke to the commissioners this night; he did not testify until October 27. Powell thought that Wynkoop testified a second time on October 18 and that is when Tall Bull and Gray Head heard him, but he only testified on October 17. Stanley was very interested in Wynkoop's testimony and would have heard him if he testified a second time. Stanley, "Medicine Lodge Peace Council," 90–94, documented the events of October 18; there is no mention of Wynkoop on that date.

26. "The Peace Commission: Indian Talks," *Missouri Democrat* (October 23, 1867), 2

27. "Indian Council," *Daily Colorado Tribune* (October 29, 1867), 2.

28. "The Council with the Southern Tribes," *RMN* (October 29, 1867), 1.

29. "Daily News," *RMN* (November 12, 1867), 4.

30. *Missouri Republican* (October 24, 1867) in Jones, *Treaty*, 98; Hoig, *Washita*, 29.

31. Taylor, "Medicine Lodge," 99.

32. Stanley, "Medicine Lodge Peace Council," 94; also see 95. Powell, *People*, 1:515.

33. Stanley, "Medicine Lodge Peace Council," 98.

34. Stanley, "Medicine Lodge Peace Council," 97; also see 95–96, 98.

35. "The Peace Council: Second Session of the Grand Council," *Missouri Democrat* (October 28, 1867), 2.

36. Kappler, *Treaties*, 977–84; Jones, *Treaty*, 136–38; Brown, *Bury*, 160; Hoig, *Washita*, 30–31.

37. "The Peace Council: Second Session of the Grand Council," *Missouri Democrat* (October 28, 1867), 2, for Black Kettle's, Henderson's, and Augur's quotes.

38. Stanley, "Medicine Lodge Peace Council" (October 27, 1867), 114.

39. Taylor, "Medicine Lodge," 108.

40. Stanley, "Medicine Lodge Peace Council" (October 27, 1867), 115.

41. *New York Tribune* (November 8, 1867), in Hoig, *Peace*, 90.

42. Stanley, "Medicine Lodge Peace Council" (October 27, 1867), 115.

43. Barnitz Journal (October 27, 1867), in Utley, *Life*, 114.

44. Stanley, "Medicine Lodge Peace Council" (October 27, 1867), 113, including Stanley's quote. Also see 112.

45. Halaas, *Halfbreed*, 239; Hoig, *Washita*, 35–36; Hoig, *Paper Trail*, 151.

46. Jones, *Treaty*, 181–82.

47. Kappler, *Treaties*, 984–89.

48. Barnitz Journal (October 28, 1868), in Utley, *Life*, 115 (emphasis in original).

49. Senator Edmund Ross letter entitled "The Indian Commission," *New York Times* (November 5, 1867).

50. George Bent to Joseph Thoburn (September 29, 1910), Thoburn Papers. Also see Halaas, *Halfbreed,* 244.

51. Stanley, "Medicine Lodge Peace Council" (October 28, 1867), 125.

52. Kraft, "Wynkoop & Black Kettle," 13. The distribution took place on October 28, not October 29. Also, there were only two piles of goods; not three. See also Barnitz journal entries for October 28 and 29, in Utley, *Life,* 115.

53. Wynkoop to John Tappan (September 13, 1869) and Murphy to John Tappan (December 21, 1869), NA RG75 M234, Roll 880.

54. Barnitz journal (October 28, 1867), in Utley, *Life,* 115.

55. "The Indian Peace Treaty," *Harper's Weekly* (November 16, 1867), 725.

56. Cited in Prucha, *Great Father,* 497.

57. Smith to Taylor (October 30, 1867), NA RG75, M234, Roll 879.

58. Wynkoop to Murphy (three letters all dated October 31, 1867), NA RG75, M234, Roll 879.

59. Wynkoop to Murphy (January 21, 1868), NA RG75, M234, Roll 880.

60. Crawford, *Kansas,* 284.

61. Olive Clark, "Solomon Valley," 720. Also see Crawford, *Kansas,* 287.

62. Charles Mix, Acting Commissioner, to John Tappan (December 24, 1867), NA RG75, M234, Roll 880.

63. G. J. Lawler, clerk Indian office, to Mix (December 16, 1867); Wynkoop to Murphy (December 18, 1867); Murphy to Mix (December 23, 1867), NA RG75, M234, Roll 279.

64. Wynkoop to Murphy (January 7, 1868). Also see Wynkoop to Murphy (January 8, 1868); McCusker to Murphy (February 4, 1868), NA RG75, M234, Roll 880; and "Daily News," *RMN* (January 20, 1868), 4. Wynkoop handed his reports to Murphy.

65. Murphy to Charles E. Mix (January 14, 1868). Also see Wynkoop to Murphy (January 7 and 8, 1868); Murphy to Mix (January 14, 1868), NA RG75, M234, Roll 880.

66. Tuttle to N. G. Taylor (January 15, 1868), NA RG75, M234, Roll 880.

67. Wynkoop to Murphy (January 21, 1868), NA RG75, M234, Roll 880.

68. Wynkoop to Murphy (January 8, 1868), NA RG75, M234, Roll 880.

69. Murphy to Charles Mix (January 15, 1868), NA RG75, M234, Roll 880, for this and the "large expense" quote.

70. Taylor to Murphy (January 28, 1868), NA RG75, M21, Roll 85.

71. RMN (February 28, 1868), 4. Some of Wynkoop's Denver City lots sold at a Sheriff's sale in late February. His lots must have been well located for it was reported that "the figures ranged high."

72. Wynkoop to Murphy (February 1, 1868), NA.

73. Wynkoop to Murphy (2nd dated February 1, 1868), NA RG75, M234, Roll 880, for quotes through "and presume." Emphasis in original.

74. Wynkoop to Murphy (February 1, 1868), NA RG75, M234, Roll 880, through Wynkoop's quote "in my possession."

75. McCusker to Murphy (February 4, 1868), NA RG75, M234, Roll 880.

76. Smith to Murphy (February 5, 1868), NA RG75, M234, Roll 880.

77. Butterfield to Murphy (February 5, 1868), NA RG75, M234, Roll 880.

78. Murphy report (February 20, 1868), NA RG75, M234, Roll 880.

79. Taylor to Murphy (February 14 and 18, 1868), Taylor to J. E. Tappan (February 18, 1868), NA RG 75, M21, Roll 85.

80. Murphy to Taylor (February 20, 1868), NA RG75, M234, Roll 880.

81. Taylor to Wynkoop (February 25, 1868). Also see Taylor to Murphy (February 25, 1868), NA RG75, M21, Roll 85.

82. Smith to Murphy (February 25, 1868), NA RG75, M234, Roll 880. This refers to a Kiowa raid on February 17 or 18, 1868.

CHAPTER 14. A MATTER OF CONSCIENCE

1. Wynkoop to Taylor (March 5, 1868), NA RG75, M234, Roll 880.

2. Barnitz Journal (February 29, March 3, 6, 1868), in Utley, *Life,* 136–37; Leckie, *Custer,* 107; Hutton, *Sheridan,* 27–28.

3. Crawford, *Kansas,* 289. Also see 287–88; Kraft, *Custer,* 22. Halaas, *Halfbreed,* 253–54, 400n16 and n17.

4. Clerk Ind. Office to Charles E. Mix, Act. Commissioner (May 23, 1868); Thomas Murphy note (May 23, 1868), NA RG75, M234, Roll 880.

5. Wynkoop to Murphy (April 10, 1868), printed in *New York Times* (May 5, 1868), 5. Italics in original. Note that this missive to Murphy is different from another dated April 10.

6. Wynkoop receipt for supplies (April 2, 1868); Alex Banks to Charles Mix (May 1, 1868), NA RG75, M234, Roll 880.

7. Dennison to Wynkoop (April 30, 1868), NA RG75, M234, Roll 880.

8. Murphy to Taylor (August 5, 1868). Also see Murphy to Taylor (August 11, 1868), NA RG75, M234, Roll 880.

9. Wynkoop to Murphy (May 15, 1868), NA RG75, M234, Roll 880.

10. Wynkoop to A. R. Banks (May 4, 1868), NA RG75, M234, Roll 880.

11. Wynkoop distribution (April 25, 1868) witnessed by John Smith and certified by Alex Banks, NA RG75, M234, Roll 880.

12. Wynkoop to Murphy (May 15, 1868), NA RG75, M234, Roll 880, through "comfort and welfare" quote.

13. Wynkoop to Banks (May 4, 1868), NA RG75, M234, Roll 880.

14. Wynkoop to Murphy (May 15, 1868), NA RG75, M234, Roll 880.

15. Wynkoop's May 17, 1868, letter was recovered in Tall Bull's village after it was attacked and destroyed at Summit Springs, Colorado Territory, on July 11, 1869. Quoted in Broome, *Justice,* 181–82. Broome's added emphasis is not retained here.

16. Wynkoop to Murphy (May 22, 1868), NA RG75, M234, Roll 880.

17. Wynkoop to Murphy (May 23, 1868), NA RG75, M234, Roll 880.

18. Murphy to Mix (June 5, 1868), NA RG75 M234, Roll 880. Wynkoop and Murphy continued to call Fort Harker "Fort Ellsworth."

19. Wynkoop to Murphy (May 26, 1868), NA RG75, M234, Roll 880.

20. Wynkoop distribution (May 29, 1868) witnessed by John Smith and certified Alex Banks, NA, RG75, M234, Roll 880.

21. Murphy to Charles Mix (June 5, 1868), NA RG75, M234, Roll 880, including Wynkoop's comment.

22. Clark, "Solomon Valley," 723.

23. Broome, *Justice,* 7–8.

24. Murphy note on a copy of his June 5, 1868, report to Mix (June 29, 1868), NA RG75, M234, Roll 880.

25. Undated Wynkoop report in Broome, *Justice,* 9. Also see 230n12.

26. Ross to Taylor (July 9, 1868), NA RG75, M234, Roll 880.

27. Barnitz to Jennie Barnitz (July 12, 1868), in Utley, *Life,* 170.

28. Foreman, "Hazen," 329.

29. See Hart, "The Washington Fight," 14–31, for the Secretary of War William W. Belknap scandal that ended President U. S. Grant's chances of a third term in office.

30. Sherman to Browning (June 24, 1868), NA RG75, M234, Roll 880.

31. Barnitz to Jennie Barnitz (July 15, 1868), Barnitz Papers, Beinecke Library, Yale University.

32. Wynkoop to Murphy (July 20, 1868), NA RG75, M234, Roll 880.

33. Barnitz Journal, 1868 (July 21, 1868), 10, Barnitz Papers, Beinecke Library. The result is unknown.

34. Barnitz to Jennie Barnitz (July 23, 1868), Barnitz Papers, Beinecke Library.

35. Taylor to Murphy, who was present (July 23, 1868), 67; also see Taylor to Wynkoop (July 23, 1868), 66, *Report of the Commissioner of Indian Affairs* (1868).

36. Brill, *Conquest,* 277.

37. Atchison, Kansas, *Daily Free Press* (July 27, August 5 and 8, 1868), all 1; Fort Scott, Kansas, *Weekly Monitor* (August 19, 1868), 2. Although the *Free Press* stated that Thomas Murphy attended the council, this appears wrong per Murphy to Taylor (August 10, 1868), NA RG75, M234, Roll 59, wherein his words imply he was not present. Wynkoop met with the Indians perhaps as early as July 22 but not later than July 31; the most likely date being July 25.

38. Murphy to Taylor (August 10, 1868); E. M. Pease to Charles E. Mix (September 1, 1868); Wynkoop to Murphy (August 4, 1868), NA RG75, M234, Roll 59; Atchison, Kansas, *Daily Free Press* (July 27, 1868), 1. Fort Scott (Kansas) *Weekly Monitor* (August 19, 1868), 2; *San Antonio Daily Herald* (September 13, 1868), 2; Historian Scott Zesch to author (July 3, 2001), Kraft Collection. Pease was governor of Texas at this time. His letter to Mix is also in Pease Records, Texas State Archives. Melinda's father's name was Green Wayne Caudle. She may have been captured in late January. Michno, *Fate,* 386–95, details "Malinda's" abduction.

39. Murphy to Taylor (August 6, 1868), NA RG75, M234, Roll 59; Capt. Henry Asbury to E. A. Belger, AAAG, District of Upper Arkansas (July 25, 1868), Records of Fort Larned, Kansas, Letters Sent, 1859–62, 1865–Nov. 5, 1869, Microfilm Roll MS 209, Kansas State Historical Society; Atchison, Kansas, *Daily Free Press* (August 8, 1868), 1, lists her parents as dead, mere hearsay.

40. Barnitz to Jennie Barnitz (July 29, 1868), Barnitz Papers, Beinecke Library.

41. Barnitz to Jennie Barnitz (July 29, 1868), Barnitz Papers, Beinecke Library. Also see Utley, *Life,* 170, 174–75, which does not contain as much detail.

42. Murphy to Taylor (August 1, 1868) through Murphy's orders to Wynkoop regarding the Cheyennes. *Report of the Commissioner of Indian Affairs* (1868), 69. Also see 68.

43. Murphy to Taylor (August 5, 1868), NA RG75, M234, Roll 880.

44. Lt. D. W. Wallingford letter (August 6, 1868), Leavenworth, Kansas, *Daily Conservative* (August 9, 1868), 1; Edward W. Wynkoop, "Ferocious Attack by a Rabid Wolf—Four Persons Bitten," *New York Times* (August 13, 1868), 5; Frank Wynkoop, "Commemoration," 4–5.

45. Wynkoop to Murphy (August 10, 1868), NA RG75, M234, Roll 880.

46. General Orders, No. 4 (August 10, 1868). Also see Sherman to J. M. Schofield, Secretary of War (August 9, 1868), NA RG94, M619, Roll 629.

47. Sherman to E. D. Townsend, AAG (September 5, 1868). Also see Taylor to O. H. Browning (August 18, 1868); Sherman to Townsend (September 8, 1868); Mix to W. F. Otto, Acting Secretary of the Interior (September 12, 1868), NA RG94, M619, Roll 629.

48. Wynkoop estimate for 3rd and 4th quarters (August 10, 1868), NA RG75, M234, Roll 880.

49. Wynkoop estimate (August 17, 1868), NA RG75, M234, Roll 880.

50. Guerrier statement to Bvt. Lt. Col. J Schuyler Crosby (February 9, 1869), House of Representatives, 41st Cong., 2d Sess., Ex. Doc. 240, 171. Guerrier then lived with Little Rock's band. Also see Greene, *Washita,* 49–50, 222n13 and n15.

51. Wynkoop report (August 19, 1868); Wynkoop to Taylor (January 26, 1969), NA RG75, M234, Roll 880.

52. Barnitz to Jennie Barnitz (August 16, 1868), in Utley, *Life,* 180.

53. Crawford, *Kansas,* 291–92.

54. Wynkoop report (August 19, 1868), NA RG75, M234, Roll 880, through "remaining at peace" quote. See Utley, *Frontier Regulars,* 143, who questioned the war party's start date in early August and more realistically placed it two or three days prior to the August 10 attacks.

55. Murphy to Wynkoop (August 24, 1868), NA, RG75, M234, Roll 880.

56. Crawford, *Kansas,* 319 (italics in text).

57. Sherman to Townsend, AAG (September 8, 1868), RG94, M619, Roll 629. Also see Wynkoop to Murphy (September 3, 1868) and Murphy to Charles Mix (September 10, 1868), NA RG75, M234, Roll 880; Hardorff, *Washita Memories,* 101n3; Berthrong, *Cheyennes,* 318–19.

58. Wynkoop to Murphy (September 13, 1868), RG75, M234, Roll 880.

59. Murphy to Charles Mix (September 17, 1868), NA RG75, M234, Roll 880.

60. Wynkoop to Murphy (September 20, 1868), NA RG75 M234, Roll 880.

61. Monnett, *Beecher Island,* 131–35, 137, 142, 144. Monnett presents a good view of the lead-up, fight, and aftermath from both sides.

62. Wynkoop to Murphy (September 20, 1868). Also see Murphy to Charles Mix (September 21, 1868) and Murphy to Chauncey McKeever, AAG (October 31, 1868), NA RG75 M234, Roll 880; Sherman to E. Schriver, Inspector General (September 17, 1868), NA RG94 M619, Roll 629. By the middle of October Caudle lived in the home of Capt. Hensley in Leavenworth, but she was soon sent to Cherokee Town near Fort Cobb in Indian Territory. Wynkoop's mother, Angeline, lived at 511 South 3rd Street.

63. Murphy to Wynkoop (September 21, 1868), NA RG75 M234, Roll 880.

64. Sherman to J. C. Kelton, AAG (September 19, 1868), NA RG94, M619, Roll 629.

65. Mrs. Wynkoop to Mix (September 26, 1868), NA RG75 M234, Roll 880.

66. Wynkoop to Tappan (October 5, 1868), printed in unknown newspaper and enclosed in Tappan to Taylor (October 11, 1868); A. O. Fannheuse to Mix (October 6, 1868), NA RG75, M234, Roll 880.

67. Mix to Taylor (October 6, 1868), NA RG75, M234, Roll 880.

68. Wynkoop to Mix (October 7, 1868), NA RG75 M234, Roll 880.

69. Mix to Wynkoop (October 8, 1868), NA RG75 M21, Roll 88. Also see "Gleanings: Territorial and Indian News," *RMN* (November 5, 1868), 4, which erroneously named Fort Arbuckle as Wynkoop's destination.

70. Greene, *Washita,* 71.

71. Custer to Elizabeth Custer (October 4, 1868), in Elizabeth Custer, *Guidon,* 10.

72. Elliott to Davis (October 31, 1868), Taft Collection, Kansas State Historical Society. Elliott died on November 27, 1868, at the Battle of the Washita.

73. Murphy to Taylor (December 18, 1868), NA RG75 M234, Roll 880.

74. Wynkoop to Taylor (November 29, 1868), House of Representatives, 41st Cong., 2d Sess., Ex. Doc. 240, 5.

75. Custer to Sheridan (November 28, 1868), House of Representatives, 41st Cong., 2d Sess., Ex. Doc. 240, 163–64. Also see 162, 165.

76. "9,000 Indians on Reservation," *Quincy Daily Whig* (December 16, 1868), 1; "From Washington," *Daily Kansas State Journal* (December 17, 1868), 1; Wynkoop to Taylor (November 29, 1868), House of Representatives Ex. Doc. 240, 41st Congress, 2d Session, 5.

77. As printed in *Weekly RMN* (December 23, 1868), 3.

78. Morrison to Wynkoop (December 14, 1868), NA RG75, M234, Roll 880, including Morrison's comment on Custer. For additional background on Morrison, Poisal, and Fitzpatrick, see Hardorff, *Washita Memories,* 282–83.

79. "The Indian Difficulties," *New York Times* (December 22, 1868), 4.

80. "The United States Indian Commission," *New York Herald* (December 24, 1868), 5, for his talk through the comment on "desperation."

81. "Indian Affairs," *New York Times* (December 24, 1868), 1.

82. Wynkoop to Tappan (January 2, 1869), Tappan Collection, MSS 617, Box 1, Folder 8, CHS.

83. "Washita and Sand Creek Compared," *RMN* (December 29, 1868), 1.

84. Wynkoop to Tappan (January 2, 1869), Samuel Tappan Collection, MSS 617, Box 1, Folder 8, CHS.

85. *RMN* (January 6, 1869), 1.

86. "Custar's [*sic*] First Victory," *Colorado Transcript* (January 6, 1869), 2, including emphasis.

87. Browning to Wade (January 6, 1869), U.S. Senate, 40th Cong., 3d Sess., Ex. Doc. 13, 1. Also see Taylor to Browning (January 5, 1869), 1–2.

88. Wynkoop to Taylor (January 26, 1969), NA RG75, M234, Roll 880. Emphasis in Wynkoop letter.

89. Wynkoop to Tappan (February 10, 1869), Tappan Collection, MSS 617, Box 2, Reel 1, CHS.

90. Wynkoop to Tappan (January 27, 1869), Tappan Collection, MSS 617, Box 2, Reel 1, CHS.

91. Wynkoop to Tappan (February 10, 1869), Tappan Collection, MSS 617, Box 2, Reel 1, CHS.

92. Cooper to Grant (March 19, 1869), Wynkoop Collection, Chávez History Library.

93. Margaret McAdams to Murphy (January 3, 1869), Murphy to Taylor (January 25, 1869), Bent to Murphy (March 20, 1869), and Enoch Hoag to Eli Parker (August 23, 1869), NA RG75, M234, Roll 880.

EPILOGUE

1. Wynkoop to Tappan (September 13, 1869), RG75 M234, Roll 880. Also see "Colonel Edward W. Wynkoop," *The Republican* (September 14, 1891); "Stanhope Furn.," *Wynkoop Scrapbook,* 205; Edward Estill Wynkoop, "Wynkoop," 78; Frank Wynkoop, "Commemoration," Wynkoop Collection (AC 247), Chávez History Library, 5.

2. Christopher H. Wynkoop to author (June 5, 1999), Kraft Collection (AC 402), Chávez History Library.

3. "The Poor Indian, An Earnest Movement for the Amelioration of His Condition," *New York Times* (May 19, 1870), 8.

4. Wynkoop, "Descendants of EWW," 1.

5. Lubetkin, Cooke's Gamble, 283, 276–82. Also see Edward Estill Wynkoop, "Wynkoop," 78; Gerboth, *Tall Chief,* 32–33.

6. Martin to Wynkoop (May 8,1875); Thomas Vail to Wynkoop (May 20, 1875); Whipple to Wynkoop (May 24, 1875), Wynkoop Collection (AC 247), Chávez History Library.

7. "The Black Hills: An Interview with an Old Mountaineer," *Wynkoop Scrapbook,* 138. Handwritten on clipping: " '76."

8. Wynkoop, "Descendants of EWW," 1.

9. Utley, *Sitting Bull,* 128–29.

10. Black Hill Rangers flyer (May 6, 1876), *Wynkoop Scrapbook.*

11. *Field and Farm* (December 29, 1888), 6; Wynkoop, "Jim Beary," *Wynkoop Scrapbook.*

12. Frank Wynkoop, "Intimate Notes," 4.

13. Jack Crawford statement on "Neighbor's Affidavit. Condition of Soldier Since Discharge," recorded in 1895 after Wynkoop's death. Also see Louise M. Wynkoop Affidavit. Both in Wynkoop Pension File. Wynkoop received treatment for his spinal injury from 1868 to 1879, and then from 1888 until his death. Dr. J. H. Floan treated Wynkoop when he lived in Santa Fe, New Mexico. Also see Parker, *Black Hills,* 76.

14. "The Black Hills: An Interview with an Old Mountaineer," 138. Also see Wynkoop, "Jim Beary." Both in *Wynkoop Scrapbook.*

15. Frank Wynkoop, "Intimate Notes," 4.

16. See Wynkoop, "Unfinished Colorado History."

17. Widow's Declaration for Pension (November 16, 1891), Wynkoop Pension File; Christopher H. Wynkoop to author (July 30, 2007) and Wynkoop, "Descendants of EWW Wynkoop," 1.

18. Wynkoop appointment (March 23, 1882); Ten-page instructions of timber agent duties (undated/first two pages missing), Wynkoop Collection (AC 247), Chávez History Library.

19. "Return of an Old Pioneer," *RMN* (April 13, 1882), 3. Also see Frank Wynkoop, "Intimate Notes," 5; Frank Wynkoop, "Commemoration," Wynkoop Collection (AC 247), Chávez History Library, 5.

20. Frank Wynkoop, "Intimate Notes," 5.

21. Wynkoop Circular Letter No. 2 (April 7, 1884), Wynkoop Collection, Chávez History Library. Also see "The Death of Gen. Kit Carson," *New York Times* (June 8, 1868).

22. Crawford to Governor of New Mexico (December 5, 1884), Wynkoop Collection, Chávez History Library.

23. Handwritten notes on ten-page instructions of Wynkoop's timber agent duties (undated/first two pages missing), Wynkoop Collection (AC 247), Chávez History Library.

24. "Crude Oil Crumbs," *Santa Fe Daily New Mexican* (March 31, 1886), 1.

25. Frank Wynkoop, "Intimate Notes," 3.

26. "Round About Town," *Santa Fe Daily New Mexican* (May 24, 1886), 4.

27. *Articles of Association of the Toltec Mining Company,* 8.

28. "Round About Town," *Santa Fe Daily New Mexican* (October 1, 1886), 4.

29. Charles Bennett review of Wynkoop manuscript (July 26, 2007) and Bennett to author (September 1, 2007), Kraft Collection; Frémont letter quoted in "Santa Fe's Opportunity," *Wynkoop Scrapbook.*

30. Stone to Prince (August 14, 1889), New Mexico State Records Center & Archives, Santa Fe (hereafter NMSRC&A).

31. Prince entry in Territorial Archives of New Mexico Executive Record Book (December 2, 1889), NMSRC&A.

32. Handwritten notes on ten-page instructions of Wynkoop's timber agent duties (undated/first two pages missing), Wynkoop Collection (AC 247), Chávez History Library.

33. Bennett, "Frontiersman," 100–102.

34. Prince, General Orders No. 2 Territorial Archives of New Mexico Executive Record Book (March 21, 1890), NMSRC&A.

35. "The Territorial Penitentiary," *Santa Fe New Mexican* in *Wynkoop Scrapbook,* 261.

36. Report on Investigation into Wynkoop's Administration of New Mexico Penitentiary, k, Legislative Assembly (December 19, 1890–February 1891), Reel 9, NMSRC&A.

37. H. B. Davis testimony, 8–9, and Wynkoop testimony, 1, Hearing Investigating Wynkoop's Administration of New Mexico Penitentiary.

38. Wynkoop Declaration for Invalid Pensions (July 29, 1890). Also see Department of the Interior Bureau of Pensions (June 7, 1890). Both in Wynkoop Pension File.

39. R. Kelly, U.S. Pension Agency (January 20, 1893), Wynkoop Pension File, which states that Wynkoop's Certificate No. 628.398 began on June 27, 1890.

40. Hearing Investigating Wynkoop's Administration of New Mexico Penitentiary, 1–33.

41. Untitled article, *Wynkoop Scrapbook*, 259.

42. Wynkoop to Bartlett (January 22, 1891), Bartlett Papers, NMSRC&A.

43. Wynkoop to Prince (February 27, 1891), L. B. Prince Papers, Letters Received, Roll 108, NMSRC&A. Hulmes is sometimes erroneously spelled as "Humes." She always signed her name with an "l."

44. Hearing Investigating Wynkoop's Administration of New Mexico Penitentiary, 1–33.

45. Report of Special Committee to the Legislative Council of the Territory of New Mexico into Wynkoop's Administration of New Mexico Penitentiary, k. Also see 1–4 and a–j.

46. Untitled article, *Wynkoop Scrapbook,* 261.

47. "A Ridiculous Mess," *Wynkoop Scrapbook,* 259.

48. Untitled article, *The Optic,* in *Wynkoop Scrapbook,* 259.

49. "The Stub-Tailed Cow," *Field and Farm* (August 8, 1891), 6.

50. "Col. Ned Wynkoop's Death," *Santa Fe Daily New Mexican* (September 12, 1891), 6, including the obituary quotation.

51. Widow's Declaration for Pension (November 16, 1891), Wynkoop Pension File.

52. Harman H. Wynkoop to Dorothy Gardiner (April 20, 1949), Wynkoop Papers, MSS 695, CHS.

53. Bureau of Pensions (April 26, 1906); Louise M. Wynkoop Drop Report--Pensioner No. 357.641 (April 21, 1924), Wynkoop Pension File.

54. Frank Wynkoop, "Commemoration," 5.

55. Louise Wynkoop Certificate of Death (November 27, 1923); Louise M. Wynkoop Drop Report–Pensioner, No. 357.641 (April 21, 1924); Angeline Schneider Application for Reimbursement (November 22, 1923), Wynkoop Pension File. Although the death certificate states she died on November 5, this is an error, and was corrected by Clarence F. Barrett, special examiner, on the certificate.

56. See Michno, "Real Villains," 22–29, 71, for an example of this accusation.

57. Director–acting coach Robert Ellenstein, conversation with author (summer 1969).

58. George Bent to Joseph Thoburn (September 29, 1910), Thoburn Papers, Oklahoma Historical Society.

Bibliography

ARCHIVAL SOURCES

Anne E. Hemphill Collection. Byron Strom, custodian. Des Moines, Iowa. Silas and Hersa Coberly Soule Letters.

Beinecke Library, Yale University. Albert Barnitz Papers.

Braun Research Library. Autry National Center of the American West, Los Angeles. George Bird Grinnell Collection, MS.5.

    "As to the Meaning of the Word Vihio," Folder 69

    "Cheyenne Band Names From the Clark Manuscript," Folder 69

    "Cheyenne Notes/Biographies," Folder 69

    "Lame Deer 1913," Folder 69

    "Names of Noted Cheyennes and the Approximate Dates of Birth and Death," Folder 119

    "Noted Cheyennes and Cheyenne Chronology," Folder 119

    "Southern Cheyennes," November 1901, Folder 69, Item 334

    Wolf Chief, "Life of Black Kettle," Folder 69

    Hyde Research, May 1917, Folder 51E

Brigham Young University. Harold B. Lee Library. Special Collections and Manuscripts, MSS SC 194.

Colorado College, Colorado Springs. Tutt Library. Wynkoop, Frank M. "Data Concerning Col. Edward Wanshear [sic] Wynkoop and Louise Brown Wynkoop." Special Collections and Manuscripts, File Mf 0109. 7 pages.

Colorado Historical Society, Denver.

    Scott J. Anthony Papers. MSS 14.

        FF2 (Correspondence, 1864).

        FF5 (Special Orders 1863–1864).

        FF6, FF7 (Special Orders 1864–1865).

        FF 15 (Declaration for Original Invalid Pension).

    George Bent Papers. MSS 54.

    Cherry Creek Settlements. MSS 194, Box 5, FF 446–93.

        FF 484, specific to Wynkoop (March 1–August 14, 1860).

    Jean H. Cramer. "A Calendar of the papers of Scott J. Anthony, 1830–1903: A holding of the Library of the State Historical Society of Colorado" (1967), 3, MSS 14.

    John H. Kehler Collection. MSS 721, FF2, 1864.

    Silas S. Soule Papers. MSS 982.

        Box 1, FF 14, Military Returns.

        Box 1, FF 14, Hersa A. Soule Pension Claim.

        Box 1, FF 14, Emma S. Soule Pension Claim.

Samuel F. Tappan Collection. MSS 617.

Wynkoop Papers. MSS 695.

    FF5, FF6 (Correspondence).

    Wynkoop, Edward W., "Unfinished Colorado History" (1876), MSS II–20 (1876), in Wynkoop's and others' handwriting.

    FF5 (Wynkoop, Frank Murray, "Reminiscences," 1953).

Colorado State Archives Public Records Register. John Evans Personal Correspondence Collection (1833–85). FF9, Folio 94.

Denver Public Library. Western History Collection.

    Arapahoe County, Kansas Territory, Census

        Mountain City (August 1860)

        Denver (August 23, 1860)

    John M. Chivington Papers, M1594. Anonymous, "History of the Reverends John M. & Isaac Chivington in Their Relationship to the Early Methodist Church in Kansas and Nebraska," n.d. FF5.

    Silas S. Soule, WH1690.

Fort Larned National Historic Site, Kansas. Sutler's Store Folder.

Fray Angélico Chávez History Library. Palace of the Governors, Santa Fe.

    Louis Kraft Collection (AC402) (correspondence, research, lectures, articles, plays, and books relating to Edward Wynkoop).

    Wynkoop, Christopher H. "Descendants of Edward Wanshaer Wynkoop."

    Wynkoop, Christopher H. "Brown-Wakely Family Descendants."

    Wynkoop manuscript reviews.

    Edward W. Wynkoop Collection (AC247).

    Wynkoop Scrapbook.

    Wynkoop, Edward Estill, "Edward Wanshear Wynkoop," n.d., File nos. 2–3, typescript.

    Wynkoop, Edward W., "Unfinished Colorado History," typescript of manuscript in the Colorado Historical Society (Denver) by Charles Bennett.

    Wynkoop, Frank M., "Intimate Notes Relative to the Career of Colonel Edward Wynkoop Which Are Not at All or Incompletely Included in This Scrapbook," n.d. (This document accompanied the scrapbook that Edward W. Wynkoop began in 1876 but never completed.)

    Wynkoop, Frank (Francis) Murray, "Commemoration: Mrs. Louise M Wynkoop; A Biographical Sketch." Box 112 (1938).

    Various correspondence.

Kansas State Historical Society, Topeka.

    Taft Collection, Box 20, #177

    Records of Fort Larned, Letters Sent, 1859–1862, 1865–Nov. 5, 1869. Microfilm MS209.

Little Bighorn Battlefield National Monument. Crow Agency, Montana. Elizabeth B. Custer Collection, Roll 2.

National Archives, Washington, D.C.

    Edward W. Wynkoop Military File. Wynkoop Pension File.

    "Letters Received by the Office of Indian Affairs, 1824–1881." RG75, M234, Rolls 879–880.

    "Letters Sent by the Office of Indian Affairs, 1824–1881." RG75, M21, Rolls 85, 88.

"Letters Received by the Office of the Adjutant General (Main Series), 1861–1870." RG94, M619, Rolls 563, 629.

"Letters Sent by the Ninth Military Department, Department of New Mexico, 1849–1890." RG393, M1072, Roll 3.

National Archives, Southwest Region.

"Letters Received by the Office of Indian Affairs, 1824–1881." RG75, M234, Roll 59.

E. M. Pease to Charles E. Mix, Acting Commissioner of Indian Affairs (September 1, 1868).

New Mexico State Records Center and Archives, Santa Fe.

Bartlett Papers, Official, Penitentiary, Box 1, Folder 6.

Legislative Assembly (December 19, 1890–February 1891), Reel 9.

Hearing Investigating Wynkoop's Administration of New Mexico Penitentiary.

Report of Special Committee to the Legislative Council of the Territory of New Mexico into Wynkoop's Administration of New Mexico Penitentiary.

Territorial Archives of New Mexico Executive Record Book, nos. 3–4, 1882–1898.

L. B. Prince, Letters Received.

Oklahoma Historical Society, Oklahoma City. Joseph B. Thoburn Collection. 86.01, Box 8, Folder 9.

Texas State Archives, Austin. Records of Governor Elisha Marshall Pease. Box 301-59. Letter Press Book (June 18, 1868–Nov. 18, 1868).

GOVERNMENT DOCUMENTS

Report on Indian Affairs by the Acting Commissioner for the Year 1867. Washington: Government Printing Office, 1868.

Report of the Commissioner of Indian Affairs for the Year 1865. Washington: Government Printing Office, 1865.

Report of the Commissioner of Indian Affairs for the Year 1866. Washington: Government Printing Office, 1866.

Report of the Commissioner of Indian Affairs for the Year 1868. Washington: Government Printing Office, 1868.

"Report of the Commissioner of Indian Affairs." In *Message of the President of the United States, and Accompanying Documents, to the Two Houses of Congress at the Commencement of the First Session of the Thirty-ninth Congress.* Washington: Government Printing Office, 1865.

Report of the Secretary of War, Communicating, In compliance with a resolution of the Senate of February 4, 1867, a copy of the evidence taken at Denver and Fort Lyon, Colorado Territory, by a military commission, ordered to inquire into the Sand Creek massacre, November, 1864. 39th Congress, 2d Session. Senate Executive Document No. 26, 1867.

U.S. Congress. House. *Message from the President of the United States.* 41st Congress, 2d Session.

———. Executive Document No. 240. *Change Name of Grand River to Colorado River.* 67th Congress, 1st Session.

———. Report No. 97. *Report of the Joint Committee on the Conduct of the War, Massacre of Cheyenne Indians.* 38th Congress, 2d Session. Washington: Government Printing Office, 1865.

U.S. Congress. Senate. 40th Congress, 3d Session. Executive Document No. 13.

The War of the Rebellion, A Compilation of the Official Records of the Union and Confederate Armies, 4 series, 128 volumes. Washington: United States War Department, 1880–1901.

BOOKS

Alberts, Don E. *The Battle of Glorieta: Union Victory in the West*. College Station: Texas A&M University Press, 1998.

Anonymous. *Portrait and Biographical Record of the State of Colorado*. Chicago: Chapman Publishing Co., 1899.

Ball, Durwood. *Army Regulars on the Western Frontier, 1848–1861*. Norman: University of Oklahoma Press, 2001.

Berthrong, Donald J. *The Southern Cheyennes*. Norman: University of Oklahoma Press, 1963.

Brill, Charles J. *Conquest of the Southern Plains*. Oklahoma City: Golden Saga, 1938.

Bromwell, Henrietta E., comp. *Fiftyniners' Directory: Colorado Argonauts of 1858–1859* (Two Volumes). Denver: privately printed, 1926.

Broome, Jeff. *Dog Soldier Justice: The Ordeal of Susanna Alderdice in the Kansas Indian War*. Lincoln, Kans.: Lincoln County Historical Society, 2003.

Brown, Dee. *Bury My Heart at Wounded Knee*. 1970. Reprint, New York: Holt, Rinehart & Winston, 1971.

Byers, Wm. N. and Jno. H. Kellom. *Hand Book of the Gold Fields of Nebraska and Kansas*. New York: Derby and Jackson, and Chicago: D. B. Cooke & Co, 1859.

Carroll, John M. *General Custer and the Battle of the Washita: The Federal View*. Bryan, Tex.: Guidon Press, 1978.

———. Introduction. In *The Sand Creek Massacre: A Documentary History*. New York: Sol Lewis, 1973. Includes "The Chivington Massacre."

Chalfant, *William Y. Hancock's War: Conflict on the Southern Plains*. Norman: University of Oklahoma Press, Arthur H. Clark Co., 2010.

Coel, Margaret. *Chief Left Hand: Southern Arapaho*. 1981. Reprint, Norman: University of Oklahoma Press, 1987.

Craig, Reginald S. *The Fighting Parson: A Biography of Col. John M. Chivington*. Tucson, Ariz.: Westernlore Press, 1994.

Crawford, Samuel J. *Kansas in the Sixties*. 1911. Reprint, Ottawa, Kans.: Kansas Heritage Press, 1994.

Custer, Elizabeth Bacon. *Following the Guidon*. 1890. Reprint, Norman: University of Oklahoma Press, 1966.

———. *Tenting on the Plains*. 1887, revised 1895. Reprint, Williamstown, Mass.: Corner House, 1973.

Custer, George Armstrong. *My Life on the Plains*. 1874. Reprint, New York: Promontory Press, 1995.

Davis, Herman S., compiler, *Reminiscences of General William Larimer and of His Son William H. H. Larimer: Two of the Founders of Denver City*. Lancaster, Penn.: Press of the New Era Printing Company, 1918.

Decker, Peter R. *The Utes Must Go!* Golden, Colo.: Fulcrum Publishing, 2004.

Dial, Scott. *Saloons of Denver*. Ft. Collins, Colo.: The Old Army Press, 1973.

Dunlay, Tom. *Kit Carson and the Indians*. Lincoln: University of Nebraska Press, 2000.

Dunn, William R. *I Stand By Sand Creek: A Defense of Colonel John M. Chivington and the Third Colorado Cavalry*. Ft. Collins, Colo.: The Old Army Press, 1985.

Gerboth, Christopher B., editor. *The Tall Chief: The Autobiography of Edward W. Wynkoop*. Denver: Colorado Historical Society (Monograph 9), 1993.

Gihon, John H. *Geary and Kansas: Governor Geary's Administration in Kansas with a Complete History of the Territory until July 1857*. Philadelphia: Charles C. Rhodes, 1857.

Greene, Jerome A., and Douglas D. Scott. *Finding Sand Creek: History, Archeology, and the 1864 Massacre Site.* Norman: University of Oklahoma Press, 2004.

Greene, Jerome A. *Washita: The U.S. Army and the Southern Cheyennes, 1867–1869.* Norman: University of Oklahoma Press, 2004.

Grinnell, George Bird. *The Fighting Cheyennes.* 1915. Reprint, Norman: University of Oklahoma Press, 1983.

Guild, Thelma S., and Harvey L. Carter. *Kit Carson: A Pattern for Heroes.* 1984. Reprint, Lincoln: University of Nebraska Press, 1988.

Hackenburg, Randy W. *Pennsylvania in the War with Mexico: The Volunteer Regiments.* Shippensburg, Penn.: White Mane, 1992.

Hafen, LeRoy R., ed. *Colorado Gold Rush: Contemporary Letters and Reports 1858–1859.* Glendale, Calif.: Arthur H. Clark Co., 1941.

Halaas, David Fridtjof, and Andrew E. Masich. *Halfbreed: The Remarkable True Story of George Bent Caught between the Worlds of the Indian and the White Man.* Cambridge, Mass.: Da Capo Press, 2004.

Hardorff, Richard G. *Washita Memories: Eyewitness Views of Custer's Attack on Black Kettle's Village.* Norman: University of Oklahoma Press, 2006.

Hatch, Thom. *Black Kettle: The Cheyenne Chief Who Sought Peace but Found War.* Hoboken, N.J.: John Wiley & Sons, 2004.

Hodge, Frederick Webb, ed. *Handbook of American Indians North of Mexico.* 2 vols. Washington, D.C.: Government Printing Office, Fourth impression, September 1912.

Hoebel, E. Adamson. *The Cheyennes: Indians of the Great Plains.* New York: Holt, Rinehart and Winston, 1960.

Hoig, Stan. *The Battle of the Washita, The Sheridan-Custer Campaign of 1867–1869.* Garden City, N.Y.: Doubleday & Co., 1976.

———. *The Peace Chiefs of the Cheyennes.* Norman: University of Oklahoma Press, 1980.

———. *The Sand Creek Massacre.* Norman: University of Oklahoma Press, 1961.

———. *The Western Odyssey of John Simpson Smith.* Glendale, Calif.: Arthur H. Clark Co., 1974.

———. *White Man's Paper Trail.* Boulder: University Press of Colorado, 2006.

Hollister, Ovando J. *Boldly They Rode: A History of the First Colorado Regiment of Volunteers.* Lakewood, Colo.: Golden Press, 1949.

Hutton, Paul Andrew. *Phil Sheridan and His Army.* Lincoln: University of Nebraska Press, 1985.

Hyde, George E. *A Life of George Bent: Written from His Letters.* Norman: University of Oklahoma Press, 1967.

Jones, Douglas C. *The Treaty of Medicine Lodge.* Norman: University of Oklahoma Press, 1966.

Kappler, Charles J., comp. and ed. *United States Indian Affairs: Laws and Treaties.* 2 vols. Washington, D.C.: Government Printing Office, 1904.

Kennedy, W. J. D. *On the Plains with Custer and Hancock: The Journal of Isaac Coates, Army Surgeon.* Boulder, Colo.: Johnson Books, 1997.

Kraft, Louis. *Custer and the Cheyenne: George Armstrong Custer's Winter Campaign on the Southern Plains.* El Segundo, Calif.: Upton and Sons, 1995.

Leckie, Shirley A. *Elizabeth Bacon Custer and the Making of a Myth.* Norman: University of Oklahoma Press, 1993.

Leckie, William H. *The Military Conquest of the Southern Plains.* Norman: University of Oklahoma Press, 1963.

Lee, Wayne C., and Howard C. Raynesford. *Trails of the Smoky Hill*. Caldwell, Ida.: Caxton Printers, 1980.

Leonard, Stephen J., and Thomas J. Noel. *Denver: Mining Camp to Metropolis*. Niwot: University Press of Colorado, 1990.

Lubetkin, John M. *Jay Cooke's Gamble: The Northern Pacific Railroad, the Sioux, and the Panic of 1873*. Norman: University of Oklahoma Press, 2006.

Mails, Thomas E. *Plains Indians; Dog Soldiers, Bear Men and Buffalo Women*. 1973. Reprint, New York: Bonanza Books, 1985.

Malone, Dumas, ed. *Dictionary of American Biography*. 10 vols. and a supplement. 1935. Reprint, New York: Charles Scribner's Sons, 1936.

Michno, Gregory F. *Battle at Sand Creek: The Military Perspective*. El Segundo, Calif.: Upton and Sons, 2004.

———. *Encyclopedia of Indian Wars: Western Battles and Skirmishes, 1850–1890*. Missoula, Mont.: Mountain Press, 2003.

Michno, Gregory and Susan Michno. *A Fate Worse than Death: Indian Captivities in the West, 1830–1885*. Caldwell, Ida.: Caxton Press, 2007.

Monahan, Doris, *Destination: Denver City, The South Platte Trail*. Athens, Ohio: Swallow Press, 1985.

Monnett, John H. *The Battle of Beecher Island and the Indian War of 1867–1969*. Niwot: University Press of Colorado, 1992.

Moore, John H. *The Cheyenne Nation: A Social and Demographic History*. Lincoln: University of Nebraska Press, 1987.

Noel, Thomas J., Paul F. Mahoney, and Richard E. Stevens. *Historical Atlas of Colorado*. Norman: University of Oklahoma Press, 1994.

Oliva, Leo E. *Fort Dodge: Sentry of the Western Plains*. Topeka: Kansas State Historical Society, 1998

———. *Fort Harker: Defending the Journey West*. Topeka: Kansas State Historical Society, 2000.

———. *Fort Larned: Keeping Peace on the Plains*. 1980. Reprint, Topeka: Kansas State Historical Society, 1996.

Parker, Watson. *Gold in the Black Hills*. Norman: University of Oklahoma Press, 1966.

Perkin, Robert L. *The First Hundred Years: An Informal History of Denver and the Rocky Mountain News*. Garden City, N.Y.: Doubleday, 1959.

Powell, Peter John. *People of the Sacred Mountain: A History of the Northern Cheyenne Chiefs and Warrior Societies, 1830–1879; with an Epilogue, 1969–1974*. 2 vols. San Francisco: Harper & Row, 1981.

Powell, Peter J. *Sweet Medicine*. 2 vols. 1969. Reprint, Norman: University of Oklahoma Press, 1979.

Prucha, Francis Paul. *The Great Father: The United States Government and the American Indians*. 2 vols. 1984. Reprint, Lincoln: University of Nebraska Press, 1986.

Richardson, Albert D. *Beyond the Mississippi: From the Great River to the Great Ocean*. Hartford, Conn.: American Publishing Co., 1867.

Roberts, Wm. Hugh, comp. *Mexican War Veterans: A Complete Roster of the Regular and Volunteer Troops in the War Between the United States and Mexico, From 1846 to 1848*. Washington, D.C.: Brentano's, 1887.

Schoberlin, Melvin. *From Candles to Footlights: A Biography of the Pike's Peak Theatre, 1859–1876*. Denver: Old West Publishing Co., 1941.

Schultz, Duane. *Month of the Freezing Moon: The Sand Creek Massacre, November 1864*. New York: St. Martin's Press, 1990.

Smiley, Jerome C., ed. *History of Denver: With Outlines of the Earlier History of the Rocky Mountain Country.* Denver: Times-Sun Publishing Co., 1901.

Stanley, Henry M. *My Early Travels and Adventures in America and Asia.* 2 vols. New York: Charles Scribner's Sons, 1895.

Szasz, Margaret Connell, ed. *Between Indian and White Worlds: The Cultural Broker.* Norman: University of Oklahoma Press, 1994.

Thrapp, Dan L. *Encyclopedia of Frontier Biography.* 3 vols. Glendale, Calif.: Arthur H. Clark Co., 1988.

————. *Encyclopedia of Frontier Biography*, vol. 4. Spokane, Wash.: Arthur H. Clark Co., 1994.

Unknown. *Articles of Association of the Toltec Mining Company.* Santa Fe: New Mexican Printing Company, 1886.

Utley, Robert M. *Frontier Regulars: The United States Army and the Indian, 1866–1890.* New York: Macmillan Publishing Co., 1973.

————. *The Indian Frontier of the American West, 1846–1890.* Albuquerque: University of New Mexico Press, 1984.

————. *The Lance and the Shield: The Life and Times of Sitting Bull.* New York: Henry Holt, 1993.

————, ed. *Life in Custer's Cavalry: Diaries and Letters of Albert and Jennie Barnitz, 1867–1868.* New Haven: Yale University Press, 1977.

West, Elliott. *The Contested Plains: Indians, Goldseekers, and the Rush to Colorado.* Lawrence: University Press of Kansas, 1998.

Wharton, J. E. *History of the City of Denver.* Denver: Byers and Daily News Office, 1866.

White, David A., compiler and annotator. *News of the Plains and Rockies 1803–1865, Volume 7: Mailmen, 1857–1865; Gold Seekers, Pike's Peak, 1858–1865.* Spokane, Wash.: Arthur H. Clark Co., 2000.

Whitford, William C. *The Battle of Glorieta Pass: The Colorado Volunteers in the Civil War, March 26, 27, 28, 1862.* 1906. Reprint, Glorieta, N.Mex.: Rio Grande Press, 1971.

Whitlock, Flint. *Distant Bugles, Distant Drums: The Union Response to the Confederate Invasion of New Mexico.* Boulder: University Press of Colorado, 2006.

Williams, Scott C., comp. *The Indian Wars of 1864 through the Sand Creek Massacre.* Aurora, Colo.: Pick of Ware Publishing, 1997.

Wynkoop, Richard. *Wynkoop Genealogy in the United States of America, Also a Table of Dutch Given Names,* 2nd ed. New York: Press of Wynkoop & Hallenbeck, 1878.

————. *Wynkoop Genealogy in the United States of America.* 3rd ed. New York: Knickerbocker Press, 1904.

Zamonski, Stanley W., and Teddy Keller. *The '59ers: Roaring Denver in the Gold Rush Days.* 1961. Reprint Denver: Stanza-Harp, 1967.

ARTICLES

Bartles, W. L. "Massacre of Confederates by Osage Indians in 1863," in *Transactions of the Kansas State Historical Society, 1903–1904,* edited by Geo. W. Martin, Vol. 8. Topeka: Geo. A. Clark, State Printer (1904): 62–66.

Bennett, Jr., W. Charles. "Reminiscences of Edward W. Wynkoop 1856–1858." *Heritage of Kansas* 11, no. 3 (Summer 1978): 33–48.

Carey, Raymond G. "Another View of the Sand Creek Affair." *Roundup* (February 1960): 4–15.

————. "Colonel Chivington, Brigadier General Conner, and Sand Creek," in *The Western-ers Denver Posse 1960 Brand Book,* vol. 16. Boulder, Colo.: Johnson Publishing Co. (1961): 105–36.

————. "The 'Bloodless Third' Regiment, Colorado Volunteer Cavalry." *Colorado Magazine* 38, no. 4 (October 1961): 275–300.

————. "The Puzzle of Sand Creek." *Colorado Magazine* 41 (Fall 1964): 279–98.

Clark, A. L. "Denver Has Always Been a Good Show Town." *Old West* 3, no. 3 (Spring 1867): 48–49.

Clark, Mrs. Olive A. "Early Days Along the Solomon Valley," in *Collections of the Kansas State Historical Society, 1926–1928,* 17: 719–30. Topeka: B. P. Walker, State Printer (1928).

Cobb, Frank M. "The Lawrence Party of Pike's Peakers (1858) and the Founding of St. Charles (Predecessor of Denver)." *Colorado Magazine* 10, no. 5 (September 1933): 194–97.

Crawford, George A. "The Candle-box Under the Wood-pile," in *Transactions of the Kansas State Historical Society, 1907–1908* 10: 196–204. Topeka: State Printing Office (1908).

Davis, Theodore R. "A Summer on the Plains," in *Harper's New Monthly Magazine* 36 (December 1867–May 1868): 292–307. New York: Harper & Bros.

De La Torre, Lillian. "The Actress and the Gambling Man," *Denver Westerners Monthly Roundup* 16, no. 12 (December 1960): 4–9.

————. "The Haydee Star Company," *Colorado Magazine* 39, no. 3 (July 1962): 201–13.

————. "The Theatre Comes to Denver," *Colorado Magazine* 37, no. 4 (October 1960): 285–96.

Foreman, Carolyn Thomas. "General William Babcock Hazen." *Chronicles of Oklahoma* 20, no. 4 (December 1942): 322–42.

Garfield, Marvin H. "Defense of the Kansas Frontier: 1866–1867." *Kansas Historical Quarterly* 1, no. 4, (August 1932): 326–44.

————. "Defense of the Kansas Frontier: 1868–1869." *Kansas Historical Quarterly* 1, no. 5 (November 1932): 451–73.

Gower, Calvin W. "Gold Fever in Kansas Territory: Migration to the Pikes Peak Gold Fields, 1858–1860." *Kansas Historical Quarterly* 39, no. 1 (Spring 1973): 58–74.

————. "Vigilantes," *Colorado Magazine* 41, no. 2 (Spring 1964): 93–104.

Greene, Albert R. "United States Land-offices in Kansas," in *Transactions of the Kansas State Historical Society, 1903–1904,* Vol. 8, pp. 1–13. Topeka: Geo. A. Clark, State Printer.

Hafen, LeRoy R., ed. "George A. Jackson's Diary, 1858–1859," *Colorado Magazine* 12, no. 6 (November 1935): 201–14.

Halaas, David F. "'All the Camp Was Weeping': George Bent and the Sand Creek Massacre," in *Cheyenne Dog Soldiers,* Colorado Historical Society, 1997, pp. 49–64. Articles originally published in the Summer 1995 and Autumn 1996 issues of *Colorado Heritage.*

Hancock, Winfield S. "The Indians" (originally printed in *Army and Navy Journal,* September 7, 1867), in *Eyewitnesses to the Indian Wars 1865–1890: Conquering the Southern Plains,* edited by Peter Cozzens, pp. 18–28. Mechanicsburg, Penn.: Stackpole Books, 2003.

Hart, John P. "Custer's First Stand: The Washington Fight." *Research Review* 12, no. 1 (Winter 1998): 14–31.

Isern, Thomas D. "The Controversial Career of Edward W. Wynkoop." *Colorado Magazine* 56, nos. 1–2 (Winter–Spring 1979): 1–18.

Isern, Tom. "Dueling in Denver." *Denver Post Empire* (November 28, 1976): 10–11.

Johannsen, Robert W. "The Lecompton Constitutional Convention: An Analysis of Its Membership." *Kansas Historical Quarterly* 23, no. 3 (Autumn 1957): 225–47.

Kingman, Samuel A. "The Diary of Samuel A. Kingman at Indian Treaty in 1865." *Kansas Historical Quarterly* 1, no. 5 (November 1932): 442–50.

Kraft, Louis. "Between the Army and the Cheyennes." *MHQ: The Quarterly Journal of Military History* 14, no. 2 (Winter 2002): 48–55.

———. "Custer, the Little Bighorn & History." *American History* 41, no. 2 (June 2006): 46–53, 78.

———. "Edward W. Wynkoop, A Forgotten Hero," *Research Review* n.s. 1, no. 1 (June 1987): 2–11.

———. "Ned Wynkoop's Early Years on the Frontier." *Research Review* 6, no. 1 (January 1992): 20–30.

———. "Ned Wynkoop & Black Kettle," *Research Review* 9, no. 2, (June 1995): 7–17.

———. "Ned Wynkoop's Lonely Walk between the Races," in *Custer and His Times*, Book Five, pp. 85–108. John P. Hart, editor. Cordova, Tenn.: Little Big Horn Associates, 2008.

———. "When Wynkoop Was Sheriff," *Wild West* 23, no. 6 (April 2011): 58–63.

———. "Wynkoop Confronts Hancock," in *Custer and His Times*, Book Four, John P. Hart, editor, pp. 38–62. LaGrange Park, Ill.: Little Big Horn Associates, 2002.

Lambert, Julia S. "Plain Tales of the Plains," Chapter 2, *The Trail* 8, no. 10 (March 1916): 5–13.

———. "Plain Tales of the Plains," Chapter 4, *The Trail* 8, no. 12 (May 1916): 5–13.

———. "Plain Tales of the Plains," Chapter 5, *The Trail* 9, no. 13 (June 1916): 16–24.

McGaa, William. "A Statement Regarding the Formation of the St. Charles and Denver Town Companies." *Colorado Magazine* 22, no. 3 (May 1945): 125–29.

Michno, Gregory F. "The Real Villains of Sand Creek." *Wild West* 16, no. 4 (December 2003), 22–29, 71.

Milavec, Pam. "Alias Emma S. Soule: Corrected Historical Fictions Surrounding Silas Soule and the Sand Creek Massacre." *The Denver Westerners Roundup* 61, no. 4 (July–August 2005): 3–22.

Moore, Ely. "The Lecompton Party Which Located Denver," in *Transactions of the Kansas State Historical Society, 1901–1902*, vol. 7, pp. 446–52. Topeka: Morgan State Printers, 1902.

"New Light on Mrs. Lucinda Ewbanks' Experiences," *The Trail* 12, no. 2 (July 1920): 20–24.

Raine, William MacLeod. "Western Fields of Honor," *1952 Brand Book*. Denver: The Westerners (1952): 131–39.

Sayre, Hal. "Early Central City Theatricals and Other Reminiscences," *Colorado Magazine* 6, no. 2 (March 1929): 47–53.

Stanley, Henry Morton. "The Medicine Lodge Peace Council" (series of dispatches printed in the *Missouri Democrat*), in *Eyewitnesses to the Indian Wars 1865–1890: Conquering the Southern Plains*, edited by Peter Cozzens, pp. 74–126. Mechanicsburg, Penn.: Stackpole Books, 2003.

Taylor, Alfred A. "Medicine Lodge Peace Council," *Chronicles of Oklahoma* 2, no. 2 (June 1924): 98–118.

Walter, Sara. "The Rowena Hotel," *Bald Eagle* 20, no. 4 (Winter 1994): 1–5 (unnumbered pages).

Williams, Francis S. "Trials and Judgments of the People's Court of Denver," *Colorado Magazine* 27, no. 4 (October 1950): 294–302.

Wynkoop, Edward Estill. "Edward Wanshear Wynkoop," in *Collections of the Kansas Historical Society, 1913–1914*, vol. 13, pp. 71–79. Topeka: W. R. Smith, State Printer, 1915.

Wynkoop, Frank M. "He Led the Way," *New Mexico Magazine* 16, no. 12 (December 1938): 17–19, 36–38.

Zamonski, Stanley. "Colorado Gold and the Confederacy." Reprinted in Stanley W. Zamonski and Teddy Keller. *The '59ers: Roaring Denver in the Gold Rush Days*. Denver: Stanza-Harp, 1967, pp. 273–303. Originally published in *The Westerners Brand Book*. Denver, 1956.

Zwink, Timothy A. "E. W. Wynkoop and Bluff Creek Council, 1866." *Kansas Historical Quarterly* 43, no. 2 (Summer 1977): 217–39.

THESIS

Bennett, W. Charles, Jr., "Edward W. Wynkoop, Frontiersman." Albuquerque: University of New Mexico, B.A. Thesis, Department of History, December 1976.

Roberts, Gary Leland, "Sand Creek: Tragedy and Symbol." Norman: University of Oklahoma, Ph.D. dissertation, 1984.

Index

References to illustrations are in italic type.

1864–65 Indian war, 107, 110, 118, 140, 141–42
1867 Indian war, 194, 197, 198, 199, 201, 203
1868–69 Indian war, 242–45
1876 Indian war, 256, 257

Adams, James, 148
A. F. & A Masons, 53–54
Albuquerque, N.Mex. Terr., 75, 76
Amateur Dramatic Association, 58, 64
Anderson, Robert, 64
Anthony, Scott, 69, *127*, 144, 146, 147, 292n71;
    background of, 94; Glorieta campaign, 70–73;
    Sand Creek campaign and disgust with, 131,
    133, 135, 141; musters out of military, 144;
    Wynkoop, endorsement of, 129; Wynkoop,
    Indian meetings with, 127–28, 291n45;
    Wynkoop, investigates, 126
Apache Canyon, N.Mex. Terr., 72, 73, 98
Apollo Hall, Denver, 32, 37, 47, 58, 60
Apollo Theatre. *See* Apollo Hall
Arapahoe County, Kans. Terr., 15; census, 41;
    273n22
Arapahoe County Claim Club, 35
Arapaho Indians, 24, 100, 103, 113, 116, 117,
    120, 144, 154, 155, 157, 159, 162, 167, 201,
    218, 220, 225, 234, 236, 243, 244, 245; Bluff
    Creek council, 164; Confederates approach,
    84; Fort Cobb, Sherman removal to, 238;
    Fort Dodge Hancock council, 196–97; Fort
    Lyon, 116, 126; Fort Lyon Wynkoop and
    Anthony meetings, 123, 127–28; Kaws and
    Osages, war with, 227, 228; Medicine Lodge
    peace council, 204, 205, 208, 214, 215, 216;
    prisoners of war, 253; Sand Creek, 129, 131,
    174; threats of, per Sherman, 182; Utes, 85,
    176; war parties and raids, 99, 106–107, 112,
    114, 159, 239; Washington, D.C., visit, 83;
    whiskey problem, 224–25; white captives,
    164; Wynkoop, annuity distributions to, 176,
    227, 229, 232, 233, 234, 237; Wynkoop, stays
    with, 23, 275n11
Arickaree Fork, fight at, 242–43
Arkansas River, 16, 17, 70, 71, 92, 94, 95, 96, 99,
    100, 117, 118, 130, 155, 158, 159, 163, 166,
    182, 194, 197, 199, 215, 216, 218, 223

Arkansas Valley, Colo. Terr.: Wynkoop, memorial
    to, 124–25
Army and Navy Journal, Hancock justification
    article, 203–204
Asbury, Henry, 234
Ash Creek, Colo. Terr., 96, 111, 286n19
Asher, Ambrose, 114
Atchison, Kans., 151, 167, 246
Augur, Christopher C., 213
Auraria, Colo. Terr., 20, 22, 31, 35, 38, 60

Bad Wound (Oglala Sioux), 188
Baldwin, Horace, 99, 101, 102
Banks, Alex, 223, 232
Barnitz, Albert, 235; erroneous gun distribution
    comment, 236; Indians, describes, 233;
    Medicine Lodge peace council, 214, 216, 217;
    Pawnee Fork battle line and village, 186, 189;
    Wynkoop's home, 199
Bartlett, Edward L., 264
Bates, A. E., 160, 164
Bates, William, 36
Bear River, 86, 88
Bear That Walks Under The Ground (Oglala
    Sioux), 188
Bear Tongue (Cheyenne), 161
Beauregard, Pierre, 64
Belknap, William W., 307n29
Bent, Charley, 133, 134, 212
Bent, George, 106, *135*, 224, 228, 271n1, 288n4,
    289n25; background of, 97; Bluff Creek
    council, 163; Sand Creek, 134; Southern
    Cheyennes, 108, 109, 162; Medicine Lodge
    council, 205, 212, 215, 216; war parties, 116,
    239; Wynkoop, comments on, 163, 270;
    Wynkoop, employee of, 181; Wynkoop,
    translates for, 111
Bent, Robert, 106, 134
Bent, William, 94, 106, 133, 154, 155, 159, 160,
    288n4; recommends Wynkoop as Indian agent,
    157
Benteen, Frederick; Indian fight, 240; Wynkoop,
    horse race, 235
Bent's New Fort. *See* Fort Lyon, Colo. Terr.
Bent's Ranch, Colo. Terr., 101
Bernal Springs, 71–72, 282n29
Big Head (Cheyenne), 161, 171; Bluff Creek
    council counteroffer by, 163

Big Jake (Cheyenne), 229, 232

Big Mouth (Arapaho), 109, 161, 197, 229, 232; Bluff Creek village and council, 162, 163; whiskey, 224

Big Sandy, 94; called Sand Creek, 287n47, 291n45, 291n49

Big Timbers, Kans., 107, 163, 186; council at, 109–13

Big Wolf (Cheyenne), 109

Bijou Basin, Colo. Terr., 94, 130

Black Hills, Dak. Terr., 256

Black Hills Rangers, 257, 258

Black Kettle (Cheyenne), 97, 116, *124, 125*, 186, 187, 196, 228, 229, 232, 239, 247, 250, 251, 269; Ash Creek village attacked, 96, 111, 161; background of, 111, 289n25; Big Timbers, 109–13; Bluff Creek village and council, 161, 164; buffalo, permit to hunt, 168; Camp Weld council, 119, 121, 123; Cheyennes, named chief of, 154; death of, 246; delivers children, 114; false death of, 134; Fort Ellsworth council, 171; Fort Larned meeting, 173; Fort Lyon meeting, 128; letters of, 106–107, 288nn4–5; Medicine Lodge peace council, 204, 208–209, 211, 212, 214, 215, 216; Sand Creek, 128–29, 131–32, 148, 291n45; Southern Cheyennes, influence over, 132–33; threatened, 213; Wynkoop, relationship with, 111–12, 153, 161; Wynkoop, wants as agent, 154; Wynkoop, warns, 130

Bliss, L. W., 35–37, 48, 58

Bluff Creek villages, Kans., 160–61, 219, 229

Blunt, James G., 147

Bogy, Charles, 205; necessity of funds for Indian agents, 172; Wynkoop, letter for, 176

Bogy, Lewis, 172, 176, 179, 192

Boone, Albert, 245, 250

Booneville, Colo. Terr., 97, 117

Booth, Captain (district inspector), 142

Booth, John Wilkes, 148

Bosse (Arapaho), 116, *124*

Bowen, Leavitt, 131, 292n71; kills child, 139–40

Box Elder Creek, 99

Box family (death and captivity of), 172–73

Bright, Emma S.: fraudulent widow's claim, 294n44

Brindle, William, 6–7, 8, 10, 13–14, 272n19

Broadwell, James M., 36

Brown, Matilda Louise. *See* Wakely, Matilda Louise Brown

Browning, O. H., 201, 234, 250

Brûlé Sioux Indians, 99

Buchanan, James, 58

Buffalo Chief (Cheyenne), 215

Bull Bear (Cheyenne), 116, 123, *124, 125*; Big Timbers council, 109, 110–11, 112; Bluff Creek council, 161, 162, 163, 164; Fort Larned council, 181; Hancock expedition, 185–88, 188–90; Medicine Lodge peace council, 215,

216; raids of, 114, 239; tipi, Hancock trophy, 198, 204

Bummers, 60

Bunch of Timber, Kans., 108. *See also* Big Timbers

Bunkara River, 88

Butterfield, J. L.: whiskey problem, 224–25

Butterfield Overland Dispatch, 157

Butterworth, D. A., 205

Byers, William, 32, *39*, 49, 53, 81, 103, 116, 117, 119, 121, 122, 150, 172, 177, 205, 260; Denver, 38, 43–44; fear tactics of, 93, 148; gold region, interest in, 26–27, 38; McLure snub, 57; *RMN* attacks Denver bad element, 40, 42, 47, 53; *RMN*, expands and sells, 40, 260; Sand Creek, defends victory, 140, 145; Wynkoop, attacks in print, 61–62, 144, 145, 205, 211, 249; Wynkoop, changing view/ relationship with, 39, 44, 48, 53; Wynkoop, interviewed by 27–28; Wynkoop, praises in print, 62–63, 66, 166–67; Wynkoop-McLure problem, 55–56

Cache la Poudre River, 85, 100

Cahill, Lt. (Second U.S. Cavalry), 160

Calhoun, John C., 6

Camp Collins, Colo. Terr., 85, 87, 100, 285n38

Camp Evans, Colo. Terr., 130

Camp Weld, Colo. Terr., 66, 69, 81, 84, 85, 87, 89, 90, 91, 96, 98, 130, 285n38; Cheyenne-Arapaho council, 119, 121–23, 144; Wynkoop commands, 84, 93–94

Camp Wynkoop, Kans., 97, 99, 101

Canby, Edward, 69, 70, 75, 76–78

Cannon, James, 142, 147, 151, 294n53

Carleton, James H., 80

Carmichael, Catharine Sinclair, 6

Carson, Christopher H. (Kit), 154; Wynkoop, honored by, 260, 261; Wynkoop, meets, 155; Wynkoop connection, 295n69

Caudle, Melinda Ann, 237, 243, 308n62; capture of, 235–36

Central City, Colo. Terr., 37, 65

Chalk Bluff station, Kans., 175

Chaves, Frank, 251

Cherry Creek, Colo. Terr., 15, 18, 19–20, 23, 27, 28, 29, 30, 33, 36

Cheyenne Indians, 24, 25, 84, 210; background of, 92

Child, Lydia Maria, 217, 233

Chivington, John, 80, 93, 95–96, 97, 100, *132*, 136, 141, 144, 145, 209, 211, 247; background and description of, 65–66, 281n15; Camp Weld council, 119, 121–22; Civil War, 68; Colorado Sand Creek inquiry, 145, 146–47; Curtis instructions to, 121; Glorieta campaign, 70–75, 282n30; military, musters out, 150; Peralta, battle of, 76–78; politics, 101, 102, 116; popularity of, 75, 78, 139; promotion of, 75, 116, 283n54; sabotages peace effort, 117;

safe conduct pass, 101, 287n2; Sand Creek, campaign of, 130–31, 133, 291n45; Sand Creek, reports of and death count, 134, 136; Soule/Cramer problem, 131, 137; Southern Cheyenne comments, 98, 147; Ute expedition, 85–88; and Wynkoop, Louise, 266, 267; Wynkoop, relationship with, 68, 78, 81, 266, 283n46

Cimarron Crossing, Kans., fight near, 194

Cimarron River, 101–102, 111, 204, 218

Civil War, 90, 95; threat of, 57, 60; war declared, 64

Clarke, R. Watson, 130

Clear Creek, Colo. Terr., 35, 37

Cleveland, Grover, 260

Coal Creek, Colo. Terr., 99

Coberly, Hersa A.: marries Soule, 148; Wynkoop, escort for, 152

Cochrane, James, 51

Cody, Mrs. M. E., 56, 280n41, 280n42

Coleman, James T., 61–62

Colley, Dexter, 105, 118, 123, *124*; Indian scam, 106

Colley, Samuel, 100, 105, 122–23, 146, 288n4; Indian scam, 106, 287n2; Sand Creek letter, 140

Colorado City, Colo. Terr., 69

Colorado River, 276n28

Colorado Sand Creek inquiry, 144–45, 146–48, 150

Colorado Territory, 80, 82, 95, 99, 152, 267; Indian removal from, 93; statehood, 57, 116–17, 243, 280n52

Comanche Indians, 83, 84, 85, 97, 100, 106, 155, 176, 218, 224, 235, 238, 242, 244; annuities, 233; Medicine Lodge peace council, 204, 208, 212–13, 214; mule incident, 16–17; raids of, 102; white captives, 175, 235–36

Combs, James, 147–48

Confederate States of America, 65

Connor, Patrick Edward, 85, 87, 130

Cook, Samuel H., 72, *86*

Cooke, C. E., 81

Cooke, Jay, 255

Cooley, Dennis, 153, 157, 160, 164, 165, 167, 170, 171, 172, 175, 176; Wynkoop, lobbies for, 173; Wynkoop, wants accounting, 174

Cooper, James Fenimore, 17, 107

Cooper, Peter, 247, 249, 250, 251, 255; background of, 233–34; Wynkoop, recommends, 252–53

Cooper, Wickliffe, 194, 302n66

Cooper Union, New York City, 233, *248*, 255; Wynkoop speech at, 247, 249

Cossitt, Chauncey, 123, 137, 142, 148

Cottonwood Springs, Nebr. Terr., 53

Council Grove, Kans. Terr., 16, 233

Cramer, Joseph, 108, 109, 117, 123, 128, 141, 145; Chivington, protest to, 131; fight with Indians,

102–103; Wynkoop, endorsement of, 129; Sand Creek fight and letter, 133, 137, 292n71

Crawford, George, 10

Crawford, Jack, 258, 260, *263*; Wynkoop, scouts for, 257

Crawford, Samuel J., 207; Wynkoop, wants fired, 206, 212, 218; weapons, 227

Cree, Theodore, 131

Criterion Saloon, 32, 42, 43, 45, 51–52, 54–55; headquarters for secessionists, 64

Crocker, Mrs. (full-blooded Cheyenne), 247

Cross of Gold (drama), 33

Crow Chief, 94

Crow Indians, 93

"Cultural Brokers," 112

Cummings, Alexander, 164–65

Curtis, Dick, *193*, *195*; Wynkoop, translates for, 173

Curtis, Samuel, 98, 101, 103, 104, 116, 117, 123, 126, 141, 147; background of, 95; Chivington, instructions to, 121; Wynkoop problem, 136, 139

Custer City, Dak. Terr., 256, 257

Custer, Elizabeth (Libbie), "perfect day," 203

Custer, George Armstrong, 249, 250, 261; background of, 182; Hancock's scapegoat, 203; Pawnee Fork battle line and village, 186, 188, 191; pursues fleeing Indians, reports of, 192, 193, 194; Washita campaign, 245, 246, 247, 251

Cut Nose (Apache), 229, 232

Dakota Territory, 256, 257

Darlington, Brinton, 253

Davidson, J. W., 167–68, 174

Davis, Theodore, 245

Deadwood, Dak. Terr., 256, 257, 259, 261

Deadwood Gulch, Dak. Terr., 256

Denison, W. W., 123

Dennison, B., 228, 232

Denver, Colo. Terr., 53, 54, 65, 81, 82, 98, 99, 105, 106, 115, 116, 118, 129, 148, 170, 172, 256, 268; Cheyenne-Arapaho arrival, 119; Civil War, 64; Confederate supporters in, 65; "Golden City," 21–22; growth of, 22, 33, 41; homeless and unemployed, 58, 64; Hungate bodies displayed, 100; Indians, fear of, in, 93, 100; Jefferson Territory, 31, 34; lawlessness and violence, 35; Lincoln election, 48; merges with Auraria, 38; naming of, 22, 274n5; people's courts, 45, 55; Sand Creek hearings, 144, 145

Denver, James W., 14, 20, 21, 27; Wynkoop, 15, 34

Denver City. *See* Denver

Denver City Town Company, 27, 28, 35, 40, 106, 273n22; land development meetings, 15, 21

Denver Guards, 57, 60

Denver Theatre, Colo. Terr., 152, 294n57

Democratic support of Union, 81

Department of Kansas, 95, 116

Department of New Mexico, 108
Department of the Missouri, 158, 175, 227
District of Colorado, 81
District of Kansas, 158
District of the Upper Arkansas, 116, 126, 174, 242; Cheyennes and Arapahos, number in district, 165
Dodge, Grenville M., 158, 159
Dog Men, 112, 121, 134, 169, 179; Arickaree Fork fight, 242–43; background of, 92–93; Black Kettle, threaten, 211; Bluff Creek council, 161; Chalk Bluff depredations, 177; Dog Soldiers (white term), 285n4; Dunn fight, 93, 286n8; Fort Larned council, 181; Hancock expedition, 185, 188; Medicine Lodge peace council, 215, 219, 225; protective of their land, 180; Sully, attack command of, 242; war parties and raids, 99, 107, 114, 140, 159, 239; Wood Creek council, 166
Dog Soldiers (white term). See Dog Men
Dole, William P., 90, 102
Doolittle, James Rood, 140, 146, 150, 152; Wynkoop, offer to and recommendation of, 151, 167
Douglas, Henry, 179
Downing, Jacob, 45, 47, 72–73, 137, 292n71
Drunkard, The, 60
Dryer, Hiram, 158, 159, 160
Dueling and duels, 36–37, 55, 57
Dunn, Clark, Dog Men fight, 93, 285–86n5, 286n8

Eagle Head. See Min-im-mie
Eayre, George S., 97; attacks Southern Cheyennes, 94, 96, 286n19, 286n20
Elliott, Joel, 308n72; Wynkoop, rough up, 245
Ennis, James, 40
Eureka, Colo. Terr., 65, 66
Evans, John: 1864 Indian war, 90, 95, 98, 102, 103–104, 118, 146, 209; Camp Weld council, 119, 121–23; enlistment of volunteers, 103; proclamation to friendly Indians, 100; resignation, 151–52; statehood politics, 102, 116; Ute Indian treaty, 89–80
Evans, Thomas, and Wakely, Rose, 49, 51
Ewbanks, Isabelle, 114–15; death of, 289nn38–39
Ewbanks, Lucinda, 114–15
Ewbanks, Willie, 114–15
Ewbanks family: members killed, 113; spelling of name, 289n37
Ewing, Thomas, Jr., 85
Extermination, cry of, 93, 100, 152, 168, 184, 242, 251, 294

Fayel, William, 208, 210
Fifth Texas Mounted Volunteers, 68
Fifth U.S. Infantry, 71, 73–75
First Colorado Volunteer Cavalry, 82, 85, 98, 101, 278n7; Big Timbers bivouacs and mutiny threat, 109–10, 113; Denver parade, 90; name change, 75, 283n45; Sand Creek campaign, 131, 133, 136
First Colorado Volunteer Regiment, 65, 68; Glorieta campaign, 69–73; name change, 75, 283n45
First Pennsylvania Volunteers, 5
First U.S. Cavalry, 72
Fitzpatrick, Jack, 247
Fletcher, Amanda, 164–65, 296n35
Fletcher, Elizabeth, 165
Flynn, Errol: Wynkoop compared to film persona, 269
Fontaine Qui Bouille, 17, 70, 117, 290n8
"Fool, The" (Southern Cheyenne), 108, 109
Forbes, B. N., 110, 288n15
Ford, James H., 73, 86, 116, 136, 139, 151
Forsyth, George, 242–43
Fort Bridger, Nebr. Terr., 84, 87
Fort Cobb, Ind. Terr., 238, 244, 245, 247
Fort Craig, N. Mex. Terr., 70, 79, 80
Fort Dodge, Kans., 160, 161, 164, 179, 181, 210, 218, 223, 224, 225, 227, 228, 245, 247
Fort Ellsworth, Kans., 174, 175, 232; becomes Fort Harker, 176; description of, 170–71
Fort Fauntleroy, Colo. Terr., 94
Fort Garland, Colo. Terr., 80, 89, 99
Fort Halleck, Nebr. Terr., 86–87, 164, 284n27, 284–85n37
Fort Harker, Kans., 243, 306n15; Wynkoop annuities, 231
Fort Kearney, Nebr. Terr., 23, 24
Fort Laramie, Nebr. Terr., 100
Fort Larned, Kans., 84, 96, 97, 98, 100, 101, 130, 150, 158, 160, 164, 165, 196, 197, 198, 217, 218, 220, 221, 225, 227, 228, 229, 230, 233, 234, 235, 238, 242, 243, 244; poor condition of, 199; Sherman Indian council, 173, 236; wolf incident, 237–38
Fort Leavenworth, Kans., 136, 158, 159
Fort Lupton, Colo. Terr., 54
Fort Lyon, Colo. Terr., 84, 97, 98, 101, 102, 105, 107, 108, 110, 113, 115, 116, 121, 133, 144, 147, 288n3; background of, 94; Chivington seals off, 131; commissary, 94, 102, 126, 128, 143; condition of, 95; flooded, 100, 143; Sand Creek inquiry, 146–48; Wynkoop commands and fortifies, 94, 141, 145
Fort Rankin, Colo. Terr., 140
Fort Riley, Kans., 129–30, 136, 150, 151, 152, 156, 167, 170, 174, 203
Fort Sedgwick, Colo. Terr., 220
Fort Sumter, S.C., 64
Fort Union, N. Mex. Terr., 71
Fort Wallace, Colo. Terr., 167, 175, 210
Fort Zarah, Kans., 158, 159, 160, 171, 210, 230
Fosdick, H. M., 97
Foster, Charles, 12
Foster, Lafayette S., 150
Fourth Confederate Missouri Cavalry, 84
Fourth Texas Mounted Volunteers, 68

Fourth U.S. Artillery, 180, 205
Fox Tail (Cheyenne): kills Mexican herder, 210, 304n24
Freeman, Thomas R., 53–54
Frémont, John C., 261
Frémont's Orchard, Colo. Terr., 93
French, Adnah, 28–29
Friend, Lee Temple, 236
F. X. Aubry (ship), 8

Gable, Thomas P., 264–65
Geary, John W., 11
Georgia Company, 27
Georgia Gulch, Colo. Terr., 89, 285n38
Gilpin, William, 64, 65, 66, 90; background of, 60
Glorieta Mesa, 72–73
Glorieta Pass, 267; battle of, 72–73, 78, 82
Goff, Andy, 51
"Golden City." *See* Denver, Colo. Terr.
Golden City, Colo. Terr., 43, 57, 58
Gold region, Colo. Terr., 15, 29, 30, 43, 44, 84; gold found, 22; news of, 26–27; routes to, 16, 23, 30, 60, 266, 273n23; slavery issue, 41, 48
Goldrick, O. J., 45, *46*
Gordon, G. M., 160, 161, 164
Grand Army of the Republic (G.A.R.), 260, 261
Grand Island, Nebr. Terr., 24–25
Grand River, 88, 276n28
Grant, Ulysses S., 252, 253, 256, 307n29; peace policy, praised, 255
Gray, Isaac, 101, 103
Gray Head (Cheyenne), 171; Fort Larned council, 181; Medicine Lodge peace council, 208–10, 211, 212, 213; testimony and raped girl, 215; Pawnee Fork, 188
Green River, 276n28
Gregory Gulch, Colo. Terr., 38
Guerrier, Edmund, 106, 116, 167, 190, 230, *231*, 308n50; raids of, 239; Sand Creek, escapes, 133; Wynkoop, employee of, 181, 182, 219, 225; Wynkoop, translates for, 183, 184, 187–89

Hackberry Creek, 110, 113
Hadley, Major (employs Haydee Star Company), 37
Hairy Wolf (Cheyenne), 161
Halleck, H. W., 141
Hancock, Winfield Scott, *195*, 209, 210, 213, 215, 224, 246, 247; expedition, battle line, 186–88, 300n44; expedition, intentions of, 180; expedition, march of, 184–86, 300n27; Fort Dodge, Arapaho council, 196–97; Fort Dodge, Kiowa council, 194–96; Fort Larned council and threats of, 182–84; Indian agents, view of, 180–81; Indians, ignorance of, 183, 197; Pawnee Fork village, inventory, and destruction of, 189–90, 194, 196; Pawnee Fork village, trophies of, 198, 204; Southern Cheyennes, charges against,
175; Wynkoop-Hancock controversy, 250; Wynkoop, raped girl, confrontations, and warnings, 181, 184, 189, 191, 192–93, 194–95
Hancock's war, 194; cost of, 203; Wynkoop criticism of, 197–98
Hanger, Charles, 164, 165
Hardin, George, 110
Harlan, James, 157, 158, 165
Harney, William S., 207; Little Arkansas peace council, 154; Medicine Lodge peace council, 208–10, 213
Harrisburg, Penn., 255, 259
Harrison, Charles, 40, 41, 43, 49, 54, 55, 284n25; death of, 84; James Hill and trial, 51–53, 279n21; Ki Harrison, confusion with, 47, 278n6; McLure, Park, 42, 45; violence of, 42, 64, 278n23; Wynkoop relationship, 42. *See also* Criterion Saloon
Harrison, H. H. C. (Ki): Charles Harrison, confusion with, 47, 278n6; Jefferson Rangers, 57; McLure problem, 47; and Wakely, Rose, 49
Harrison's Star Saloon and Restaurant, 47
Hawley, Charles, 145
Haydee, M'lle, 32, 33, 37, 38
Haydee Star Company, 35, 38
Hazen, William, 238, 243
Heap of Bears (Kiowa), 160
Heap of Buffalo (Arapaho), 116, *124*
Hemenway, S. O., 29–30
Henderson, John B., 206, 209, 212, 213; promise to hunt buffalo, 215, 216, 234
Henning, B. S., 136
Hickok, James Butler (Wild Bill), 261
Hill City, Dak. Terr., 256
Hill, James, 51–52
Hill, R. A., 142
Hoag, Enoch, 253
Honeymoon (drama), 64
Hotame-taneo o. *See* Dog Men
Houston, Sam, 5
Howland, George W., 72
Howland, John, 207
Hubbard, Asahel W., 293n25
Hulmes, Ada, 264–65, 311n43
Humboldt, Kans., 84
Hungate family, brutal murder of, 100, 287n36

Indian agents: accusations against, 178–79
Indian removal, 11, 213, 215, 273n15
Indian Suffrage Party, 250
Indian Territory, 213, 238, 243, 244, 245
Interior Department–War Department: Indian control infighting, 177, 179, 246; Wynkoop, knowledge of infighting, 182
Iron Mountain (Comanche), 235
Iron Shirt (Apache), 229, 232
Irwin (government freighter), 93
Irwin, W. R., 205; necessity of Indian agent funds, 172; Wynkoop, letter for, 176

Jackman (government freighter), 93
Jackson, George A., diary error, 275n26
James, Amos, 148
Janis, Antoine, 28
Jefferson Rangers, 57, 60
Jefferson Territory, 31, 41, 57, 58; elections and politics, 43, 48
Jicarilla Apache Indians: attacks of, 18; Southern Cheyennes, proposed meeting, 228, 332
Johnson, Andrew, 152, 173, 179, 220, 246, 251; Wynkoop, meets, 167
Johnson's Ranch, N.Mex.Terr., 72–75
Joint Committee on the Conduct of the War (Washington, D.C.), Sand Creek investigation, 141, 145, 146–47
Joint Special Committee (Washington, D.C.), on treatment of Indian tribes, 146, 150, 293n25; views Sand Creek, 151
Jones, Fred, employee of Wynkoop, 181
Julesburg, Colo.Terr., 49, 166; attacked, 140
Jump, Ed, 32, 42
Jump's Hall, 32
Junction City, Kans., 174

Kansa Indians. See Kaw Indians
Kansas, 107, 171, 174, 218; statehood, 57; weather, 232, 233, 235
Kansas City, Kans.Terr., 13–14, 170
Kansas River. See Kaw River
Kansas Territorial Legislature, 28, 276n34
Kansas Territory, 6, 31, 34
Katie Estelle Company, 6, 39
Kaskaskia Indians, 11
Kaw Indians, 16, 212; Southern Cheyennes, war with, 219, 220, 227, 228, 232–33, 236–37
Kaw River, 8, 16
Keeper of the Sacred Arrows. See Stone Forehead
Kehler, John H., 66
Kempton, Dr.Thomas, 6
Kendrick, J. Mills, 266
Kenyon, Sgt. (First Colorado Cavalry), 102
Kerber, Charles, 69–70
Kicking Bird (Kiowa), 194, 196
Kiowa Apache Indians. See Plains Apache Indians
Kiowa Indians, 84, 85, 97, 103, 106, 155, 161, 176, 195, 218, 224, 225, 238, 243, 244; annuities, 229, 233; Fort Dodge Hancock council, 194, 196; Fort Larned meetings, 173, 235, 242; Medicine Lodge peace council, 204, 208, 212–13, 214; mule incident, 16–17; raids of 99, 102; threats of, per Sherman, 182; Washington, D.C., visit, 83; white captives, 173
Kozlowski's Ranch, N.Mex.Terr., 72–73, 75, 282n33, 282n37

Lambert, Julia, 42, 143
Langrishe, Jack, 64
Larimer, John, 273n22
Larimer, William H. H., 18

Larimer, William, Jr., 19–22, 28, 30, 32, 38, 45; background of, 18; threat by, 21, 274n4
Las Gorras Blancas, 262
Las Vegas, N.Mex.Terr., 71, 150, 151
Las Vegas Land Grant, 262
Lawrence, Charles A., 18, 28, 30
Lawrence, Kans.Terr./Kans., 16, 20, 95, 159, 245
Lean Bear (Cheyenne), 96, 111
Leavenworth, Jesse, 154, 169, 195, 206, 208, 243; Hancock expedition, 184, 185; Wynkoop, comments on, 191
Leavenworth City, Kans.Terr., 14, 18, 243
Lecompton, Kans.Terr., 8, 14–15, 21, 27–28; growth of and slavery issue, 10, 11
Left Hand (Arapaho), 97, 109, 112, 123, 126, 128, 148; Sand Creek, moves to, 128–29; Sand Creek, protection of, 148
Left Hand (Oglala Sioux), 188
"Let Neddy plant the Willow, &c" (Anna Wynkoop), 5
Lewis, William, 71, 73, 74
Lincoln, Abraham, 48, 53, 148
Little Arkansas River, Kans., 153
Little Bear (Oglala Sioux), 188
Little Black Kettle (Cheyenne), 171
Little Blue River, 113
Little Bull (Oglala Sioux), 188
Little Creek, 161
Little Heart (Cheyenne), 86
Little Raven (Arapaho), 109, 112, 123, 126, 161, 207, 228, 229, 232, 237, 249; Bluff Creek council, 161, 164; description of, 206; Fort Dodge Hancock council, 196–97; Fort Larned meeting, needs weapons, 173; Little Arkansas peace council, 155; Medicine Lodge peace council, 212, 214, 215; Wynkoop, wants as agent, 154
Little Robe (Arapaho), 171, 229; Bluff Creek council, 161; false death of, 134; Fort Larned council, not at, 299n18; Medicine Lodge peace council, 213, 215; raids Kaws, 232; Wynkoop, meetings with, 233
Little Rock (Cheyenne), 241, 308n50; Wynkoop, meetings with, 239, 240
Little Sage Woman (Black Kettle's wife; Cheyenne), 111
Little Wolf (Cheyenne), 171
Lone Wolf (Kiowa), 196; Wynkoop, meeting with, 235
Lookout Station, Kans., murders at, 192, 194
Lord, Capt. (First U.S. Cavalry), 72
Los Lunas, N.Mex.Terr., 76, 78
Louderback, David H., 130, 142, 148

Maahótse. See Sacred Arrows
Madam Wakely. See Wakely, Matilda Louise Brown
Maid of Croisay. See Cross of Gold
Man That Moves (Kiowa), 194
Man That Shot The Ree, The (Cheyenne), 171

Man Who Breaks The Marrow Bones (Cheyenne), 239
Marble, Daniel, 114, 289n38
Marcy, Lt. (Palmer Divide), 18, 19
Marrs, Isaac, kills Little Heart, 85–86
Martin, Benjamin, Wynkoop recommends, 255–56
Maynard, J. L., 145
McAdams, Margaret, 154, 212; Wynkoop employs, 162, 228, 237, 239
McCannon, John, 133
McCook, A. McDowell, 150, 153, 294n49
McCusker, Philip, 224
McGaa, William, 20–21, 22, 28
McKensie, Charles. See Wynkoop, Charles Shippen
McKensie's Vaudeville Troupe, 6
McLure, Park, 41, 43, 46, 62; "judge," 49; attacked by press, 48; Byers snub, 57; death of, 84; Denver Guards, 57; spelling of name, 278n1; trial and standoff, 45, 47; Wynkoop mail problem, 54, 55–56, 58, 279–80n38, 280n42; Wynkoop, relationship with, 42
McMasters, Rachel (wife of William Larimer, Jr.), 22
Medary, Samuel, 27, 30
Medicine Arrow (or Medicine Arrows). See Stone Forehead (Cheyenne)
Medicine Wolf (Cheyenne), 188
Medicine Woman Later (Black Kettle's wife; Cheyenne), 132
Mexican man, killed by Fox Tail, 210, 304n24
Mexican War, 5, 6, 15, 60, 68
Miami Indians, 11, 13
Middle Park, Colo. Terr., 88, 89
Military District of Colorado, 144
Military District of Utah and Nevada, 85, 130
Military Division of the Missouri, 158
Min-im-mie (Cheyenne), 106, 108, 109; white captives, 165
Minton, William, 128, 142, 148
Missouri River, 11, 13, 158
Mix, Charles, 232, 238, 244
Mixed-blood Indians, white hatred of, 133
Montana City, Colo. Terr., 19
Montande, Charles, lodges with Wynkoop, 41
Montoya, José Manuel, 264–65
Moonlight, Thomas, 144
Moore, Ely, 272n19
Morris & Hanger, 164
Morrison, James, 197, 217, 218, 221, 237; Washita death count, 247, 249, 251
Morrow (killer of Soule), 150
Morton, Nancy, 114–15, 289n38
Mountain City, Colo. Terr., 37, 38, 41
Murphy, Thomas, 154, 157, 160, 169, 224, 233, 250, 253; background of, 151; Medicine Lodge peace council, 204, 205, 206; views on war, 241, 242; Wynkoop, working relationship with, 159, 176, 178, 197, 198, 199, 201, 203, 217,

218, 219, 220–21, 222–23, 225, 228, 229, 230, 231–232, 235, 236–37, 244, 245, 246

Nance, R. M., 31
Navajo City, Colo., 261
Navajo Indian Agency, Wynkoop's interest in, 251
Navajo Indians, 68, 251
Nebraska Territory, 15, 18, 65, 87, 113, 239, 284n37
Neva (Arapaho), 109, 113, 116, 124
New Mexico Penitentiary, 262. See also Wynkoop, Edward Wanshaer
New Mexico Territory, 15, 69, 70, 79, 84, 264. See also Southwest
New York City, 14, 209, 233; Wynkoop in, 157, 244, 246, 247, 251, 255
Nichols, Charles, 20, 21, 28
Nichols, David H., 128
Ninth U.S. Kansas Cavalry, 84
"Noble savages," 17
Northern Cheyenne Indians, 93
Northern Pacific Railroad, 255
North Park, Colo. Terr., 87–88, 285n38
North Platte River, 87, 155, 285n38
No-ta-nee (Arapaho), 116, 124, 130

Oglala Sioux Indians, 166, 181, 209, 222, 256; Pawnee Fork, 184, 185, 186, 188, 189, 190, 191, 192, 194, 196, 198; Powder River village, attacked, 256
Ohméséhesos. See Northern Cheyenne Indians
Ojo Caliente, N.Mex. Terr., 266
Old Park, Colo. Terr., 88
Olney, James, sworn statement of, 149
Omaha, Nebr. Terr., 26, 28, 38
One-Eye (Cheyenne), 106, 108, 109, 112, 114, 124, 147, 288n15; death of, 134; safe conduct pass, 101; Wynkoop, meets, 107, 287n2
Oro City, Colo. Terr., 94
Osage Indians, 246; kill Confederate soldiers, 84; Southern Cheyennes, war with, 220, 227, 228, 236–37
Oster, John, 100
Overland Stage Line, 86
Overland Trail, 87, 284n27

Palmer, I. N., 171
Palmer, Lucian, 148
Palmer Divide, Colo. Terr., 18, 19, 21, 274n25
Panic of 1873, 256
Paola, Kans. Terr., 11–13
Parker, Eli, 253
Paul, Gabriel René, 71, 76–77
Pawnee Fork village, Kans., 179, 181, 190, 196, 204, 210, 215, 222, 250, 268; described and Indians' flight from, 189, 191, 192, 301n46; destruction of, 194, 205; inventory of, 196; later camps on, 218, 228, 232, 239; raped girl, 191, 215, 217

Pawnee Indians, 197, 204, 212; Southern Cheyennes, tribal conflict with, 116, 239; Wynkoop held captive by, 24–26

Pawnee Killer (Oglala Sioux): Fort Larned council, not at, 299n18; Hancock expedition, 184–85, 186, 188; White Rock massacre, 222; Wynkoop safe conduct letter, 166

Pawnee Land Office, 6, 8, 9, 27, 29; land sales, 11

Peck, Dr. (Charles Hill's doctor), 52

Pennsylvania, 3, 5, 38, 157, 260; Wynkoop in, 153, 157, 254, 255, 256, 259

People's court, 45, 55

Peoria Indians, 11

Peralta, N.Mex.Terr., battle of, 76–78

Perrin, Edwin O., 12

"Pet Lambs" (First Colorado Volunteers), 68, 75

Petrikin, Hardman, 10, 272–73n7

Petrikin, Henry, 10, 272–73n7

Philadelphia, Penn., 4, 5, 6, 91, 243, 254; Wynkoop, in city; 244, 249, 250

Phillips, Charles, 94, 109

Piankeshaw Indians, 11

Pigeon's Ranch, N.Mex.Terr., 72, 73, 74, 79, 98

Pike's Peak, 15, 16, 17, 42

Pike's Peakers. See First Colorado Volunteer Regiment

Pizarro, 57–58

Plains Apache Indians, 83, 85, 106, 155, 259, 205, 233, 244; Bluff Creek council, 161; Fort Larned meeting, 173; Medicine Lodge Creek peace council, 204, 208, 212, 213, 214; Wynkoop, agent for, 174; Wynkoop, annuity distributions to, 176, 229, 232, 234

Plains Indians: background of, 82, fight for future of, 249; well armed, 179

Platte River, 23, 24, 30, 93, 96, 97, 99, 107, 118, 121, 150, 155, 158, 197, 216; concentration of soldiers, 179

Plum Creek Ranch, Nebr.Terr., 114

Poisal, John, Jr. See Poysell, John, Jr.

Polvadera, N.Mex.Terr., 80, 283n6

Pollock, Dr. (Wynkoop's doctor), 81

Pond Creek, Colo.Terr., 167, 174

Poor Bear (Apache): Bluff Creek council, 161; Medicine Lodge peace council, 208, 212

"Poor Lo" (eastern press term), 17

Pope, John, 158, 165

Porcupine Bear (Cheyenne): Bluff Creek council and threat, 161, 162, 163–64

Porcupine Bear (father of Porcupine Bear; Cheyenne), turns Dog Men into outlaws, 161

Pottsville, Penn., 4–5, 254

Powder Bull (Arapaho), 241

Poysell, John, Jr., and Washita death count, 247

Prather, John, claim of, 198

Prince, L. Bradford, 261–62, 264

Prowers, John, 147

"Puebla," Colo.Terr., 17, 274n25

Pueblo, Colo.Terr., 147, 260

Purgatoire River, 70

Pyron, Charles L., 72–73

Quakers: Wynkoop connection to, 10–11, 13, 249

Quantrill, William, 95, 278n6, 284n25

Quinby, Ira, 101, 103

Raguet, Henry, 79–80

Rath, Charles, 154

Raton Pass, 71

Red Canyon, Dak.Terr., 257

Red Iron (Cheyenne), 161

Red Nose (Cheyenne), 239

Red River, 71, 95, 96, 99, 213

Republican River, 16, 94, 96, 116, 121, 140, 163, 180, 222, 243, 273n23

Richmond, Harry, kills captives, 149

Río Grande, 70, 76, 78, 80

Ritter, Private, wounded at Johnson's Ranch, 74

Roan, George, 148

Robbins, Samuel M., 86, 103, 119

Rocky Mountains, 15, 31, 60. See also Gold region, Colo.Terr.

Rocky Mountain News: 1864 Indian war, mixed reporting on, 119 123–24, 144, 145; defends Colorado volunteers, 140; Wynkoop, success of and welcomes back, 165, 259. See also Byers, William

Rhodes, Halsey, 266

Ripley, W. D., 93

Rogers, Hickory, 15, 17, 18–19, 20, 274n27

Roman Nose (Cheyenne), 214, 269; death of, 243; description of, 187; Fort Ellsworth, meets Wynkoop, 171–72; Fort Larned, Wynkoop meeting, 179; Hancock expedition, 186, 188, 189–90, 300n44; mistaken as chief, 224, 298n69; tipi, Hancock trophy, 198, 204; Wynkoop, attempts to kill, 205–206, 303n13

Rood family, killed, 101

Roper, Laura, 113

Ross, Edmund G., 207, 233

Ross, Lewis W., 150

Rucker, John, 40

Russell, Majors and Waddell Co., 24

Rutledge, Joseph, 260

Sacred Arrows: meaning of, 161; ceremony of, 204, 213, 214

Saline River, Kans., 232, 251; August 1868 raid, 239

Sanborn, George L., 73

Sanborn, John B., 154–55, 206, 210, 215

Sand Creek, 94, 161, 190, 197, 211, 249, 266, 267, 268; American flag, 131, 146; attack at, 131–33, 136; atrocities at, 134, 136–37, 142, 292n71; Chivington's command, size of, 131; Chivington's victory, questioned, 140; controversy over, 144, 148; Indian casualties, 134, 135, 140, 142, 146; missing children, 172;

Southern Cheyennes move to, 129, 291n45; victims of, 157
Sand Creek letters, 136–37
Sand Hill, 165
Santa Ana, Antonio López de, 5, 68
Santa Fe, N.Mex. Terr., 71, 72, 75, 79, 80; Wynkoop's final home, 259, 260, 261, 262, 266
Santa Fe Trail, 16, 118
Satank (Kiowa), 235
Satanta (Kiowa), 196, 229, 235, 249; description of, 206; Medicine Lodge peace council, 208, 212; needless killing of animals, 208; raids of, 97, 101–102, 172; white men, will live like, 242; Wynkoop, calls his agent, 173
Sayre, Hal, 131, 292n71; M'lle Haydee confusion, 38; spelling of name, 277n8
Scott, Winfield, 5
Scurry, William R., 75
Sears, J. P., Jr., 123
Second Colorado Volunteer Regiment, 73, 150
Second Texas Mounted Rifles, 72
Second U.S. Cavalry, 160
Senate Committee on Indian Affairs, 140, 246
Seventh Texas Mounted Volunteers, 68
Seventh U.S. Cavalry, 180, 205, 242, 245–46
Seward, William H., 152
Shaffer, James, 58, 86; Civil War, 66, 76; Glorieta campaign, 73, 74; marshal, election as, 61–62; McLure and Wynkoop, 45, 47
Sheldon, Lionel Allen, 260
Sheridan, Philip H., 246, 249, 250, 258; Fort Dodge Indian councils, 227; Indians, surrender to, 241; Sherman, war comments to, 242; winter campaign, 245; Wynkoop, shares Indian plans with, 243
Sherman, William T., 210, 245, 250, 255; buffalo promise, 215–16; Fort Cobb, move Indians to, 238; Fort Larned, Wynkoop-Indian meeting, 173; Hancock, gives free rein, 182; Indian agents, 178–79; Indians, 1868 comments on, 242, 244; Indians, denies weapons distribution to, 234, 235; Wynkoop, receives formal protest of, 192; Wynkoop's agency, shuts down, 243
Shippen, Charles, 272n7
Shortridge, W. T., 53, 55
Shoshonee Terr., 15
Shoshone Indians, 85
Shoup, George L., 119, 131
Sibley, Henry H., background of, 68; invasion of Southwest, 70–71, 75–76; retreat of, 78
Sibley's Brigade, 68–69
Sioux Indians, 20, 24, 25, 90, 100, 106, 115, 121, 197, 204, 256, 261; Arickaree Fork fight, 243; raids of, 130, 239, 257; white captives, 115; Wynkoop, called Sioux agent, 206
Sitting Bear (Cheyenne), 171
Skatara, the Mountain Chieftain (Steinberger), 34, 47
Slaughter, William M., 52
Slavery issue, 6, 7, 10, 11, 12, 14, 18, 41, 48, 95

Slim Face (Cheyenne), 181
Slough, John, 281n12; Glorieta campaign, 69–70, 71, 73, 75
Smith, A. J., 188, 192, 194, 203, 211, 246; Wynkoop comment, 217–18
Smith, H. P. A., 15, 16, 17–18, 20–21, 22
Smith, Jack: death of, 135–36
Smith, John Simpson, 108, 117, 124, 136, 142, 146, 150, 154, 171, 232, 239; background of, 106; Black Kettle, lives with, 168; Bluff Creek village, 160; Camp Weld council, 119, 122, 123; Cheyennes, comment on, 225; Medicine Lodge peace council, 206, 215; Sand Creek village, 130, 135; St. Charles Town Company, 20–21, 275n25; Wynkoop, complains about, 224; Wynkoop, translates for, 107, 109, 110, 111, 113, 114, 162, 173
Smoky Hill River, 16, 93, 96, 107, 108, 109, 110, 130, 159, 163, 166, 170, 176, 180, 182, 199, 286n20; Indian camps along, 133
Snake River, 86
Snyder, Naman D., 146
Solomon River, Kans., 232; August 1868 raid, 239; isolated 1866 attacks on whites, 168
Soule, Silas S., 85, 86, 98, 101, 103, 117, 120, 129, 141, 149, 152; Big Timbers, 108, 109, 113; Camp Weld, 119, 123; Chivington, protests to, 131; Coberly, Hersa, marries, 148; Denver, threats and death, 150; Fort Lyon, Indian meeting, 128; Sand Creek battle, 133; Sand Creek letter, 136–37, 139; Sand Creek testimony, 145
South Carolina: secession, 48, 53
Southern Cheyenne Indians, 99, 105, 117, 120, 144, 167, 195–96, 198, 199, 201, 244, 252, 268, 269; annuities, deliveries and anger, 171, 176, 226, 227, 229, 232; annuities, refuse, 234; Arickaree Fork fight, 243; Big Timbers, battle line and council, 108–13; Bluff Creek village and council, 161, 162, 163, 164, 169; Camp Weld meeting, 119, 121–22; chief control over warriors, 197, 204; Confederates approach, 84; depredations, accused of, 230; clans and warrior societies, 111, 161, 171; Cooper fight, 194, 302n66; council of 44, 297n43; Dunn fight, 93; First Colorado bivouac, invades, 110; Fort Cobb, Sherman removal to, 238; Fort Ellsworth council, 172; Fort Larned council, 182–84; Fort Lyon, 116, 288n3; Hancock expedition, fear, battle line, and flight, 184, 185, 186–88, 189, 190, 191, 192; intertribal conflict, 85, 176, 197, 220; January 1865 raids, 140; Kaws and Osages, war with, 227, 228, 236–37; Little Arkansas Treaty, to abide by, 153–55, 162; Medicine Lodge peace council, 204, 208, 211, 213, 214, 215, 216, 217; prime hunting ground, invasion of, 180; prisoners of war, 253; raped girl, 191, 210; Sand Creek, attacked at, 129, 131–34, 291n45; Sand Creek,

Southern Cheyenne Indians (*continued*)
fear of repeat, 174; surveying parties, 223;
threats of, per Sherman, 182; villages attacked,
94, 96, 131, 246; war faction, 160, 242; war
parties and raids, 97, 106, 232–33, 239,
240; warriors, hungry for food, 173, 179;
Washington, D.C., visit, 83; Washita battle,
death count, 246, 247; whiskey problem, 224;
White Butte Creek, villagers murdered, 128;
white captives, 113–14, 115, 164, 165; Wood
Creek council 166; Wynkoop, agent for, 174;
Wynkoop, relationship with, 157, 219. *See also*
Sacred Arrows; Wynkoop, Ned
Southern Ute Indians, 89
South Park, Colo. Terr., 89
South Platte River, 16, 19, 20, 22, 23, 27, 36–37,
49, 55, 85, 93, 100, 140, 199, 215, 216,
274n27
Southwest: invasion of, 65, 68–69, 78; second
invasion, fear of, 79, 80, 84, 95, 99
Spotted Wolf (Arapaho), 229, 232
Spotted Wolf Bull (Arapaho), 241
Spring Bottom, Colo. Terr., 147
Spring Creek, Dak. Terr., 256
Spring Garden, Philadelphia, 4, 271n4, 272n7
Squiers, Charles, 150, 151
Standing Bear (Arapaho), 241
Stanley, Henry, 207, 209, 211; background
of, 181–82; Fort Larned council, 299n19;
Medicine Lodge peace council, 212, 214,
215; Pawnee Fork village, describes, 191;
Wynkoop, comments about, 182, 185, 206,
210
Stanton, Edwin M., 91, 103; Wynkoop, denies
request 201
Stark, murder of, 42
Starr carbines: malfunction of, 102–103
St. Charles Town Company, 20, 21, 27–29, 30, 40,
276n34
Steck, Amos, 56, 82, 145
Steele, George, 40
Steele, Robert, 43
Steinberger, Albert B., 22, 23–27, 28, 29, 34, 58,
274n10
Stevens, Robert, 12
St. Joseph, Mo., 245
St. Louis, Mo., 13–14, 156, 158, 159
Stock market crash of 1857, 14
Stone, Dr. Joseph S., 35–37, 48, 58
Stone Forehead (Cheyenne), 214, 229, 232, 241,
269; August 1868 raid, 239, 240; background
of, 161, 296n20, 304n24; Bluff Creek council,
163; control over warriors, 204
Storm (Arapaho), 229, 232, 241
Stout, E. P., 21
Streeter, James, 144, 293n18
Stumbling Bear (Kiowa), 194, 206
Sully, Alfred, 245; Dog Men attack, 242

Tall Bear (Oglala Sioux), 188
Tall Bull (Cheyenne): Arickaree Fork fight, 243;
Fort Larned annuities, 229; Fort Larned
council, 181, 183–84; Hancock expedition,
186; Pawnee Fork village, 189; Medicine
Lodge peace council, 208–10, 211, 215; raids
Kaws, 232; Wynkoop, safe conduct letter, 230,
306n15
Tall Chief, The (Gerboth, ed.), errors, 271n2,
272n3
Tappan, John E., 198, 230, 254
Tappan, Samuel S., 77, 99, 145, 152, 207; Glorieta
campaign, 71, 75; Sand Creek Denver
hearings, 144, 145; Wynkoop, impressed by,
65, 66; Wynkoop, Indian rights, 244, 249, 250,
251, 252, 255; Wynkoop, Peralta accusation of,
78, 283n54
Taylor, Alfred A., 211–12
Taylor, I. J., 164, 165; alcohol problem, 159; Dog
Men, exterminate them, 168; Indian annuities,
158; Satanta, Box captives, 173; Wynkoop,
relationship with, 160, 171, 172;
Taylor, Nathanial J., 233, 238, 250, 253; Medicine
Lodge peace council, 207, 208, 209, 211, 212;
Murphy, Thomas, updated by, 197, 198, 205;
Wynkoop, working relationship with, 192,
196, 206, 217, 218, 221–22, 225, 227, 228,
235, 245
Teller, Henry M., 102
Ten Bears (Comanche), 235; Medicine Lodge
peace council, 208, 212
Terry, Alfred H., 207
Third Colorado Volunteer Cavalry, 117, 123, 118,
142; enlistment of, 103; first Cheyenne fight,
128; Sand Creek campaign, 130–31, 133, 139;
villains, except in West, 145
Third U.S. Cavalry, 72
Third U.S. Infantry, 179, 242
Thirty-seventh U.S. Infantry, 180
Thomas, O. B., 51–52
Thompson, Lt., bitten by wolf, 237
Thorne, Charles R., 32–33, 35, 37
Thorne, Thomas W. (son), 35
Tijeras, N. Mex. Terr., 75
Timber Mountain, 235
Toltec Mining Company, 261
Topeka, Kans. Terr., 15, 16
Treaty of Little Arkansas River, 153–56; changed,
160; ratification of, 295n68
Treaty of Medicine Lodge Creek, 204, 205, 212,
218, 219, 222; commissioners at Fort Larned,
206; Henderson's buffalo promise, 215, 234;
Indians' understanding of, 223, 232; major
points of, 213, 216; opinions about treaty, 217,
220; ratification of, 235; Southern Cheyennes,
fear of attack and arrival at, 208, 214;
Wynkoop, testimony at, 209–10
Trinidad, Colo. Terr., 70

Tsistsistas: meaning of, 92, 285n3. *See also* Southern Cheyenne Indians
Tuttle, E. B., 220
Two Face (Sioux), 115
Two Gregories (comedy), 33

Union Pacific Railroad, 158, 163
Union Pacific Railroad, Eastern Division, 163, 178, 180
United States Indian Commission, 234, 247, 255
Upper Arkansas Indian Agency, Kans., *200*
Ute Indians, 83, 90, 91, 118; attacks and raids, 18, 84, 85, 86, 87, 88; Southern Cheyennes, problems with, 97, 111, 228, 232; treaty with, 89–90, 285n40

Valverde, N.Mex.Terr.: battle at, 70
Van Wormer, Isaac, 99–100
Veracruz, Mex., 5
Verdigris River, 84
Vi'ho'i, meaning of, 161
Virginia Dale Stage Station, Colo.Terr., 87

Wade, B. F., 141, 250
Waggoner, Judge (Wynkoop friend), 54
Wakely, Flora (Louise's sister), 32, 33, 41, 49, 57, 58
Wakely, George D. (Louise's stepfather), 32, 41; chief's arrival in Denver, 119
Wakely, Louise Matilda Brown. *See* Wynkoop, Louise
Wakely, Matilda Louise Brown (Louise's mother), 32, 37, 41
Wakely, Rose M. (Louise's sister), 32, 33, 41, *50*; artistic capabilities of, 37; death of, 277n21; M'lle Haydee confusion, 38; Thomas Evans, elopement and marriage to, 49, 51
Walker, Charles J., 72, 73
Walker, Robert J., 11, 12
Wall Street panic of 1873, 255
Walnut Creek, Kans., 240; annuity distribution at, 176
Walsh, Hugh Sleight, 27
Wanless, John, 53, 55
War Bonnet (Cheyenne), 137
Warren, Thomas, 36, 37
Washington, D.C., 43, 65, 83, 141, 144, 145, 146, 152, 196, 235, 253; Wynkoop in capital, 157, 167, 169, 170, 172, 173, 174, 179, 246, 250, 251, 258
Washita, Battle of the, 246, 250; death count and controversy, 247, 251. *See also* Custer, George Armstrong
Washita River, Ind.Terr., 197, 245
Waters, Patrick, 53–55, 279n35
Watson, W. H.: Wynkoop, criticism of and agenda, 168–69
Wea Indians, 11
Wedeles, Hugo, claim of, 198

Weichselbaum, Theodore, 230; background of, 198–99
Whipple, H. B., 256
White, A. S. H., 207
White Antelope (Cheyenne), 109, 116, 123, *124*; death of, 131–32, 134, 137
White Butte Creek, Colo.Terr., 128
White Caps. *See* Las Gorras Blancas
White captives, 113–15, 164–65, 173, 235, 289n38
White hatred and fear, 97, 100, 130; atrocities feed, 134
White Horse (Cheyenne), 181, 188, 213, 215, 243; demented mother, 191
Whiteley, Simeon, 122
White River, 86, 88
White Wood Gulch, Dak.Terr., 256
Whitsett, Richard E., 18
Williams, J. Elliott, alleges Indian fraud, 205
Wilmarth, Margaret. *See* McAdams, Margaret
Wilson, Luther, 97, 99, 131, 133
Wimsatt, John, 30, 31
Winchester, Lucillias J., 15
Wind Woman (Black Kettle's sister; Cheyenne), 289n25
Wood, Carl, 40, 277n17
Wood Creek council, Kans., 166
Wyatt, H. P., 173–74
Wynkoop, Angeline Catherine (daughter), 159
Wynkoop, Angeline Catherine Estill (mother), 4, 91; death, 259
Wynkoop, Anna Maria (sister), 4, 5
Wynkoop, Charles Shippen (brother), 4, 6, 39
Wynkoop, Charles Wanshaer (son), 255
Wynkoop, Edward Estill (son), 80, 117, 125, 137, 152, *202*; birth of, 68, 281n17; errors in writing, 294n54
Wynkoop, Edward Wanshaer (Ned), 7, *67*, *83*, *86*, *120*, 116, *124*, 132, *193*, *195*, 208, *258*, *263*, 243, 288n4, 289n25; annuities, deliveries and weapon problems, 219, 223, 225, 227, 228, 229, 230, 232, 233, 234, 237, 238, 242; appearance and descriptions of, 6, 8, 10, 26, 42–43, 182, 206, 265; Arapahos, stays with, 23, 275n11; attacked in print, 58, 62, 144, 211; background and birth, 3, 4, 6, 272n14; Big Timbers, battle line and council, 108–13; Black Hills Rangers, 257, 258; Black Kettle, relationship with, 111–12, 153, 213, 214; Bliss-Stone duel, 36–37; Bluff Creek, council and threat, 162–64; budgets and expenses, 175, 176, 178, 201, 219, 222, 228, 238–39, 242; Byers, changing relationship with, 39, 44, 53, 57, 66; Camp Weld council, 119, 121–22, 123, 290n8; celebrity and popularity of, 29, 30, 31, 81, 82, 151, 212, 257, 259, 261, 267; Chivington, changing relationship, 68, 81, 131, 139, 266; Confederates, watches for, 95–96, 98, 99; Cramer endorsement of, 129;

Wynkoop, Edward Wanshaer (Ned) (*continued*)
dead man, 56–57; death of, 266; Denver, city lot sales, 35, 40, 305n71; Denver, named by, 22; Denver City Town Company, efforts for, 27–28; Denver parade, 90; detached duty, special agent, 157–61; Evans, meets with, 118; Ewbanks, Isabelle, comment on, 114; Fort Ellsworth council, 171–72; Fort Larned council, 181, 183; Fort Lyon, Indian meetings, 123, 127–28; Glorieta campaign, 69–75; gold region, trips to, 15–19, 31–32, 33, 276n36, 276n38; guarantees safety of villages, 128, 197; Hancock expedition, fear of and battle line, 180, 185, 186–88; Harrison and Hill Criterion Saloon incident, 42, 51–52; health of, 84, 257, 258, 262, 264, 265, 310n13; honored, 82; horse accident, 81; Indian agent fraud, not linked to, 179, 181, 299n3; "Indian fighter," 87, 89; "Indian lover," 177; Indians, changing views and comments on, 17, 24–25, 107, 123, 142, 150, 167, 169, 174, 221, 228–29, 249, 251; Indians want as agent, 154; Interior Department problems, funds and scouts, 179, 221–22, 223–24, 225, 228, 237; Interior Department, special agent, 170; Jefferson Territory, refuses to support, 43; Kiowa, races, 17; La Fonda rats, 79; land development, 15, 20–21; Las Gorras Blancas, 262; Lecompton, discontent, 10, 11; Lecompton, trips to, 8, 22–27, 274n10, 275n20; Little Arkansas Treaty, 153–56; marshal election, 61–63; McLure mail problem, 54, 55–56, 279n36, 279–80n38, 280n40, 280n42; McLure trial and standoff, 45, 47–48; Medicine Lodge peace council, testimony of, 209–10, 215; memoirs, 259, 261; Miami Indian woman, 13; military, enlistment/muster out, 65, 169, 281n8; military rank of, 66, 75–76, 146, 283n46; mining, 37–38, 41, 42, 256, 260, 261; mother, visits, 91–92, 153, 244; names of, 5, 272n9; New Mexico Penitentiary, 262–64, 265; newspapers, use of, 29, 58, 87, 119, 246; Paola, 11–12; Paola gold, transports, 14; Pawnee Fork village, Hancock and raped girl, 191, 210; Pawnee Fork village, waits, 190, 192; Pawnee Land Office, 8, 10; Pawnees, robbed by, 24–26; Peralta, battle of, 76–78; political parties of, 48, 81, 264, 278n7; Polvadera and caravan from, 80; removal from command and banishment, 125–26, 129, 136, 139; Roman Nose attempts to kill, 205–206; rumors about, 117; Sand Creek, blamed for, 187; Sand Creek, horses lost, 172, 173; Sand Creek, Fort Lyon hearings, 146–47; Sand Creek, outrage over and report, 137–38, 139, 140, 141–42; Satanta, pursuit of, 101–102; secession, 61; sheriff, election as, 43–44; sheriff of Arapahoe County, appointment and resignation, 15, 22, 34; Smith, John, relationship with, 106;

son, plays with, 152; Southern Cheyennes, interrogates, 107; "speculator," 41; speeches of, 65, 69, 82, 247, 249; stub-tailed cow, 42; summation of, 267–270; superintendent of Indian Affairs, 253; tall tales, 261; Tappan accusation, 78, 283n54; theater involvement and reviews of, 34–35, 57, 58, 60, 64–65, 69; timber agent/inspector, 259, 260, 261; Upper Arkansas Agency, housing/food problems, 177, 198–99, 201, 222; U.S. Indian agent, appointment and resignation, 167, 173, 174, 245, 250; Ute expedition, 84–89, 91, 284n29, 284–85n37, 285n38; Wakely, Rose, rescue of, 49; Walnut Creek council, 176; Washington, D.C., wants to take chiefs to, 165, 219; Washita, negative press, 249, 250; Waters case, 53–54, 55; weapons, skill with, 10, 55–56; white hostages, receives, 113–14, 164, 236; Wood Creek council, 166; Wynkoop, Louise, relationship with, 35, 37, 38, 41, 57, 66, 68, 277n9, 281n17. *See also* Byers, William; Hancock, Winfield Scott; Murphy, Thomas; One-Eye (Cheyenne); Smith, John Simpson; Tappan, Samuel S.; Taylor, Nathaniel J.; Washington, D.C.

Wynkoop, Emily (sister), 4, 5, 6, 7, 8, 10
Wynkoop, Emily Reveille (daughter), 81, 137
Wynkoop, Francis Murray (brother), 4, 5, 15, 272n10
Wynkoop, Francis "Frank" Murray (son), 81, 254, 260
Wynkoop, George (brother), 4, 30, 35, 38; as actor, 34; Bluff Creek, 160, 162, 163; death of, 170; Denver City Town Company, sues, 40; Lecompton, 27, 28; Wynkoop, Ned, reunion with, 159
Wynkoop, George Campbell (uncle), 4
Wynkoop, Harman Henry (son), 255; Chivington, 266
Wynkoop, John Estill (brother), 4, 5, 254, 255
Wynkoop, John Wanshaer (father), 3, 4
Wynkoop, Louise (wife), 35, 40, 41, 42, 49, *59*, 80, 107, 117, 123, 137, 151, 152, 156, *202*, 234, 243, 250; and Caudle, Melinda, 236; Chivington, 266, 267; death of, 267, 311n55; Fort Riley Indian encounter, 152; La Fonda rats, 79; M'lle Haydee confusion, 38; New Mexico Penitentiary, 262, 264, 265; Pennsylvania, 153, 157, 254, 260; pension of, 266, 267; pregnancies, 66, 79, 81, 148, 159, 256, 259; sings for soldiers, 235; theatrical career and reviews of, 32–34, 37, 57–58. *See also* Wynkoop, Edward Wanshaer (Ned)
Wynkoop, Mai Twiggs, 39
Wynkoop, Rose M. (daughter), 259, 266
Wynkoop, Thomas Atwood (son), 256
Wynkoop's Shanty, 5

Yellow Bear (Arapaho), 229, 232
Young Chief (Apache), 229, 232